# ACQUIRING CULTURE: CROSS-CULTURAL STUDIES IN CHILD DEVELOPMENT

Until recently anthropologists studying different cultures have mainly confined themselves to the behaviour and idea systems of adults. Psychologists, on the other hand, working mainly in Europe and America, have studied child development in their own settings and simply assumed the universality of their findings. Thus both disciplines have largely ignored a crucial problem area: the way in which children from birth onwards learn to become competent members of their culture. This process, which has been called 'the quintessential human adaptation', constitutes the theme of this volume.

It derives from a workshop held at the London School of Economics which brought together fieldworkers who in their studies had paid more than usual attention to children in their cultures. Their experiences and foci of interest were varied but this very diversity serves to illuminate different facets of the acquisition of culture by children, ranging in age from pre-verbal infants to adolescents.

Evolutionarily primed for culture-learning, children are responsive to a rich web of influences from subtle and indirect as in their music and dance to direct teaching in the family guided by culture-specific ideas about child psychology. Some of the salient things they learn relate to gender, status and power, critical for the functioning of all societies.

The introductory essay provides the necessary historical background of the development of child study in both anthropology and psychology and outlines how future research in the ethnography of childhood should proceed. The book concludes with an annotated bibliography providing a guide to the literature from 1970 onwards.

Gustav Jahoda is Professor Emeritus at the University of Strathclyde.

I.M. Lewis is Professor of Anthropology at the London School of Economics and Political Science, and Honorary Director of the International African Institute.

# Acquiring Culture:

## Cross Cultural Studies in Child Development

Edited by
GUSTAV JAHODA and I. M. LEWIS

CROOM HELM
London • New York • Sydney

© G. Jahoda and I.M. Lewis
Croom Helm Ltd, Provident House, Burrell Row,
Beckenham, Kent, BR3 1AT

Croom Helm Australia, 44-50 Waterloo Road,
North Ryde, 2113, New South Wales

Published in the USA by Croom Helm
in association with Routledge, Chapman & Hall, Inc.
29 West 35th Street, New York, NY 10001

British Library Cataloguing in Publication Data

Acquiring culture: cross-cultural studies
  in child development.
  1. Child psychology — Cross-cultural
  studies 2. Child development
  I. Jahoda, Gustav II. Lewis, I.M.
  ISBN 0-7099-4335-0

**Library of Congress Cataloging-in-Publication Data**
ISBN 0-7099-4335-0

Typeset by Ace Filmsetting Ltd, Frome, Somerset
Printed and bound in Great Britain by
Biddles Ltd, Guildford and King's Lynn

# Contents

| | |
|---|---|
| List of Contributors | vii |
| Preface | ix |
| Introduction: Child Development in Psychology and Anthropology<br>*Gustav Jahoda* and *I. M. Lewis* | 1 |

**Part I: Non-verbal Processes in the Acquisition of Culture** — 35

1. Universal Co-operative Motives: How Infants begin to know the Language and Culture of their Parents — 37
   *Colwyn Trevarthen*
2. Dance and Music in Venda Children's Cognitive Development, 1956–8 — 91
   *John Blacking*
3. The Shadow Play and Operetta as Mediums of Education in Bali — 113
   *Angela Hobart*

**Part II: Cognitive Development and Indigenous Psychology** — 145

4. From Child to Human: Chewong Concepts of Self — 147
   *Signe Howell*
5. Personal Autonomy and the Domestication of the Self in Piaroa Society — 169
   *Joanna Overing*
6. Concepts and Learning among the Punan Bah of Sarawak — 193
   *Ida Nicolaisen*

**Part III: Cognitive Development, Gender and Hierarchy** — 223

7. Children's Perceptions of Gender and Hierarchy in Fiji — 225
   *Christina Toren*
8. Cognitive Development and Sex Roles on the Kerkennah Islands of Tunisia — 271
   *Katherine Platt*
9. Sex Roles and State Roles in Soviet Georgia: Two Styles of Infant Socialisation — 288
   *Tarama Dragadze*

Annotated Bibliography: Recent Studies of Ethnography of Childhood — 307
*Christina Toren*

Index — 334

# Contributors

**John Blacking** is Professor of Social Anthropology, Queen's University, Belfast, N. Ireland. Author of *How musical is man?* (1976) and *Worlds of music* (in press), editor of *The anthropology of the body* (1977).

**Tamara Dragadze** is a freelance anthropologist, specialist on Eastern Europe, PhD (Cambridge) and editor of *Kinship and marriage in the Soviet Union* (1984).

**Angela Hobart** of Goldsmith's College and School of Contemporary Dance, London, PhD (London) is the author of *Dancing shadows of Bali: theatre and myth* (1987).

**Signe Howell** is Lecturer in Anthropology, University of Edinburgh, specialist on indigenous peoples of Malaysia and Eastern Indonesia and author of *Society and cosmos: Chewong of Peninsular Malaysia* (1984).

**Gustav Jahoda** is emeritus Professor of Psychology, University of Strathclyde, Scotland; his recent books include *Psychology and anthropology* (1982).

**I. M. Lewis** is Professor of Anthropology, London School of Economics and editor of *Symbols and sentiments* (1977).

**Ida Nicolaisen** is a lecturer at the Institute of Cultural Sociology, University of Copenhagen.

**Joanna Overing** is Senior Lecturer in the Social Anthropology of Latin America, London School of Economics and editor of *Reason and morality* (1985).

**Katherine Platt** is a research fellow at the Center for the Philosophy and History of Science, Boston University. Her PhD research was in social anthropology, Kerkennah Islands, Tunisia, 1977–8.

CONTRIBUTORS

**Christina Toren** is at London School of Economics. Her PhD research was in social anthropology, Fiji, 1983–4.

**Colwyn Trevarthen** is Professor of Child Psychology and Psychobiology, University of Edinburgh, Scotland. His recent publications include 'Form, significance and psychological potential of hand gestures of infants', in J-L. Nespoulous, P. Perron, and A. Roch Lecours (eds), *The biological foundation of gestures: motor and semiotic aspects*, MIT Press, 149–202 (1986).

# Preface

This book has grown out of a workshop which we organised at the London School of Economics in 1982 in an effort to focus attention on the neglected theme of how children actually acquire the cultures in which they are socialised. As we discuss in our Introductory chapter, apart from the generally unproductive efforts of the American Culture and Personality School (and its subsidiary derivatives), this crucial issue has been studiously avoided by most social anthropologists in the British tradition and approached in an insufficiently culturally sensitive fashion by most (Eurocentric) psychologists concerned with child development and 'cognition' (a problematic concept as we show). Our exhaustive correspondence with our social anthropology colleagues in Britain has indeed convinced us of the remarkable paucity of systematic ethnographic reporting in this field. We cannot therefore claim that the studies assembled and discussed here are representative in any global sense. As we point out, they do, however, contain sufficiently varied evidence to cast serious doubt on a number of current views of child development.

In the absence of a geographically wider array of adequately documented information, it would be rash to claim too much for our conclusions. The necessarily tentative character of our findings will, we hope, nevertheless further serve to encourage other psychologists and social (and cultural) anthropologists to join forces to elucidate the 'ethnography of childhood' which we see as crucial to a fuller understanding of the mechanisms by which cultures (and societies) are actually reproduced as ideological and moral systems.

We wish to thank the British Social Science Research Council for a conference grant, and the London School of Economics Staff Research Fund for a research assistance grant. As always, we are also extremely grateful to our hard-pressed and long-suffering secretaries at the University of Strathclyde, Dept. of Psychology, and London School of Economics, Dept. of Anthropology. The examples of Jacqueline Rabain and of Meyer Fortes (who died before he could write his promised paper for us) have been a constant inspiration.

G. Jahoda
I.M. Lewis

# Introduction

# Child Development in Psychology and Anthropology

## Gustav Jahoda and I.M. Lewis

To describe how the child is socialised, to grasp how it acquires its social ways of being, amounts to recording and studying the teaching and learning of the cultural code; this code we shall define for the moment, very generally, as a collection of verbal or non-verbal rules of conduct by which society recognises one of its members. (Jacqueline Rabain, 1979, p. 25).

**HISTORICAL BACKGROUND**

**The evolutionary phase**

The beginnings of the systematic study of child development can, like so much else, be traced back to Darwin when the idea of evolution dominated the imagination of those concerned with the study of man (see e.g. Burrow, 1966). At that time a division was taking place into anthropology (Stocking, 1968; Langham, 1981) and psychology (Wertheimer, 1979), both these emerging disciplines sharing the view of a close parallel between phylogenetic and ontogenetic development. Anthropologists proposed that each culture undergoes progressive evolutionary development from savagery to civilisation, while psychologists and educators believed that the development of the child recapitulates the stages in the development of human societies. Hence early writers on child psychology like Sully (1895) made extensive use of anthropological accounts in order to illustrate such common evolutionary schemes. Stanley Hall, the founder of child psychology in the United States, systematised this approach. According to his 'recapitulation theory' children instinctively re-enacted the activities of their distant ancestors, beginning with those most remote in the history of the human race. From this it follows that observation of children should also help to understand the beliefs and institutions of 'primitives'. Thus in an article on dolls (Ellis and Hall, 1896) the forms of doll play among 'savages' were considered, and the question discussed as to how this might relate to 'idolatry'. This assumed of course that the spontaneous activities of children of various ages are innately determined: 'The best index and guide to the stated activities of adults in past ages is found in the instinctive, untaught and non-imitative plays of children' (Hall, 1904, p. 202).[1]

By the second decade of the twentieth century, the doctrine of 'recapitulation' had become discredited. Accordingly, references to other cultures were dropped from works on child psychology for more than half a century (although, of course, persisting in the Freudian psychoanalytic tradition). Child development came to be regarded, in the phrasing of Piaget's earlier writings, as a 'psychobiological' field which had no need for comparative anthropological contributions referring to 'other cultures'.

The scene on the other side of the academic fence saw changes in the opposite direction. Nineteenth-century anthropologists were only peripherally concerned with childhood, to the extent that aspects of it provided grist for their theories. Edward Tylor, the 'father of anthropology', only made occasional reference to children in the grand sweep of his *Origins of culture*. 'Child language' in different cultures is mentioned in the context of speculations about the origin of language; and children's games are discussed as culturally (as opposed to Hall's postulated genetically) transmitted 'survivals' (i.e. relics of earlier stages). This was characteristic of the older tradition that consisted of the use of varied materials, drawn from a heterogeneous collection of societies, in order to delineate some broad evolutionary schema.

In this period an exceptional, pioneering work in the ethnography of children was Kidd's (1906) *Savage childhood*. This is a detailed, generally sympathetic and insightful account of the lives of Bantu children in South Africa, as the following extract from a description of a children's party indicates:

> For several days before a party, the children are very busy in the kraal; the girls bring out small grinding-stones very similar

to those used by grown women for grinding corn; soft white stone is then broken into little pieces which are ground into a fine powder between the grinding-stones. This white powder is mixed with water, or fat, and smeared on the body. The children frequently paint their bodies in very fantastic ways, invariably making themselves look extremely ugly from the European point of view. There is much variety as to the colours used for painting, and as to the parts of the body painted. In Basutoland the girls are fond of red paint, while in Fingoland they prefer white. In these tribes the boys do not often paint themselves for parties; but in Zululand the boys frequently smear their head, trunk and legs with white paint, the girls only painting a white circle or band round their waists, sometimes adding a few touches of white on the cheeks.

The bigger children make extremely pretty bead-work, choosing very good combinations of colour. Bangles are made with grass, or with brass wire, and are worn round the ankle, calf, knee, waist, neck, elbow and wrist. Blankets are well rubbed with red clay, and often have their edges very prettily ornamented with bead-work. The skins of wild animals are worked up with grease until they are very soft and supple, and the tails of wild cats are made into ornaments for the loins. The children frequently tatoo themselves specially for these parties, using a pointed stick, which makes whitish marks in the skin; these marks only last for a few days. Thus the face and arms can be richly tatooed without leaving any permanent marks, as would be the case if they used hot embers. However, the girls sometimes make permanent marks on their skin; they cover a small portion of the arm with cow-dung, and then place glowing embers against the protected flesh. As soon as the heat reaches the skin small circular burns are made. When these burns heal, smooth circular patches of lightish colour are left. The girls think such patches very beautiful.

On the day of the party the girls sometimes make garlands or coronets of leaves, very occasionally adding a few wild flowers to heighten the effect. The contrast of the bright green leaves against the dark burnt-sienna skin is very effective. The children have a special coating of grease given to their bodies so as to make them look smart and clean. It is striking how much improved in appearance are the boys after they have received a good rubbing with grease, for the scratches, which usually cover the body as a result of playing in the veld, are thus hidden.

The anxious mothers are also busy for days in advance of the party, telling the boys to be sure not to quarrel with other boys, lest it should be said they come from a quarrelsome kraal, and so the whole family should be disgraced publicly. They specially impress on the children not to eat too much; they tell them that if they show any signs of greediness the people will all say, 'See, those children come from a kraal where there is famine.' After that cutting sarcasm no one in the kraal could look the world in the face for many a day. But in spite of these days of coaching by anxious mothers, the children always eat too much, and the boys always quarrel and fight. As the children go off to the party the parents finally impress on the boys that they must not annoy the girls, nor forget to be very polite to the owners of the kraal who are giving the party.

The children are all very excited as they put the last touches on their toilette, which is very simple and strangely scant according to our ideas of what is decent. Europeans are inclined to call children un-dressed when they are thus decked out in bead-work. As the twilight dies and a rich afterglow of the deepest purple or violet suffuses the sky, there can be seen a string of little children streaming out of a hut on hands and knees—all silhouetted against a few low-lying clouds of orange colour—and hurrying over the veld in single file along the narrow Kafir footpath. At length this thin, wavy line of excited, talkative, chattering children arrives at the kraal, which is the focus of many other groups of children, dimly seen to be converging on it in the dusk.

On arriving at the kraal the guests have to salute the head-man of the place. If there should happen to be a chief present, the children walk up to him in single file, and as each child passes the chief, he or she has to stand still, shuffle the feet, point to the sky with the right hand, and say, 'Bayete.' If the greatest man present is only an ordinary head-man, the children shuffle their feet, and say, 'Numzaan,' rarely pointing with the hand to the sky. In some tribes it is not correct etiquette for guests to speak first on arriving at a kraal; it is expected that they should sit down in silence until the head-man first addresses them.

The greeting of the head-man of the kraal is one of the ways in which a Kafir shows respect and honour to him. But it has another very practical aspect. It is an excellent way of attracting attention, not so much to the head-man, as to one's self. It is as if the person were to say, 'Take notice, all ye people; it is I who have arrived at the kraal.' A Kafir loves to draw attention to himself and to obtain recognition; and of course he thinks a person cannot start too early in shuffling to the front in the race of life.

When the guests have saluted the great person, they next go and shake hands with his 'great' wife, and after that they shake hands with the other women present and with the various guests, not a little kissing being indulged in between the women and the small children. When this process is over, the guests are told which huts are set apart for the evening, and, if the weather be cold, the children are ushered into one of the other huts, where the girls of the kraal usually hang up their blankets on a leather thong stretched between two poles. The guests pile their blankets on these leather ropes; they will not need their blankets again till the morning, for there are fires kept burning in every hut all night.

Since the party is to last till dawn, any children who may get unduly tired are free to go to one of the huts and enjoy a sleep whenever they like; when refreshed they can return to the party. If the party does not last the whole night, the children all sleep at the kraal of the person inviting them. Beds are quite unknown, for the people sleep in their blankets on grass mats, using blocks of wood for pillows. It is therefore a simple matter to find floor-space for a hundred visitors.

It is difficult for us nowadays to appreciate how far in advance of his contemporaries Kidd was, given the then prevalent ideas about 'savage' life even by those who saw it at first hand. Take for instance this account of childhood in Rhodesia by a missionary writing just before the First World War:

> The children of this land are non-entities. Nothing at all is done for them. They feed, sit about and sleep, and in this manner they grow until it comes time for them to get about for themselves, to do something in the gardens, or to seek work from the white man. They have no nurseries, no toys, no books, no tea-parties and no instructions from their parents and friends. They are here and that is all. Their lives are one big nothing. (Baker, 1913, quoted in Schwartzman and Barbera, 1976)

INTRODUCTION

The ethnocentric absurdity of such a view is vividly brought out by modern studies such as that of Gelfand (1979), which documents in detail the richness of the lives of Shona children. However, even anthropologists at this time generally played little part in modifying these very misleading prevailing stereotypes. In Britain during the inter-war years anthropology, employing the intensive participant-observation fieldwork techniques patented if not invented by Malinowski, was, of course, dominated by the functionalists (see Kuper, 1973; Lewis, 1985, pp. 52–60).

**Contributions from British functionalist anthropology**

Although famous even among psychologists for his alleged demolition of the universality of the Oedipus complex, Malinowski had relatively little to report or say about the lives of Trobriand children. He recorded stages of development and gender differentiation (Malinowski, 1922, p. 51), but his theory of needs apparently led him to regard child behaviour from the standpoint of its function in preparing children for their future participation in the social and economic life of the community, yet lacked a more detailed analysis of such processes. Malinowski also had recourse to a principle then popular in psychology as well as anthropology, namely 'imitation'. Notwithstanding these limitations, Malinowski did, however, encourage his disciples to include, within the study of kinship, interaction between parents and children in the socialisation process and to observe how knowledge of specialised techniques was taught and passed on (Richards, 1970, pp. 1–3). Such data are contained in the work of a number of his pupils, including, among others, Firth (1936), Kaberry (1939), Krige (1943) and Richards (1932, 1939, 1964).

This emphasis is particularly prominent in the work of two other members of this Malinowskian circle, Meyer Fortes and Margaret Read. Here Meyer Fortes broke radically new ground. It was probably because he had originally been trained as an educational psychologist that he produced his classical *Social and psychological aspects of education in Taleland* (1938 reprinted as 1970). This study, to which Bruner (1966) has paid tribute, is now widely known and quoted by psychologists so that only a few comments will be necessary here.

Fortes describes the process of informal education in a non-literate culture, showing in graphic detail how as a consequence of the unity of the social sphere learning is not an isolated activity but woven into the general texture of practical life: 'Tale children receive their education not only from adults but also from older children and adolescents who are always transmitting what they know of the cultural heritage to their younger brothers and sisters and cousins' (1970, p. 211). The ways in which adherence to moral and conventional rules develops are traced, and the structure of parent–child relationships delineated, which explains the fact that there is rarely need for coercion. Important aspects of cognitive development are also considered, and here Fortès implicitly rejected a then fashionable behaviourism in favour of Bartlett's 'schema' approach:

> These total patterns which constitute the texture of Tale culture are not built up bit by bit, by addition, during the course of a child's life. They are present as *schemas* from the beginning. . . . A child's knowledge of the kinship structure evolves in the same way. The schema, rudimentary, and unstable as yet, can be detected in the 3–4 year old. He or she discriminates kinsfolk from non-kinsfolk, equating the former mainly with people living in close proximity. He knows his own father and mother precisely, but already calls his mother's co-wives 'mother'. Similarly, he knows that 'father' is his own father, but that other men—in the first instance those of the same joint family—are also 'fathers', and he knows that the other kinsfolk frequently are brothers, sisters, grandfather, grandmother. But he is still unable to discriminate genealogical differences; he groups people by generation and spatial proximity. (1970, pp. 238/9)[2]

On the basis of his data, Fortes also criticised the notion of play as imitation of adult activities, pointing out that play 'is never simple and mechanical reproduction; it is always imaginative construction, based on the themes of adult life and the life of older children' (1970, p. 244). This formulation anticipates Piaget's (1945) views about symbolic play. Altogether, Fortes' monograph remains today an unsurpassed contribution to our understanding of childhood in a non-European traditional culture. One of the few recent works that comes closest to it is the extensive study of Wolof children by Rabain (1979) who also has a background in both psychology and anthropology.

Not long after Fortes, another well-known work appeared by

Otto Raum (1940), entitled *Chaga Childhood*. Longer and more detailed in its descriptions, this is a perceptive account which also criticises the simple imitation theory of play. Yet it lacks the depth of psychological insight that characterises Fortes. Margaret Read, another contemporary student of Malinowski and the only one in Britain to pursue a professional university career in education, between 1933 and 1939 carried out an unusually extensive field study of child development and formal and informal education amongst the Ngoni of Central Africa (Read, 1960). In contrast to the American Culture and Personality School (see below), Read treated values and the indigenous Ngoni 'ideal personality' as *determining* child-training practices. She also concluded that ostensibly harsh weaning procedures seemed to have little adverse impact on Ngoni children who were characteristically 'happy, busy, friendly, helpful, endlessly inventive and full of initiative'.

Few of these studies, however, had much influence at the time on psychologists, nor was this exemplary focus on the ethnography of childhood pursued seriously and systematically by many other social anthropologists in the British 'structural–functional' tradition. This was in conformity with the strongly antipsychological posture assumed, under the influence of Durkheim, by the other founding-father of modern British social anthropology, A.R. Radcliffe-Brown (1881–1955) despite (or perhaps because of) the implicit psychological assumptions of most of his 'sociological' interpretations of kinship and ritual behaviour (Lewis, 1977, pp. 6–8).

This rather striking neglect of the sharp edge in the transmission of cultural knowledge and in the inculcation of social norms contrasts intriguingly with the continuing provision of professional guidance on the appropriate questions to ask and observations to make here. The standard fieldwork manual, *Notes and queries on anthropology* (first edition 1874, sixth edition 1951), which every social anthropologist was supposed to carry into the field as his bible included a comprehensive chapter devoted to the 'Social life of the individual' with detailed sections on children and education, formal and informal. This reminded the ethnographer that, 'careful field studies of the training of children should be made. Observations of child behaviour in simple societies are of great value as checks on current psychological theories of child development'.[3]

Until very recently, this eminently sensible directive reads like a 'survival' (a throw-back to the Malinowskian and pre-Malinowskian era of W.H.R. Rivers and C.G. Seligman (Lewis, 1977, pp. 2–3)), and was largely ignored by British social anthropologists for whom children, in the societies they studied, were not only not heard but also not seen. This, of course, was particularly ironical since the classic fieldwork situation involved a European (or other foreign) anthropologist having, like a child, to 'learn his way' into the culture under study. Later field studies in the 1950s and 1960s in this British tradition, with few exceptions (see e.g. Richards, 1964; 1970), continued to disregard these issues. Thus, for example, in his studies of Somali culture and society Lewis (1961; 1982), noted but did not closely investigate the intriguing fact that in this extremely patrilineal society children were taught their *father*'s genealogy (conveying their multiple political identity) by their *mother* (who normally belonged to a different lineage). These social anthropologists, indeed, usually restricted their description and discussion of formal education processes to the meaning and significance of institutionally dramatic (and often apparently traumatic) rites of passage in the individual's life cycle and to initiation rituals generally. In this vein, although the evidence advanced is often circumstantial rather than conclusive (Ottenberg, 1982), most structural functionalist interpretations of rituals emphasise their didactic force (see e.g. Richards, 1956, 1970; Spencer, 1965; Barth, 1975; La Fontaine, 1985). They rarely, however, attempt to locate such analyses within the wider framework of a society's educational system in the most general sense. As late as 1970, Philip Mayer could write with justice, 'we do not even know how far simpler societies have or lack specialised educational institutions, we only know that anthropologists have often not reported any' (Mayer, 1970, p. xviii).

This increasingly blatant (at least in retrospect) neglect of socialisation in social anthropology while conforming to what his British anthropological successors took to be Durkheim's aversion to psychology (ironically despite Durkheim's very strong pedagogical interests) may also be seen to reflect the priority attached to *society* rather than *culture* in their (sociological) schema. Culture, in this perspective, is the vehicle or medium rather than prime mover for social relations (Lewis, 1985, pp. 380–1). Hence, enculturation is disregarded and, paradoxically, at the same time by definition 'socialisation', since this is really assumed to mean learning one's culture. Further reinforcement for this rather blinkered insistence on this doctrinal position in British social anthropology was readily provided by alienating developments in American cultural anthropology to which we now turn.

## Margaret Mead and the Culture and Personality School

In this transatlantic tradition which treated society rather than culture as a secondary phenomenon, Margaret Mead placed child development at the centre of her interpretation of culture. At a time when few psychologists, not to mention anthropologists, had even heard of Piaget, she attempted to test his theory of animism with children in the Admiralty Islands (Mead, 1932) and claimed to have refuted it. As she described her aims reflectively much later:

> Without a knowledge of the specific cultural patterning of the experiences of early childhood, we could not at that time interrelate the three sets of materials with which Freud worked: the recorded behaviour of individual children, the recollected behaviour of neurotics and the rituals and beliefs of different primitive cultures. It would be necessary to know in concrete and specific detail, how early childhood thinking—which Piaget described and regarded as universal—is fostered, cultivated, or discouraged in those cultures where there is a respected pattern of belief and practise, and also what the equivalent of neurosis is when rituals similar to those reported for individual neurotics are available to everyone in a given culture. (Mead, 1962, p. 123.)

Much of Mead's ensuing work dealt with child and adolescent development, though focusing on affect more than cognition. This was particularly true of her later research, increasingly influenced by psychoanalysis. However tinged with ethnocentricism these latter influences may have been, Mead was nevertheless largely responsible for popularising the important anthropological understanding of 'childhood' as a stage in development which was culturally relative both in duration and content.

Mead's approach paralleled that of the Culture and Personality School that came to prominence in America during the 1940s and 1950s. Although concerned with childhood, this influential movement celebrating the idea of human plasticity concentrated on socialisation and emotional growth taken to be the foundations of adult personality. Preoccupied with children's responses to emotional crises such as weaning and their assumed or attributed effects, members of the School had little to say about the ways children's ideas were actually formed or how they acquired particular skills; and from these writings one learns remarkably little about children's everyday lives. Much the same is true of the so-called 'hologeistic' approach based on the Human Relations Area Files, which followed the decline of the original Culture and Personality School.[4] Its aim is to test hypotheses, mainly about the relationship between early socialisation and adult personality. As the term implies, such relationships are taken to range across all world cultures and the technique is therefore confined to features that are very general.

Here it is generally argued, for instance, that harsh parental treatment in infancy produces beliefs that the spirit world is correspondingly severe and hostile. This is ultimately claimed to be linked with the way in which patterns of livelihood determine socialisation and personality type. So, Barry, Child and Bacon (1959, 1967) claim to have demonstrated, that herding and agricultural societies produce compliant, nurturant personalities, whereas hunting and fishing cultures, lacking storage facilities, inculcate self-reliance, initiative and 'achievement motivation'. So in 'societies in which one succeeds by being obedient, responsible and nurturant, in short by being compliant, we may expect that such behaviour towards elders and those in power will also be appropriate toward powerful spirit beings' (Bourguignon, 1976, p. 48). In this style of identifying (rather arbitrarily) causal chains, these writers posit an explicit linkage between infrastructure and superstructure in a less shadowy fashion than many of their explicitly Marxian colleagues.

Various limitations of this holocultural approach (discussed in Jahoda, 1982) led the Whitings, who were at one time its foremost exponents, to turn later towards observational studies employing time-sampling (Whiting and Whiting, 1975). While these yielded more information about children's behaviour, the aim still remained that of generalising across cultures. This involved isolating specific aspects of mainly social behaviour for the purpose of comparison. Although the findings were often intriguing, they once again only tell us about the presumed effects of rather broad features of the cultures studied, and are confined to what was common to these cultures. The accounts of behavioural episodes, lifted out of their context, are largely meaningless in themselves.

**Cross-cultural psychology**

The aim of arriving at generalisations that transcend cultures has also been dominant in psychology. Piaget originally regarded his theory as a psychobiological one and thus universally valid. His position came to be modified in the course of interdisciplinary discussions held during the 1950s, when Margaret Mead forcefully impressed upon him the role of culture in development. Thereafter he and his followers modified their views (Piaget, 1966), marking the beginning of a veritable industry of worldwide comparative studies, whose outcome has been summarised by Dasen (1972, 1977). However, most of this work was concerned mainly to test the cross-cultural validity of Piagetian theory and to propose such modifications of it as were dictated by the new data.

An entirely different approach has been taken by Cole and his associates (Cole, Gay and Sharp, 1971; Laboratory of Comparative Human Cognition, 1982, 1983), based on the culture-historical Soviet school of Vygotsky and Luria. Unlike Piaget, whose bias was biological, they regarded cognitive development as primarily a social process whereby children acquire cognitive skills as a result of interaction with others in culturally defined situations. This implied an entirely different research strategy from that of the Piagetians who presented their subjects with tasks invented in Geneva, though substituting whenever possible culturally familiar materials. Cole and his colleagues took as their starting point the everyday activities of people within their own indigenous culture, devising their tasks on this basis; and at one time Cole called his approach 'experimental anthropology'.

In the course of the past decade there has been considerable convergence of what were at one time diametrically opposed approaches; Piagetians especially now recognise the need to consider specifically cultural factors, and one of the more impressive Piagetian studies of Ivory Coast children (Dasen, Inhelder, Lavallee and Retschitzki, 1978) takes considerable account of the ethnographic background.

Another more general movement in the same direction has

been the rise of 'environmental' psychology, initially mainly concerned with the physical but later increasingly with the social environment. An important contribution was made by Bronfenbrenner (1979, p. xiii) in an influential book whose preface contains the following passage where he describes the impact on his outlook of cross-cultural experience:

> Seen in different contexts, human nature, which I had previously thought of as a singular noun, became plural and pluralistic; for the different environments were producing discernible differences, not only across but also within societies, in talent, temperament, human relations, and particularly in the ways in which the culture, or subculture, brought up its next generation.

While this is not exactly a new revelation for anthropologists, this 'conversion' of one of the major figures in American psychology indicates that it does constitute a fresh perspective for most psychologists, many of whom still labour under the misapprehension that one can learn universal truths about human nature by studying one's fellow-citizens (and in practice most frequently just one's undergraduate students). As Campbell and Naroll (1972) put it: 'the laboratory psychologist still assumes that his college sophomores provide an adequate base for a general psychology of man'. These strictures apply, or at least did so until recently, to what one might call 'mainstream' psychology in the USA and western Europe. They do not apply, of course, to the same extent, to the small minority of cross-cultural psychologists whose influence on the main body still falls far short of constituting a critical mass. Moreover, while lip service is regularly paid to ecological factors by cross-cultural psychologists, it all too frequently remains just that. The jet-setting transnational researcher flitting from continent to continent handing out questionnaires to high-school and university students is intent on global comparisons; there is no opportunity to learn very much about the local ecologies and cultures whose surface is barely scratched by such an approach.

Others, like Berry, have taken ecology seriously. He has conducted both large-scale comparisons of the apparent effects on visual and spatial perception of different ecologies (Berry, 1976) and, together with a group of colleagues, carried out an intensive study of neighbouring Pygmy and Bantu populations (Berry et al., 1986) in the Central African Republic. This entailed repeated visits over a period of years, thereby approximating more closely the anthropological style. Generally it is becoming more common for cross-cultural psychologists to have, like anthropologists, *their* people to whom they return. For instance Super and Harkness have worked for many years with the Kipsigis of Kenya, concentrating on childhood. Narrowing down Bronfenbrenner's rather general notion of ecology, they put forward the concept of the 'development niche' (Super and Harkness, 1986). This is intended to summarise three major aspects of culture as experienced by an individual at various life stages. They are (a) 'the physical and social settings of everyday life', (b) 'culturally regulated customs of care and rearing' and (c) 'the cognitive and affective orientations of parents and other caretakers'. This approach has enabled them to explore cognitive, and to some extent affective development in novel and fruitful ways. Their narrow focus is in many ways a virtue, since it enables them to apply the quantitative tools valued by psychologists in a meaningful manner.

Of course, this does not mean that, however elegant, the causal nexus sometimes adduced is necessarily completely convincing, since in the Culture and Personality Tradition it still tends to have a self-fulfilling or teleological focus. So, for instance, from a series of ecological studies in Kenya, Munroe and Munroe (1977) trace out a causal chain in which the larger the plot of land a woman cultivates, the less patience she shows towards her children, and this is deemed to entail stricter child discipline and, so it is argued, consequently a decrease in their cognitive growth.

At the same time, such psychological studies may be criticised on the grounds that they do not seriously attempt to relate child development to the broader features of the social structure. Despite the failings of the Culture and Personality School referred to above, this is surely an important part of the task that should be undertaken. Those concerned probably would agree that the skills of the anthropologist are required for this purpose.

There are in fact now several examples of joint work between psychologists and anthropologists intended to bridge the gap between individual behaviour and higher-level structural aspects of a culture. Thus an anthropologist was part of the team in the previously mentioned Pygmy–Bantu project. In another study of cognitive development of children in New Guinea, some puzzling inter-tribal differences in developmental trends were illuminated by the contribution of an anthropologist (Lancy and Strathern, 1981). It was shown that the differences could be explained in terms of variations in folk taxonomies and the nature of social relationships. It is likely that such joint ventures will become increasingly common in future, thereby enlarging our understanding of the processes linking the macro-levels of society and culture with the micro-levels of individual development.

## INTRODUCTION TO THE CHILD STUDIES

### Preliminary methodological and conceptual considerations

Since the studies presented in this book are intended at least as much for psychologists as for anthropologists between whom there is apt to be much misunderstanding, several issues need to be clarified at the outset. Prominent among them is that of methods of research on which mainstream psychology and anthropology remained until recently most deeply divided. Many psychologists draw a sharp distinction between data obtained by formal empirical methods, usually involving some kind of 'hypothesis-testing', and material collected in other ways which they are apt to dismiss as 'unscientific'. Bronfenbrenner (1979) for instance, who, as has been shown, advocates a program that has a good deal in common with that sketched out here, in one place derides anthropological research as 'heavily anecdotal'. Some anthropologists reply in kind, as when La Barre (1978, p. 264) characterises academic psychology as 'a new method-obsessed scholasticism that to obtain the reliable has given up the threateningly significant'. Such mutual recriminations, although containing more than a grain of truth, are not helpful.

There was a time when controlled experiments were not merely regarded as important, but considered the only reliable method for getting at what was believed to be *the* scientific truth. Now it must be acknowledged that experiments are the only method that permits us to arrive at secure causal inferences, and none of the critics of experiments have been able to suggest an adequate substitute. However, there are severe limitations to the application of experimental methods in the social sciences. As has already been mentioned, they are used in psychology for the study of such part-functions of the human organism as perception. When it comes to behaviour involving the whole person, both ethical and practical constraints mean that experiments other than relatively trivial and artificial ones are not feasible. This is even more obvious when, as with most of the studies in this book, our concern is with the relationship between the cognitive growth and socialisation of the child in relation to the broader socio-cultural environment. Bronfenbrenner (1979, p. 37) rejects this point of view: 'If you wish to understand the relation between the developing person and some aspect of his environment, try to budge the one, and see what happens to the other'.

As is apparent from this passage he is not concerned with experimentation in the strict sense, but proposes the disturbance of an existing equilibrium in order to discover the properties of the system that have created it. While no doubt an admirable aim in principle, no detailed account is given of how one might proceed to achieve this on a sufficiently large scale to gain important information. There is no way (perhaps fortunately) that psychologists or anthropologists can routinely manipulate individual people or social structures. Yet it is possible to take advantage of naturally occurring variations to gain insights into the functioning of either person-environment or larger systems. In this spirit anthropologists make use of what they call 'case and situation analysis' (cf. Mitchell, 1983), and it is the atypical case that often proves most illuminating. Anthropologists also look to historical (cf. Lewis, 1968) and ecological (Burnham and Ellen, 1979) change and variation to provide insight into structural dynamics. On the other hand in psychology recently and especially in the study of child development (as the paper by Trevarthen with which we open our special studies demonstrates), systematic, anthropological-style ethnographic observation of natural behaviour is coming to play an increasingly important role. In fact, such prominent psychological researchers as Cole (1978) who started out as 'tough-minded' experimentalists have come to relegate experiments to a rather subordinate place.

This, of course, is not to dispute that anthropology is not sometimes guilty of a cavalier lack of concern for methodological rigour—and not least when it claims to be most theoretically rigorous. Yet in the last analysis the task of the anthropological observer must, by its very nature, be more dependent on subjective judgement and personal insights than is the case in most fields of psychology other than the clinical. It is important to understand, however, that these weaknesses (including psychological naïveté) usually apply more to the models of society and culture constructed by anthropologists than to their basic building blocks of ethnographic description, problematic though that may also be (see e.g. Malinowski, 1922, pp. 3–4; Wagner, 1975; Clifford, 1980; Stocking, 1983). In this respect their professional training equips them with skills usually superior to those acquired by psychologists for observing the key features of the socio-cultural setting in which children grow up—at least in Third World contexts. Anthropologists also have, in the main, a very different style in presenting their findings. The actual observations made and conversations with informants are recorded in voluminous field notes. From these materials a generalised account is gradually distilled, a process that often takes several years and as mentioned above involves a good deal of subjective judgement. It should be added, though, that anthropologists are generally well aware of the risks entailed thereby and seek to guard against them by checking internal consistency and comparisons with other accounts by their predecessors and/or contemporaries. They certainly are by no means naive regarding methodological problems, as may be illustrated with reference to the previously mentioned study by Meyer Fortes (1938/1970). In his introduction to this classical work he specifically discusses sampling problems, especially in relation to variations in behaviour. He also considered the tricky question as to how far it might be possible to account for such variations in terms of specific causes:

> For example, the first case of thumb-sucking I observed was that of a girl infant 3–4 years old whose mother had recently died. Could it be assumed that this was a clear-cut instance of the thumb being substituted for the nipple? Some time later I came across a little girl, about the same age, thumb-sucking, but her mother was alive and she was not yet fully weaned. Further observation brought a few more cases of this habit to light, but it is so infrequent among Tale children that *a single year's observation* (our italics) does not yield sufficient instances to suggest any correlation (1970, p. 204).

It is of course not suggested that all anthropologists are, even today, equally sophisticated, but it would be very mistaken to underestimate them. At the same time it is as well to recognise that many of their conceptual tools are considerably different from those of psychologists, sometimes employing the same terminology in a rather different sense. A highly pertinent case in point is the term 'cognition'. Psychologists normally understand this to refer to the inferred processes of thinking at the *individual* level. Anthropologists, on the other hand, employ 'cognition' primarily to designate *what* people think, their collective cultural representations, particular cosmologies, 'belief systems' and the like. What people think, in terms of the cultural content of their thoughts, is not necessarily at all the same as *how* they think, the actual (cognitive) processes of thinking, the form of their thinking (cf. Shweder, 1977). There is abundant anthropological evidence that people in different cultures and societies think similarly with different cultural constructs and cosmologies. Differences in cosmologies and standardised beliefs do not, therefore, necessarily imply different processes of thinking (cognition in the psychological sense). This unfortunate confusion is encouraged by glib anthropological references to 'getting inside their informants' heads'—in 'Cognitive Anthropology' and to the assimilation of individual, personal and collective cosmologies in, for example, the work of Mary Douglas (1970). The notion 'modes of thought' in the tradition of Evans-Pritchard's and his students' subtle work (see e.g. Finnegan and Horton, 1973) on religious ideas (sometimes dubbed 'thought structuralists') also risks blurring this important distinction between content and form. Of course, just as artists maintain that form *is* content, there is likely to be some relationship here, but this has to be convincingly demonstrated rather than buried in conceptual confusion. The current revival of interest among psychologists in what they call 'social representations' (Farr and Moscovici, 1984) as well as of anthropologists in 'collective representations' (Hallpike, 1979; Toren, 1983; Sperber, 1985) may facilitate clarification of this confusing issue.[5]

These divergencies should be kept in mind when perusing the essays in this volume, where the usage is not always entirely consistent. However, most contributors most of the time use the expression 'cognitive development' in a descriptive sense, similar to that in much psychological work, to denote children's increasing intellectual skills in understanding their environment. This includes, of course, their social as well as physical environment: they learn, for instance, the kinship categories of their society and associated norms and rules.

This brings us to the second important concept, namely 'socialisation', and unlike 'cognition' it is not viewed very differently by psychologists and anthropologists. The reason is probably not that all agree on a clear definition, but on the contrary that the notion is so diffuse in both disciplines as to guarantee considerable overlap. The common core of meaning is the process whereby children become effectively functioning members of a particular society.[6] Most attempts at formal definition refer to both cognition and affect: 'inculcation of the skills and attitudes necessary for playing given social roles' (Mayer, 1970, p. xiii); 'learns the ways of a given social group ... acquires behavior, attitudes, values and other personality traits' (Dager, 1971, pp. ix/x). Yet in practice until recently most studies concerned with the issue, from the Culture and Personality School onwards, have tended to focus on values, attitudes and personality dispostions rather than on knowledge and skills. Thus the *Handbook of cross-cultural human development* (Munroe, Munroe and Whiting, 1981) has two quite separate sections dealing respectively with 'Cognitive and moral development' and 'Socialization and outcomes'. Others have come closer to a recognition of the relevance of both aspects, though still distinguishing between 'The socialization of affect' and 'Cognitive socialization' (Schwartz, 1975).

In fact, both are merely different facets of one and the same process. The line drawn between 'cognitive' and 'affective' socialisation is an arbitrary one, prompted by the interests and methods of different researchers. Although this issue is hardly touched upon directly by our contributors, several of the essays bring out the close interweaving of cognitive and affective features of development. The ethnographic account, at its best, can provide a perspective that is relatively less distorted by preconceived categories and divisions.

Having concluded that, apart from some specific purposes, it makes little sense to split socialisation into the cognitive and affective, one may go on to ask what the nature of the process is and how it is conceived by those who deal with children. Beginning with the former, three different theoretical models can be distinguished in the literature:[7]

(1) *The 'unfolding' model.* Prominent in the history of European thought at least from Rousseau onwards, this held that the function of caretakers is merely that of providing a suitable

environment that is essentially passive for permitting 'natural' development to occur. Such a notion, though still supported by Gesell about a generation ago, has now been largely abandoned.

(2) *The clay moulding model.* Here the child is regarded as mainly passive, being shaped by society in the proper mould. Such a view also goes far back in European history and has until recently remained dominant in twentieth-century social science.

(3) *The interactive model.* This portrays socialisation as a struggle between the child wishing to gratify impulses and assert independence while society in the form of caretakers and authority figures seeks to make the child conform. Again this is not a new idea, but one that governs most current socialisation research.

Although this sketch is grossly over-simplified, it should be enough to indicate the existence of very different notions about socialisation. Moreover, when thus crudely formulated it is easier to recognise that beliefs similar to one or other of these notions can also be found in the cultures described in this volume. These beliefs, in turn, are related to the institutions and cosmologies of these societies. Several of the case studies document the links between collective representations and childrearing, sometimes offering striking illustration of the manner in which these affected adult–child interactions. This work prompts the thought that perhaps some of the western ideas about socialisation may be little more than social representations (in Moscovici's sense) dressed up as scientific theories! At any rate there are now many psychologists ready to accept that the socio-cultural system in which a child grows up channels the development of both cognition and affective disposition. As Rogoff (1984, p. 5) puts it: 'The formal institutions of society and the informal interactions of its members are thus central to the process of development.' Such a general claim is difficult to establish in a modern large-scale and heterogeneous society, but its validity can be more clearly seen to be supported in the case studies presented here.

**Ethnographic case studies**

It was with the strengths of this ethnographic reportage in mind that we approached a number of our social anthropological colleagues to discover what data they had managed to collect on child development and the acquisition of culture. The response we received confirmed our impressions that this was still a relatively neglected subject and one which accordingly merited attention. This led us to organise the workshop at the London School of Economics in 1982 from which the present volume has developed.

Since all the original participants (except Jahoda) were social anthropologists, we felt it crucial to include an account of current ethological research on child development and we thus invited Colwyn Trevarthen to contribute our opening chapter. This vigorous exposition of a Chomskian view of the acquisition of culture, based on biological programming in early infancy, provides a challenging point of departure, not least for the cross-cultural universality it claims for its findings on developmental stages in the first two years of childhood. Trevarthen shows convincingly how very young infants play a much more active, eliciting role than is conventionally assumed. Age-linked changes, he argues, are universal in all cultures and races, and these provide the limits within which, contrary to Piagetian assumptions, cultural differences may be instilled in the process of mobilising innate 'co-operative motives'. Some of the other, social anthropological studies in later chapters suggest greater cultural variability here than these trenchantly expressed findings based on a few intensive cross-cultural comparisons indicate. But the complex issue of how much is biologically universal in infant performance requires much further research both by ethologists, prepared like Trevarthen, to utilise ethnographic observational techniques, and by those anthropologists who take these techniques for granted but who (with the exception of the Culture and Personality School) have so far seldom made infancy a primary focus of their research.

Concentrating on the first two years of infancy, by which time children as they learn to speak are seen as making a significant entry into cultural activities, Trevarthen deals primarily with pre-verbal transactions in the acquisition and transmission of culture. John Blacking and Angela Hobart, writing as social anthropologists, evaluate the didactic significance of other non-verbal media in these early stages and in later phases of growth with reference to cultures where music and the theatre play major (if infrequently recognised) roles in education in its broadest sense. Drawing on his experience of Venda music and dance, Blacking argues persuasively for the formative influence of the non-verbal experience of affective culture in cognitive development and creativity. Cognitive development itself, Blacking insists, should be assessed not only in specific social contexts but also in terms of indigenous psychological concepts about growth, motivation and intelligence—the focus of the chapters in the second part of this volume.

More specifically, what Blacking sees as the open-textured, adaptive character of the 'traditional' Venda world view enabled individuals to achieve self-actualisation creatively in a variety of achieved rather than ascribed roles. Here dance and music provide a means of testing the experience of self, body and other. The underlying principles of the Venda socio-cultural system itself are communicated through music and dance, communal music reinforcing group identity with sensuous satisfaction as the reward for the individual musician's altruism.

In Bali, in turn, Angela Hobart shows how intrinsic traditional theatre is to the process by which moral attitudes and values are inculcated. She points to the crucial cultural importance in Bali of the visual medium in the transmission of knowledge; information received through the other senses being regarded as less authoritative. Here, appropriately, the eyes are the most vital feature of dancers and actors. Thus the visually dependent (traditional) shadow play, a veritable sacred drama reflecting hallowed tales from the sacred texts, for its male (and child) audiences celebrates core values. The lighter operetta, despised by men, caters for a female public.

The second part of this book presents three studies, based on anthropological fieldwork in widely separate geographical areas, which focus centrally on childhood and cognitive development viewed in the context of indigenous (or ethno) psychology. As Signe Howell justly notes in her consideration of Chewong (Malaysia) childhood, this is an orientation hitherto largely ignored by British social anthropologists. Moreover, as she observes, if we are to examine the process of cognitive growth in an unfamiliar cultural context we need first to establish the local cultural understanding of what constitutes personality and selfhood. While in line with Trevarthen's views the Chewong assume behaviour to be largely innate and make little effort to encourage socially desirable features; they also regard cognitive development as starting in the womb and continuing until death (and sometimes beyond that).

Joanna Overing's intriguing account of childhood and maturation amongst the Piaora Indians of Venezuela similarly concentrates on the indigenous understanding of growth as a long and continuing process of acquiring knowledge. Initiation into the secrets of power is necessary at every stage in the individual's general education. This involves the incorporation of extraneous forces which are domesticated and become a kind of inner (internalised) clothing. Such knowledge, typically, of hunting and sorcery in the case of men, and of fertility in the case of women is reified in the form of the 'beads of life' which cumulatively constitute the self's inner clothing. Here, it seems, a cultural account of cognitive development is actually central to an understanding of Piaora society in general.

Although the cultural circumstances of the Bornean Punan Bah rice-cultivators of Sarawak described in rich detail by Ida Nicolaisen are very different, the individual's development is similarly conceived of as a gradual process involving the increasing acquisition of spiritual power. Nicolaisen demonstrates, again, how adult expectations and treatment of children have to be set within a fuller cosmological context in which the cultural construct of selfhood is clearly elucidated. Particularly interesting is that gender role differentiation, traceable to age two and pronounced about age five or six, seems to precede the corresponding sex-linked soul distinctions which occur at sexual adolescence. There is here an interesting hiatus between the development of distinctive roles in infancy and the later attribution of the associated cosmological constructs. In this subtle study, Nicolaisen also makes the intriguing observation that children are more concerned about gender than adults in a culture where men readily adopt women's domestic roles. She suggests that, in this hierarchical society, boys who are unable otherwise to assert themselves because of their junior status, may thus seek to emphasise and manipulate their gender identity as a basis for precedence. In any event, children, or boys, are evidently exaggerating the adult cultural construction of gender.

The socio-cultural inculcation of gender differences is the integrating focus of the three chapters in the final section of this book. In the first of these Christina Toren, a social anthropologist whose earlier training is in psychology, adopts a hybrid approach to elucidate children's construction of gender and hierarchy in Fiji. In this context she questions the influential anthropological view that in hierarchical societies rank takes precedence over gender as an organising principle. The sociological analysis of cultural constructs cannot on its own, Toren maintains, reveal their centrality in organising people's perceptions. A satisfactory elucidation of the relative weighting of the two principles, she argues, requires a technical study of children's cognitive development. Systematic analysis of the development, at different ages, of children's perceptions offers an objective assessment of the relative significance of rank and gender as conceptual ordering principles in Fijian culture. This procedure does not merely elucidate *how* children learn their culture, but offers new insight into the meaning and relative primacy of cultural constructs themselves. What psychologists will surely regard as the most technically sophisticated of the contributions we present here, concludes that in Fijian ideas gender and rank are equally dominant salient principles. More generally, hierarchy is seen to be a principle no more absolute and no less subject to cultural construction (and relativisation) than gender.

Gender provides the dominant theme in indigenous ideas of child development amongst the Muslim population of the Tunisian island of Kerkennah analysed by Katherine Platt. Crucial areas here are the idea of the self, self-expression, and attitudes towards activity or passivity. Here Platt argues, while girls may learn physical independence earlier than boys, the latter develop psychological independence and a sense of identity earlier and more fully. This may be consistent with a more individualised pattern of work for males than females in adult life in this particular Islamic society, where the distinction between work and play applies virtually only to the male sex. This sexual disparity in culturally constructed development, as Platt notes, is also reflected in a greater tendency for adults to censor conversation more carefully in the presence of male than female children. More generally as might be anticipated, there is correspondingly a much sharper distinction between the ages at which men and women attain maturity than in the other ethnographic examples discussed above. Women mature early: men have to wait until old age. This is also consistent with the age differential between the sexes at marriage.

Tamara Dragadze's fascinating ethnographic vignette of childhood in Soviet Georgia, our concluding study, describes a rural context in which there is less emphatic sexual differentiation. This village setting has very different relations with the external Soviet world of which it is part compared to the corresponding relationship between Kerkennah island and its wider (Tunisian) Islamic hinterland. In the latter case there seems to be a high degree of congruity between local and regional values and hence the tightly integrated pattern of socialisation discussed by Platt. In Soviet Georgia, there are clearly two worlds with different, conflicting values, implying different socialisation requirements. The local Georgian culture is a 'great' literate tradition which has been to some extent marginalised by the Soviet system and yet remains the ultimate treasurehouse of fundamental values. Women, who like men may work outside the household and farm, are the guardians of this Georgian literacy, and the secure repositories of Georgian values. Girls learn more poetry and kinship than boys. Here, *pace* Trevarthen, the local ethnopsychology assumes that children enter the world in a state of complete ignorance and have to be taught everything. In this process, Dragadze stresses the importance of non-verbal communication between parents and children, especially for those external state contexts in which children are taught to pay lip service to official instructions and to divulge as little information as possible. There is a sharp contrast between the actually collectivist village world of shared solidarity and the officially collectivist state world where actual survival depends on guarded individual opportunism. Georgian values are imparted with confidence and pride, the reticence and evasions regarded as essential to confronting the external official world and its capricious demands are inculcated in a more authoritarian and didactic style, typically without explanation. Here, despite the common structural situation of Georgian rural families in relation to the state, Dragadze found no homogeneous set of rules for dealing with this context. She throws out the interesting suggestion that, given these two levels of experience, cognitive development might vary according to the different styles used by adults to develop children's identity as related co-villagers on the one hand, and as 'citizens' in a hostile, remote external context, on the other. Dragadze recognises that this plural setting is by no means unique, and (in line with Blacking's comments on the Venda) gently questions the routine assumption in socialisation studies that the 'traditional' cultural context forms a perfectly integrated, self-perpetuating system where childrearing practices harmoniously (and mechanically) inculcate the appropriate perennial parental values and expectations.

INTRODUCTION

## Socialisation: towards an ethnography of childhood

The training of children to operate in two or more incompatible contexts and to deal with the ensuing conflicts is a remarkably under-researched area, especially when one considers the contemporary prominence in plural societies all over the world of ethnic minorities to say nothing of the yawning 'generation gap' associated with rapid social change. It is, of course, also of theoretical as well as practical interest, since it provides a 'natural' experimental setting in which to re-examine the validity of such analytical syndromes as 'cognitive dissonance'. Whatever may have been the case in the past, such pluralist contexts are evidently today increasingly common.

Children's apparent tolerance of such conflicting principles tends to reinforce the evidence of the ethnographic contributions in this volume on the absence of demonstrably tight linkages between ecology, culture and personality. Although child development was not in every case the primary focus in our colleagues' research, these case studies illustrate the crucial importance of grounding studies of children's education in the local ethnographic context with as full an account as possible of indigenous psychological assumptions, general values and cosmological beliefs. It is naturally very difficult even for a researcher proficient in the local language to cover all this ground systematically (whether or not using hybrid approaches such as Toren's) within the scope of a single extended ethnographic field study and to record it in a corresponding full-length monograph, far less chapter or article. When we add that such research should distinguish carefully between indigenous psychological theories and ideals of child training and their actual implementation (the effects of variability in which needs also to be considered) the task seems impossibly daunting. It is not surprising therefore that, as we have been insisting, there are so few accounts of childhood and child development which satisfy the anthropological canons of ethnographic fullness and fidelity. However, if we are to proceed beyond the just-so, anecdotal accounts of culture, personality and cosmology—whether by anthropologists or psychologists—with which the literature abounds, this difficult task needs to be confronted. Varied in their coverage as they are, the ethnographically orientated contributions presented here will have fulfilled a useful purpose if they serve to highlight the inadequacies that we find in so many current psychological studies of socialisation.

Notwithstanding their limited geographical range, our case studies take us beyond the dubious conclusions of the Culture and Personality School. They demonstrate that 'socialisation' involves a more complex and subtle range of processes than is generally supposed by those who approach it in such simplistic terms as the global effects imputed to traumatic (or non-traumatic) weaning. Although it seems that it is commonly about age seven that children are generally considered to become morally responsible and capable of intellectual development, there are wide differences in the phases and gradations drawn between 'child' and 'adult' in different cultures. The processes by which individuals of either sex move from one pole to the other vary widely and often involve much more than merely achieving the married state.

More significantly, variations in socialisation are not only matters of the nature of didactic procedures, formal and informal, verbal and non-verbal, aesthetic etc., or of different ways of punctuating the life cycle (in 'rites of passage' cf. Bernardi, 1985). They also crucially reflect contrasting views of children's innate learning capacity and of the role of nurture in human development. At one end of the scale, in Georgia, children are regarded virtually as blank slates where everything has to be taught. With their stress on learning through initiation into the powerful secrets of human culture, the Piaora Indians seem to share a similar view of education as an externally imposed process. With less elaborate initiatory rituals, The Chewong and Punan Bah nevertheless place great emphasis on the development of self-control and the avoidance of overt displays of emotion. In both these cases, there is little in the way of explicit education. Behaviour is largely assumed to be innate, children are virtually self-taught and left to develop speech and motor skills at their own, individual pace. Amongst the Venda and in Fiji, on the other hand, the influence of nurture is emphasised in interactive theories of child development which, in line with Trevarthen's views, stress the active role of the child.

Of course, it is difficult to securely characterise these apparently culturally contrasting assumptions concerning child development since much depends on the impressions of the ethnographer who records them. As we should expect, the situation is even more complicated when we include gender variations within the same culture. Where there is a strong emphasis on contrasting gender stereotypes, it would be quite remarkable if boys and girls were subject to the *same* socialising process. That is self-evident. What is more interesting and not necessarily predictable, is the nature of the developmental process according to sex. Our case studies of Kerkennah and Punan Bah both indicate a much smoother transition from childhood to adult in the case of girls than boys. In each case these differences in childhood expectations and behaviour and in the transition to later years seem to anticipate stereotyped adult male and female roles. So in Kerkennah, boys are weaned later than girls. Their circumcision, following weaning, abruptly moves a boy's centre of gravity from his mother to the world of male peers, where he is expected to behave aggressively and irresponsibly, settling down later 'naturally' as a responsible, mature adult. Weaned earlier and without ritual punctuation marks, girls move more smoothly into the wider intergenerational female community.

These sex-linked differences in socialisation serve to illustrate the complexity of processes which are often assumed (by anthropologists as well as psychologists) to operate teleologically, automatically producing stereotypical exemplars of a particular society. There is an urgent need here for more sensitive and subtle cross-cultural research on the means by which cultures are reproduced. Despite the formidable difficulties facing effective research here, the rewards go beyond merely elucidating and documenting (important though that is) the intergenerational transmission of culture. Apart from offering access to the often overlooked mechanisms and processes (so regularly taken for granted by social anthropologists) by which children actually absorb adult culture, we may thus hope to gain additional and often novel insight into the meaning of childhood, parenthood and gender in particular societies. Through examining the earliest contexts in which they are produced and reproduced in a person's life, we are also provided with a new point of entry (and an opportunity to test interpretations made in other contexts) to understanding dominant cultural symbols.

So in her extraordinarily rich study of Wolof infancy and childhood, Jacqualine Rabain (1979) shows how in this society where descent is traced bilaterally, and mother's milk designates matrifiliation, the pattern of breast-feeding is not to be understood simply as a matter of (casually or idiosyncratically) gratifying infant demands. Rather these maternal responses are what designates the mother as mother and signify her relationship to the child which, in turn, is part of a wider circle of matrilateral kinship. When the mother breast-feeds her child she responds to the moral commands of this kinship principle: her breast milk is not entirely her own. 'Your child is not your possession, your thing, it is a relative, it is our child', the mother is told. The child, in turn, has to learn that it does not own and cannot monopolise its mother, since both are subject to the Wolof code (Rabain, 1979, pp. 42–43). Rabain describes in meticulous detail how the child's breast-feeding and maternal body contact is extended and transformed as it is weaned about 22–24 months within the wider family circle where the infant's changing feeding pattern constitutes a veritable apprenticeship in the meaning of exchange relationships. Such minutely detailed information on non-verbal and verbal patterns of interaction between parents and infants, set in an equally comprehensive semantic account of the wider cultural context, provides unusual, if not unique, insight into cultural processes and the production and reproduction of cultural meanings.

We are not alone, of course, in stressing the importance of this more comprehensive style of ethnographic reportage which pays proper attention to children as objects and agents in the transmission of culture. Particularly in France,[8] but to some extent elsewhere also, there are signs of welcome recent developments here, [9] which the current emphasis on the cultural (and social) 'construction' of beliefs and behaviour might be expected to further encourage. Finally, as far as research strategies are concerned, we have already indicated a number of promising interdisciplinary studies. It seems to us, however, that sometimes the efforts of a mixed anthropological and psychological team may be less effective than those of single hybrid professionals such as Meyer Fortes, Jacqualine Rabain and, in the present volume, Christina Toren. The existing record of team work here, in our opinion, tends to confirm the validity of Meyer Fortes' shrewd observation that the best interdisciplinary co-operation is often that carried out in the mind of a single researcher. However that may be, it is beginning to be more widely recognised that we must now move beyond the relatively narrow confines of cognitive development in cross-cultural studies. We need to advance our understanding of the manner in which children come to adopt the prevailing social categories, values and norms in the context of their widening social relationships. We want to know not merely how children grow up thinking, but also feeling and acting as members of a particular society—in other words the aim is to throw light on the actual processes involved in the acquisition of culture.

## NOTES

1. In contrast, a generation earlier Galton had already displayed a more enlightened attitude, devising a questionnaire requesting information about children of 'savages' who had been removed from their parents and brought up in 'civilised' conditions. His aim seems to have been to explore the relative contributions of heredity and environment (Pearson, 1924).
2. For a more recent study of the acquisition of kinship concepts among Hausa children, see Levine and Price-Williams (1974).
3. *Notes and Queries on Anthropology*, Royal Anthropological Institute, London 1951, p. 101.
4. Useful overviews are provided by Barnouw (1973) and Bock (1980).
5. If the connection here between psychological and anthropological interpretative assumptions is particularly obvious, this of course is not to suggest that other areas of anthropological theory are immune from psychological assumptions, however unacknowledged. For fuller discussion of some of these see Richards (1970); Lewis (1977); Jahoda (1982); Sperber (1985).
6. Some anthropologists favour the term 'enculturation' coined by Herskovits and distinguish this from 'socialisation'. However, as shown by Bourguignon (1973), the usage is inconsistent and will therefore not be further considered here.
7. Here we are indebted to the excellent discussion of this topic by Schaffer (1984).
8. See e.g. *L'Usage social des enfants, Anthropologie et Sociétés* (Special issue), 1980, *4*, 2.
9. For example on children's games and play. See Lancy and Tindall (1977); Schwartzman (1978); Le Moal (1981); and S. Ottenberg (1982).

## BIBLIOGRAPHY

Barnouw, V. (1973) *Culture and personality*. Homewood, Illinois: Dorsey Press.
Barry, H. III, Child, I.L. and Bacon, M.K. (1959) 'Relations of child training to subsistence economy'. *American Anthropologist 61*, 51–63. Reprinted in C.S. Ford (ed.), (1967) *Cross-cultural approaches: readings in comparative research*. New Haven: HRAF Press.

Barth, F. (1975) *Ritual and knowledge among the Baktaman of New Guinea*. New Haven: Yale University Press.
Bernardi, B. (1985) *Age class systems: social institutions and politics based on age*. Cambridge: Cambridge University Press.
Berry, J.W. (1976) *Human ecology and cognitive style*. New York: Wiley.
Berry, J.W. et al. (eds.) (1986) *Cultural adaptation and cognitive development in Central Africa*. Lisse: Swets & Zeitlinger.
Bock, P.K. (1980) *Continuities in psychological anthropology*. San Francisco: Freeman.
Bourguignon, E. (1973) 'Psychological anthropology'. In J.J. Honigman (ed.), *Handbook of social and cultural anthropology*. Chicago: Rand McNally.
—— (1976) *Possession*. San Francisco: Chandler and Sharp.
Bronfenbrenner, U. (1979) *The ecology of human development*. Cambridge, Mass.: Harvard University Press.
Bruner, J.S. (1966) 'On cognitive growth II'. In J.S. Bruner et al., *Studies in cognitive growth*. New York: Wiley.
Burnham, P.C. and Ellen, R.F. (eds) (1979) *Social and ecological systems*. London: Academic Press.
Burrow, J.W. (1966) *Evolution and society*. Cambridge: Cambridge University Press.
Campbell, D.T. and Naroll, R. (1972) 'The mutual methodological relevance of anthropology and psychology'. In F.L.K. Hsu (ed.) *Psychological anthropology*. Cambridge, Mass.: Schenkman.
Clifford, J. (1980) 'Fieldwork, reciprocity and the making of ethnographic texts: the example of Maurice Lienhardt', *Man*, *15*, 3.
Cole, M. (1978) Ethnographic psychology of cognition—so far. In G.D. Spindler (ed.), *The making of psychological anthropology*. Berkeley: University of California Press.
—— Gay, J. and Sharp, D. (1971) *The cultural context of learning and thinking*. New York: Basic Books.
Dager, E.Z. (ed.) (1971) *Socialization*. Chicago: Markham.
Dasen, P.R. (1972) 'Cross-cultural Piagetian research: a summary'. *Journal of Cross-cultural Psychology* PS *3*, 23–39.
—— (1977) 'Are cognitive processes universal? A contribution to cross-cultural Piagetian psychology'. In N. Warren (ed.), *Studies in cross-cultural psychology* vol. 1. London: Academic Press.
—— Inhelder, B., Lavallee, M. and Retschitzki, J. (1978) *Naissance de l'intelligence chez l'enfant Baoule de Côte d'Ivoire*. Berne: Hans Huber.
Douglas, M. (1970) *Natural symbols*. London: Barrie and Rockliff.
Ellis, A.C. and Hall, G.S. (1896) 'A study of dolls'. *Pedagogical Seminary*, *4*, 129–75.
Farr, R.M. and Moscovici, S. (eds) (1984) *Social representations*. Cambridge: Cambridge University Press.
Finnegan, R. and Horton, R. (eds) (1973) *Modes of thought*. Faber.
Firth, R. (1936) *We the Tikopia*. London: Allen & Unwin.
Fortes, M. (1938) 'Social and psychological aspects of education in Taleland'. Supplement to *Africa*, *2* (4). Reprinted in: M. Fortes

(1970) *Time and social structure and other essays*. London: Athlone Press.
Gelfand, M. (1979) *Growing up in Shona society*. Gwelo: Mambo Press.
Hall, G.S. (1904) *Adolescence* vol. 1. New York: Appleton.
Hallpike, C.R. (1979) *The foundations of primitive thought*. Oxford: The Clarendon Press.
Jahoda, G. (1982) *Psychology and anthropology*. London: Academic Press.
Kaberry, P.M. (1939) *Aboriginal women*. London: Routledge & Kegan Paul.
Krige, J.D. and Krige, E.J. (1943) *The realm of a rain-queen*. London: Oxford University Press.
Kuper, A. (1973) *Anthropologists and anthropology: The British School*. London: Allan Lane.
La Barre, W. (1978) 'The clinic and the field'. In G.D. Spindler (ed.), *The making of psychological anthropology*. Berkeley: University of California Press.
Laboratory of Comparative Human Cognition (1982) 'Culture and intelligence'. In R.J. Sternberg (ed.), *Handbook of human intelligence*. Cambridge: Cambridge University Press.
—— (1983) 'Culture and cognitive development'. In W. Kessen (ed.), *Handbook of child psychology* (4th ed.) vol. 1. New York: Wiley.
La Fontaine, J. (1985) *Initiation: ritual drama and secret knowledge across the world*. Harmondsworth: Penguin Books.
Lancy, D.F. and Tindall, B.A. (1977) *The study of play*. New York: Leisure Press.
—— and Strathern, A.J. (1981) ' "Making twos": pairing as an alternative to the taxonomic mode of representation'. *American Anthropologist 83*, 773–95.
Langham, I. (1981) *The building of British social anthropology*. Dordrecht: D. Reidel Publishing Company.
LeVine, R.A. and Price-Williams, D.R. (1974) 'Children's kinship concepts: cognitive development and early experience among the Hausa'. *Ethnology 13*, 25–44.
Lewis, I.M. (1961) *A pastoral democracy: a study of pastoralism and politics among the northern Somali of the Horn of Africa*. London: Oxford University Press. (Revised edition, New York: Holmes and Meir, 1982).
—— (ed.) (1968) *History and social anthropology*. London: Tavistock.
—— (ed.) (1977) *Symbols and sentiments*. London: Academic Press.
—— (1985) *Social anthropology in perspective*. Cambridge: Cambridge University Press.
Malinowski, B. (1922) *Argonauts of the Western Pacific*. London: Routledge & Kegan Paul.
Mayer, P. (ed.) (1970) *Socialization. The approach from social anthropology*. London: Tavistock.
Mead, M. (1932) 'An investigation of the thought of primitive children with special reference to animism'. *Journal of the Royal Anthropological Institute 62*, 173–89.
—— (1962) 'Retrospects and Prospects' in T. Gladwin and W. Sturtevant (eds) *Anthropology and Human Behaviour*, Washington DC; Anthropological Society of Washington.

Mitchell, J.C. (1983) 'Case and situation analysis'. *The Sociological Review 31*, 187–211.
Munroe, R.L. and Munroe, R.H. (1977) 'Land, labor and the child's cognitive performance among the Logoli'. *American Ethnologist 4*, 309–20.
Munroe, R.H., Munroe, R.L. and Whiting, B.B. (eds) (1981) *Handbook of cross-cultural human development*. New York: Garland STPM Press.
Ottenberg, S. (1982) 'Illusion, communication and psychology in West African masquerades', *Ethos*, *10* (2) 149–85.
Pearson, K. (1924) *The life, letters and labour of Francis Galton*. Cambridge: Cambridge University Press.
Piaget, J. (1945) *La formation du symbole chez l'enfant*. Paris: Presses Universitaires de France.
—— (1966) 'Necessité et signification des recherches comparatives en psychologie génétique'. *International Journal of Psychology 1*, 3–13.
Rabain, J. (1979) *L'enfant du lignage. Du sevrage à la classe d'âge*. Paris: Payot.
Raum, O. (1940) *Chaga childhood*. London: Oxford University Press.
Read, M. (1960) *Children of their fathers: Growing up among the Ngoni of Nyasaland*. New Haven: Yale University Press.
Richards, A.I. (1970) 'Socialization and contemporary British Anthropology'. In P. Mayer (ed.), *Socialization. The approach from social anthropology*. London: Tavistock.
—— (1932) *Hunger and work in a savage tribe*. London: Routledge.
—— (1939) *Land, labour and diet in Northern Rhodesia: an economic study of the Bemba tribe*. London: Oxford University Press.
—— (1964) 'Authority patterns in traditional Buganda'. In L.A. Fallers (ed.), *The king's men*. London: Oxford University Press.
—— (1956) *Chisungu: A girl's initiation ceremony among the Bemba of Northern Rhodesia*. London: Faber and Faber.
Rogoff, B. (1984) In B. Rogoff and J. Lave (eds) *Everyday cognition: its development in social context*. Cambridge, Mass.: Harvard University Press.
Schaffer, R.H. (1984) *The child's entry into a social world*. London: Academic Press.
Schwartz, T. (ed.) (1975) *Socialization as cultural communication*. Berkeley: University of California Press.
Schwartzman, H.B. (1978) *Transformations: the anthropology of children's play*. New York: Plenum Press.
—— and Barbera, L. (1976) 'Children's play in Africa and South America'. In D.F. Lancy and B. Allan Tindall (eds), *The anthropological study of play: problems and prospects*. Cornwall, N.Y.: Leisure Press.
Shweder, R.A. (1977) 'Likeness and likelihood in everyday thought: magical thinking in judgements of personality'. *Current Anthropology 18*, 637–58.
Spencer, P. (1965) *The Samburu: a study of gerontocracy in a nomadic tribe*. London: Routledge & Kegan Paul.
Sperber, D. (1985) 'Anthropology and psychology: towards an epidemiology of representations' *Man*, *20* (1) 73–89.

Stocking, G. (1968) *Race, culture and evolution.* New York.
—— (ed.) (1983) *Observers observed, history of anthropology* vol. 1. Madison: University of Wisconsin.
Sully, J. (1895) *Studies of childhood.* London: Longmans.
Super, C.M. and Harkness, S. (1986) 'The developmental niche: a conceptualization at the interface of child and culture'. *International Journal of Behavioral Development, 9*, 545–69.
Toren, C. (1983) 'Thinking symbols: a critique of Sperber (1979)', *Man, 18,* 260–8.
Wagner, R. (1975) *The invention of culture.* Chicago: Chicago University Press.
Wertheimer, M. (1979) *A brief history of psychology.* New York: Holt, Rinehart and Winston.
Whiting, B.B. and Whiting, J.W.M. (1975) *Children of six cultures.* Cambridge, Mass.: Harvard University Press.

# Part I:
# Non-verbal Processes in the Acquisition of Culture

# 1

# Universal Co-operative Motives: How Infants begin to know the Language and Culture of their Parents

Colwyn Trevarthen

## INTRODUCTION: TOWARDS A THEORY OF INNATE COGNITION FOR SOCIAL AND CULTURAL SKILLS

In recent years, detailed examination of how normal infants respond to the adult who gives affectionate care has brought evidence for potent control behaviours in the infant that stimulate a particular diet or syllabus of supportive and instructive behaviour from caretakers (Trevarthen, 1979a, 1983; Stern, 1985; Trevarthen and Marwick, 1986). Some of the newly chartered behaviours, additional to the behaviours that make sure the infant is adequately fed and protected from harm, or healed if sick, are purely psychological in function and consequence. They ensure an increasingly elaborate mental and behavioural engagement between the infant and other persons and appear to be produced by innate self-regulatory brain systems that are, in effect, representations or primitive concepts of persons and how one has to communicate with them, verbally or non-verbally. In time, and by controlling relationships with persons who teach, they set the direction of development for cognitive processes of culture.

This theory of socio-cultural development to explain these phenomena has been called Innate Intersubjectivity Theory (Trevarthen, 1979b, 1980). It claims that infants possess an inherent readiness to link their subjective evaluations of experience with those of other persons. It sees children starting cognitive learning in a co-operative and imitative relationship to other more experienced companions and actively contributing to the propagation of collective knowledge.

Modern psychological theories, I submit, systematically

undervalue the competence of the infant for having feelings and desires, for acting with purpose, for dealing with persons and for co-operative life. They consequently misrepresent the process by which children become 'socialised' or taken into the culture as contributing and creative members. Clearly I am in agreement with Elizabeth Tonkin (1982) who argues we must seek to understand what children give to the process of socialisation, and also with Vygotsky's theory of mental development (Wertsch, 1985).

Behaviourist learning theories admit as innate certain biological needs regulating survival of the organism. In social learning theory the importance of modelling and imitation is stressed; but no explanation is offered for the origin of the capacity to imitate some behaviours and not others. Freudian psychoanalytic theory considers mental representations from the point of view of their relationship to sensations of pleasure or pain. Fantasy is a means of separating out a self-image from a reality that is challenging or life-threatening, life being presumed to begin with no clear representation of the 'self' in relation to objects or others. Piagetian cognitive theory, while it does accept that self-generated action is the 'motor' of learning, considers adaptations to social conditions to be of the same kind as adaptations to physical conditions for actions. The child gains symbolic, moral and co-operative abilities as it gains concepts, schemata to represent objects and processes in the physical world, by building up memories of the sensory effects of acting and by organising these into control programs. This occurs after the child develops an egocentric intentionality by linking up internal representations and thoughts about the sensory feedback from motor operations that originate in the child. Imitations of others are based on self-imitations, and play with others grows out of play for the self. Morality is an internalisation of rules of play that peers impose to regulate competitive games.

Theories, such as Piaget's, that concentrate on the mind of an individual on its own, do not grasp that human societies depend upon the skills individuals have for knowing and using historically created cultural meanings and symbols for their communication (Trevarthen and Logotheti, 1987). Persons have mastery of meaning; in language, in traditional beliefs, in customary co-operative actions and in the accepted perception of the artificial tools, institutions and rituals that they use together (Trevarthen, 1987). This is 'cognition' in the anthropological sense—the working knowledge of a culture, especially talk about that knowledge and hence the store of meanings in words. Children must learn the skills and 'sense' of culture as they learn to talk. The question is, how do they do it? Must we assume that cognition as the anthropologists define it, is historically created, absorbed by every new generation with the language? This is classical dualism, 'nature' and 'culture' essentially different, unreconciled.

The experimental psychologist defines cognition as the perceiving by the individual of the physical circumstances that condition his action. In a mature person, cognitive activity 'processes' the input of sensory information with intelligence, attaching it to categories that previous experience has proved are real, or useful. Most developmental psychologists assume that social cognitions are, like the vocabulary of language or word lists in an experiment, taken in by learning. The human brain, starting as biological (non-mental and non-social) matter, is made consciously effective by a process of 'socialisation'; that is, by conditioning the construction of meaningful social habits. True, social learning theory recognises that there are some special mental processes that govern cognition of the actions of other persons in the subject's mind; but those crucial and ever-present features of children's behaviour, imitation, observational learning and imaginative play, are given no satisfactory explanation. An effort is made to prove that the underlying empathic motivations are learned in infancy by a brain that is empty at first of all ideas of persons and what special things can be done with them.

The recent research with infants indicates a contrary thesis. Humans are born with a self-regulating strategy for getting knowledge by human negotiation and co-operative action. Children learn social behaviours and language tasks in an intermental 'zone of proximal development' where they are supported by responses older persons give to their communicative expressions (Vygotsky, 1962, 1978). Thus socialisation is as natural, innate or 'biological' for a human brain as breathing or walking; both the latter, by the way, attain full proficiency epigenetically through practice and learning. The systematic steps by which a baby, incapable of speech, with extremely limited behavioural effectance of any kind, and capable of recognising only very few kinds of event within a short distance of its body, nevertheless gains awareness of the social and co-operative value of things and actions, carry vital supportive evidence for the theory that the individual is programmed for social development. Age-related changes occur which should be universal in all cultures and races. In these matters, I would propose, cultures have to adapt to (learn) what infants and children want, the young everywhere asserting control of important and culturally significant psychological values and properties. This sets quite a new problem for anthropological study of children. The theory of innate intersubjectivity leads to novel interpretations of personality, of emotional regulations of behaviour and emotional disorders, and of the universals in underlying structure of all historically created cultural skills, including languages and other forms of symbolic expression. It also leads us to a functional or ecological interpretation of differences between cultures. It helps explain the different ways in which humans in society choose to satisfy and use their co-operative motives to live together, and how each culture propagates its particular way of life through the generations (cf. Wertsch, 1985, for discussions, in a Vygotskian perspective, of the relationship between development of children and the history of society, and Trevarthen and Logotheti, 1987, for a critical examination of theories of how symbols are learned).

## A SYNOPSIS OF DEVELOPMENTS OBSERVED WITH WESTERN WHITE SUBJECTS IN THE US AND SCOTLAND

### Reactions of new-borns to mothers

Accurate description of the patterning of spontaneous movements when new-borns are alert and contented proves the existence of a core nervous network that links all motor organs and all special receptors in one co-ordinated sensory-motor system (Trevarthen, Murray and Hubley, 1981; Trevarthen, 1984a, c). The head and limbs are capable of adopting different well-formed complementary settings with reference to a body-space or orientation field. Arm and hand movements are co-ordinated spontaneously to places outside the body, and this orienting can be excited by objects that the infant sees or hears in gentle motion in near space. The object's stimuli can guide the orienting. Cyclic internal changes over the day, and subtle responses of the infant's state of arousal and emotion to human attentions, govern a highly selective sampling of the earliest contacts with the outside world (Mehler and Fox, 1985).

Human beings show preferential responses to persons from before birth (Sander, 1983; Stern, 1985; Trevarthen, 1987). New-borns show almost no outward-directed sociability controlled by perception of its effect on others, but they do fixate a human face (Maurer and Salapatek, 1976); when aroused they can make specific imitations of exaggerated face expressions (Meltzoff and Moore, 1977; Field, Woodson, Greenberg and Cohen, 1982; Kugiumutzakis, 1985). A baby that is calm but alert after an easy delivery, will turn to look at a soft human voice calling from one side, even if the speaker is completely concealed from sight (Alegria and Noirot, 1978). The unborn foetus can hear and learn distinctive features of the human speech through the intrauterine media, because a new-born may prefer orienting to the mother's particular voice, her individual vocal quality, as compared to other female voices (De Casper and Fifer, 1980). This would appear to prime a rapid 'imprinting', perhaps in hours, to the appearance of the mother's face, so she is soon recognised on sight. Microanalysis of expressions of new-borns reveals that the numerous muscles of the baby's face (a uniquely human organ for communication, more complex than the homologous structure of any other species) are already co-ordinated into configurations of contraction that closely resemble expressions by which adults universally express basic emotions (Trevarthen, 1984b, 1985). The 'knit' brow of concentrated attention accompanies visual fixations, and the smile of recognition is stimulated by a mother's gentle holding, looking and vocalisation (Oster, 1978). A condition of distress is signalled by expressions of sadness or anger.

Mothers learn to detect and regulate the contentment or distress of their new-borns, to stop them crying, by holding them, shielding them from discomfort or cold with their own bodies or in soft cloth or animal pelts, patting and rocking (with regular beat) feeding, cuddling and gently humming or singing. A new-born's expressive protest elicits this comforting, and a healthy baby calms quickly when it is received. The infant has sensitivity to direct human response, pretuned to many 'higher order invariants', including dynamic invariants, of maternal olfactory, visual, auditory, tactual and gestatory stimulation and to the affection signalled in her transporting, holding and nursing. It has been shown that these infant sensitivities may be rapidly conditioned, but the adverse effects of unaffectionate mothering, even when adequate food and physical attention is presented, indicate that the new-born is primed with standards for 'good' mothering. New-borns show a pattern of excessive sleep, inertia and silence when affectionate human care is withheld. Moderate and temporary withdrawal of a healthy new-born to inactivity can assist a caretaker who, while busy with other tasks, may temporarily have to treat the baby as an object to be carried or put aside.

In comparing the care of new-borns in different cultures, we need to attend to the most intimate aspects of neonatal care that are relevant to the sensitivities and responses of the baby. Many strikingly different customs for mother–infant interaction and baby care may not change the quality of this basic human contact. The neonate period is one in which avoiding behaviours and sleep give 'protective concealment' to maturing brain mechanisms for perception and expression. It is not a period for exercise of exploratory, communicative or object handling skills, and communication, is, at this stage, highly specialised to regulate maternal 'holding' and care.

**Primary intersubjectivity—awakening to human communication in the second month**

At 46 weeks gestational age $\pm 1$ there is an outward-reaching, actively seeking response to people; now social (or interpersonal) orienting may be said to begin. New-born sleepiness and concealment of motives for exploration of outside phenomena clear away. The mother notices the new alertness, and feels more attended to. Her receptive, encouraging responses in turn elicit intent regard (Figure 1.1A), alternating with 'social' smiles.

We have examined the exchanges that develop between mothers and two-month-olds when they are seated facing one another and the mother is asked to 'chat' with her baby (Trevarthen, 1974, 1979b). By speaking with a finely modulated and repetitive 'baby talk', a mother can excite repeated cycles of expression in the baby that include rudiments of speaking, and of gesticulating with a preferred hand (Trevarthen, 1986a). Detailed description of behaviours of mother and baby and their precise timing and interactions are presented elsewhere (Trevarthen, 1979a, b, 1983, 1985, 1986b; Trevarthen and Marwick, 1986).

The mother's contribution to the 'protoconversational'

interactions show that she possesses a motivation to generate vocalisations, face movements and gestures that are supportive in quality, intensity, temporal organisation and responsiveness (Sylvester-Bradley and Trevarthen, 1978; Trevarthen and Marwick, 1986). She assumes a position with her face in front of her baby at a distance of 25 to 50 cm and watches and listens attentively. Her movements of head, brows and eyes, mouth and tongue, and her vocalisations become regular and delicately modulated; with successions of short, evenly spaced utterances synchronised with large smooth and undulating movements of her head and face (Trevarthen, 1985, 1986b). She may touch her infant's hands, face or body in time with her speech. Her voice is coaxing, questioning or appreciative and encouraging. What she says indicates her belief that her infant is aware of her; she is trying to understand what her infant feels (Murray and Trevarthen, 1986). The vocal contours of her baby talk define emotions that are simultaneously conveyed in head nodding and turning and movements of eyebrows and lips. In experiments where the mother's reactions to two-month-olds are interfered with, to distort them or make them non-contingent with respect to the infant's behaviour, the distress reactions of infants prove the expectations they have for supportive and appropriately modulated and timed responses from her (Murray and Trevarthen, 1984; Trevarthen, 1984b, 1985). Sylvester-Bradley (1980, 1981) charted instances where the mother was unsympathetically projecting 'mistaken' interpretations of the infant's feelings. In every case this produced avoidance. He concludes that an important form of co-ordinated motivation in the infant is that which permits rejection and avoidance of the mother. Jaffe, Stern and Peery (1973) and Stern (1974) have shown how the infant can regulate contact with the mother by seeking eye contact or looking away.

The descriptive and experimental evidence shows that Primary Intersubjectivity is a genuine two-party communication that depends on the mother adapting to the infant and infant adapting to the mother (see Beebe, Jaffe, Feldstein, Mays and Alson, 1985 for an analysis of timing of engagement with slightly older infants). Their contact and mirroring of expressions is regulated by a set of emotions that mean the same for both parties, and the same to any human onlooker (Trevarthen, 1984b, 1985). The rate, smoothness, pattern of repetition of expressive movements linked together, especially eye orientations and the momentary configurations of face expression and vocal setting, convey states of interpersonal contact without ambiguity and allow motivational interaction to occur directly, even when mother and baby are not touching each other.

It is important to explain that evidence for the most elaborate emotional and expressive functions in two-month-olds has been obtained by analysis of selected portions of quiet and intimate interactions recorded by cine or television in protected situations. At times, the 'state' of the infant or the mood of the situation may preclude such behaviour. Healthy young infants observed at random will often be asleep, inert, 'tuned out' or fretful. They can be relied on to enter into alert responsive and expressive interaction in optimal situations with persons they know, but only sometimes and in 'safe' places. In strange surroundings and in situations that are too loud or confused, they are quiet and inactive; if not protesting because they are frightened, hungry or hurt. Field-working anthropologists observing young infants should keep this in mind.

It seems likely that all human societies recognise that full-term babies become more sociable and 'human' at about six weeks old, that from then on they are sometimes much more interested in people at a short distance away, and more clearly communicative (smiling on eye contact, cooing, gesturing, making pre-speech). Differences in treatment of babies (swaddling, restricting contact with the mother or otherwise regulating her expressions of affection, placing the baby in a cot, handing the baby over to other less affectionate or less familiar caretakers, exposure of infants to contact with many persons, including young children) may cause large changes in the frequency of 'protoconversation'. But this does not automatically alter subsequent development. The indications are that normal developments occur in a wide range of culturally regulated 'treatments' or regimes of mothering, as long as mothering is what Winnicott (1965) called 'an adequate facilitating environment'.

It is said that in some cultures mothers do not speak to infants and do not stimulate 'protoconversations', (e.g. Ochs and Schieffelin, 1983), but such claims require critical examination. First, the restrictions on this intimate communication may apply only to public situations where the mother is 'on stage' in adult company. Second, the above described responses of the two-month-olds when they are played with in face-to-face interactions undoubtedly mean that there are intrinsic abilities in babies to be expressive in a human way. It does not follow, however, that exercise of these activities at this early stage is necessary for their further development and for learning of language. If infant behaviours are manifestations of motives that persist until the child is actually speaking and gesturing in conversation with other people, they do not depend on maternal behaviours for their beginnings and may develop autonomously through infancy as long as the human environment is 'good enough' in the satisfaction of more general motivations. Given the attractive communication that two-month-olds are capable of, it is highly unlikely that a human 'baby talk' response to the infant expressions is totally withheld in any but a pathological type of family with impoverished feelings. Of course, the affectionate human response may come principally from someone other than the natural mother, and a transfer of the baby from the mother may be regulated by cultural rules. But someone will be susceptible to the 'affordances' of the infant for joyful social play, and will support them. Ochs (1983, p. 190) claims that Margaret Mead discovered in Samoa that 'the child is not considered socially responsive or responsible' during the first year. I don't know what 'responsive' and 'responsible' mean here, but they would seem to be on quite a different plane from the affectionate communication play I have been describing. If absence of belief in the latter is claimed, I believe that Margaret Mead was mistaken.

**Growth of an affectionate bond to a companion in early infancy**

It is frequently asserted, as a tenet of Attachment Theory in its original form, that the young infant, under three months, will respond positively to any friendly person, indiscriminately. This conclusion was encouraged by experimental studies of early smiling by Spitz and Wolf (1946), using masks. Two-month-olds we have studied show a subdued observation of strangers and frequently avoid them, struggling or becoming inert if picked up by them. The contrast with recognition and smiling given to the mother is clear (Trevarthen, 1984b, 1985, 1986a). Even a newborn may show wariness of a strange person.

Developments in negative social behaviours with older babies give important signs of increasing social awareness, but they do not constitute evidence for the creation out of nothing of a capacity to differentiate self from other and to distinguish familiar caretakers from unfamiliar persons. Younger infants are more elastic than one-year-olds in responses to different adults, and less exacting or precise in their demands from preferred caretakers and companions. Moreover, they are, in many cultures, attended to by a number of different people. They can adapt with little sign of distress to a new caretaker if the mother abandons them or dies. But the capacity to focus affection and readiness to communicate on a responsive, kind individual who supplies consistent care is evident from the first months.

**Games at three to five months: new interests in surroundings, and new humour**

A second change in responsiveness of infants to mothers is observed around twelve weeks after birth (Sylvester-Bradley and Trevarthen, 1978; Sylvester-Bradley, 1981; Trevarthen, 1983, 1986b; Trevarthen and Marwick, 1986) (Figure 1.1A). This is connected with perceptual, cognitive and motivational changes that increase the infant's involvement in the world at several feet from its body. Visual and auditory tracking of events strengthens (Owen and Lee, 1986), there is greater exploratory curiosity in unfamiliar places, and the baby makes increasingly successful efforts to seize graspable objects (Figure 1.1B), being particularly responsive to objects in motion at near 'reaching distance'. Reaching is co-ordinated by an elaboration of innate orienting mechanisms (Trevarthen, 1984a); it can be adjusted in extent and rapidity to the velocity of a moving object from the first efforts (Von Hofsten, 1980).

The interpersonal change is reflected in looking away from the mother's face when she offers communication. The tendency to avoid her and explore surroundings may outweigh the preference for looking at her and communicating. Counteracting this is a playfulness marked by laughter. If the mother plays a vigorous game involving bouncing or touching and surprising use of face expression and/or voice, a three-month-old turns to look at her, smiling, and may laugh. This stimulates the mother to become more playful or teasing, and to laugh herself (Trevarthen and Hubley, 1978; Trevarthen, 1986b).

Cognitive psychologists concentrate on the three-month-old's increased powers for perceptual monitoring of the sensory con-

**Figure 1.1:**
*A*: Summary of behaviours of infants and mothers in the Edinburgh sample: Percentage of time infant attends to the mother's face, to her hands, or away from her into the room or to nearby objects (mutually exclusive categories); percentage of time showing happiness by smiling or laughing.
*B*: Development of controlled reaching for a ball, presented, suspended on a thread, by the mother; loss of interest in the ball after about eight months; mother's playfulness in face-to-face play and when presenting the ball. (At each age, results from three to five infants averaged.)

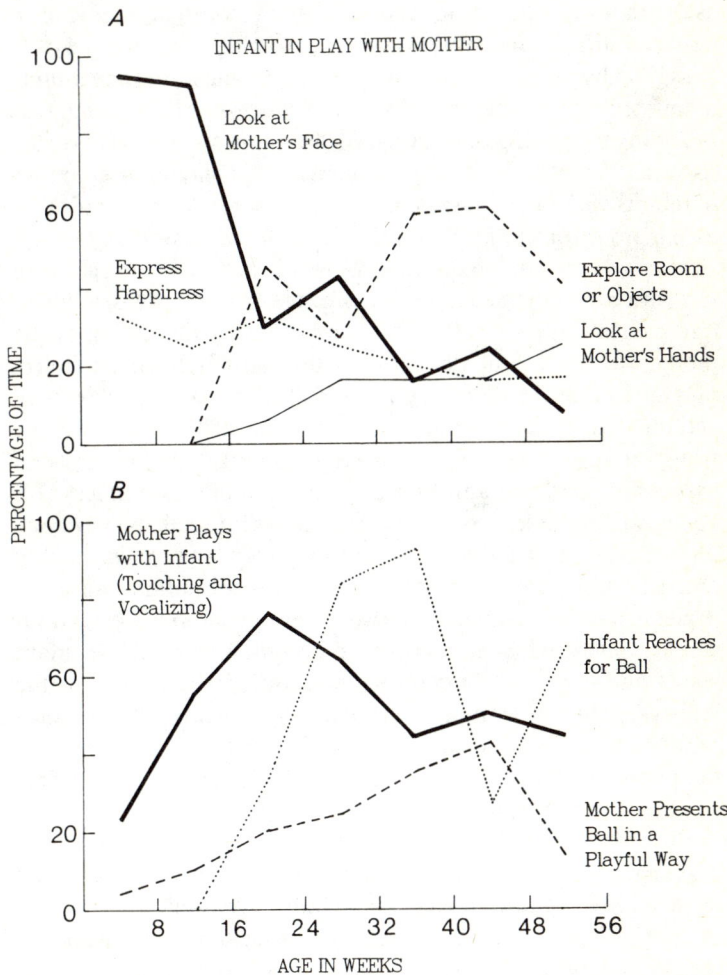

sequences of their own actions. Experiments show that learning gains in power at this age and the infant makes more sustained following and predicting of recurrent or progressive events (Watson, 1977). Most effective reinforcers of the baby's actions are mechanisms that exhibit bursts of visible motion and/or sound when displaced or struck. Rattles, bells, and mobiles stimulate repeated efforts, and the infant shows excitement and pleasure when successful in recreating sought-for effects, and frustration or distress if failing (Papousek, 1967). Mouth, head, arm and leg movements or jumping of the whole body can serve as operant activities. But, study of spontaneous communication between infants and other persons shows that infants' playfulness is really best adapted to human communication. The infants manifest awareness of emotions, and express universal patterns of feeling by moving their faces, vocal system and hands (Trevarthen, 1986a, b). It is illogical to describe the playful interactions of infants with physical systems in experiments as prototypical or explanatory for the more usual interpersonal games.

Mother's respond to the 15 to 20-week-old's changing sense of fun with carefully measured jokes or teasing that are developed into games (Figure 1.1B). The success of this adaptation of the mother to the infant depends on the mother having a warm playful feeling for the baby and a rich repertoire of expressive actions. She is clearly the most proficient of the two. But the transaction also requires a corresponding set of feelings and expressions in the infant. Because the infant moves with less skill and power and is less sophisticated and less rational, the mother's 'baby games' and 'baby music' must be scaled in rate, variability and emotional range of action to a level the infant can comprehend and at least partly control. Thus the mother's behaviour can be construed as an elaborated imitation of what the infant wants and can use. Changes in the mother's behaviour as the baby gets older permit one to chart developments in the infant's motivation (Sylvester-Bradley and Trevarthen, 1978; Trevarthen and Hubley, 1978; Trevarthen, 1984a, 1986b, 1987; Trevarthen and Marwick, 1986).

Recordings of baby games and baby songs reveal remarkable regularities that we would attribute to the structure of infant motivation for play (Trevarthen, 1986b). Cross-cultural study of these forms will provide valuable data on universals in infant motives for play, and for learning to play better.

Figure 1.1B outlines changes in the playful behaviour of 16

mothers in the Edinburgh sample. The changes are, as far as we can determine, not due to any external syllabus given to the mother. Mothers noticed that at three to five months their children were becoming more playful and humorous and that before about twelve weeks it was not worth trying such play. Evidently a mother has musical sense that motivates affective communication between her and her infant before any co-operative use of objects is possible and long before the child masters the language (Trevarthen, 1986b). Traditional action songs, like 'Round and round the garden' or 'Clappa, Clappa Handies' were used soon after the infant was twelve weeks old by nearly all mothers. The culture supplied the mothers, out of their past experience of being played with when they were children, or from observation of other parents, with effective musical forms of song or dance. When we interrogated the mothers, several expressed puzzlement as to how they knew the rhymes, they could not remember when they had heard them. All felt they were responding directly to the animation, watchfulness, smiling, laughter and vocalisation of their infants. Some fathers, siblings and grandparents also began playing games with the infants, but, in our experience, play with mothers is in advance of play with other persons by at least a few weeks. In Edinburgh, parents closely supervised toddlers who wanted to play with infants, and they often moderated the older child's efforts to create action games with the baby.

Play behaviour in humans and social animals is characteristically structured about affective regulation of intersubjective encounters with familiar partners (Bateson, 1955; Herron and Sutton-Smith, 1971; Shotter, 1973; Aldis, 1975; Bruner and Sherwood, 1976; Garvey, 1977; Tizard and Harvey, 1977; Plooij, 1979). Affectionate or affiliative behaviours, and aggressive or defensive behaviours, are mingled in teasing as the interactants attempt to predict one another's moves, and jump ahead or forstall each other. In mother–infant play a young baby's interest and movement is closely observed by the mother who attempts to stimulate the child at precise points in the action. The infant is attracted to watch the mother's actions closely and this tracking gives way to vocal or manual reposte at particular points. The older babies are acting boldly and precisely to thwart or confirm the mother's actions or experience. In this way they take increasing initiative until they themselves are capable of starting a game, or making a joke (Hubley and Trevarthen, 1979; Trevarthen, 1986a).

## Development of object awareness and perceiving what other persons' hands are doing

From four months infants can reach for and grasp neaby objects (Figure 1.1B). We observed this in two situations, with a decorated ping pong ball dangling from a thread held by the mother, and with a small wooden toy truck containing three wooden dolls (Trevarthen and Hubley, 1978; Hubley and Trevarthen, 1979; Trevarthen, 1984a, 1986a). Intent visual exploration and tracking with clumsy swipes and grabs develops into efficient grasping at four to five months. At this age infants are usually seriously intent in this activity and unresponsive to efforts by the mother to use toys in interactive play. Mothers in Edinburgh became playful in presenting themselves and in moving the baby's body and touching it from the time the baby was four months old, but it was not until after six months, when infants were skillful in reaching and grasping the ball on the thread, that mothers became playful when presenting this elusive object (Figure 1.1B).

Infants imitate hand clapping in early weeks (Kugiumutzakis, 1985; Trevarthen, 1986a, b) and this proves infants perceive intersubjective or mirroring equivalence for hands before they can reach properly. In our recordings infants look more at mother's hands as well as less at mother's face and eyes after three months (Figure 1.1A). Hubley found mothers incorporating objects in teasing games from about four months (Trevarthen and Hubley, 1978), and this has been confirmed in our subsequent recordings. However, below six months infants are normally intent upon their own efforts at grasping and manipulating and they often withdraw from objects presented in a teasing manner.

## Mirroring of actions on objects linked to self-awareness and fear of strangers

In the second half-year, infants look at their mother's face and may imitate her speech and gestures while the two of them are playing (Trevarthen and Hubley, 1978; Bretherton and Bates, 1979; Hubley and Trevarthen, 1979). This development comes at the same time as the baby starts to imitate other people's actions on objects; it is part of a development in observational awareness of others. Infants can imitate game playing, mannerisms and gestures before nine months; that is, before development of awareness of the usefulness or purpose of another person's actions on an object (Trevarthen, 1986a, b). The imitative behaviour is linked with self-conscious 'showing-off' to the mother or to a friendly stranger, or to the baby's own mirror reflection, as when the baby reacts to sight of his or her image in the camera window by behaving in a cheerful and amusing way (Trevarthen, 1984b, 1986a, b).

From being amused by the mother's teasing, infants over seven or eight months started to tease or act comical themselves, taking the initiative. They also acted mock angry or aggressive when 'attacking' their mothers, giving many expressive signs of mirroring their mother's experience as receiver of their act. From six months the infants also laughed more when the mother teased them with the swinging ping pong ball. They found it funny to have their reaching attempts dodged, and to be playfully 'attacked' with the ball. In a case study of play, Trevarthen and Hubley (1978) described how one girl progressed from enjoyment of body play (the mother teasing by touching or moving the baby's body), to games with their facial and vocal communication (as in peek-a-boo), and then to amusement at the mother mimicking the movement of an object with face movements and voice sounds. The baby laughed at six months when the mother moved her head in time with a toy the baby was shaking or pulling.

The growing ability to mirror a familiar playmate is also manifest as self-conscious shyness and withdrawal when an unfamiliar person intrudes into the infant's 'personal space', overstepping some boundary of the self. An infant who laughs at a mother's comical expressions and her chanting, dancing or clapping, will look away from a strange intruder, then either smiles or actswithdrawn and 'self-absorbed', or stares at the stranger unsmiling. Infants three to six months old may alternate awkwardly between being playful and being wary with strangers, but after six months they may express their anxiety or embarassment by making rather forced and usually incomprehended efforts to display the games or 'tricks' they have learned with their mothers or other familiar companions. They do not perform as triumphantly or happily as when encouraged by their mothers; indeed they act as if aware that the performance cannot 'work'. The younger baby challenges the stranger with a tense coquettish smile, the older one with a defiant gesture or learned display of the hands (Trevarthen, 1986a).

A part for learning, and for teaching by the mother, in these developments is not to be questioned. However, it is equally certain, on the evidence from the parallel developments age-for-age in different subjects, that each infant is growing an organised personal awareness of its own actions that can be compared to, but is not confused with, the personal identities of other people. It is a set of relationships between the infant's 'self' and the identified 'others' that is growing.

Research on infant–adult attachments in different cultures has revealed large differences in the emotional quality of relationships between infants and their caretakers, and in the infants' reactions to strangers (LeVine, 1980; Chilsholm, 1983; Bretherton and Waters, 1985; Lamb, Thompson, Gardner and Charnov, 1985; Shand and Kowasa, 1985; Tronick, Winn and Morelli, 1985). Inherent sexual differences are modified by gender roles that may have effects from an early age. The evidence suggests that a considerable variety of socio-emotional systems of relationship work well in sustaining entry of the child to awareness of the co-operative principles of the society in which he or she has been born. Nevertheless, it is also clear that there are universal principles of communication that regulate care and companionship for infants, and the link between the emotional systems and cognition. Moreover, these principles manifest consistent age-related changes. A balanced investigation of developments in caretaking and infants' attachments and fears for other people will give attention to both the universal features of motivation in infants and the adults, and the special interpersonal behaviours cultivated in a given society.

**Co-operation with objects—secondary intersubjectivity**

Several recent studies concur in recording an important advance in infant intelligence in the last quarter of the first year (Bates, Camaioni and Volterra, 1975; Halliday, 1975, 1978; Sroufe and Waters, 1976; Emde, Kligman, Reich and Wade, 1978; Bretherton and Bates, 1979; Lewis and Brooks-Gunn, 1979; Sroufe, 1979; Freeman, Lloyd and Sinha, 1980; Bretherton, McNew and Beeghly-Smith, 1981; Campos and Sternberg, 1981). These findings define a high level change that transforms the infant's awareness and evaluation of other persons and what they can do and that increases communication through mutual orientations, expressions of feeling (including laughter), gestures and vocalisation. The actions of other persons become of direct interest to the infant and are selectively attended to. Other-centred states more frequently influence what the infant chooses to do and how he or she feels about experiences and actions. The infant behaves with more deliberate intention to communicate by gesture and vocalisation. Penelope Hubley and I have defined the person-person-object play that develops at about 40 weeks after birth as Secondary Intersubjectivity (Trevarthen and Hubley, 1978; Trevarthen, 1979a).

From this point the infant does not just respond empathically to the emotions of others and accommodate to or resist their movements of caretaking, or their teasing and presentations of objects in play. Now the reactions of the observed person to the infant, and to other persons or things, are perceived as models, or as messages about each other and about shared surroundings (Trevarthen, 1987). Infants also begin at this age to show numerous signs of being aware of the way they and their actions may seem to others (Stern, 1985). This permits the infant both to give messages in a more directed way, and to comply with messages that require interpretation of how others orient to and evaluate their goals. Imitations of gestures, mannerisms, vocalisations and ways of handling objects become common, and vocalisations and gestures are combined in well-formed 'acts of meaning' or protolanguage, to regulate self-presentation or to gain 'goods and services' from others (Halliday, 1975). All of these sharing behaviours are manifested most richly to loved and trusted individuals who have frequently played games, teased and joked with the infants in preceding months, and who draw out the infants' self-expression and acting in a supportive manner (Trevarthen, 1987).

The immediate benefit of this mental growth at the end of the first year is that it sets in motion a particular form of learning. All experiences, even those acquired first by private exploratory play, now have the potential to be evaluated in conjunction with what other persons feel and know. Within a few weeks the infant is more observant of the ways others act with objects and feel about them, and more adept at learning by observing what others do and by listening to what they say. A task involving combining objects in a particular way can be defined for the infant by the indicating gestures and speech of another person. Compliance with instructions, requests for help, giving on request, co-operative acts that require awareness of a joint evaluation of a situation if they are to be well-planned and executed with control, occur with increasing frequency (Hubley and Trevarthen, 1979; Trevarthen and Marwick, 1986).

In short, objects and actions have gained a 'symbolic potential' in the infant's mind, in that their evaluation is, or could be, the goal of a meeting of attitudes or a convention of experiences. The ball is no longer a thing that rolls when bumped, or that bounces when dropped, or that can be chewed, or even something that a mother can use to tease the infant's sense of prediction in playful combat with her. It becomes something to be possessed, to be thrown on the floor so the mother will be irritated, to be pointed to, to be called for, and, finally, to be named with a voice-sound like 'ball'. It can now be seen as an object another wants to hold and be given in compliance with a request, or as something to be refused or protested about in a contest with a peer or sibling. In all of these uses the ball falls within two or more persons' awareness. Its existence is not merely a distal object in one mind, it is an intermental 'meaning' that is ready to be represented by a symbol, any symbol, be it iconic or entirely arbitrary in form (Trevarthen and Logotheti, 1987).

The learning capacities of the infant are revolutionised when objects become meaningful with others, and when familiar situations become places to observe and use both gestures and things in customary manner. Attentive pupil-like activity in the child encourages instructive teacher-like behaviour in companions. This transformation of mother–infant co-operation takes different patterns in different pairs, and social classes may show consistent differences in style of communication about joint tasks (Trevarthen and Marwick, 1986; Trevarthen, 1987).

In a few months the developmental product of this learning is the mind of a toddler who, though barely able to speak a word, is immediately sensitive to the meaningful utility and recollective value of many tools, tasks, possessions, gestures, postures and experiences. When speech floods the child's mind at the age of two, there are already abundant categories of meaning that have served both interpersonally and pragmatically in preceding months.

Subhuman primates, indeed many mammals, show evidence of mutual and collective awareness, and doubtless many species are capable of observational learning to gain more effective exploitation of the environment's resources of food, shelter, escape, etc. But only humans have the kind of appetite a one-year-old begins to show for sharing the arbitrary use of tools, places, manners and experiences. I would propose that the developments that have been described in affective and playful communication of infants from birth to one year are universal in human societies. From the start the infant's impulses to interact with other persons are tending systematically, step-by-step towards construction of cultural awareness. The individual's cognitive processes are always ready to be moulded by the collective cognition for which they are performed. Thus human intelligence is an innate strategy for picking up the skills of human social life, and it causes the child to deliberately learn to become a person who has a role in the community.

## DEVELOPMENT OF COMMUNICATION IN THE FIRST YEAR IN LAGOS

To test the concept of universal co-operative motives, Mundy-Castle and I observed Yoruba infants from an area surrounding a large hospital in Idi Araba, a poor section of Lagos city (see Mundy-Castle, 1980, for a preliminary account). Mothers and infants were transported in two's and three's by Landrover to a TV recording room constructed for our study in the Teaching Hospital. We attempted to give the same schedule of treatments as used in Edinburgh in repeated visits (Table 1.1).

Conditions in Lagos were not as conducive to quiet intimate play as in Edinburgh, partly because the hospital was a busy place from which only partial sound-isolation could be obtained. Mothers, although used to noisy public spaces and generally cheerful and remarkably co-operative, were possibly less in touch with the aims of the observers than those who helped in the Edinburgh study of infants' play. Furthermore, Lagos mothers had to sit and wait their turn in a hospital passage. Edinburgh mothers came separately and did not meet each other. Nigerian infants, who are normally free to crawl about when not carried on their mother's hip or back, struggled to get out of our infant seat, a new experience for most of them. With infants older than nine months, some recordings were made with the young subjects seated on the table in front of their mothers.

We processed the Lagos tapes with the same descriptions and analysis as for the Edinburgh data. Comparison of the frequen-

**Table 1.1:** Lagos subjects (ages in weeks)

| Subjects | | Sex | Laboratory visits | | | | | Home descriptions | Photographs at home |
|---|---|---|---|---|---|---|---|---|---|
| **Group I** | | | | | | | | | |
| 1 Olasumbo | A. | F | | 5 | 9 | 13 | 16 | 6 | 9, 10 |
| 2 Abimbola | F. | F | | 6 | 9 | 14 | 18 | 22 | 12 | — |
| 3 Adijatu | M. | F | 3 | 4 | 8 | — | — | 7 | — |
| 4 Olutola | O. | F | | — | — | 12 | 17 | — | 11 |
| 5 Toyin | Ok. | F | | 4 | 8 | 14 | 20 | 9 | — |
| 6 Faruk | L. | M | | 4 | 8 | 14 | 18 | 9 | 13 |
| 7 Obenga | O. | M | | 6 | 9 | 13 | 18 | 9 | — |
| 8 Busayo | O. | M | | — | 8 | 14 | 18 | — | — |
| **Group II** | | | | | | | | | |
| 9 Taiwo | A. ⎫ Twins | F | | 18 | 26 | 36 | — | 21 | 26 |
| 10 Kehinde | A. ⎭ | F | | 18 | 26 | 36 | — | 21 | 26 |
| 11 Serilatu | A. | F | | 18 | 26 | — | — | 18 | 28 |
| 12 Oyebanji | A. | M | | 19 | 27 | — | — | 19 | 27 |
| 13 Ganiyu | A. | M | | — | 24 | — | — | — | — |
| 14 Lanrewaju | O. | M | | 17 | 26 | — | — | 21 | 28 |
| **Group III** | | | | | | | | | |
| 15 Taibatu | A. | F | | — | — | 43 | 50 | 46 | 51, 52 |
| 16 Ronke | A. | F | | 38 | — | — | — | — | — |
| 17 Abiola | D. | F | | 35 | — | 43 | — | 41 | — |
| 18 Toyin | Od. | F | | 37 | — | 43 | 52 | 40 | 44 |
| 19 Lookman | A. | M | | 37 | 38 | 43 | 52 | 42 | — |
| 20 Abegbenro | A. | M | | 36 | 38 | 43 | 52 | 40 | 48, 49 |
| 21 Adewale | S. | M | 32 | 37 | 38 | 43 | — | 42 | 49 |

cies of time units occupied with different categories of behaviour enables us to draw preliminary conclusions regarding developmental changes and the kind of mental adaptations between mothers and infants in the two communities. Comparison of Figures 1.1 and 1.2 shows a clear difference in maternal playfulness and the amount of time that the infants looked at their mothers after three months of age. This reflects a considerable difference in style of co-operative interaction in the two communities, at least in our recording situations. In general the Lagos interactions were more coercive, mothers expecting to be ordered what to do and generally being very manipulative and instructive with their infants, overriding them when they were angry and fretting. This forceful and direct quality of communication was usually full of good humour and not unkind, but it contrasted with the response of the Edinburgh mothers who were more inclined to let their infants express themselves spontaneously.

The middle class mothers, especially, in Edinburgh were more often giving way to their infants, encouraging verbally rather than physically forcing them to become playful, and generally deferring to infants' moods. When infants were looking away from the mother in some task or exploration, they were generally left alone. A gentle politeness, with much more talking and less touching, characterised the communication of the educated middle class mothers and their play was less boisterous and 'physical' than that of mothers from either the Scottish working class or Lagos. We have not examined for social class differences yet, except for the speech acts the mothers used at the start of protolanguage (Trevarthen and Marwick, 1986), and here treat the Scottish and Lagos groups as if each were homogenous.

Information on the normal life in the homes of our African subjects was obtained in visits by Esther Akinsola, a developmental psychology graduate of the Lagos Department of Psychology. She made a running description of activities, particularly interactive play and communication between the mother or other persons and each infant over a $1\frac{1}{2}$ to 2 hour period when the infant was awake. In many cases she made two visits (see Table 1.1).

Details of the economic situation of the family and cohabitants of the family room and compound were recorded from an interview with the mother. Further information came from a detailed photographic study undertaken in April 1978 by John and Penelope Hubley from Edinburgh, of some of the mothers and

**Figure 1.2**: Summary of behaviours of infants and mothers in the Lagos sample. As in Figure 1.1; at each age, results from three to four infants averaged. Note that, in *B*, mothers are more active in play, and, in *A*, gain more attention from the infants, in comparison with the Edinburgh mothers.

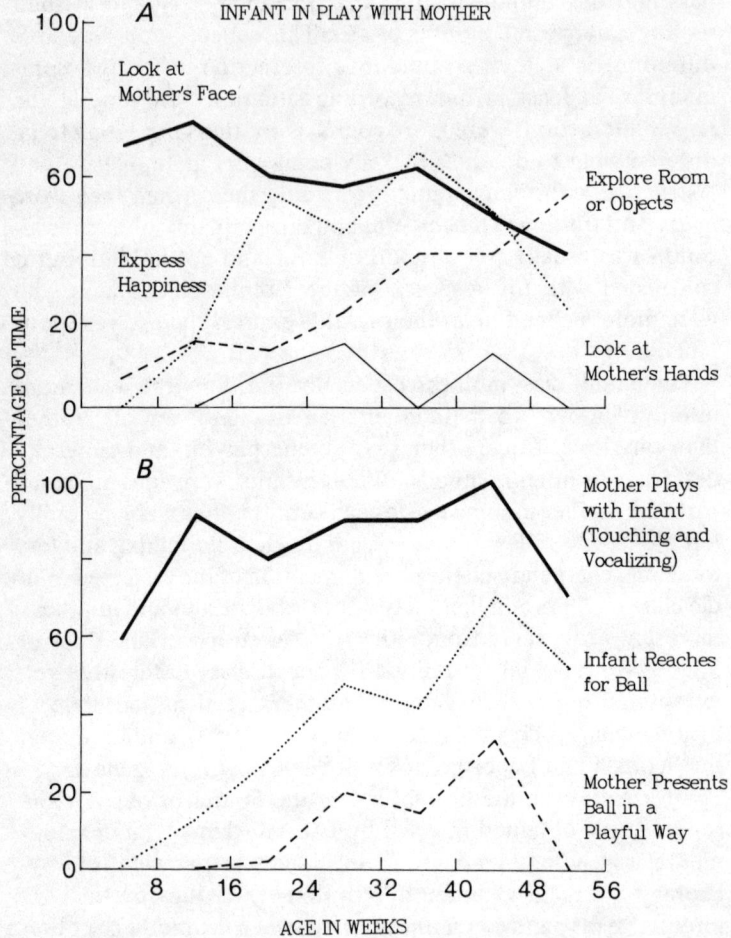

infants at home, of persons known to the infant and of the living quarters and surrounding environment. Additional photographs were taken wherever possible at the place of work of the mother where this was outside the home. Lagos infants often accompanied their mothers to work. No mother worked more than a short walk from her home.

We make no claim that these observations are more than a small sample of the life of our subjects, but they provide a wealth of data on typical opportunities of the infants to observe and participate in activities of people round them. We did not ask questions directly about the way infants are perceived and described by adults.

### Descriptions of video tapes taken in the hospital laboratory

One-month-olds were watchful of their mother's movements as she sat in front of them, but their gaze frequently wandered and it was never clearly focused. They rarely smiled and then did so spontaneously, or when stimulated by sounds or touching, rather than to sight of the mother. Co-ordinated visual tracking and prereaching were observed when the mother presented the suspended ball. The infants also made expressive movements of the mouth, accompanied by upward gestures of one hand at a time, when they were spoken to.

Lagos mothers used pulsating touches and jiggling to the infant's cheeks when attempting to stimulate smiles, and they also touched and jiggled the hands or chest of the baby, making all these movements in bursts over a slow regular beat (one every 1 or 2 seconds). Their vocalisations were gentle chanting at the same slow tempo as their touching (Trevarthen, 1986b). They looked closely at their babies' faces, trying to get recognition and reply.

When mothers kept their faces immobile, at our request, new-borns became restless, waving their arms and vocalising with grimaces. Most looked soberly and silently at strangers, but one was stimulated by the stranger's musical baby talk to smile. One infant stared at her mother's protruded tongue, then opened her lips and moved her tongue in clear imitation.

All two-month-olds smiled on sight of the mother who became more active, touching and vocalising at a brisker beat than with the new-borns. When asked to get the baby to smile, every mother immediately touched one of the infant's cheeks with her finger tips, or both cheeks with one hand each side, and jiggled in short bursts. In some cases there was no accompanying vocalisation, in others the mother repeated double sounds like 'ba *ba*', with the second syllable sharply accented, each time she touched. Mothers used their hands, more than Edinburgh mothers, for all kinds of interactions with their babies, touching cheeks or lips for smiling, squeezing lips or putting a finger in the mouth to touch the tongue when asked to get the baby to protrude the tongue, and in one case trying to get an eight-week-old to look at somebody to the side of the baby, touching the baby's eyes and moving the hand away towards that person.

One two-month-old became animated with her mother's two-second clapping, smiled, waved her right hand then brought her hands together in a rough imitation. The same kind of impulsive effort to bring hands together in imitation of the mother's clapping was seen with under three-month-olds in Edinburgh. Edinburgh mothers made slow demonstrations of one, two or three quiet claps, they did not clap with such an insistent steady beat as did the Africans.

When asked to sing, Nigerian mothers tended to produce a dance-like pattern (Trevarthen, 1986b). They accompanied their songs with clapping or jiggled the baby's hand. Songs became more elaborate and lively with infants over two months of age, and mothers produced them more spontaneously.

After the babies were three months old, mothers' songs were more brisk and humorous. They made a much greater variety of attention-getting noises, including hissing loudly, clicking their tongue or lips, making loud kissing noises with their lips. Their infants were sitting upright and looking about the room, often glancing at their mothers and smiling or grinning in a teasing way with lively gestures and vocalisations, but also frequently looking quickly away.

Just as with the Edinburgh infants, play became more joking and teasing in the fifth month, at the same time as the infants developed the ability to reach and grasp at objects with effective arm control. Mothers were not so helpful as the Edinburgh mothers in presenting the ball on the string, frequently keeping it out of reach of the infants and swinging it quickly about. This caused infants to be less forthcoming in reaching although they were perfectly capable of doing so when the ball was nearer. The babies often just watched the ball and sometimes stared at their mother's hand.

The four- and five-month-olds become increasingly vocal, joining in games with squeals, yodelling and growling noises which the mothers imitated. They also watched their mother's hand move, and in some cases appeared to be trying to imitate hand clapping. Usually they just watched their mothers clapping and smiled or laughed. More attention was given to mothers' efforts to point to events in surroundings.

When mothers kept their face immobile the three to five-month-olds stared at them then looked away to explore the room; or they become vocal and flapped their arms about. They did not become distressed. When the mother spoke again, they immediately smiled. With strangers infants at this stage were ambivalent, but not frightened or sad. They sometimes stared without smiling, sometimes gave brief smiles, but usually looked away. Several were prepared to have their hands touched and moved.

Between six and nine months the Lagos Infants became more vocal, more vigorous in reaching for the ball and more playful with it, laughing and squealing when unable to catch it, intensely interested in manipulating and mouthing the wooden dolls with the truck and greatly amused by teasing games with the mother. They also began to imitate her expressions, mouth opening, vocalisations and gestures and to begin to attend to her instructions with the truck. They often became vocal and demonstrative when mothers kept their faces still, and they showed increasing fear of strangers, tending to stare with a sad expression, to drop eyes and even cry, especially if the stranger laughed. Most babies greeted the mothers with an immediate smile on her return. When the mother poked her tongue out the infant tried to touch it, and a game of touching each other's tongue developed. When the mother kept her face still and remained silent, the Lagos infants became vocal and tended to 'show off'. These behaviours were essentially the same as those observed with Edinburgh subjects.

Lagos infants over six months began to learn quickly to clap hands in imitation of the mother, to look to where she pointed and to imitate her vocalisations (which were originally imitations of baby noises). One pair developed a game at eight months which involved the mother saying 'hoo! hoo' and pointing up and raising her eyebrows high and lifting her head. The infant immediately looked at her then pointed, vocalised and looked up at the ceiling. This game was played for the next two or three months and was seen in the infant's home when the infant was nine months old. The mother explained that the baby had begun by pointing up and vocalising, and she had imitated to create the game. Mothers attempted to teach their infants to point, clap hands and wave 'bye bye'. Lagos babies over six months often 'dance' on cue, jumping rhythmically, waving their arms up and down or banging their feet on the table when in the infant seat. By nine months they are frequently immediately responsive to an invitation to dance to rhythmic chanting or clapping, or to being stood up on the mother's lap. One eight-month-old flapped his hands and vocalised in a falsetto, imitating singing. At this stage the infants made longer, articulated vocalisations or babbling, often in a playful showing-off manner.

The nine to twelve-month-olds were more observant of the mother's instructions with the truck. Dolls held by the baby in one or both hands were watched and repeatedly moved together; they were exchanged between the hands and pushed against the truck, and they were not brought so frequently to the mouth as was the case with younger subjects. As the mothers tapped dolls against the truck or pointed into it, infants watched. They were less resistant than earlier when the mothers tried to manipulate a hand holding a doll so that the doll went in the truck. Finally, on several occasions the infants showed a definite comprehension of their mother's wishes, putting the doll in the truck to comply with her speech and gesture.

The older infants were discontented in the seat and often protested at being kept on the table, being already used to considerable locomotor freedom. They cried with strangers and when angry threw toys on the floor and cried loudly. They were comforted when their mothers picked them up to be held.

**Conclusions**

These observations from the video records indicate that in spite of the more vigorous, intrusive and 'dictatorial' manner of the mothers and the less relaxed recording situation, Lagos infants and their mothers showed the same developmental progression as we have observed in Edinburgh. The interpersonal awareness that was weakly manifested in facial expression, eye contact, vocalisations and gestures at one month became subtle, confident and self-consciously playful by six months. At one year, infants were clearly trying to co-operate with their mother's game displays, and to act in compliance with her gestures. They happily imitated many simple forms of movement, vocalisation, gesture and facial expression. In some cases they created humorous actions which the mothers developed into shared and often repeated jokes or games. At the same time, strangers, who were recognised as different from early weeks, now became more of a threat or a cause for withdrawal and crying.

## Observations made in visits to Lagos homes

The house visits confirmed that in everyday life the developing behaviours that we have described are common; they must have a profound influence over the infant's experience of people and surroundings.

Olasumbo, Abimbola, Adijatu, and Toyin No. 1 (females) and Faruk and Oligbenga (males) were visited when they were between five and ten weeks of age. The youngest smiled little but already showed an acute awareness of the mother, reacting to the sounds of her movement and voice by becoming alert and looking at her. They were wary when a stranger picked them up, but responded socially with lip and tongue movement, cooing and small gestures. They slept on a large bed with the mothers and lay there during the day when not carried in arms or on the mother's back under a cloth. Infants cried frequently to be fed or cleaned and they were responded to quickly by the mother, or by someone else who picked them up in the mother's absence. All infants were breast-fed by their mothers.

After two months the babies were smiling, cooing and raising their arms readily to their mothers who played more with them when picking them up, making little jokes about their hunger or dirtiness. Some also smiled at strangers, but all showed preference for the mother and other very familiar children or adults. Mothers were observed tickling infants on the cheek to make them smile, kissing, chanting rhythmic songs or speech, mostly asking about the baby's state. Adijatu, at seven weeks, was observed to coo in alternation with her mother's gentle vocalisations, as if replying. Toyin, at five weeks, was looking towards mother and father (home for lunch), smiling and vocalising while sitting on the visitor's lap. Mothers, 'aunts', siblings etc. spoke to babies in short musical phases, often using their names in shortened form (e.g. 'Sumbo, 'Bola, 'Gbenga).

The infants under four months possessed toys (rattles and other colourful plastic objects), but could not handle these. Adults used them in attempts to get the infant's attention or to pacify them. When tired and complaining infants were put on their mother's back where they immediately settled and slept. To assist this 'Gbenga's mother (when he was ten weeks old) danced for him, singing rhythmically '*oto o, oto o*' (stop crying, stop crying).

Taiwo and Kehinde (twins) and Serilatu (female) and Oyebanji and Olanrewaju (male) were visited between 18 and 22 weeks. They were much more alert to the busy life of the home than the younger infants, especially to lively goings on of young children, and they followed familiar persons preferentially, smiling and vocalising to them or raising their arms as if asking to be picked up. Mothers and other family members frequently played with and teased them, tickling, throwing them up in the air, shaking toys for them (the infants were more attentive to these than when younger and reached for them when they were close enough), bouncing the infants' hands or legs, blowing on their stomachs, singing and dancing for them. Infants were noted to watch people's mouths and hands when they sang and clapped, and to be attentive to objects handed to them.

They all possessed rattles (*woro woro*, usually made of plastic, though traditional rattles were made of plant material) which they were expected to enjoy shaking. They were more vocal and often people questioned them about what they were 'saying'.

Taibatu, Abiola and Toyin No. 2 (female) and Lookman, Adegbenro and Adewale (male) were seen at home when they were between nine and ten-and-a-half months. These infants were often placed sitting on the floor where they played with two to five-year-olds from the families of the compound, whom they recognised with affectionate smiles and playful vocalisations. Even two or three-year-olds took some responsibility for baby minding; calling the mother to clean infants who had soiled themselves or to rescue them from danger or unfairness of other playmates, and showing toys or playing games with vocalisations, dancing about, etc. Adewale laughed and squealed when his three-year-old brother covered his face with paper and made noises. The infants were highly responsive to gestures and speech by familiar adults or children, recognising their own names, receiving gifts of toys or food and imitating amusing vocalisations and actions. Their own vocalisations were also frequently mimicked. There were fights, too, with mean or jealous playmates, and the infants protested loudly when things they wanted were removed from them.

Mothers were strongly preferred company for these ten-month-olds, quickly responded to with smiles and vocalisations when they spoke. Whenever they were present the infant was attentive to their movements and mothers talked often to their infants, instructing them and joking as if expecting to be understood. They teased their infants often, by throwing them up in the air, tickling, patting their cheeks and in one case playing a Yoruba form of 'peek-a-boo': Adegbenro's mother covered her face with her hands then removed them saying '*Wuya!*', and the baby laughed. Several infants pulled themselves up by their mother's clothing to stand, and they tugged at her to get attention, or, as the mother usually acknowledged, to see what she was doing when she was working.

Several babies were allowed to play with objects the mother used in her work. Taibatu held the keys while her mother prepared a meal, perched on her mother's back, watching her chop firewood, cut up food, draw water, stir the pot. Abiola watched her mother sewing and, seated on the work table, played with scissors, tape measure, cloth, reel and thread. She also tried to manipulate parts of the sewing machine, but was prevented from doing that. She played with her can of baby powder and took the comb from her mother after her hair had been washed and combed, and she reached to the top of her head, trying to comb her own hair. Adegbenro also watched his mother sew. Lookman crawled to his mother to take fish she had peeled to eat, and to his sister to take beans from a pot, recognising the solid food immediately. Mothers often interrupted their work to tease and play with their infants, recognising their curiosity and desire for companionship, making a game of it. Several infants played with magazines, paper or plastic wrappers.

These older infants observed strangers with calm curiosity and occasionally smiled or vocalised to them, or they looked with suspicious fear and crying. When comforted after crying by being held by her mother, Abiola turned to smile at the stranger, and Toyin did the same. Adewale, who had been sick and was fretful, cried whenever looked at by a stranger and closed his eyes. He cried when put beside a strange one-year-old, but played happily with familiar children and adults.

There were some amusing examples of infants deliberately teasing their mothers. Abiola crawled by stages toward a mirror after being told not to, looking back to the mother and laughing. She also threw a ball down steps repeatedly for her mother to fetch it, after being told not to, and once bit her mother's nipple after feeding, causing her mother to shout '*Cruelty!*' which made Abiola laugh. Adegbenro repeatedly threw down a toy tortoise to defy his mother.

Adegbenro had a toy metallophone in the form of a piano with plastic keys that many people played with. The baby enjoyed sharing this toy with other children admiring their play and attempting to imitate. When the mother played the piano he imitated saying '*ee, ee, ee*'. He fought with his three-year-old brother over his plastic tortoise, crying for adult help, then imitated his brother's singing.

Several infants showed deliberate use of vocalisation to communicate in 'protolanguage'. Abiola played the game of saying '*Hoo hoo*' and pointing up and looking at the ceiling and his mother imitated him. When crying for his mother he said '*mama, mama*'. Adegbenro used sound-like vocalisations which his mother imitated, he made a rueful sound with a serious face when scolded for urinating on his mother's dress. There were frequent examples of vocal requests for objects with pointing or reaching, and refusals or denials.

We saw games turn into displays of learned performance. Taibatu danced, jumping up and down to her mother's singing and clapping; she also imitated hand clapping. Adegbenro, we have seen, imitated his mother's 'piano' playing while making singing noises, and also clapped with singing noises in imitation of a song his three-year-old brother performed for him. When playing the infants often spontaneously made comical sounds or gestures, or pulled faces, much to the amusement of their companions.

The notes of the home visits give a clear picture of lively atmosphere in which the infants were treated affectionately and given much social stimulation from a number of people. Their behaviour appeared to develop along lines that were remarkably like those of the Edinburgh sample, especially in details of expressive and gestural communication, and in curiosity to explore and manipulate the environment with other people. Photographs, in many cases, precisely illustrated behaviours that had been described three to nine weeks before by Esther Akinsola.

**The Lagos environment**

Lagos is, of course, famous as a huge, chaotic city growing too fast; squalid shanty towns cluster round rich new buildings with inadequate services. Its inhabitants make many ironic jokes about its rutted streets littered with wrecked cars, rampaging buses and taxis, open drains choked with stagnant water and garbage overflowing in the rains, crowded apartments and lawlessness. Yet, in spite of its disease, its extremes of wealth and poverty and occasional violence, the courtyards, streets, shops and markets have an exhilarating spirit of survival and good fellowship.

Our mothers were, with one exception who was a photographer, poor seamstresses or traders in foodstuffs and plastic goods. But, most of them were financially independent of their husbands many of whom, while they kept traditional pride and loyalty for their children, only visited occasionally.

Families lived in single sleeping/living rooms about 4 metres square with one or two windows and one door opening into a passage way or the courtyard of a compound. A typical compound had eight or nine family rooms round the courtyard, partially isolated from the street. Some houses had two storeys with balconies on the second level. Windows were protected with shutters or metal grilles against burglars. Mothers drew water from a tap or well in the courtyard and cooked on wood fires or primus stoves in passage ways or under lean-to's in front of their rooms. Infants slept with their mothers and other children on a large bed, played in the courtyard with children of the compound and were bathed in plastic tubs or at the courtyard tap. Treasured possessions were a transistor radio, a fan, a sewing machine with which the mother makes her living. Life was much as Oscar Lewis (1959) describes for the poor families of Mexico City.

**DEVELOPMENTS IN CO-OPERATIVE AWARENESS IN THE SECOND YEAR: MEANINGS IN A RELATIONSHIP**

Attachment theorists (Bowlby, 1969; Ainsworth, Blehar, Waters and Wall, 1978), taking evidence from the intensity of emotional displays and approach or withdrawal behaviour where the child is separated from the mother in strange surroundings and reunited with her, recognise that an infant's feeling for the mother becomes more intense at about nine months (the beginning of Bowlby's phase of 'Clear-Cut Attachment'). This development is ascribed to formations for 'increasingly sophisticated behavioural systems organized cybernetically and incorporating representational models of the environment and self' (Bowlby, 1979, P. 131). Alternatively, a similar concept of cognitive representation is formulated in terms of Piaget's Stage III Object Concept.

In Ainsworth's strange situation with toys, the securely attached infant uses the mother as a source of security or 'refuelling base' from which to explore objects, apparently for private cognitive satisfaction. In concentrating on the importance of the mother's *presence* for a state of happiness and curiosity in the child, this theory fails to observe that play frequently involves active sharing of experiences with the mother. The infant brings objects to her, follows her demonstration and directives and joins in co-operative games. In other words, a constructive component of the securely attached child's motivations, part of the secure relationship, is a ready meeting of their consciousnesses in appreciation of a shared world. The infant depends on the mother not just for protection, not just out of familiarity, and not even primarily for affection and emotional support, but because she is the curator of meaning with whom the child best understands objects. She is a familiar, affectionate and willing partner in the discovery and use of meanings in the child's world. Much of what the infant does alone (egocentrically), in the way of problem solving or play with experiences, is practice of what has been, or could easily be, shared with someone who is familiar with the child's history of experience.

After the first birthday the conventionalisation of a child's actions and their meaningfulness to others increases rapidly. To study this, Helen Marwick and I observed five of the subjects at 19 months of age in Edinburgh. We placed three different collections of objects on a low table that the toddler could easily look down on and grasp from when standing (Trevarthen and Marwick, 1982, 1986; Trevarthen, 1983, 1986b, 1987). The mother sat behind the child and they were left to improvise play. Toy set No. 1 consisted of the following easily recognised things made of plastic and cloth: cot with mattress, cover and pillow; hair brush; pair of cups, saucers, knives, forks and spoons, plates; a milk jug and teapot; a bath with sponge and towel, a tip-up truck, a small train engine, a female doll with removable clothes, baby bottle for the doll and a fluffy dog. The child had never seen these objects before. Set No. 2 comprised unusual 'unconnected' objects (three pheasant tail feathers; a large cloth doll with very long arms and legs and square head with no face; a small red wooden spinning top, a sheet of cardboard and a lump of plasticine). The child also played with a selection of his or her own toys from home, chosen by the mother because they were well-liked and easily transportable in her bag. We televised the child performing the following with imaginary substances (indicated by quotation marks): 'water' was swilled about, or wiped off hands, or dried off dishes; plates were laid out for a meal of 'food' that was eaten with cutlery or picked up and passed to the mother; cups were filled with 'tea' from a pot, and drunk from; 'milk' and 'sugar' were added to the 'tea'; spilled 'milk' was wiped with a 'cloth' from the floor; hair of infant, doll or dog was brushed.

The mother contributed by generating ideas, adding to the child's imagination, prompting, correcting some misuse of objects, or helping physically; but it was striking how most children resisted advice, taking only occasional single directives. They tended to keep their backs to the mother and obviously they wanted to take responsibility themselves for making useful actions. If what the mother did was helpful and complementary, it was more likely to be accepted. Frequently when the mother suggested new actions, the child ignored the instruction, deliberately acted differently, or said, 'No!'.

Differences between individual children appeared to hinge on differences in the mother's style and her sensitivity, flexibility, supportiveness, 'respect'. That is, mothers who gave less recognition to the child's independent but sharing will had children that either awkwardly, passively and insecurely submitted to being controlled by the mother, or disobediently acted in a contrary, often disorganised and meaningless way. For example, the hands of one child were held from behind so his mother could completely regulate their joint moves. He behaved in an unenthusiastic, confused way. One or two children misused objects in a way the mothers said was 'silly', or they marched away from the table after treating the objects with mistrust, or threw objects on the floor. It seems clear that the optimal play was one where the child confidently and affectionately shared awareness of what to do with a mother who accepted that the child could know, and have fun knowing. Of course the unfamiliar situation may have been more stressful for some infants and/or their mothers.

However, there is evidence that the different styles of relationship between mothers and their children, whatever their cause, were highly consistent through infancy from early weeks to this mid point in the second year.

With the strange objects, children were more cautious and looked for the mother's reaction. They turned to her for support, asking to be shown what to do with feathers or top, for example. With their own toys, however, many much-practised skills and knowledge were demonstrated immediately, giving proof of learning with help from older members of the family.

We repeated this test with the same five children and an additional nine from the group studied in the first year when they were two years old, observing behaviour that was similar but significantly enriched. The main development was, in most cases, a considerable gain in speech and a marked increase in the child's ability and willingness to have the mother add to the imaginative situation. Fantasy games were created where mother and child shared a complex sequence of actions. For example, there were extended tea parties where, in proper sequence, the table was laid, cups were put in saucers, 'tea' was poured, 'milk' and 'sugar' were added, 'cake' was eaten with plate and fork. Again, the doll was sat on the chair, given a 'meal', bathed, dried, and put to bed. In the most developed play the infant showed elaborate fantasy which the mother totally shared. The transcript in the Appendix illustrates this vividly.

This same child, from our poorest working class family, demonstrated a remarkable repertoire of 'performances' learned in play with mother and father. In the laboratory she sang and performed verses from the following: Allie, Ballie, Allie Ballie Bee, Sitting on his mother's knee; Jack and Jill went up the Hill; Little Jack Horner sat in the corner; Horsey, Horsey; Humpty Dumpty sat on a wall; Little Miss Muffet; Peter Rabbit; Polly had a dolly.

The key element in this child's behaviour appears to be the intense parental enjoyment of the E's personality and her world. In spite of firm, even rough discipline, mother and father showed ready pride in letting the child express herself as a capable person who knows how to do some things well. We can trace this quality in the relationship back to when this child was five months old playing teasing games with her mother.

## Conclusions

A number of features of this development in the second year merit emphasis. First, although speech assists the mother in designating significant meaningful objects and actions alerting the child to their potentialities for use, and the child comprehends an increasing number of words in the context of a co-operative game with relevant objects, the child's awareness of the meaningfulness of these objects is not dependent on an ability to speak, nor is it dependent on an understanding of words. The stock of comprehensions (cognitions) for recognising meaningful things is at first practical, visual and largely independent of language. At 18 months the child has a considerable non-verbal, or partly verbalised, semantic repertoire of ideas that have developed in a consciousness that seeks to comprehend the world as others do, by observing them.

Secondly, the development of this co-operative and imitative consciousness of meanings is actively motivated in the child. It is not simply an automatic outcome of learning by a cognitive cerebral system that has gained representation of permanent objects and is sensitive to contingent reinforcement from parents. The strong age-related uniformities in development of communication between infant and mother, in spite of individual variations in their customary joint style of expression, speak at least for intrinsic anatomical limitations in learning. The mother's behaviour appears at best to be responding to an emergent role-playing impulse in the child. A fascinating aspect, indicative of a lateralised brain system responsible for directing these processes, is that as imaginative object play appears, infants demonstrate a consistent handedness for the appropriate actions (Trevarthen, 1986a). Finally, absence of productive meaningful play with objects appears to be indicative of a difficulty in the relationship between infant and mother where there is mistrust and insensitivity with respect to each other's motives. Whatever their cause, and it could be that either mother or infant is deficient in capacity for understanding co-operatively, the mutuality of action is in some cases distorted so that negative meaning is generated. The child can also imitate unco-operative and destructive devaluation of cultural objects, because this too can be a style of sharing and communicating. Cultural, subcultural or ideosyncratic parental influences on children at this stage can shape different styles of co-operative self-expression, but they cannot create or deny inherent aptitudes in the child to be co-operative, and to have a self-confidence based on success in achieving co-operation.

## Is co-operative use of meanings a product of general cognitive development?

A number of recent psychological studies, attending not to responses in artificial and highly simplified psychophysical experiments, or to mastery of problem-solving tests, but to free expressions of social and object-using behaviours by older infants and toddlers, have found it necessary to consider the child's personality, self-awareness, social interactions, cognitive mastery of problems and language to be inextricably interacting in development. They have found that in the second year infants gain in mastery of symbolic behaviours of many kinds, and in the process they act more 'self-aware', that is, they appear to control their image of themselves in relation to the awareness of others (MacNamara, 1972; Bloom, 1973; Nelson, 1973; Halliday, 1975, 1978; Bates, 1976; Bruner and Sherwood, 1976; Dore, 1978; Bretherton and Bates, 1979). There is apparently a compulsion in most of those who have made these important studies to see the development as due to some central cognitive development. They think that if the child has a better recall of experiences, a better representation of events related to what the child does and a better capacity for inferring consequences of action, it will develop all of the observed new social, communicative and problem-solving skills, automatically.

The more one contemplates the rich behaviours actually recorded the more unsatisfactory this general notion of rational and impersonal 'cognition' seems to be. Perhaps there is no need to find an alternative explanation than the obvious one. What seems to be a universal advance in co-operative intelligence that automatically relates the child's awareness of self-produced actions with the actions of other persons may be just that. The cognitive, intellectual, perceptual, motivational empathetic and moral changes may all be incidental. Even the development of language seems at first to be a symptom of a general change in co-operative awareness, not its cause (Trevarthen 1987; Trevarthen and Logotheti, 1987).

Our observations indicate that by the end of infancy a child has an expressed sense ot personal individuality, can take a role with a sense of worth, fears ridicule, is interested in sharing 'standard' behaviours with others, has a sense of moral involvement and shame because of an awareness of trust and dependency with familiars. All of these interpersonal evaluations are linked to knowledge of a world that is perceived in semantic categories. These 'meanings' qualify all the child's pragmatic behaviours and all the objects the child perceives by referring to the approval and uses that others make of those actions and objects. There is strong preference in the child's mind for taking up and remembering evaluated or meaning-bearing objects *before* the child speaks, and the child can first comprehend (hear and retain) words best in a context of joint praxis and joint curiosity. Later the child seeks to express emergent 'nodes', 'foci' or 'peaks' of meaning and intention in articulated vocal forms that others endorse as words in the mother tongue. Likewise a language of representative symbols and signs can be made of hand gestures, as long as the child's expressive hand movements are endorsed by others communicating with them (Goldin-Meadow and Feldman, 1975; Volterra and Caselli, 1985). But before language there is a rich importation of expressions, attitudes and deeds by observational learning, because the child is inherently co-operative and co-conscious with the family.

## Cross-cultural comparisons for the second year and a study of rural Indian children

We are seeking evidence that the developmental changes that we attribute to an inherent program of growth in interpersonal and subjective understanding in the second and third year are universal. Do parallel phases of personality and social competence appear in the toddlers of cultures that differ radically from those in Europe and the US?

Jerome Kagan has reported remarkable similarities in three groups of one to three-year-olds, accentuating a major developmental change about the second birthday which he described as the appearance of 'one of the most significant sets of competences to appear in our species' (Kagan 1982, p. 379). American middle class children, Fijian children growing up in isolated Pacific atolls and Vietnamese children recently arrived in California all showed increasing awareness of parental standards of good and bad objects and actions, increasing anxiety and distress when left to imitate an activity modelled by an examiner (anxiety was seen with the mother as model, but less), smiling privately when performing a task correctly and ability to remember where an examiner had hidden a prize. Kagan also notes that American children at the same time start to use directives to adults and self-descriptive utterances and to perform 'symbolic acts' for other than self (e.g. helping mother or doll use the telephone). It is the same age at which Lewis and Brooks-Gunn (1979) found experimental evidence for increasing self-recognition in studies of children's reactions to televised images of themselves. Kagan (1982) attempted to explain these far-reaching developments in 'self-awareness' in terms of an advance in inferential reasoning and ability to accept standards of competence, or 'an ability to sustain ideas and action plans' (p. 375), or again the 'capacity to hold cognitive representations or the stage of active memory'. He said: 'I believe that the growth of the functions I have called self-consciousness is composed of the maturation of at least five competences: recognition of the past, retrieval of prior schemata, inference, awareness of one's potentiality for action, and, finally awareness of self as an entity *with symbolic attributes*' (p. 379, my italics). Furthermore, he concluded:

> It is possible that the American children in Cambridge, the Fijians and the Vietnamese refugees all displayed signs of apprehension to the modelling of acts during the last half of the second year because their patterns of social experience were similar. However, the remarkable temporal concordance for the appearance of distress to the model, across all samples, exceeded that for the onset of speech, which most scientists acknowledge depends in part on the maturation of new capacities. Perhaps no special class of social interactions is necessary for these competences to develop. Perhaps all that is required for the capacities called 'self-awareness' to appear is *any information resulting from the child's actions and feelings*. (p. 377, again my italics)

Thus we are left with the child as source of necessities for this development. Kagan concludes that co-ordinated growth in the cerebral anatomical substrate must be responsible.

I would account for Kagan's observations in terms of the

child's attainment of a critical capacity to represent relationships between him- or herself and familiar others; to be a person who knows, and is known to know, significant ways of acting with others, or the proper performance of tasks that others, too, recognise. Selective attention to blemishes can be understood as a selective modelling of occasional parental dismay or annoyance at broken toys, dirtied clothes, etc. Indeed, we have recorded a fine precursor of this in a baby under one year of age, a girl of 41 weeks who wiped a doll with her hand after taking it from her mother when the mother said 'Dirty!' in a disgusted voice (Trevarthen, 1986a), and many acts of our 19-month-olds are of this kind. The embarrassment or fear of the two-year-old asked to imitate an action performed by a stranger seems easily compared to our eight or nine-month-olds' suspicions or fearful withdrawal from a stranger who tries to initiate task sharing. The difference is that the two-year-old has a new and more elaborate sense of both task and responsibility, as Kagan says.

It may be that the period of acute sensitivity to failure observed before most children begin a rapid surge in learning of words is an example of a negative or 'fragile' phase of ego development on the threshold of the differentiation of new skills in communication, such as has been described for other ages (cf. Trevarthen, 1982).

An Edinburgh postgraduate student, Kevan Bundell, has carried out an important comparative study of the communicative abilities of three girls and three boys 15–24 months of age. Bundell lived for eight months in 1980 in a small village in the Madurai District of Tamilnadu State, a rural part of South India. With the aid of an English-speaking resident assistant the six children were selected and filmed once a month and extensive notebook observations were made in more normal situations.

The films of these children seated on the ground outside their homes playing in the company of several familiar people (parents, siblings, neighbours, grandparents) with toy domestic objects sold in the Madurai Temple market (cups, water pots, pestle and mortar, roller and block, grinding stone), and with a toothbrush, a spoon, dishes, a comb, pens and pencils, coffee beans, a half-coconut, stones and Alphabet picture books, reveal an extraordinary likeness of expressive acts to those observed with our Edinburgh boys and girls of the same age. The children in India and Scotland presented themselves with the same self-confident or self-conscious, independent yet imitative wilfulness.

Indian children used stones to make a fire place, sticks to fuel imaginary flames under the coconut shell pot in which dirt and water was placed to be stirred with a stick to make curry. (Fourteen-year-old sister asks Krishnaveni 'What curry are you going to make?' 'Pooli-curry!' replies K. with a grin.) In 'cooking', many actions to prepare food were performed with the appropriate miniature objects. Water was poured from high, just as adults pour tea to cool it. The children imitated writing and looked at pictures in books.

The children were observed to imagine 'talcum powder' (spread on face), 'cloth' (to wipe face), 'vermillion paste' (for dot on forehead), 'black paste' (for eyebrows). One boy had a doll which in imaginative play he bathed, dried, 'powdered' and dressed in a 'sari' (rag); then he put a 'dot' on the doll's forehead. Many traditional gestures were performed, such as bringing the palms of the hands together (Namaste) for prayer or greeting, nodding the head to give a command, tossing the head to say 'No!' and wobbling the head to say 'yes!'. The children actually cleaned their teeth using powder with the right fingers (the left was forbidden), and washed themselves in the morning. Children at the village school ritually sit up straight with crossed arms and legs to learn lessons and the two-year-olds were often seen to imitate this when being given instructions.

The following extracts from Bundell's notebook give an impression of the intelligent participation in domestic and cultural acitivities of these children when they were 18 to 24 months old.

(1) Manjula is playing, as usual, with her $3\frac{1}{2}$-year-old sister outside the house in the communal yard. The sister takes a stone and props it up against a wall. 'Look Manju, Swami!' (i.e. God, lit: Lord), she ways, kneeling and bowing. Manjula, watches, then half imitates, but seems unaware of what's going on, and changes to something else.

(2) My assistant and I arrive at Veli's house. He 'invites' us to sit down beside the house with a clear polite gesture of his hand and arm. It is customary to offer a seat when visitors come.

(3) Usha takes plates and pots one by one from her mother, washes one, hands it back, asking for another. This is a real practical task, clearing up after a meal.

(4) Usha holds spoonful of food to her sister (aged four) and says 'Ah' with open mouth.

(5) Velmurugan takes a calendar with a picture of God, puts his hands together, and puts dot of ash on his father's forehead (in imitation of worship, or *puja*, performed daily in the house).

In early film sessions, when his presence evoked much curiosity and excitement, Bundell noticed that the children were somewhat intimidated by the many people who came about. Later, after it was less interesting, they were more forthcoming in games with family playmates. Several (particularly the girls) showed a clear increase in confidence and co-operativeness towards two years, and they were more actively involved in sharing play with their partners.

Bundell's findings confirm that two-year-olds are making a significant entry into cultural activities of this traditional semi-literate community, at the same time as they are beginning to learn to speak.

## Conclusions

Two-year-olds, in Edinburgh, Lagos, Fiji or Madurai, are beginning to act like convention-sensitive beings. They are using objects as instruments to do the tasks for which the objects were made, they are performing formal gestures and attitudes in social interaction with others, they are assuming social roles with pride and confidence, or showing self-conscious lack of confidence and sensitivity to ridicule and unfairness; and they are beginning to have fluent comprehension of speech and to talk with imaginative recall of semantic entities that have been given meaning through negotiations with other persons.

As we trace developmental antecedents to these complex psychological achievements we can detect a remarkable preparation for human interaction. This inbuilt motivation is asserting itself clearly in early face-to-face interactions, a few weeks after birth. Play between mothers and two-month-olds is built about a mutual emotional response. Mutual awareness is expressed and emotional signals are used to create brief finely tuned engagements. We find that mothers obtain this kind of reaction by presenting a wealth of measured sights, sounds and touches that make up a characteristic 'baby talk' display that gives direct information concerning infant preferences for experiencing a receptive human 'object'. The infant, in turn, makes spontaneous communications that include rudimentary speech and gestures. In their detailed structure these movements give evidence of elaborate cerebral machinery for human expression. The learning process that turns these emissions into voluntary acts of meaning within twelve months is one to which the infant certainly contributes directive impulses or motives. The development is constructed intrinsically, as well as extrinsically by environmental reinforcement (Trevarthen, 1987).

The games that amuse older infants at the time they begin deliberately to explore objects with hands and mouth reveal an inbuilt measure of tempo and cadence. Play movements of infants, and most conspicuously the play movements of mothers that successfully entertain these three- to six-month-olds, have musical control in their beat, phrasing and melodic line (Trevarthen, 1986b).

I have emphasised co-operative awareness, defining it as a cognitive process that identifies objects not merely within the field of potential actions of the infant as isolated subject, but within a joint or shared intersubjective field. There is evidence that infants can identify with, mirror others' actions on objects *before* the infants can themselves control comparable actions. But perhaps we should regard this evidence, from imitation of hand movements and selective curiosity for objects that are being given 'presentation movement' by another person, as merely suggestive at this point in our researches. There is no doubt, however, that infants can, by nine months of age, start to take note of the manipulative actions and directions of attention of others, as well as their emotional evaluation of objects that they manipulate or attend to. The evidence for neonatal imitation of expressive movements is, to my mind, conclusive; but a new, deliberate and much more selective quality appears in the imitations of play movements and object use in the last semester of the first year.

The plainest explanation of observed behaviours over this important stage of psychological development, before words are picked up as vocabulary for language, is that the infant, already endowed with capacity to mirror and respond to emotional expressions of interpersonal contact, has expanded his interpersonal awareness to include acts by persons on things. The evidence is not in agreement with the dominant Piagetian hypothesis that before the child can pick up conventions from society it must proceed as an individual actor, solving alone the problem of perceiving objects as permanent entities separate from its own moveable and receptive body. Such child–environment interactive learning must contribute to refinement, tuning, etc. of representations of objects which cannot be 'known' innately in their specific properties and qualities. At the same time, the child is discovering objects as much by observing and identifying with the actions and reactions of other subjects as by carrying out the tests itself. At the very least, the child is evaluating object properties by the social, intersubjective co-operative route as early as it is by the private, intellectual, problem-solving route (Trevarthen and Logotheti, 1987).

Leaving aside the now open question about how the 'object concept' arises, and how intermediary objects or instruments are first conceived, I wish to pass to the, for me, much more entertaining question of fantasy and role-taking imagination. In the second year children develop a powerful capacity to take on performatory and expressive roles that others find easy to see and generally endearing and amusing, provided they are not destructive or dangerous. This socio-dramatic play part of child behaviour is not the frill it may be considered to be by the serious rationalists wrapped up in his private struggle of abstract thought and problem solving. Playing a part, doing an act or task for 'fun' is at the heart of human mental development and its motivation is close to the cause of co-operative culture. In this kind of behaviour the child's independence is again actually a dependence on the approval, assistance and appreciation of others (Trevarthen and Logotheti, 1987). Our 'play with useful objects' test shows that the mother of an 18-month-old, as a familiar trusted person who understands, is influencing the play, even though the child may seem to be refusing, turning its back on, what the mother wants to contribute to it. From this stage it is a straightforward step to the more confident, more knowledgeable two-year-old who is prepared to take more advice and interested to put words onto the more outstanding elements of a jointly understood world.

Descriptive research has recently brought to light a wonderful richness of social awareness in toddlers. They present themselves with clear personalities who react to older persons as individuals, expressing clear preferences or attachments, and avoiding or repulsing advances from 'strangers'. They exhibit a rich array of mannerisms, attitudes and performances that have 'symbolic' character. Many psychological theorists have accommodated to this naturalistic information by strengthening a social learning theory. Followers of G.H. Meade (1934) consider the meanings of gestures and words to be injected into the child by an intensive education process in which parents interpret initially meaningless 'biological' movements, rewarding them for adherence to 'social' significance (e.g. Berger and Luckmann, 1966; Harre and Secord, 1972; Shotter, 1973; Lewis and Brooks, 1975; Lock, 1980). Human children become socially co-operative members of cultures entirely because they are quick to learn and because they are treated by their culture-dependent guardians 'as if' they are intending to mean. The developments, which are easy to observe, do not necessarily support this constructivist conception.

The evidence from the few studies of cooperative object use and the more extensive data on early language, on the contrary, shows infants to be active in setting intermental, co-operative, meaning-seeking goals from the start (Trevarthen and Logotheti, 1987). Stages of development are intrinsically regulated and gestures have an expressive value that needs response from others for its maturation, but not for its initiation. Most importantly, the phases of co-operative awareness, which I suggest are genuine universals, are conclusive evidence of intrinsic developmental control. We will never understand linguistic, cognitive, perceptual or motor development of children without a correct appreciation of their motives for co-operative awareness.

A final point on the origins of differences in temperament and personality. Without going deeply into this complex and difficult question, I should like to comment on the evidence for a universal emotional code in mother–infant interaction (Trevarthen, 1974, 1984b, 1985), and the indications of considerable differences in different families, social classes and cultures in evaluation and reinforcement of expressive styles. Our infant subjects were treated with widely different gentleness, permissiveness, indulgence, and given different degrees of affectionate caressing or poking, smacking etc. They were spoken to with differing intimacy, playfulness and gentleness and given widely differing degrees of social intimacy with a range of individuals. The Nigerian babies were, as a group, certainly touched more on the face, teased more, handled and cared for by more people (including children) with more physical vigour than were the Edinburgh babies, as a group. It may be that the Lagos mothers behave towards their infants in some ways more like American fathers studied by Lamb (1981). Lagos babies were, I would judge, correspondingly both more attentive to their mothers when the latter made themselves available, and more 'stoical' and capable of either shutting out noisy situations and physical pulling about, or protesting loudly. Their protests were often left to wear themselves down. On the other hand all infants were treated with essentially the same affectionate playful and responsive mothering at times, and I feel that the evidence is clear that their communication and co-operative awareness developed along the same lines with constant emotional guidance of the human contacts. Mental achievements of all the infants seemed to depend on these contacts.

I would conclude that, just as infants learn different actions, to use different tools and to speak different languages, they adapt to different interpersonal styles and social conventions in expression of feeling. That does not mean they have an historically fabricated emotional code put into them, that they are born with nothing but crude instinctive reactions to stimuli to control body state, that emotions are reflections of CNS arousal or a density of neural information flow (see Trevarthen, 1985). Spontaneous emotions in mother–infant interaction are easily comprehended across cultures, as is their use in play and co-operative evaluation of people, things and events. Different social units, families or cultures, create different ways of using this universal mechanism that regulates personalities and their dependence and independence. I would accept Hogan's thesis of 'cultural character' (Hogan, Johnson and Emler, 1978) and would expect children to be adopting these conventions, too, along with culture-specific sex roles, by the end of infancy.

## ACKNOWLEDGEMENTS

Work reported in this chapter was supported by grants from the Spencer Foundation of Chicago and the Social Science Research Council of the United Kingdom. I wish to thank my colleagues: Penelope Hubley, Lynne Murray, Benjamin Sylvester-Bradley, Helen Marwick, Kevin Bundell and Katerina Logotheti. The work in Lagos would not have been possible without the enthusiastic collaboration of Professor Alistair Mundy-Castle and his associates at the Department of Psychology, University of Lagos.

## APPENDIX

Transcript: Emma (two years) and her mother share fantasies in play with a box of laboratory toys that Emma had not seen before.

(*The toys are taken from the box on the floor by her mother and placed on a low table in front of Emma*)
E: Oh, gimme the dolly, Mum.
M: What's this? You wantin' this for her? (*M. puts bed on table*)
E: Baby go in.
M: Baby go in cot?
E: Aye. She goin sss... (*Rocks doll in cot, looks at M*)
M: Is she going to sleep? Gi' her the bottle. (*E. finds the bottle and puts it in doll's mouth with left hand*)
E: (*Mumble*) The bottle. (*Takes doll out, rocks on right arm feeding with bottle*)
M: She taken' it? (*E. nods*)
M: Mm that's clever. (*E. continues rocking and feeding*)
M: She tired? Eh? (*E. nods. After feeding doll for several seconds, puts doll on table and looks in toy box*)
E: Baby's going in that. (*Reaches for chair, M. hands chair to her and E. places it in the bed*) Baby's goin' in.
M: (*Interrupting sternly*) A chair doesne' go in a baby's cot! (*E. ignores this and carefully sits the doll in the chair which is balanced in the rocking cot*)
E: Mummy, baby's sitting on the seat.
M: What a clever baby, Eh?
E: What a clever baby! Baby not fall. (*Shaking head*)
M: What's your baby's name? (*No reply. Mother looks away. E. lifts doll*)
M: Here's the cover for it I think. (*E. takes the doll and vigorously forces it into the bed for which it is too long. M. smiles but says nothing*)
E: Baby's got a cover.
M: Uhuh. Is she OK?
E: (*Whispers*) She's going to bed (*while busily putting on the cover, pats foot of bed with left hand when finished. Picks up bottle and feeds doll with left hand, carefully moving the covers from the doll's face with the right hand. Mutters something like Take. Removes bottle. Covers doll's face and turns aside, patting the foot of the bed with her left hand again.*)

M: Uhuh! Is that good? (*E. removes the cover, dropping it on the floor. Picks up the cot containing the doll and hands it to M.*)
E: Mumma. Hold that!
M: Right! (*taking on lap*) What are you going to do? (*E. picks up cover from floor and puts it over the doll in cot on M's knee, saying*) Put on.
M: Put it on the table. Mm, Cosy (*helping to tuck doll in*) She has to go on the table, see. Put her there. (*M. places the cot etc. on the table in front of the camera. E. Attends, pulls cloth over doll's head and pats the bed with her left hand*)
M: Oh, you've covered her head! (*E. folds back the cover and tucks it in leaving the doll's face clear. Picks up chair*)
M: What's the chair? (*E. takes off the cover, throws out the bottle and picks up the doll holding it in the left hand, takes the chair with her left hand and puts it in the cot. Sits doll on chair*)
E: Mum. Baby put her (*mumble*) on.
M: Uhuh! (*E. reaches for the cup with her right hand and knocks the doll and chair out of the bed*)
M: Oops!
E: Mum. Baby's fall off, Mum.
M: Uhuh. She alright? (*E. nods slowly putting the doll in bed with left hand, then taking doll out and sitting it on the edge of the table, from which it immediately falls off*)
E: Oop! Bump'd her heid.
M: Bumped her head?
E: (*Rubbing doll's head with left hand*) She bumped her head. (*E. takes the chair with her right hand and places it in the cot*)
M: The chair doesne go in the cot! (*E. puts the doll down and with both hands carefully but firmly puts the chair in the cot. Sits the doll balanced on the chair and pushes it back. As the doll falls M. says*) Now she's goin' to fall off! Take that oot o' there (*firm order. M. pulls the bed towards her and puts it aside saying*) she'll only fall! (*E. grabs the chair and, with a frown, puts it on the table with her right hand, holding the doll in her left hand.*)
M: And get a cup of tea. (*E. tries to sit the doll in the chair, contemplatively; then seeing the bare behind and back of the doll through the dress open at back, starts to remove clothes*)
E: Mumma, take it. (*Pulls at dress*)
M: Dinna take her clothes off! (*E. takes off the dress*)
E: Mum, take her clothes off.
M: Are you going to bath her? (*E. tries to take off the hat. Turns to her mother with an impatient effort noise.*)

*E: (Looks at mother)* Take her hat off. (*M. tries to remove hat, but the chin tape is knotted. E. impatiently takes the doll from M. and tries to untie the tape with her left hand.*
E: Mumma, canne (*turning for help*)
M: Doesne' come off! It's all tight, see. (*She tries to untie the knot, E. waits impatiently. E. pulls at the hat trying to force it over the doll's head*).
E: Oh!
M: It's stuck. (*E. pulls at the hat so the tape draws tight across doll's throat and E. imitates a coughing sound, as if the doll is choking*)
M: You'll have to keep it on. Just bath her like that. (*E. places the doll on the table. M. looks in the box and brings out the bath saying*, Oh look! (*E. gives a loud sigh of pleasure*)
E: 'There's a bath!'
M: Uhah (*E. puts the doll in the bath then looks aside, picks up spoon with left hand and puts it to doll's mouth*)
E: Get up. (*Lifts doll from the bath saying*) She's washed. (*Notices taps, puts doll roughly on table, turns on plastic taps, waiting quietly. Puts hands in bath*)
M: Are you filling the bath for her? (*E. swills both hands in the imaginary water and brings them out carefully together, to avoid dripping*)
E: The water's too hot Mum. (*Continues dipping her hands in bath and rubs them together*)
M: Is it too hot? (*E. continues, then turns taps off. She looks into the box. M. points to the doll behind on the table saying*) Oh she's over there! (*E. pulls fluffy dog from box and dumps it in the bath*)
E: Doggie's having a bath.
M: Is your doggie wanting a bath? (*E. lifts 'water' up around dog—wipes hands on dress*)
(*After this E. gave her mother a dinner*)
M: Thank you that's nice. (*E. mimes eating food with a spoon from a plastic plate*)
M: That nice? (*E. scrapes food from one dish to another*)
E: Here you are.
M: Is that for my dinner? (*E. nods*)
M: Thank you (*taking the plate*)
(*E. continues with elaborate meal preparations then cleans up and washes dishes*)

*Note:* E. showed left-handedness for imitated gestures at seven months. At two years she is strongly left-handed for gestures and use of artefacts. Both her parents are right-handed (see Trevarthen, 1986a for a detailed analysis of handedness in the Edinburgh subjects).

## BIBLIOGRAPHY

Ainsworth, M.D., Blehar, M.C., Waters, E. and Wall, S. (1978) *Patterns of attachment*. Hillsdale, N.J.: Erlbaum.
Aldis, O. (1975) *Play fighting*. New York: Academic Press.
Alegria, J. and Noirot, E. (1978) 'Neonate orientation behaviour towards the human voice'. *Early Human Development*, *1*, 291–312.
Bates, E. (1976) *Language and context: the acquisition of pragmatics*. New York and London: Academic Press.
——, Camaioni, L. and Volterra, V. (1975) 'The acquisition of performative prior to speech'. *Merrill-Palmer Quarterly*, *21*, 205–26.
Bateson, G. (1955) 'A theory of play and fantasy'. *Psychiatric Research Reports*, *2*, 39–51.
Beebe, B., Jaffe, J., Feldstein, S., Mays, K. and Alson, D. (1985) 'Interpersonal timing: the application of an adult dialogue model to mother–infant vocal and kinesthetic interactions'. In: T.M. Field and N. Fox (eds), *Social perception in infants*. Norwood, N.J.: Ablex, 217–47.
Berger, P.L. and Luckman, T. (1966) *The social construction of reality*. New York: Doubleday.
Bloom, L. (1973) *One word at a time: the use of single word utterances before syntax*. The Hague: Mouton.
Bowlby, J. (1969) *Attachment and loss* Vol. 1. *Attachment*. New York: Basic Books.
—— (1979) *The making and breaking of affectional bonds*. London: Tavistock.
Bretherton, I. and Bates, E. (1979) 'The emergence of intentional communication'. In: I.C. Uzgiris (ed.), *Social interaction during infancy: new directions for child development* Vol. 4. San Francisco: Jossey-Bass, 81–100.
——, McNew, S. and Beeghly-Smith, M. (1981) 'Early person knowledge as expressed in gestural and verbal communication: when do infants acquire a "Theory of Mind"?' In: M.E. Lamb and L.R. Sherrod (eds), *Infant social cognition: empirical and theoretical considerations*. Hillsdale, N.J.: Erlbaum, 333–72.
—— and Waters, E. (eds) (1985) 'Growing points of attachment theory and research'. *Monographs of the Society for Research in Child Development*, Serial No. 209, *50*, 1–2.
Bruner, J.S. (1975) 'From communication to language—a psychological perspective'. *Cognition*, *3*, 255–87.
—— and Sherwood, V. (1976) 'Early rule structure: The case of peekaboo'. In: J.S. Bruner, A. Jolly and K. Sylva (eds), *Play—its role in development and evolution*. New York: Penguin Books.

Campos, J. and Sternberg, C. (1981) 'Perception, appraisal and emotion: the onset of social referencing'. In: M. Lamb and L. Sherrod (eds), *Infant social cognition*. Hillsdale, N.J.: Erlbaum.

Chisholm, J. (1983) *Navaho infancy. An ethological study of child development*. New York: Aldine.

De Casper, A.J. and Fifer, W.P. (1980) 'Of human bonding: newborns prefer their mothers' voices'. *Science*, 208, 1174–6.

Dore, J. (1978) 'Conditions for the acquisition of speech acts'. In: I. Markova (ed.), *The social context of language*. Wiley: Chichester, New York.

Emde, R.N., Kligman, D.H., Reich, J.H. and Wade, T.O.(1978) '*Emotional expression in infancy 1*. Initial studies of social signalling and an emergent model'. In: M. Lewis and L.A. Rosenblum (eds), *The development of affect*. New York: John Wiley and Sons, 125–48.

Field, T.M., Woodson, R., Greenberg, R. and Cohen, D. (1982) 'Discrimination and imitation of facial expressions by neonates'. *Science*, 218, 179–81.

Freeman, N.H., Lloyd, S. and Sinhan, C.G. (1980) 'Infant search tasks reveal early concepts of containment and canonical usage of objects'. *Cognition*, 8, 243–62.

Garvey, C. (1977) *Play*. Fontana Paperback.

Goldin-Meadow, S. and Feldman, H. (1975) 'The creation of a communication system: a study of deaf children of hearing parents'. *Sign Language Studies*, 8, 225–36.

Halliday, M.A.K. (1975) *Learning how to mean: explorations in the development of language*. London: Arnold.

—— (1978) 'Meaning and construction of reality in early childhood'. In: H.I. Pick, Jr. and E. Saltzman (eds), *Modes of perceiving and processing information*. Hillsdale, N.J.: Erlbaum, 67–96.

Harre, R. and Secord, P.F. (1972) *The explanation of social behaviour*. Oxford: Blackwell.

Herron, R.E. and Sutton-Smith, B. (1971) *Child's play*. New York: Wiley.

Hofsten, C. von (1980) 'Predictive reaching for moving objects by human infants'. *Journal of experimental Child Psychology*, 30, 369–82.

Hogan, R., Johnson, J.A. and Emler, N.P. (1978) 'A socioanalytical theory of moral development'. *New Directions for Child Development*, 2, 1–18.

Hubley, P. and Trevarthen, C. (1979) 'Sharing a task in infancy'. In: I. Uzgiris (ed.), *Social interaction during infancy, new directions for child development* Vol. 4. San Francisco: Jossey-Bass, 57–80.

Jaffe, J., Stern, D. and Peery, J. (1973) ' "Conversational" coupling of gaze behaviour in prelinguistic human development'. *Journal of Psycholinguistics*, 2, 321–29.

Kagan, J. (1982) 'The emergence of self'. *Journal of Child Psychology and Psychiatry*, 23, 363–81.

Kugiumutzakis, J.E. (1985) *The origin, development and function of early infant imitation*. Uppsala University Ph.D. Thesis (*Acta Universitatis Uppsaliensis*, 35).

**Figure 1.3:** Lagos infants and mothers at home and in market or fields.

**Figure 1.3: A:** Mother, a seamstress, in her small shop.

(These photographs, and Figure 1.4, were taken by John and Penelope Hubley in Lagos, April 1978. Copyright John and Penelope Hubley.)

**Figure 1.3: B:** Olugbenga's mother with baby, 14 weeks, at her stall.

**Figure 1.3: C:** Olugbenga, male, 14 weeks, held by his father while mother sings a clapping song. Christian, father a cleaner.

**Figure 1.3: D-H:** Toyin, female, twelve weeks, with her mother: selling dried fish; preparing a meal in the passage; baby exercised after a bath. Family (Moslem) share one room with mother's sister.

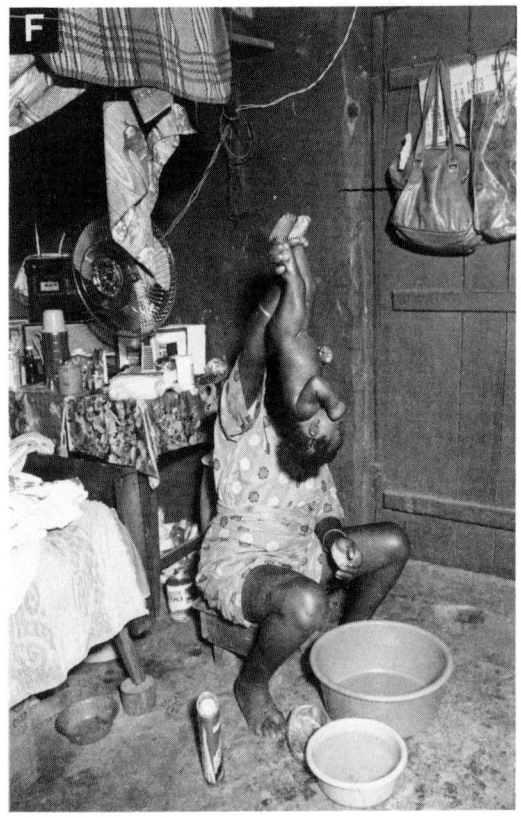

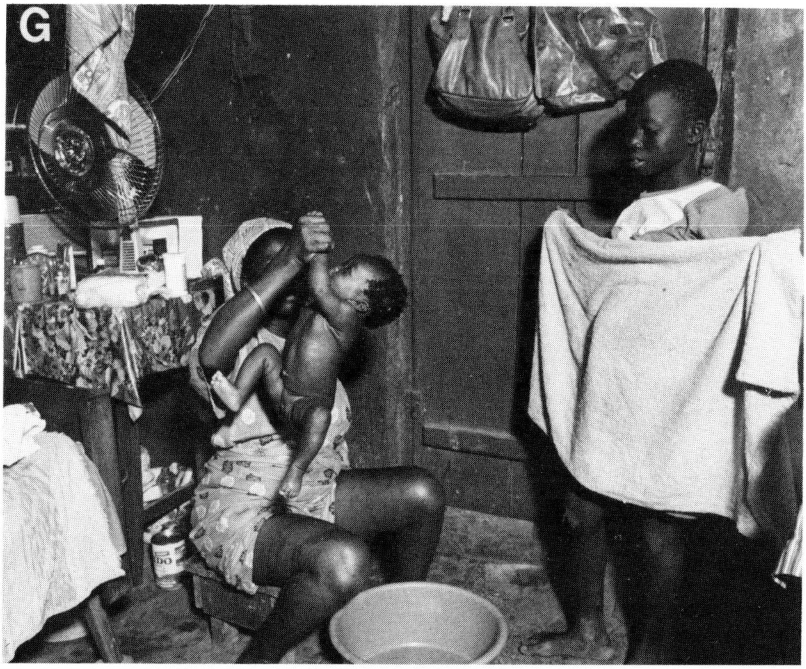

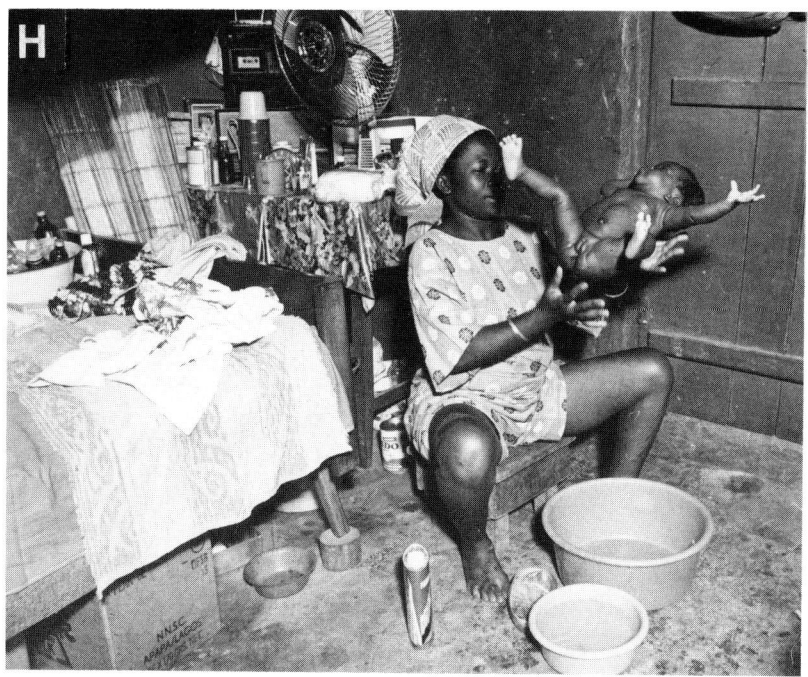

**Figure 1.3: I-K:** Ajayi twin, female, 27 weeks, with mother's sister (twin's elder brother in background); mother bathes twin in courtyard with brother standing by. Christian.

**Figure 1.3: L-M:** Adewale, male, 49 weeks, with mother and a neighbour, who is the infant's principal caretaker, in first floor room where family lives. Baby who has been unwell, avoids caretaker, fusses when dressed by mother.

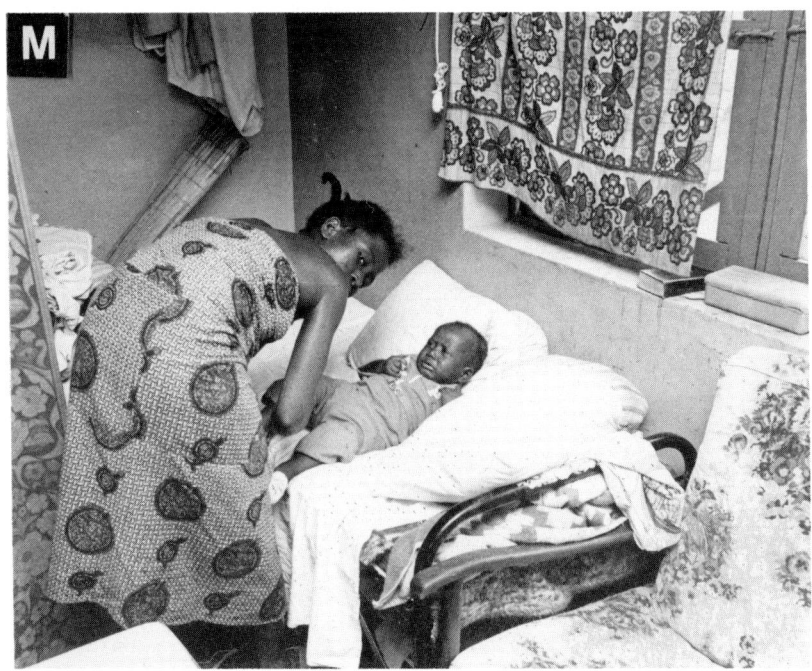

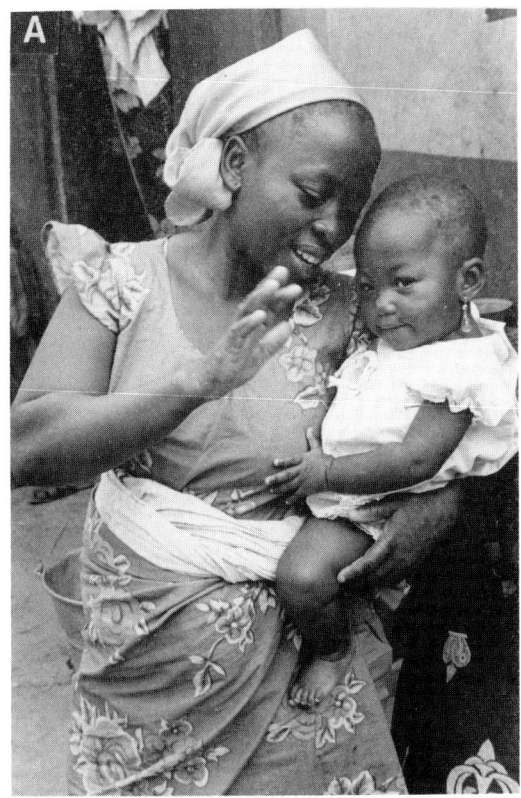

**Figure 1.4: A-D:** Taibatu, female, 52 weeks: Mother shows greeting to photographer, baby coy; baby watches while mother prepares a meal, chops firewood, builds fire. Moslem; father wharf official, mother trader.

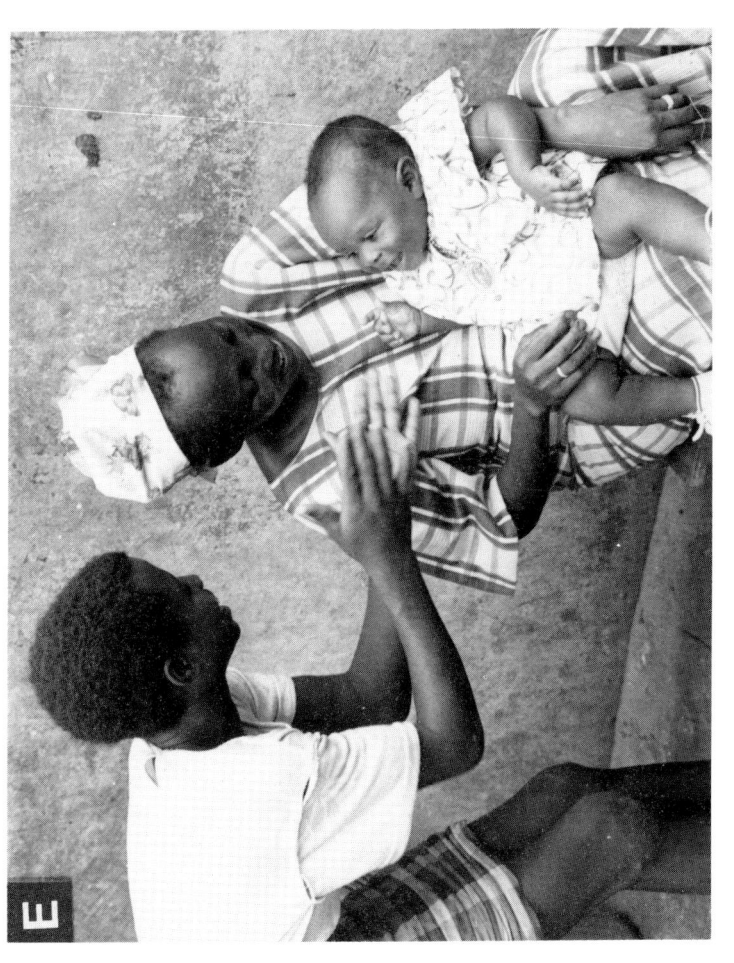

**Figure 1.4: E:** Oyabanji, male, 27 weeks. Playing with mother's sister, clapping song. Christian; father plumber, mother trader.

**Figure 1.4: F:** Adewale, male, 49 weeks. Shows neighbour, who is main caretaker, a piece of food.

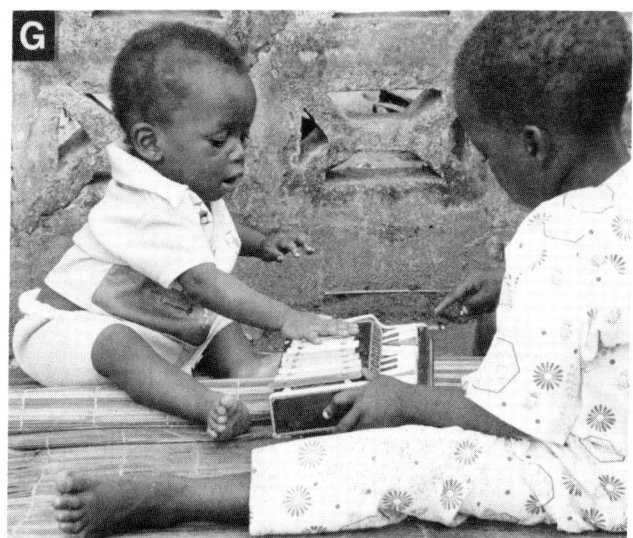

**Figure 1.4: G-H:** Adegbenro, male, 49 weeks; playing plastic piano and 'singing' with brother (five years), and sharing toy with mother.

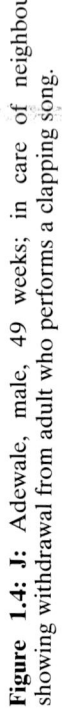

**Figure 1.4: J:** Adewale, male, 49 weeks; in care of neighbour, showing withdrawal from adult who performs a clapping song.

**Figure 1.4: I:** Ajayi twin, female, 27 weeks; with mother's sister.

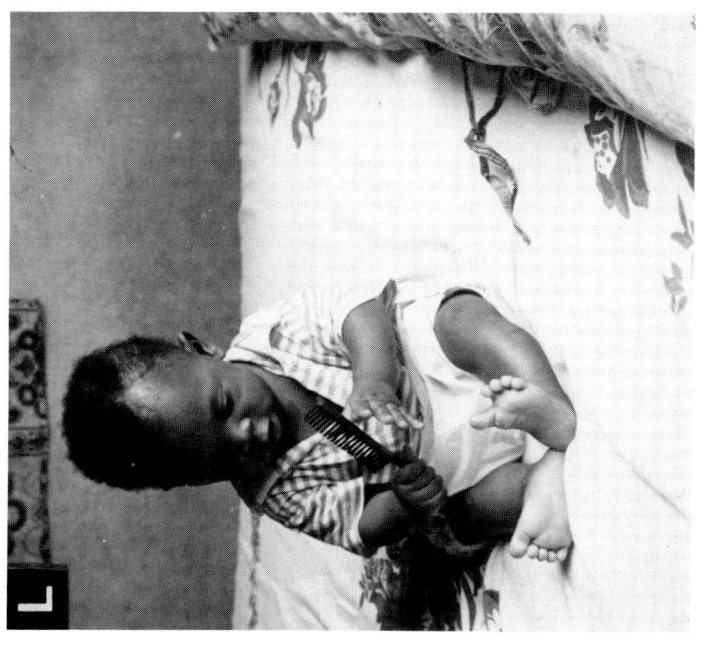
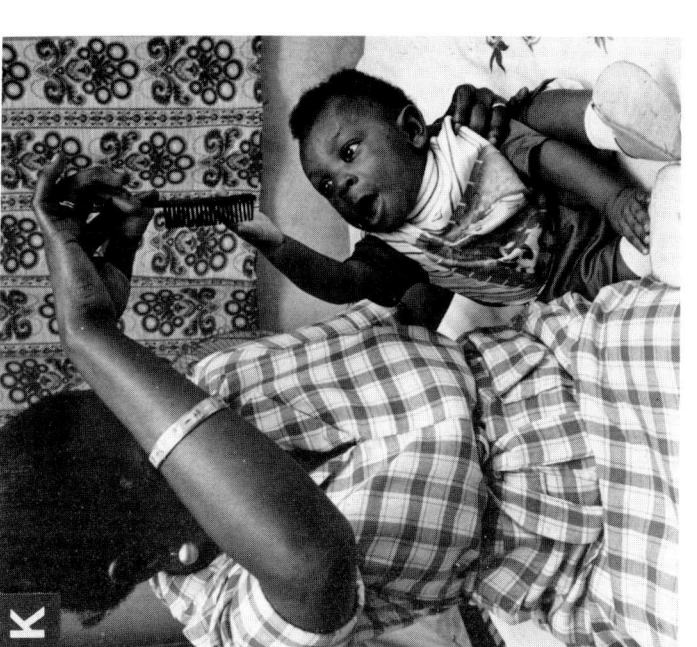

**Figure 1.4: K-L:** Olanrewaju, male, 28 weeks. Reaches for comb and plays with it on parents' bed. Father businessman, mother photographer; richer than other families. Christian.

**Figure 1.4: M:** Adegbenro, male, 49 weeks. Took comb and used it on his own hair. Typical courtyard scene.

Lamb, M.E. (1981) 'The development of father–infant relationships'. In: M.E. Lamb (ed.), *The father's role in child development*. New York: Wiley.

——, Thompson, R.A., Gardner, W. and Charnov, E. (1985) *Infant–mother attachment: the origins and developmental significance of individual differences in strange situation behavior*. Hillsdale, N.J.: Erlbaum.

LeVine, R.A. (1980) 'A cross-cultural perspective on parenting'. In: M.D. Fantini and R. Gardenas (eds), *Parenting in a multicultural society*. New York: Longman, 17–26.

Lewis, M. and Brooks, J. (1975) 'Infants' social perception: a constructivist view'. In: L.B. Cohen and P. Salapatek (eds), *Infant perception: from sensation to cognition* Vol. 2. New York: John Wiley and Sons, 102–43.

—— and Brooks-Gunn, J. (1979) *Social cognition and the acquisition of self*. New York: Plenum Press.

Lewis, O. (1959) *Five families*. New York: Basic Books.

Lock, A. (1980) *The guided reinvention of language*. London: Academic Press.

MacNamara, J. (1972) 'Cognitive basis of language learning in infants'. *Psychological Review*, 79, 1–13.

Maurer, D. and Salapatek, P. (1976) 'Developmental changes in the scanning of faces by young infants'. *Child Development*, 47, 523–7.

Mehler, J. and Fox, R. (1985) *Neonate cognition: beyond the blooming, buzzing confusion*. Hillsdale, N.J.: Erlbaum.

Meade, G.H. (1934) *Mind, self and society*. Chicago: University of Chicago Press.

Meltzoff, A.N. and Moore, M.H. (1977) 'Imitation of facial and manual gestures by human neonates'. *Science*, 198, 75–8.

Mundy-Castle, A. (1980) 'Perception and communication in infancy: A cross-cultural study'. In: Olson, D. (ed.), *The social foundations of language and thought*. New York: Norton and Co.

Murray, L. and Trevarthen, C. (1984) 'Emotional regulation of interactions between two-month-olds and their mothers'. In: T. Field and N. Fox (eds), *Social perception in infants*. Norwood, N.J.: Ablex, 177–97.

—— and Trevarthen, C. (1986) 'The infant's role in mother–infant communication'. *Journal of Child Language*, 13, 15–29.

Nelson, K. (1973) 'Structure and strategy in learning to talk'. *Monographs of the Society for Research in Child Development*, Serial No. 149, 38: 1–2.

Ochs, E. (1983) 'Cultural dimensions of language acquisition'. In: E. Ochs and B. B. Schieffelin (eds), *Acquiring conversational competence*. New York: Routledge and Kegan Paul.

—— and Schieffelin, B. B. (1983) *Acquiring conversational competence*. New York: Routledge and Kegan Paul.

Oster, H. (1978) 'Facial expression and affect development'. In: M. Lewis and L.A. Rosenblum (eds), *The development of affect*. New York: Plenum Press, 43–75.

Owen, B.M. and Lee, D.N. (1986) 'Establishing a frame of reference for action'. In: M.G. Wade and H.T.A. Whiting (eds), *Motor development in children: aspects of co-ordination and control*. Dordrecht: Martinus Nijhoff, 287–308.

Papousek, H. (1967) 'Experimental studies of appetitional behaviour in human newborns and infants'. In: H.W. Stevenson, E.H. Hess and H.L. Rheingold (eds), *Early behaviour: comparative and developmental approaches*. New York: John Wiley and Sons, 249–77.

Plooij, F. (1979) 'How wild chimpanzee babies trigger the onset of mother–infant play—and what the mother makes of it'. In: M. Bullowa (ed.), *Before speech*. Cambridge: Cambridge University Press, 223–43.

Sander, L. (1983) 'Polarity, paradox and the organizing process in development'. In: J.D. Call, E. Galenson and R.L. Tyson (eds), *Frontiers of infant psychology* Vol. 1. New York: Basic Books.

Shand, N. and Kowasa, Y. (1985) 'Japanese and American behaviour types at three months: Infants and infant–mother dyads'. *Infant Behaviour and Development*, 8, 225–40.

Shotter, J.D. (1973) 'Acquired powers: The transformation of natural into personal powers'. *Journal for the Theory of Social Behaviour*, 3, 140–56.

Spitz, R.A. and Wolf, K.M. (1946) 'The smiling response. A contribution to the ontogenesis of social relations'. *Genet. Psychol. Monogr.*, 34, 57–125.

Sroufe, L.A. (1979) 'Socioemotional development'. In: J. Osofsky (ed.), *Handbook of infancy*. New York: Wiley, 462–516.

—— and Waters, E. (1976) 'The ontogenesis of smiling and laughter: a perspective on the organization of development in infancy'. *Psychological Reviews*, 83, 173–89.

Stern, D.N. (1974) 'Mother and infant at play: The dyadic interaction involving facial, vocal and gaze behaviours'. In: M. Lewis and L.A. Rosenblum (eds), *The effect of the infant on its caregiver*. New York: Wiley.

—— (1985) *The interpersonal world of the infant*. New York: Basic Books.

Sylvester-Bradley, B. (1980) *A study of young infants as social beings*. PhD Thesis, University of Edinburgh.

—— (1981) 'Negativity in early infant–adult exchanges and its developmental significance'. In: P. Robinson (ed.), *Communication in development*. London: Academic Press, 1–37.

—— and Trevarthen, C. (1978) 'Baby talk as an adapatation to the infant's communication'. In: N. Waterson and C.E. Snow (eds), *The development of communication*. New York: John Wiley and Sons, 75–92.

Tizard, B. and Harvey, D. (eds) (1977) *Biology of play*. London: Heinemann.

Tonkin, E. (1982) 'Rethinking socialization'. *Journal of Anthropological Society of Oxford*, 13, 243–56.

Trevarthen, C. (1974) 'Conversations with a two-month old'. *New Scientist*, 2 May, 230–5.

—— (1979a) 'Instincts for human understanding and for cultural co-operation: their development in infancy'. In: M. von Cranach, K. Foppa, W. Lepenies and D. Plooij (eds), *Human ethology*. Cambridge: Cambridge University Press, 530–71.

—— (1979b) 'Communication and cooperation in early infancy. A description of primary intersubjectivity'. In: M. Bullowa (ed.), *Before speech: The beginnings of human communication*. London: Cambridge University Press.

—— (1980) 'The foundations of intersubjectivity: development of interpersonal and cooperative understanding in infants'. In: D. Olson (ed), *The social foundations of language and thought: essays in honor of J.S. Bruner*. New York: W.W. Norton, 316–42.

—— (1982) 'The primary motives for cooperative understanding'. In: G. Butterworth and P. Light (eds), *Social cognition: studies of the development of understanding*. Brighton: Harvester Press, 77–109.

—— (1983) 'Interpersonal abilities of infants as generators for transmission of language and culture'. In: A. Oliverio and M. Zapella (eds), *The behaviour of human infants*. London and New York: Plenum, 145–76.

—— (1984a) 'How control of movements develops'. In: H.T.A. Whiting (ed.), *Human motor actions: Bernstein reassessed*. Amsterdam: Elsevier (North-Holland), 223–61.

—— (1984b) 'Emotions in infancy: Regulators of contacts and relationships with persons'. In: K. Scherer and P. Ekman (eds), *Approaches to emotion*. Hillsdale, N.J.: Erlbaum, 129–57.

—— (1984c) 'Biodynamic structures, cognitive correlates of motive sets and development of motives in infants'. In: W. Prinz and A.F. Saunders (eds), *Cognition and motor processes*. Berlin-Heidelberg-New York: Springer Verlag, 327–50.

—— (1985) 'Facial expressions of emotion in mother–infant interaction'. *Human Neurobiology*, 4, 21–32.

—— (1986a) 'Form, significance and psychological potential of hand gestures of infants'. In: J.-L. Nespoulos, P. Perron and A.R. Lecours (eds), *The biological foundations of gestures: motor and semiotic aspects*. Cambridge, Mass: The MIT Press, 149–202.

—— (1986b) 'Development of intersubjective motor control in infants'. In: M. Wade and H.T.A. Whiting (eds), *Motor development in children*. The Hague: Martinus Nijhoff.

—— (1987) 'Sharing makes sense: Intersubjectivity and the making of an infant's meaning'. In: R. Steele and T. Threadgold (eds), *Language topics: essays in honour of Michael Halliday*. Amsterdam and Philadelphia: John Benjamins (in press).

—— and Hubley, P. (1978) 'Secondary intersubjectivity: confidence, confiding and acts of meaning in the first year'. In: A. Lock (ed.), *Action, gesture and symbol*. London: Academic Press, 183–229.

—— and Logotheti, K. (1987) 'First symbols and the nature of human knowledge'. *Cahiers de la Fondation Archives Piaget* (in press).

—— and Marwick, H. (1982) *Cooperative understanding in infants*. Project Report to the Spencer Foundation. Department of Psychology, University of Edinburgh.

—— and Marwick, H. (1986) 'Signs of motivation for speech in infants, and the nature of a mother's support for development of language'. In: B. Lindblom and R. Zetterstrom (eds), *Precursors of early speech*. Basingstoke, Hampshire: MacMillan.

——, Murray, L. and Hubley, P. (1981) 'Psychology of infants'. In: J. Davis and J. Dobbing (eds), *Scientific foundations of clinical paediatrics*. London: W. Heinemann Medical Books Ltd., (2nd edition) 211–74.

Tronick, E.Z., Winn, S. and Morelli, G.A. (1985) 'Multiple caretaking in the context of human evolution. Why don't the Efe know the Western prescription of child-care?' In: M. Reite and T. Field (eds), *Psychobiology of attachment*. New York: Academic Press.

Volterra, V. and Caselli, M.C.C. (1985) From gestures and vocalizations to signs and words. In: W. Stokoe and V. Volterra (eds), *Sign language research*. Silver Spring, Maryland: Linstok Press, 1–9.

Vygotsky, L. S. (1962) *Thought and language*. Cambridge, Mass: The MIT Press.

—— (1978) *Mind in society*. Cambridge, Mass: The MIT Press.

Watson, J.S. (1977) 'Perception of contingency as a determinant of social responsiveness'. In: E.B. Thomam (ed.), *Origins of the infant's social responsiveness*. Hillsdale, N.J.: Erlbaum, 33–63.

Wertsch, J.V. (ed.) (1985) *Culture, communication and cognition: Vygotskian perspectives*. Cambridge: Cambridge University Press.

Winnicott, D.W. (1965) *The maturational process and the facilitating environment*. London: Hogarth Press.

# 2

# Dance and Music in Venda Children's Cognitive Development, 1956–8[1]

John Blacking

## AFFECTIVE CULTURE AND COGNITIVE DEVELOPMENT

In tribal and peasant societies much of the formal and informal education of young people was effected through 'affective culture', and especially by systems of non-verbal communication such as 'dance' and 'music'.[2] During the 1960s and 1970s in the United Kingdom and other industrialised countries, concern for the development of the emotions increased greatly in arguments about educational policy and in the practice of primary and secondary education.

Are then dance, music and other artistic activities peripheral or central to general cognitive development? Are they simply optional extras which can help children to learn in a pleasant way word-based social and technical skills and moral values, and to acquire a sense of group identity? Or are they essential forms of knowledge which are necessary not only for a balanced personality but also for the development of cognitive capacities?

Arguments for and against the cognitive value of 'affective culture' have centred round issues such as the transfers of skills from one activity to another, the different modes of consciousness of the hemispheres of the brain and the need to maintain a balance in using them, the value of 'the intelligence of feeling' (cf. Witkin, 1976) and rejection of a division between emotion and reason, and the conflicting claims that the arts can be used to restrict or enhance creative thinking. A major problem in assessing arguments about relationships between affective culture and cognitive development is that they must rely on words to investigate forms of knowledge and action that are predominantly non-verbal. Nevertheless, a case cannot be made for the influence of affective culture on cognitive development unless we adopt the notion of a 'thinking artist' (e.g. musician or dancer) who acts consciously and intentionally, but often with a mode of discourse that is not generally used in ordinary social interaction; and unless we recognise that the institutionalisation of intuition is a source of cultural creativity and accept that the capacity to appreciate and interpret this discourse is common to the human species and not only to a few people: 'art and the equipment to grasp it are made in the same shop' (Geertz, 1976, p. 1497).

The most easily accepted argument for the positive influence of affective culture on cognitive development is that which asserts that people learn best in a warm and familiar environment, in which new knowledge can be easily related to the values, symbols and social experience of the home and neighbourhood. In a study of changes in the traditional dances of Bali and Hawaii, Joann Keali'inohomoku (1979, p. 47) defined affective culture as 'those cultural manifestations that implicitly and explicitly reflect the values of a given group of people through consciously devised means that arouse emotional responses and that strongly reinforce group identity'. The performing arts of music and dance, in particular, can provide powerful symbols of ethnic identity, but their emotional impact is a very personal matter of individual response and interpretation. If dance and music 'reinforce group identity', it is because people assign certain social meanings to their symbols, and because their commitment to the associated institutions is reinforced by the sensuous impact of the artistic forms.

Experiences of affective culture can sometimes take people by surprise, especially in childhood, because of some resonance that is created, an unintended consequence of intentional action. Edmund Gosse described such an experience in his autobiographical account, *Father and son: a study of two temperaments*, when, at the age of ten, he read his first piece of fiction in a home dedicated to 'the truth'. 'There were certain scenes and images in *Tom Cringle's Log* which made not merely a lasting impression on my mind, but tinged my outlook on life' (Gosse, 1974; pp. 113–14).

Psychologists recognise that affects are primary motives, which have profound effects on cognition and action, and yet they often ignore the influence of 'affective culture' on individual development. In a number of standard works on children's social and cognitive development (e.g. Connolly and Bruner, 1974;

Hamilton and Vernon, 1976), there is no discussion of the kind of experience that precipitated a leap forward in Edmund Gosse's life, or on the effects of artistic practice in general. Judging by the results of experimental research on artistic development (see, for instance, Gardner, 1973, chs 5 and 7), artistic practice can affect human development in many ways. A person's cognitive growth and actions are affected more by feelings and commitment associated with particular people and events than by objective assessments of situations. Passion is as important in scientific endeavour as is compassion in artistic vision. But the young Gosse's passion and commitment could only affect his subsequent thought and actions because he was able to integrate and use different kinds of experience.

Thus the role of affective culture in cognitive development cannot usefully be considered apart from the different ways in which societies conceptualise and use non-verbal symbols, not only because verbally assigned meanings provide the links between people's experiences of affective culture and their cognitive development in other spheres of life, but also because they are a part of the processes of constructing and making sense of non-verbal forms (cf. Feld, 1982). Experiences of dance and music are personal, but the feelings engendered by them are relevant to other aspects of a person's life only in so far as they are noted and interpreted. This is a creative act that presupposes other 'labelled' experiences and knowledge of at least some of 'the public images of sentiment that only ritual, myth, and arts can provide' (Geertz, 1975, p. 82).

An anthropological approach to dance and music therefore requires some qualification of the view that practice of the arts provides special kinds of knowledge that can be had in no other way. In so far as this knowledge is private, there can be no objection to David Best's argument that since the 'feelings expressed in dance are inseparable from the physical movements employed, these feelings can be experienced in no other art form' (Best, 1974, p. 200); moreover, there is no guarantee that all people who perform or perceive the same movements will have the same feelings. But when dance is a social institution and the interrelationships of dancers and spectators are a part of public life, then the private experiences can become public knowledge. To dancers, no less than to spectators who do not literally experience the physical movement, private feelings will be interpreted in the light of common-sense knowledge of artistic conventions and of the cultural institutions in which they are embedded. Whether or not different art forms are closely interrelated, as they are in many African societies, and whether or not different forms of affective culture are expressions of a common mode of 'artistic cognition', people's interpretations and uses of artistic experience invariably transcend the performance situation, and in reflection they invoke notions and even feelings that are extrinsic to the actual artistic experience. These external experiences in turn affect each individual's artistic experience (cf. Wachsmann, 1982).

Performances of dance and music can indeed have value in themselves, and the private experiences of those involved do not need to be justified by any form of public expression. But even such conditions and responses would be cultural conventions, and as such would be related to ideas about the performing arts and about performing as a way of knowing which presuppose ideas about the types and purposes of knowledge. Thus, David Best's critique of Modern Educational Gymnastics, which followed on from his general argument about the uniqueness of artistic experiences, also invokes kinds of intelligence which are not distinguished in all cultures. He argues that Modern Educational Gymnastics cannot teach people to think as they do in other spheres of education, with words or mathematical symbols, although movement by itself could be described as a mode of thought. An able performer might exhibit 'kinaesthetic intelligence. But ... the able mover who is not intellectually gifted will perform physical activities more competently, will exhibit greater kinaesthetic intelligence, than the intellectually gifted who is not an able mover' (Best, 1978, p. 58).

Taken to its extreme, this argument demolishes the notion that affective culture can have any direct influence on cognitive development. It suggests that different art forms require not only different skills but also different kinds of intelligence, which are to some extent mutually exclusive. If this is so, then the contribution of affective culture to cognitive development depends on people's ability to integrate and relate these different intelligences. Consequently, experiences of affective culture become intellectually redundant, and what matters is the integrating faculty. If this faculty is a manifestation of creative thinking rather than of any specific kind of intelligence, then there is evidence that at least the practice of music enhances it.

Barkóczi and Pléh's longitudinal study of Hungarian children,

*Music makes a difference* (1982), showed that although intensive musical education by the Kodály method did not affect the general level of children's intelligence, it had a positive effect on their creativity and produced a 'more harmonic relation between creativity and intelligence, divergent and convergent thought' (p. 31). The special musical education also seemed to have beneficial effects on personality development and on the educational performance of previously disadvantaged children. Similarly, Leon Crickmore (1968) found that people's ability to comprehend music structures was independent of their personality, measured intellectual capacity, and musical intelligence as assessed by the Wing tests. Since measurements of musical intelligence are culture-specific, Crickmore's subjects were using either more general musical capacities than those measured by the Wing tests or a non-specific creative faculty.

What emerges from these and other studies is a picture not so much of a bewildering variety of different kinds of intelligence as of different cultural systems in which affective culture and other intellectual activities are constituted in many different ways: dance and music are not universal phenomena produced by some specific kinaesthetic or musical intelligence, but the products of processes whose differences are culturally selected. If the varieties of affective culture do have a common intellectual base, then perhaps it is what might be called 'artistic cognition', which, according to the biologist J.Z. Young, must have had an important evolutionary function, because of its capacity to provide new variations of existing knowledge freed from the immediate requirements of the environment (Young, 1971, p. 519; De Bono, 1969, p. 130). Mihaly Csikszentmihalyi has also argued (1978, p. 118) that 'artistic cognition can provide the novel concepts and the unthought of rules constituting the variation without which knowledge could not evolve'.

I have suggested (Blacking, 1976) that aesthetic/artistic cognition, embodied in non-verbal communication, was a key constituent in early developments of the 'power of mind', the phrase which E.B. Tylor coined to refer to the collective thought and action which made cultural evolution possible. Although the power of mind is a social fact, it is not entirely independent of the operations of the brain, and especially the differential but complementary functions of its two hemispheres. Capacities for artistic cognition in general, and for dance and music in particular, appear to be located in the right hemisphere of the brain. But this does not mean that all artistic activities are exclusively products of right hemisphere activity: for example, many professional musicians use the *left* hemisphere for music-making. Thus it seems that the cognitive capacities used for dance and music, or speech, or any other activity, are related, *not to the activity but to how it is processed*. We should be looking not for species-specific abilities for dance or music, but for species-specific modes of thought that can be used in processing, structuring and communicating sensory data, and for one or two in particular that are most characteristically realised in 'dance' and 'music'.

Although verbal modes of communication are used in the production of what some societies label as 'the arts', the processes as well as the products of dance and music are most typically non-verbal. And non-verbal modes are the most ancient and affecting of all the source of intellectual imagination and creativity. They are particularly appropriate for the expression of the quality and intensity of feelings (Bateson, 1973, p. 388). Nonverbal modes of communication are most closely related to the activities of the right hemisphere of the brain and can be linked to what has been described as 'artistic cognition'.

In spite of the reservations that have been expressed about the specialisation of the two hemispheres of the brain and the lateralisation of cognitive function, I find the model of hemispherical differentiation the most useful as a general guide to understanding the languages, uses, and functions of dance and music in different societies. Not only does it correspond with contrasts in communication that are commonly described as 'propositional/discursive' or 'performative/expressive', and with many folk classifications of different kinds of dance and music and of contrasts between 'artistic' and 'non-artistic' systems; it also explains in a more powerful way the intellectual significance of dance and music as systems of non-verbal symbols, and hence the structural relationships between affective culture and cognitive development.

The model of hemispherical differentiation disposes of the argument that experiences of affective culture could be self-contained and intellectually redundant, because it relates the specific forms of all skills and modes of communication to more general cognitive processes, of which the abilities to create and integrate are a part, rather than a dominant, organising feature. That is to say, creative thinking and the ability to integrate and relate different skills and experiences are essential to cognitive development, but they are also *parts* of cognitive development. More particularly, they are a function of *balanced* cognitive development, in which the two modes of thought characteristic of the left and right hemispheres are as far as possible used together, although most occupations and skills value one mode over the other (Ornstein, 1973, p. 92; 1975, pp. 67–8).

I am not suggesting that affective culture in particular, and the variety of human inventions and activities in general, should or could be reduced to applications of these two contrasting modes of thought to human sensory-motor capacities, or that we can now abandon the search for subsets of a larger domain of knowing, for more specific mental structures and schemata. We should ask the same sort of questions about the arts that Lévi-Strauss has asked about myth and kinship. If such a mode as 'musical cognition' exists, is it necessarily connected specifically with the organisation of tones, rhythm, and timbre? Or could it be a more general mode of thought whose most effective and characteristic embodiment is with musical symbols? If so, in what other forms can 'musical cognition' appear? Is architecture, for example, an embodiment of musical thought? Are mathematics or any of the sciences organised with musical thought?

If there is a basic mode of musical cognition, perhaps similar to speech as a primary modelling system, it does not follow that all extant musical systems should be derived from it, since different musics can be and have been produced with very different principles. Similarly, a theory of music that does not try to account for all musical systems, first in their own terms and then perhaps in more general terms, can never be more than the self-fulfilling prophecy of a social group that sets its own ground rules. The true nature of 'musical cognition' as a subset of a larger domain of cognition could only be revealed by cross-cultural musical analyses that transcend any one body of ethno-theory; and the same must apply to the discovery of any other type of 'artistic cognition'. If such modes of cognition exist, they extend in space and time, and would have been available as much to the ancient Greeks and the Stone Age hunters of Europe as to all contemporary peoples of the world.

The model of hemispherical differentiation cannot usefully be applied to analyses of dance and music without considering individual motivation and cultural context. First, we cannot produce a coherent analysis of relationships between dance and music and cognitive development unless we assume that people make conscious choices about whom they wish to interact with and in what modes they prefer to communicate.

Second, the reasons for people's choices cannot always be explained in terms of motives which are said to be basic to all human beings by 'Western' psychology: motivation must be understood in terms of people's own ethnopsychologies.

Third, the relevance of dance and music in human interaction and decision-making cannot properly be assessed unless their symbolic as well as social implications are taken into account. People can engage in dance and music for social, political, or economic reasons, and hence process the experience verbally in a variety of ways. But they can also process the experience nonverbally, in terms of the essential characteristics of the media of communication, deriving satisfaction from the special kinds of social activity, and so transcending their social contexts. Because dance and music are culturally encoded, dance and music codes, as dance and music and not with reference to something else, enable people to establish connections between their inner worlds and social reality when there are structural links between people's organisation of feelings and their constructions of social reality. These links enable people to associate, by 'resonance', qualitatively and functionally different but structurally similar experiences.

The model of hemispherical differentiation can be most satisfactorily combined with Rogers's and Maslow's notions of 'growth motivation' and 'self-actualisation' (Maslow, 1954), to provide a framework for analysis that can be adapted to different cultural systems and can account for individuals' decisions and cognitive development in relation to their participation in affective culture. If we assume that people constantly seek to use their brains as they use other parts of the body, it follows that they will wish to use both parts of the brain, although the mental equivalent of right-handedness may allow more habitual use of one hemisphere rather than the other without undue stress. The greatest sense of fulfilment and successful self-actualisation should be derived from the complementary use of both hemispheres/modes of thought (cf. Ornstein, 1973, 1975) which in itself is a source of new kinetic and intellectual energy. People would be motivated by the 'need' to establish a balance between their use of different modes of thought, and might therefore choose, whenever possible, to do something that was missing from their current activities, if only to re-charge their reserves of energy. This is supported, for example, by reports of people who worked hard in the fields all day until they were tired, but were able to recover their energy and strength in the evening with dancing, which used different movements and required different mental attitudes.

## COGNITION AND COGNITIVE DEVELOPMENT

In their introductory chapter, Jahoda and Lewis distinguish between the anthropologist's treatment of cognition as the acquisition and assimilation of a particular society's world view, and the psychologist's interest in the cognitive development of individuals in different social and cultural contexts. They argue that anthropologists should be concerned not only with what children are expected to do and learn, but how they actually absorb a society's rule system, how they are instructed, and how they learn to think and act and relate to others. The first section of this paper has maintained that the process of cognitive development, which interests psychologists, cannot be properly assessed without considering the effects of people's world view and ethnopsychology on their motivation and commitment to different types of learning.

Here I suggest that the various theories of Piaget, Vygotsky and Witkin can be usefully treated as complementary, rather than as contradictory. For example, Piaget's four stages in the development of thought might perhaps be more usefully regarded as four types of thought, which are present in the thinking capacities of normal individuals but are most commonly brought into play in the order specified. I suggest that the third and fourth types (concrete and formal operations) can be used before the age of seven, and that at least the second type (preoperational) may be used in adulthood. For example, some of the beliefs that people in most societies hold in politics and religion are hardly different from the apparent inability of small children to see that two differently shaped glasses are in fact holding the same amount of water.

If Piaget's scheme is qualified by the notion of 'situational intelligence', which I have found to make more sense in interpreting what I observed both in Venda in 1956–8 and in the development of my own children, we have something much closer to Vygotsky's approach, which in turn could be regarded as a variation of E.B. Tylor's notion of 'the power of mind'. Tylor argued that the 'power of mind' was created by the combined enterprise of individuals who possessed basically the same intellectual potential. Piaget's 'stages' may therefore be seen in much the same way as Vygotsky's 'functional systems', as modes of thought that have been found generally appropriate in the socialisation of children in many societies, perhaps in all known societies. In this sense, they may be super-species of functional systems that transcend the culture-specific functional systems that Vygotsky described.

H.A. Witkin's theory of psychological differentiation becomes necessary to explain the inevitable contradictions that must arise from conflicts between the demands on individuals of general and of culture-specific functional systems. Both Piaget's and Vygotsky's models are restrictive in the sense that they underestimate the imagination and creative potential of children. They are frequently confounded by the evidence of child prodigies. If prodigies are genetic freaks, then there is no more to be said. But if they are children who have developed certain cognitive skills exceptionally quickly, because of commitment to a particular activity and/or a person or persons associated with it, then the interesting and crucial question is not: Why are they prodigies? but Why aren't thousands of other children performing as well as they? This was one of the problems that stimulated me to study children's development in a skill in which child prodigies have always been significant, namely, music; and also the relationships between skills in music and in other activities.[3]

## A VENDA WORLD VIEW, 1956–8

In the first section of this paper, I argued that cognitive development must be assessed not only in specific social contexts but also in terms of people's psychological concepts about growth, motivation and intelligence. Because I was concerned primarily with the performance of traditional Venda music between 1956 and 1958, I will describe only the current world view of those involved in its performance. Many Venda Christians held a modified world view and shared different musical experiences, which will not be discussed here. (See Blacking (1981) for a discussion of Christian music.)

### Self-actualisation and individual development

In traditional Venda society, each individual birth, in theory, marked the return of an ancestral spirit in human form, and the death of every 'identifiable', fulfilled person marked the birth of a new ancestral spirit. Thus every human being began life as a reincarnation of a deceased person (who maintained his/her autonomy as an ancestral spirit), and could eventually become an autonomous ancestral spirit in his/her own right. The cycle of existence was not a closed, self-perpetuating system, but cumulative as a result of the fruitful social life of individual human beings. Self could only be realised through others, but significant others only existed because of fully developed selves.

The Venda theory of personality and cognitive development therefore began with the assumption that a 'child is an *active* rather than a passive participant in his/her own development' (Ault, 1977, p. 12). The second assumptions was that of the interactionist position. If an infant survived the first, physically dangerous year of life, the innate characteristics of the deceased ancestral spirit lodged in the child's body would gradually be modified by the different social experiences of the new person, who could eventually develop a strong and independent personality.

The Venda theory of human development was encapsulated in a well-known saying: *a hu aluwi muthu: hu aluwa mbilu*, 'it is not the person who grows up, but the heart'. Although *-aluwa* referred to biological maturation in general, the concept of the person was not biological. A person could only become a person through social interaction with other persons (*muthu ndi muthu nga vhañwe*). And the essential definition of personhood, or humanity (*vhuthu*) was that it referred to a person's kindness, neighbourliness (*vhuhura*) and compassion (*vhuhwavho*). Sheer self-interest was not regarded as a human attribute. People explained the apparent egoism of very small babies with the observation that they had not yet developed human characteristics. They did not yet belong to the *mu/vha* class of nouns reserved for human beings: they were *lushie* or *lutshetshe*.

The importance of co-operation and sharing permeated the whole Venda education system. The purpose of the formal education of girls from puberty to marriage, through three important rites, *vhusha*, *tskikanda* and *domba*, was to prepare them for motherhood by learning all the techniques of being human: how to be polite, neighbourly and kind, to maintain good relations with seniors, age mates and children, with officials, relatives and visitors. Individuality was valued and cultivated, but pretentiousness and failure were criticised. People were judged in terms of what they set out to do, and above all by what they were as people.

Thus, Mrs N. might have been a poor cook and her gardens might not have been as good as her neighbour's, but she need never have felt an outcast as long as her intentions and behaviour were charitable. On the other hand, if Mr N. ventured into a specialist field such as medicine or teaching because he wanted to help his people, he would be harshly criticised if he were technically incompetent. Assuming that Mrs N. and Mr N. were both good people, Mr N.'s fault would have been to try to do something for which he had no true vocation. The development of children's abilities was likewise associated with the idea that exceptional ability in skills such as dance, music, or medicine, was a consequence of working at the skill, and that this obsession must be inherited from an ancestor or validated by a dream. The notions of possession and of union with the other self were prominent in Venda thinking and were constantly invoked as explanations of experience.

The peculiar nature of white domination inevitably distorted patterns of change in Venda during the past century, because it was impossible for any black South African to share freely the life and skills of European industrial cultures. Nevertheless, the traditional Venda ethos predominated. In an analysis of occupational prestige among urban Venda school children in 1961, I found that teaching, clerical work, nursing and shopkeeping were high in the list of preferred jobs and that doing socially necessary work remained the highest ideal, though personal independence and scope for the use of the intellect were important considerations in assessing occupations.

**Venda concepts of intelligence and cognitive development**

The head was regarded as the centre of thinking, of *strategic intelligence*, and the heart the centre of understanding. Because of the basic importance of co-operation, the earliest manifestation of general intelligence was widely held to be a child's willingness and ability to co-operate with others. The following extract from a life history is typical (italics mine):

When I was three years old and *rather more intelligent*, my mother had long ceased to carry me on her back, and I was happy to stay at home and play with other little children. (Blacking, 1964, p. 61)

The verb used in this passage to refer to *general intelligence* (*-thanya*) was morally neutral. The intellect could be applied to 'teach' and 'impart wisdom' to others (*-thanyisa*), to 'outwit' them in a straight confrontation (*-thanyela*) or to be too clever by half and outwit by deceit or dishonesty (*-thanyesa*). The mind was meant to be used to realise human potential, and in particular to enlarge the range of social interaction within prescribed limits: 'being too clever causes your downfall' (*u thanya hu a wedza-wedza*), and a person's downfall was measured in terms of loss of friends or followers, of influence or public trust and respect. (In the context of white domination, the deception of white administrators and businessmen became a legitimate use of intelligence, and several kinds of 'downfall' were not regarded as such.)

There was a noun which was semantically similar to *-thanya*, though not etymologically related. *Maano* could be said to refer to *situational intelligence*, and especially to the ability to discriminate between *actions* that were or were not culturally appropriate. A child might show ample evidence of general intelligence (*u thanya*) but still do 'senseless' things on occasions. I often heard people explain away children's behaviour with the words, '*Ha na maano*', 's/he's not with sense (of what is the right thing to do)'. When I made similar errors, as for example in matters of etiquette, people said kindly, 'He does not know the custom'. '*Ha na maano*' could also be said of an adult who did something naive, stupid, or socially inept, but was said critically and not in the almost apologetic tones used for children, and it referred to particular responses rather than a person's general state of mind. *Maano* could be 'stretched out' (*-vhambwa*), like a wet hide or a skin over a drum, to deal with a particular situation; but, as a Venda proverb said, 'it doesn't last a year' (*maano ha fhedzi nwaha*). It referred to people's ability to organise consciously their basic intellectual competence in response to situational challenges. No adult human being could consistently lack *maano* unless s/he were suffering from some sickness, such as congenital lunacy or the madness of bewitchment.

*Vhutali* was another word for intellect, but it was used only in a complimentary way, to refer to a person's socially productive intelligence, to insight and understanding more than sheer cleverness.

Two related words for 'stupidity' (*vhutsilu*) and 'fool' (*tsilu*) also seemed to be most generally used for situational rather than absolute judgements. In another Venda proverb, 'labour for the chief hurts (lit. kills) only the fool (who works for others who fail to turn up)': *mushumo wa musanda u vhulaha tsilu*. Such a man could not really be said to lack *maano*, because he was doing the right thing at the right time. Another word for 'fool' (*phuphula*) would be inappropriate in the context of that proverb: derived from the verb *-phuphula*, its basic meaning was 'to fail to produce any fruit, have no cob or ear (of maize or millet), or, if so, very few grains on it'; it stressed the norm of the *socially* productive use of intelligence. People were only said to act '*like* fools' on certain occasions: they were not *called* 'fools' unless they really were half-witted, and then the word was used more in a compassionate rather than a contemptuous tone.

In traditional Venda society, the absence of an extensive division of labour and of writing imposed constraints on any one person's monopoly of knowledge. Most members of the society were involved most of the time in a cultural system which was essentially adaptive and open, and whose situational challenges exercised the 'head' as much as the 'heart'. The proper celebration of ritual, and experience of its forms, accurate performances of music, punctilious observance of etiquette and of the formalities of social relations, knowledge of proverbs and of the many *milayo* formulae taught at initiation, all exercised the intelligence and were believed to increase personal and spiritual power. Although the aim was to internalise those skills and take them to heart, no one was excused for slapdash behaviour on the grounds that her/his heart was in the right place. They were part of the rules of membership of different social groups, and to ignore them would have been an affront to the group and to the basic 'human' principle of co-operation. Furthermore, human co-operation was believed to be intricately connected with the balance of forces and the 'real' harmony which existed in the world, and knowledge and understanding of this were the keys to all forms of power and control of them.

Thus cognition and cognitive development were as complementary as self-actualisation and communal life. Just as individuals could satisfy themselves best by serving and sharing with others, so a profound and personal understanding of the Venda world view could give individuals the most stimulating intellectual challenge and emotional satisfaction. This was possible because the Venda world view was an open and not a closed system. That is, it was not meant to *determine* individuals' lives and ambitions, but rather to provide a framework for self-actualisation and cognitive development, whose ultimate sanction was personal experience of the spiritual foundations of the universe. For example, if a man's strong desire to make drums conflicted with his role expectations (e.g. because there were no drum-makers in his family), he could still go ahead and try. Public acceptance depended not only on the quality of his work but on proof of his spiritual calling, which would appear in the conviction that he showed as a result of his inner experience.

## DANCE AND MUSIC AS SCHEMATA, SYMBOLS, CONCEPTS AND RULES

Music is always multi-media communication, in that the 'raw material' of organised sound is embedded in and accompanied by other verbal and non-verbal messages. Cognitively, it is also multi-*level* communication; its ambiguity allows performances of a single piece of music to be perceived and remembered as schemata, symbols, concepts, or rules.

In the context of social life, musical systems are groups of *schemata* and *symbols* which are linked by certain *concepts* and governed by *rules*. A child can grasp the schemata without having any idea of their significance as symbols, simply by performing them and remembering them. The same material can be rehearsed and interpreted as symbols and concepts that relate to other cultural phenomena, and then *rules* are discovered and used for creating new forms. It might be more correct to describe music as 'symbolised schemata' of sound, since the sounds have no intrinsic meaning and only become symbols in so far as they can be related to other cultural and social phenomena.

One of the first songs that all Venda children acquired *as a recognised musical skill* was the four-tone counting song *Potilo* (Blacking, 1967, No. 13). Each phrase was accompanied by a rhythmical touching or grasping of the fingers and thumbs—from left little finger to thumb by the thumb and first finger of the right hand, and then right thumb to third finger by the thumb and first finger of the left hand—until the concluding tenth phrase was reinforced by a clap of the hands. Infants were often encouraged to perform this song before they could speak sentences of Venda. Between the ages of twenty-four and thirty-six months most children first produced an erratic melody, unstable words and rhythmic movements that were regular but did not necessarily coincide with the melodic phrases, and then they graduated effortlessly to co-ordinated performances that were publicly accepted as correct. By the age of three they also appreciated the symbolic significance of *Poṱilo* and other similar schemata as 'counting songs' (see Blacking, 1967, plate 14 and songs Nos 13–17). They related them to counting-out games, and began to associate them with other singing games and musical activities that were categorised as 'songs' or 'games', such as verses that were sung by all present as part of children's stories (*ngano*) told on winter evenings, or the *tshigombela* dance of girls (Blacking, 1967, plate 6), which was called a 'game' (*mutambo*).

Assimilation of the concepts of singing, playing and dancing as skills and social activities was helped on by attempts to perform during intervals in adult music-making (Blacking, 1967, plates 9A and B), by imitation while standing alongside girls and boys who were rehearsing their dances, and by performing children's play-dances (*dzhombo*). The variety of contexts in which children experienced or tried to perform music and dance helped them to understand the relationship of artistic skills to social institutions, and to value them as means of communication no less important than speech.

During my fieldwork children between the ages of five and eight years taught me concepts and rules relating to musical symbols. Not only could they outline the classifications of different types of children's song and several different musical styles, but they had grasped the essential difference between Venda speech and song (Blacking, 1976, pp. 27–8). They had also discovered rules of music-making to the extent that they could correct my mistakes (Blacking, 1976, p. 69) and could adapt a given melody to new words, because they understood the principles of interaction of patterns of melody and speech-tone (Blacking, 1967, pp. 167–71; Blacking, 1976, pp. 69–70). They had grasped the basic principles of harmony and could recognise two different melodies as transformations of a single harmonic framework (Blacking, 1976, pp. 23–4); they understood the principles of repeating rhythmic patterns (Blacking, 1967, pp. 157ff), and also appreciated that repeated melodic patterns could be transformed by the organising principles of tonality and mode (cf. Blacking, 1967, p. 186 and song No. 36A).

As children grew up, they began to explore available musical instruments (e.g. Blacking, 1967, plate No. 9A) and tried to participate in performances. By the age of five or six some had begun to learn certain solo instruments for pleasure and reflection, but all participated in the boys' and girls' play-dances (*dzhombo*) on moonlit nights, where they first learnt to improvise words and dance-steps, use additive rhythms, and lead songs—all good training for *malende* songs and dances, which were a major musical activity of adults. At about this stage, they learnt that the 'call' sections of songs provided singers with opportunities for improvising words of protest or social comment, and they would have heard many women doing this when pounding maize at night. A good singer (*nambi*) was one who had not only a strong, clear voice but also a rich storehouse of different verses and the ability to adapt them to a topical issue.

In most cases, children acquired the skills of music and dance indirectly by attending a wide variety of performances, and directly by learning from their peers and immediate seniors. Even at initiation schools, songs and dances were learnt not so much from instructors as from those who had recently graduated. There was, in fact, surprisingly little direct adult–child interaction involving music and dance, and comparatively little mother–child interaction except in the early pre-verbal stages. The critical appreciation of adults provided an incentive to perform well, but it was not an important factor in learning *how* to perform.

## EXPERIENCES OF DANCE AND MUSIC AS EVIDENCE OF WORLD VIEW, STIMULI TO SELF-ACTUALISATION, AND GUIDES TO THINKING, FEELING AND ACTING

I argued that the sensuous impact of the performing arts depends on people's ability to integrate and use different kinds of experience, and that the symbolic structures of dance and music are created and interpreted by individuals with the same cognitive equipment as other features of the socio-cultural system. The effectiveness of dance and music in Venda children's cognitive development therefore depended on the ways in which they used and made sense of them. There were early milestones in Venda children's acquisition of dance and music skills which helped them to develop relationships and affect, and to link musical experience and performance to daily life.

For the first eighteen months of their lives, infants spent much time first on their mother's backs, and then on the backs of siblings and other children. They therefore heard songs and felt rhythmical movements as their mothers and minders sang and danced or played singing games in many different social contexts. After feeding, most mothers held their babies in front of them in face-to-face interaction, singing to them and 'dancing' them up and down. When an infant started spontaneous banging with some object, s/he was not told to shut up: invariably an adult or older child would convert the spontaneous behaviour into intentional musical action by adding a second part in polyrhythm. Polyrhythm was an essential feature of all Venda music, and although it has been argued that all children's songs ought to be isorhythmic—as a necessary phase of human cognitive development—Venda children played polyrhythms at a very early age. The experience of polyrhythmic performance was a necessary step on the path to understanding the human predicament, which I discussed earlier, *muthu ndi muthu nga vhañwe*.

If tone-stress and ideal motion in music portray nervous tension and motor impulse and so stimulate emotional experience, it is because people have learnt to make the connections. From early childhood, Venda grew accustomed to experiences of bodily change and animation that could be had through systematic body movements with others. When two children played together a succession of beats or an iambic figure (short–long beat), they generally played in different tempi or in canon, rather than in unison. Thus one could play two to a partner's three beats, or synchronise the short beats of an iambic figure with the other's long beats, producing a stream of short beats (Blacking, 1976, pp. 27ff). To do this was an exercise of individuality in community. Each player had to hold fast to her/his part, and the collective effort produced both new cultural forms for the ears of performers and listeners, and a richer bodily experience for the participants. The right sound of the music could not be divorced from the experience of 'falling into phase' that players shared. Musical sounds were always associated with a rhythmical stirring of the body; and I remember an old, blind master musician criticising a performance on one of my tape recordings on the grounds that the drummers could not have been moving their shoulders and arms correctly.

The process of increasing participation in dance and music helped Venda children to learn how to think and act, how to feel, and how to relate. Emotion and reason, affect and cognition, were not separate but integrated aspects of social life. Codes of affect could not easily be distinguished from patterns of non-verbal cognition. Much of public life was ritualised, especially in dance and music, and displays of emotion were regarded as unintelligent, except when appropriate for certain stages or crises of life, such as shyness for young girls (and even sulking on occasion) and grief for mourners.

Distinctions between emotion and cognition were not sharply drawn, as people emphasised feeling in general as a quality of mind, and especially fellow-feeling and sensitivity to other self and to the world of nature. Dance and music were means of testing theories about self, body, other self, and other persons (cf. Blacking, 1983). The balance between types of cognition, between 'propositional/discursive' and 'performative/expressive', was recognised in the contrasting forms of institutions (Blacking, 1982, Table II) and worked out in movement and music. Feeling was structured in ways that had implications for human relationships and cognitive development.

Thus sensuous, bodily experience was a consequence of correct musical performance, which was to be attained by rehearsal, and correct musical performance was a way of feeling. Having feelings through music could be an end in itself or a means to an end, depending on the context of the feelings and the person having them. In Venda the underlying principles of the socio-cultural system were explained in ways that could be assimilated at a very personal level, through communal music and dance, without the kind of political indoctrination that Maurice Bloch reported from Malagasy (1974). The order of succession of different styles learnt by every Venda and the varied composition of their ensembles reflected a process of induction into and reinforcement of the Venda system of government (Blacking, 1976, p. 77, Figure 7); but the processes of music-making were structured so that there was always scope for individual creativity and imaginative improvisation within a framework that itself was organised to allow for the exercise of individuality in community. The ways in which communal music was used reinforced group identity, and the ways in which it was performed offered personal, sensuous satisfaction in return for unselfish behaviour. The polyrhythmic and polyphonic principles of musical performance ensured that self-satisfaction could not be gained by self-seeking, but that the best musical results were obtained when all participants combined the maximum of individual skill and fellow-feeling in the realisation and elaboration of a basic musical pattern. Pleasing others and pleasing oneself in musical performance were two interrelated aspects of the same activity. Self-actualisation included social service, and vice versa. Dance and music-making provided Venda people with experiential evidence of their system of ideas about self and other, their concept of intelligence and of the soul, and the balance that must exist between personal and corporate power.

**NOTES**

1. I avoid the ethnographic present tense and wish to place the analysis in a specific historical context. Although I carried out research among Venda people who lived in urban areas and have maintained contacts with friends and scholars like Mr Alfred Tshibalanganda and Dr Nkhumeleni Ralushai, to whom I am grateful for assistance on many occasions, most of my data and experience of children's life was gained during a period of intensive fieldwork in Venda in 1956–8. Unfortunately, for political reasons, I have been unable to do any further fieldwork in Venda. But even if I had been able to check the continuity of various ideas and institutions, I would be unhappy about extrapolating so-called norms of action in Venda society on the basis of only twenty-two months of close contact.

2. I have placed 'dance' and 'music' in inverted commas to emphasis that the concepts are not universal, although dance-like and music-like activities seem to be found in almost all known societies. The Venda happened to have terms and concepts which corresponded quite well with what is generally understood by 'dance' and 'music' in the English language, and in any case I consider that the terms are analytically acceptable as gloss words, like 'religion'. They are therefore used without inverted commas in the rest of the discussion.

3. Howard Gardner pointed out that 'musical ability is also found quite frequently among children who are not outstanding and may even be retarded in other areas' (Gardner, 1973, p. 188). He also observed that 'the boy Mozart probably did play as finely as anybody else alive ... but Picasso at 16 was not drawing as well as Degas', and he suggested that differences between the acquisition of music and painting 'reflect the preeminently formal nature of the medium and the fact that music is more self-contained' (p. 198). On the other hand, those differences may themselves have been a consequence of the nature of the particular symbol systems and their relations to others *in the context of European*

*cultures*. Robert Serpell (1976) has argued convincingly that cultural differences influence the choice of cognitive styles and the degrees of complexity and types of congruence of different skills.

**BIBLIOGRAPHY**

Ault, R.L. (1977) *Children's cognitive development*. New York: Oxford University Press.
Barkóczi, I. and Pléh, C. (1982) *Music makes a difference*. Budapest: Zoltán Kodály Pedagogical Institute of Music.
Bateson, G. (1973) *Steps to an ecology of mind*. St. Albans: Paladin.
Best, D. (1974) *Expression in movement and the arts*. London: Lepus Books.
—— (1978) *Philosophy and human movement*. London: George Allen and Unwin.
Blacking, J. (1964) *Black background: the childhood of a South African girl*. New York and London: Abelard Schuman.
—— (1967) *Venda children's songs: a study in ethnomusicological analysis*. Johannesburg: Witwatersrand University Press.
—— (1976) *How musical is man?* London: Faber and Faber.
—— (1976A) 'Dance, conceptual thought and production in the archaeological record'. In G. de G. Sieveking, I.H. Longworth and K.E. Wilson (eds), *Problems in economic and social archaeology*. London: Duckworth, 1–13.
—— (1981) 'Political and musical freedom in the music of some black South African churches'. In L. Holy and M. Stuchlik (eds), *The structure of folk models*. London: Academic Press, 35–62.
—— (1982) 'Songs and dances of the Venda people'. In D. Tunley (ed.), *Music and dance*, Fourth National Symposium of the Musicological Society of Australia, Perth: University of Western Australia, Department of Music, 90–105.
—— (1983) 'The concept of identity and folk concepts of self: A Venda case study'. In A. Jacobson-Widding (ed.), *Identity: personal and socio-cultural*. Uppsala: Acta Universitatis Uppsaliensis, 47–65.
Bloch, M. (1974) 'Symbols, song, dance and features of articulation: is religion an extreme form of traditional authority?' *Archives of European Sociology 15*, 55–81.
Connolly, K. and Bruner, J. (1974) *The growth of competence*. London: Academic Press.
Crickmore, L. (1968) 'An approach to the measurement of music appreciation'. *Journal of Research in Music Education*, XVI (3, 4), 239–53, 291–301.
Csikszentmihalyi, M. (1978) 'Phylogenetic and ontogenetic functions of artistic cognition'. In S. Madeja (ed.), *The arts, cognition, and basic skills*. St. Louis: Cemrel, 114–27.
De Bono, E. (1969) *The mechanism of mind*. London: Jonathan Cape.
Feld, S. (1982) *Sound and sentiment: birds, weeping, poetics and song in Kaluli expression*. Philadephia: University of Pennsylvania Press.

Gardner, H. (1973) *The arts and human development.* New York: John Wiley & Sons.
Geertz, C. (1975) *The interpretation of cultures.* London: Hutchinson (c. 1973).
—— (1976) 'Art as a cultural system'. *Modern Language Notes, 91,* 1473–99.
Gosse, E. (1974) *Father and son: a study of two temperaments* (edited with introduction by J. Hepburn). London: Oxford University Press.
Hamilton, V. and Vernon, M.D. (eds) (1976) *The development of cognitive processes.* London: Academic Press.
Keali'inohomoku, J.W. (1979) 'Culture change: functional and dysfunctional expressions of dance, a form of affective culture'. In J. Blacking and J.W. Keali'inohomoku (eds), *The performing arts: music and dance.* The Hague: Mouton, 47–64.
Maslow, A. (1954) *Motivation and personality.* New York: Harper.
Ornstein, R. (1973) Right and left thinking. *Psychology Today,* May, 87–92.
—— (1975) *The psychology of consciousness.* Harmondsworth: Penguin.
Serpell, R. (1976) *Culture's influence on behaviour.* London: Methuen.
Wachsmann, K.P. (1982) 'The changeability of musical experience'. *Ethnomusicology, XXVI* (2) May, 197–215.
Witkin, R. (1976) *The intelligence of feeling.* London: Heinemann Educational Books.
Young, J.Z. (1971) *An introduction to the study of Man.* Oxford: Clarendon Press.

# 3

# The Shadow Play and Operetta as Mediums of Education in Bali

Angela Hobart

Theatre is the most flourishing art form in Bali. Traditionally it was also considered one of the principal mediums of education. During the course of its history the island has been subject to a variety of influences from both the East, and more recently also the West, but theatre has retained an important educational role in the society. Hence it is an integral part of the child's cognitive development whereby he gains awareness and knowledge of the world.

This chapter will focus on two genres of theatre, the shadow play and the operetta. They are of special interest as they tend to be the most popular genres. The shadow play, though, primarily appeals to males, and the operetta to females. Both genres express through highly standardised stimuli selective patterns of meanings, or in Durkheimian terms, 'collective representations'. These should not, however, just be viewed as self-contained entities, for the child must become conscious of the social categories and assimilate them. So theatre is intrinsic to the child's education in the widest sense, involving both individual processes and the collective level. In order for the cultural heritage to be passed on from one generation to another, via in this case the medium of theatre, interaction must occur between both levels.

There exist a number of works on Asian theatre, but most scholars have studied the subject from a literary, artistic or historical point of view. Singer's (1966) analysis of the role of the Radha-Krishna devotional songs in Madras City or Peacock's (1968) work on Javanese proletarian drama are notable exceptions. Mead (1970) also briefly looked at Balinese theatre from the perspective of the Culture and Personality School. In this chapter the focus is on the didactic significance of theatre and concomitantly the ethical content of both the shadow play and operetta. It is to the moral system represented on the stage that the Balinese that I interviewed drew special attention when discussing the influence of the shadow play or the operetta. Such an approach has of course its limitations; the aesthetic nature of theatre, for example, can only be touched on in passing here.

The following discussion is divided into three main parts. After an introduction to Bali and to theatre on the island, the shadow play and operetta are first described. Then the moral values, norms and ideals expressed by the two genres are examined. It will emerge that the pattern of meanings transmitted by each of them respectively, relate to the differential place of males and females in the society. Finally, children's education through theatre is discussed, with a view to understanding how they acquire knowledge through this medium.

Bali is a small island covering about two thousand square miles. It lies just off the equator, to the east of Java and to the west of Lombok. The backbone of the island consists of a range of volcanoes. Set within these are large crater lakes which are the main source of fertility for the land.

The Balinese today comprise a population of over two million. They are a Malayo–Polynesian people who practise a variant form of Hinduism which reached Bali from Java, and ultimately from India, over one thousand years ago. They have a peasant economy based on irrigated rice cultivation where there is sufficient water. Elsewhere they depend on dry crops and small-scale husbandry of pigs and cattle. The island is predominantly rural. The population is concentrated in the south central part of Bali. This area is particularly fertile as it is intersected by streams and rivers which flow down slopes from the volcanic lakes. Villages tend to be tightly clustered and situated on high ground, surrounded by rice-fields. These vary from small hamlets to large residential complexes, which comprise from a few hundred to several thousand inhabitants. The villages are formally ruled by princes who are descended from aristocratic families who claim the status of Ksatriyas.

Balinese social structure is complex. It is notable for its stratification into ranked descent groups, or *wangsa* (peoples)—Brahmans, Ksatriyas, Wesyas and Sudras—according to an ideology similar to the Indian caste system, with spiritual and temporal power being distinguished between the Brahmans and Ksatriyas. The three high castes, known as *triwangsa*, are said to be aristocrats who came over principally from the last great Javanese kingdom of Majapahit about the fourteenth century. The Sudras, who are for the most part peasants, comprise over 90 per cent of the population. They are commonly called *jaba*, meaning literally outsiders to the courts where the princes live. At the same time the Balinese possess a complementary system which cuts across the hierarchical structure and which emphasises the equality of men. This is especially evident in such corporate activities as the voluntary rice harvesting association, the village council or orchestral and drama associations.

Traditionally Bali contained some eight small kingdoms. There have, however, been successive changes in the structure of the administration, so that by 1970 the island comprised one province of the Indonesian government. The former kingdoms have become local administrative centres. According to indigenous accounts the heartland of Balinese culture is in the southern part of the island which was the area exposed to early Indo-Javanese influences. It is in this area that I did my research (1970–2 and 1980), for it is here that most dramatic performances are given.

**BACKGROUND TO BALINESE THEATRE**

There are four main genres of theatre in Bali: the shadow play, the masked dance, operetta and a relatively new form simply called drama. Performances of any of these can attract up to several thousand spectators. Because of their significance and popularity on the island, I am for the purpose of this chapter exclusively focusing on the shadow play and operetta.

As Brandon has pointed out, theatre in all countries of South-East Asia is more than just entertainment, for it is through the medium of performances that the 'religious, metaphysical, social and intellectual values of the ruling elite were disseminated to the most unsophisticated villagers' (1970, p. 278). This statement, though, should be qualified. While most stories dramatised relate the adventures of the mythic aristocrats, it is the servants or clowns, representing the 'unsophisticated villagers', who give the stories shape by interpreting and commenting on the doings of the other characters. It is largely through the servants that the audience is made aware of the instruction inherent in the plays.

The use of theatre to instruct is of course not unique to South-East Asia. Works of tragedy in classical Greece were meant to illustrate the moral quality of men's lives by producing, in an unspecified manner, 'catharsis' which resulted from arousing pity and fear in the spectators. The miracle and mystery plays of medieval Europe sought to dramatise the theological mysteries and instruct in Christian doctrine. In modern times numerous playwrights have used the theatre to educate, as well as to entertain. We need but think of plays by Strindberg, Shaw or Bertolt Brecht.

In order to understand why the Balinese consider theatre such an important vehicle of education of the young in particular, it should be linked to certain indigenous philosophical ideas. Foremost is the emphasis placed on sense information for comprehending the world of men. Sight is initially the most important sense of knowing, as the information received from the other senses is said to be less reliable. In view of this, it is unsurprising that one of the greatest misfortunes is to be blind, *buta*, a term which also implies ogre or demon. Such a being dwells in the underworld and is characterised by his inability to discriminate between right and wrong. The Balinese seem here to be echoing Leach, who in 'Virgin birth' refutes Tylor, Frazer and the latter-day neo-Tylorians in speculating 'about causes which are inaccessible to observation and verification' (1966, p. 45). An ambiguity is, however, evident in the people's approach for they clearly recognise that there are various levels of comprehension. It is only the common man who cannot establish the truth-value of beliefs. An enlightened man may transcend his senses and gain comprehension of a higher order of reality.

A number of points stem from the above. First, the philosophical background helps explain the high regard given to texts. Words, it is pointed out, owe nothing to external reality. When they are written down, however, they fix the tradition; it is then that they become sacred. Plots dramatised in plays are partly based on texts, but some pertain more to them than others. The shadow play is of all the genres the one which adheres closest to the mythic texts, versions of which were written down in palmleaf manuscripts. This helps explain the esteem in which it is held, which exceeds that of other genres. The language used in operetta is freer and described as more ornamental and less consequential. Several scholars (see Goody, 1978) have discussed the significance that language may acquire once coded and visible. None the less, it is essential to draw attention to the power that the spoken word may have. This will emerge when we examine the Balinese servants in theatre. The interrelationship between the written and oral level is, however, a complex topic which cannot be dealt with in detail in this paper.

Second, it accounts for the importance given to the visual element in theatre. According to Else's (1967, p. 28) translation of *The Poetics*, Aristotle wrote that the basic principle of tragedies was the plot, and the character came second. Western theatre has continued to stress these two principles. What is important in Bali, however, is not the telling of the story, which in any case is often known, but dancing. The same word *sesolahan* in fact refers to both, for theatre, as de Zoete and Spies put it, 'is only conveyed through the heightened rhythm of dance, never at the flat pitch of reality' (1973, p. 18). The characters, apart from the servants, show little individualisation; most can be categorised into types which are easily recognised by dress, manner of dance and physical features, which are fixed by tradition. The other dramatic components used all accord with the visual.

This harmony which is demanded between all the dramatic elements contributes to the didactic role of theatre. Dissonance between appearance, actions, speech and thought exists in life, but not in theatre. So the kiss of Judas which Gombrich describes as the 'use of ritual of love as a signal of aggression' (1966, p. 398) would not convince Balinese spectators, as a character in a play is unable to conceal his intentions and feelings. It is of interest here to note that in folk terminology *sesolahan*, dance and drama (or acting) is derived from *solah*, or character, as on the stage this is said to be revealed by the visual.

The significance the body attains in dance can also be viewed in relation to the indigenous philosophical ideas. Numerous scholars have been aware of the evocative power of the body (cf. Blacking, 1977). Douglas's (1980, p. 115) approach to the body as a symbol of society is perhaps most pertinent to Bali. The Balinese, like the Indians (and others), consider the head to be the most elevated part of the body. It is identified with the Brahman caste, and the other castes with progressively lower parts. It is thus unsurprising that the eyes are singly the most important feature of dancers and actors.

The impact of drama is of course so considerable as performances are often given through the island. The main occasion for a play is in conjunction with the anniversary, *odalan*, of a temple which occurs once in the Hindu–Balinese year of 210 days. It is customary to have a form of entertainment on the three final days of the anniversary for which the temple congregation pays. Performances may also be given spontaneously in the village.

In order to understand the significance of the shadow play and operetta, I shall first focus on a given genre itself. Spectators vary in their responses to a play and, in any case, mainly appraise its technical aspects. As Langer (1976, pp. 51–2), moreover, pointed out, content and form are intimately related, the symbolic import permeating the latter. Because of the complexity of the subject I shall only draw attention to the most expressive features of each genre.

## MEN'S AND WOMEN'S THEATRE

### Men's theatre: wayang kulit or the shadow play

The shadow play has explicit religious and didactic value for all Balinese. It is, however, almost exclusively watched by men and children, who may include young girls and boys of all ages. The spectators squat on the ground or stand further back watching the shadows of the puppets during the performance. The shadow play is not a commercial enterprise as no admission is charged. Most women, when asked, apart from a few Chinese, emphatically say that they do not like the shadow play as they neither understand the stories nor enjoy watching war scenes.

The shadow play is often performed in conjunction with religious rites in the temple or household. The performance lasts for about four hours. It takes place in a temporarily erected booth with a transparent screen on which the shadows of the puppets are projected by a coconut-oil lamp which hangs over the cross-legged puppeteer. Behind him four musicians play metallophones.

The stories dramatised in Bali, as well as Java, are primarily drawn from the great Hindu epics, the *Mahabharata* and *Ramayana*. Plays based on the former epic are, however, by far more numerous and popular, as the characters are more complex and the stories more intricate, relating to social, political and spiritual issues. The *Mahabharata*, on which I will concentrate, recounts the conflict of two families of the Kuru clan, the five semi-divine Pandawa brothers and their first cousins, the hundred Korawa brothers who are seen as ogres incarnate. The conflict centres on who are the rightful heirs to the throne of Nastina and culminates in the great war, the *Bharatayuddha*, in which the Korawas are defeated. Problems with women add fuel to the conflict. The heroes of most stories are the three eldest Pandawa brothers whose progenitors are gods: the gentle Yudistira, the tempestuous Bima and the noble Arjuna. Throughout they are aided by their mentor Kresna.

The puppeteer is one of the recognised ritual practitioners in Bali. Ideally, he ought to be one of the Brahman caste, but in practice he is usually a Sudra. Generally the art of being a puppeteer is transmitted patrilineally. Traditionally he is said to be one of the 'teachers' on the island, the others being the Brahman priest, the ruler and the father. The puppeteer was, and still is, considered the main pedagogue who teaches the sacred classical literature from a stage, which is ritually purified by offerings and ritual incantations he recites.

The puppets are the most constraining dramatic component in a play, and the other stimuli harmonise with them. New puppets are made by copying old ones, and hence a continuity of style is ensured. The puppets are flat cut-outs of buffalo hide and are painted in traditional colours. There are about one hundred puppets in a collection, which include the following main categories: gods, the four castes, and ogres.

I want here to focus on only two iconographic features, the eyes and the body colours. They are of special interest for the meanings attributed to them, and they are articulated during a performance. Although Sperber (1979, pp. 17–34) has ably criticised the 'cryptological' conception of symbols typified by Turner, the exegesis is an important source of meaning in Bali, for the people are explicit in their interpretations of the features. The interpretations are highly standardised and tally with those given of the same features in other artistic or social contexts. The fixed nature of the dramatic stimuli, moreover, ensures stability in the interpretations. For example, new puppets have always a lingering affinity with figures on reliefs of east Javanese temples of the thirteenth and fourteenth centuries. In line with Sperber it is, though, perhaps best to view the exegesis as an extension of the symbolic, and not just constituting an interpretation of it.

There are two eye-shapes depicted on puppets: slit and round eyes. These are linked to specific social values. Round-eyed characters are coarse and hot-tempered while slit-eyed characters are refined and controlled.

A number of scholars have written about body colour. This is a complex subject which I will only touch on. Five basic colours are always used in painting puppets: blue, black, white, red and yellow. These are combined in varying proportions to produce the mixed colours. Almost all the bodies of puppets are painted in a mixed colour.

In discussing the Balinese colour system, it is first important to point out that the five basic colours are considered to be the purest manifestations of the Hindu–Balinese gods, whose mystic nature they are said to reflect. Hence, the body colours, which are derived from mixing the basic colours, are the most significant iconographic feature. In examining the body colours of the puppets these are best understood as involving a number of contrasts which are terminologically distinguished (cf. Conklin, 1955). These can be arranged according to three levels which are indicated in Figure 3.1. These opposites are associated with extraneous dimensions and give expression to certain core values in the society.

**Figure 3.1**: The colour contrasts

| Level 1 | *Light* | | | as opposed to | *dark* | |
| --- | --- | --- | --- | --- | --- | --- |
| | | white | | | black | |
| Level 2 | *cool* | | | as opposed to | *hot* | |
| | blue | white | (black) | | yellow | red |
| Level 3 | | | mixed colours | | | |

Level 1  *light:dark colours*::supernatural power of the right: supernatural power of the left

Level 2  *cool:hot colours*:: fecundity: infecundity:: order: disorder[a]::refinement: coarseness:: restraint: lack of control:: modesty: pride

Level 3  *mixed colours*: depending on the different proportions of basic colours used, they reflect the values of levels 1 and 2.

---

a. The relationship of cool/hot to fecundity/infecundity and order/disorder is not immediately clear and is best explained as follows. Cool colours are associated with water which brings fertility to the land. This is said to lead to peace, prosperity and order in the kingdom. In the same way, hot colours are associated with fire and disorder. In passing I want to point out that colours may have ambiguous meanings. This comes to the fore with black and red. The former is also linked to night, witchcraft and destruction; the core of the latter is purity. For the purpose of this discussion, though, it is sufficient to lay out the above colour contrasts.

During the actual play all the characters are polarised into two distinct camps: the Pandawas and Korawas. Each comprises the particular set of brothers and their followers, but the Pandawas are supported by the gods and the Korawas by the ogres. The Pandawas always enter the stage from the right of the puppeteer and the Korawas from the left. In view of the meaning attributed to the iconographic features, it is unsurprising that most members of the Pandawa camp should have slit eyes and cool, light body colours, mainly in whitish yellow, while most of the members of the Karawa camp have round eyes and hot, dark body colours, in tones of reddish and yellowish brown. For reasons which will emerge more clearly later, the colour contrasts are not seen by most of the spectators, as we are dealing with a play of shadows. None the less, the very standardisation and familiarity of these contrasts implies that they articulate meaning. War occurs in every performance, in which the Pandawas always defeat the Korawas. From a purely visual point of view their victory is appropriate for, as the two above features alone indicate, they are nobler than the relatively coarse Korawas.

Apart from the puppets' iconography, attention should be drawn to the behaviour of the figures on the stage as it is an index of their caste *dharma*, or duty. The Brahmans generally teach and give advice. Ksatriyas are mainly involved in battle. It is uncouth behaviour of the Sudra servants which primarily highlights their caste position. As in life, they also lower themselves bodily when addressing their masters, indicative of the caste difference between them.

The emphasis in describing the shadow play has been on the puppets as they are the main fixed referent during a performance, and the principles underlying them are evident in all other traditional art forms. Of these, the shadow play is considered the oldest and most sacred, and hence also the most influential. The narration is, however, more prominent in the shadow theatre than in other genres. While the puppeteer derives the skeleton of his plot from the epic poetry, he improvises and develops the dialogues extensively. All the high-caste characters on the stage speak a version of Old Javanese, or *Kawi*, which is inaccessible to most of the audience. It is the servants who translate and comment on what they say. Because of their importance in any performance, irrespective of the genre, a special section is later devoted to them.

**Women's theatre: arja or operetta**

Arja is best translated as operetta or musical comedy (cf. de Zoete and Spies, 1973, p. 196), as it is a form of romantic play which combines dance, singing and spoken lines and comic scenes. A performance can continue for interminable hours, from the evening until late into the next morning. It draws a large audience of primarily low-caste married women with their children. Most sit squashed together on seats for which they have paid minimal prices. The majority of the women in the past were illiterate, but many of the younger ones in the meantime have had some schooling. Balinese men in general view operetta as light-hearted entertainment for women and they rarely attend, saying they do not comprehend the songs and find the stories too sentimental.

As productions of operetta have become so accomplished and expensive (for the community), they are generally only given in larger villages in connection with the anniversary of one of the temples. Formerly small troupes of actors, often in simple, tattered clothes, and musicians wandered from village to village giving performances. For a few years operetta has been serialised once a week on television. As a television now exists in almost every village, even the humblest villager has the occasion of witnessing shows. A present-day performance will require about thirteen actors and it takes place in the community pavilion. Formerly some of the actors were males who took on the roles of coarse or masculine characters. Nowadays they are all pretty girls who are usually trained in the village context by an elderly actor known for his expertise.

Most of the stories are based on mythical or romantic versions of Javanese history. In Java these belong to the *Panji* cycle, the Balinese version of which is called *Malat*. A few modern Chinese tales are also popular. The heroine of most stories is the refined, sweet, *manis* princess Galuh. She is opposed by the ugly coarse princess Liku who is always described as mad, *buluh* (*gila* in

Indonesian). The Balinese say, though, that her madness must be clearly distinguished from that of the insane in the one mental hospital in Bali. In this section I will merely describe how madness manifests itself in the play. Liku manages to usurp the place of Galuh in her husband's affection. It is only after endless trials that the unhappy Galuh is reconciled with her husband, who realises that Liku has beguiled him into thinking she was beautiful.

The dancing in operetta is a combination of fluidity and rigid accents which relate to the music and songs. There are numerous characteristic, fixed movements in operetta, for dancing in Bali is as precise an art as in Java or other countries which have inherited the Dramatic Code (*Natya Sastra*) from India. Each character dances in a definite manner according to his or her type. So Galuh, who is a slender girl with a pale white face as appropriate to her type (see the shadow play), dances slowly and gracefully, creating winding patterns through space. She often droops in lament. Liku used to be enacted by an ugly, burlesque man. Now a sturdy girl is chosen. Her eyes are made up to look dark and round and her face is given a pinkish tint. A characteristic feature of hers are the bushy eyebrows which she can move rapidly up and down alternately. These give her a comical and eccentric expression. Liku dances less than Galuh and in a somewhat directionless and gawky fashion.

The appeal of operetta, however, relies primarily on the songs, which are sung in high-pitched voices which have a thin, bright and vibrant quality. They are lyrical and sentimental and are accompanied nowadays by a full-scale percussion instrument, *gamelan gong*. As in the past, though, the most important instruments are still the bamboo flutes, *suling*. Their clear, sweet, somewhat reedy tones weave ornamental configurations around the voices. The songs cannot for the most part be understood as the words flow freely into one another. The servants, as in the shadow play, translate and explain each line of a stanza. This is shown in the following brief excerpt from a play. Liku sings while her female servant translates:

*Liku*: (My) attractively coiled hair, (it) pleases hearts (of men).
*Servant*: Yes, it is true princess, *palungguh cokorda déwa i ratu*, what you say about your hair. It is attractively coiled and has a dark, velvety sheen which will please men.

123

*Liku*: (My hair) resembles (the) clouds (of the) seventh month.
*Servant*: Yes, it is true princess, your hair resembles the clouds of the seventh month.
*Liku*: (These are) rain clouds.
*Servant*: It is true, princess, the colour is like the dark rain clouds which conceal the sun from view.
*Liku*: (My) side-curls (are) delicate.
*Servant*: Yes, princess, the men will find your side-curls delicate.
*Liku*: (Men will desire) to kiss (my) cheeks.
*Servant*: Yes, it is true, princess, what you say. Men will be attracted to you.

Liku's song is well known in Bali. Although only a few lines are included, they given an indication of Liku's ostentatious character. She swells in importance as she sings. Liku's manner of singing is strikingly different to that of Galuh who always appears refined, modest and restrained.

**The servants, clowns or jesters in theatre**

The importance of the Sudra servants, clowns or jesters has already been hinted at. They are in many ways the most relevant characters in a performance. It is through their translations and commentaries that the predominantly Sudra audience, many of whom were illiterate in the past, became acquainted with the classical literature, which was written in Old Javanese. This is an archaic language containing a large number of Sanskrit words (Zoetmulder, 1974, p. 7). Formerly only the intellectual elite could read the texts. This comprised mainly Brahmans and scattered individuals, to whom among others the puppeteers belonged. The servants also give comic relief to the otherwise serious mood of the main plot evolving around the Ksatriyas.

There are four main servants in any play, who are all males. In the shadow play an elderly father and his son serve the Pandawas and two brothers the Korawas. In operetta there are two pairs of brothers, who may be 'real' or classificatory brothers, as they may be called if they have the same prince as master. Historically the servants may relate back to misshapen wards or dwarfs of the former rulers of the kingdoms of Java. Such dwarfs or jesters are of course not only found in Bali. Apart from other countries in South-East Asia, it is known that they existed in India, medieval Europe, and Africa. In Shakespeare's *King Lear* and others of his plays, jesters, who were usually low-class men, comment wittily on the foibles of their masters while fooling around. This role the servants also have in Balinese theatre, for they not only translate what their masters say but rebuke them for their faults, reminding them of their duties.

The servants are also the main characters in the subplots which in all performances intersperse the main plot drawn from the classical literature. In contrast to the main plot, the subplots are largely derived from daily village life. However, the two are subtly woven together by either the puppeteer or the actors in operetta to create a coherent story. It is here that the servants may dance, weep, tell jokes, frolic around, or make advances to the opposite sex. In operetta the subplots are spinkled with light-hearted romantic songs, such as the one included below. It is sung by one of the servants.

> Were I rich I would take you to Den Pasar
> And we would go to the Bali Hotel. (the most luxurious hotel in Bali)
> There the bedspreads are woven with gold.
> The sheets are soft and green.
> The pillows come from Java.
> And when we had made love
> We'd leave in a car, honking the horn.
> 
> (see McPhee, 1966, p. 303)

The instructive element comes more to the fore in the subplots of the shadow play than those of operetta. In these the servants often discuss and evaluate the ethics of the masters' intentions and behaviour. This emerges in the following dialogue which is between the hereditary servants of the Korawas. Sangut, the younger brother, is quick-witted and intuitive. He realises that the Pandawas, though not his masters, are more virtuous than the Korawas. He upbraids his elder brother, Dèlem, who is stupid and bombastic, for always believing what the Korawa king says. The dialogue is drawn from a play that I witnessed.

*Sangut*: You are often taken in by others who are clever, Dèlem. This is like an expression at the coffee stall: everyone

knows now and has known in the past that there are three things: actions, speech and thoughts, *bayu-sabda-idep*. These cannot be separated. That which appears as one has diverse elements; that which appears as diverse has an underlying unity.
*Dèlem*: What do you mean?
*Sangut*: If the thoughts are evil, it is clear that the actions are evil. If the actions are evil, it is clear that the thoughts are evil. It must be so. If only the speech is clever, the actions and thoughts are still evil.
*Dèlem*: Oh!
*Sangut*: Why do you say oh? As he (Duryodana, the king of the Korawas) is clever with words he can hide his thoughts and actions from others.
*Dèlem*: Oh, Sangut knows how to philosophise.

In this short dialogue Sangut is explaining to Dèlem how crucial it is to interrelate actions, speech and thoughts. The dialogue refers to the issue brought up earlier of the importance of visual information for understanding the world of men. Of the three, actions, which are visible, are the most reliable information; thoughts are concealed, while words are tenuous. At the same time, we see the power that the spoken word may have for the servants in this dialogue have departed from the texts and are freely discussing folk philosophy.

It is evident that the servants have great authority in the plays. Not only do they spice the stories with shrewd comments and jokes, but it is in large part through their eyes that the characters are interpreted and evaluated. Spectators simply tend to walk off if the servants fail to stimulate and amuse them. As such, the servants can be said to be the mediators in a play between the world of myth or legend, inhabited by princes and princesses, and the world of the village which they represent.

## THE SIGNIFICANCE OF THE SHADOW PLAY AND OPERETTA IN RELATION TO THE PLACE OF MALES AND FEMALES IN SOCIETY

So far the focus has been on the form and content of the shadow play and operetta. I want here to suggest that the different pattern of meanings expressed by each genre can only be understood in relation to the traditional place of males and females in society, and that this has a bearing on their educational role. My approach is ably illustrated by Strathern (1980, p. 186), who points out that the 'nature/culture' opposition cannot simply be applied cross-culturally in an unanalysed way. The same can be said of such contrasting concepts as 'refinement/coarseness' or 'sweetness/madness' which are enacted on the Balinese stage.

In order to appreciate the significance of operetta and the shadow play, it is useful to lay out first their dramatic components, see Figure 3.2.

**Figure 3.2**

|  | *Operetta* | *Shadow play* |
| --- | --- | --- |
| Actors | humans | puppets (shadows) |
| Spheres represented | men | gods<br>men<br>ogres |
| Setting | domestic<br>private | cosmic<br>public |
| Symbolism | centripetal | centrifugal |
| Language | Balinese | Old Javanese<br>Balinese |
| Music | full-scale orchestra (flutes) | four metallophones |
| Story | legendary romance | mythic<br>conflict, war<br>inheritance issues<br>spiritual striving<br>romance |
| Tone of play | lyrical | reflective |

As the chart shows, the shadow play and operetta vary considerably in their make-up. There are, though, some basic similarities between these two genres to which I want to draw attention. Of prime importance is the fact that each exemplifies on the stage the appropriate social and religious duties, *dharma*, of the four castes in Bali. This hierarchical axis is, however, crosscut by a horizontal one where the Sudra servants come to the fore. As we have seen, they have equal, if not at times greater, authority than their masters in the play.

There is another similarity which relates to their dramatic structure: an opposition is always set up on the stage between two groups, one of which is nobler than the other. The tension which ensues between them is only resolved when the nobler aspirations of man subdue his baser instincts and desires. An examination of the contrasting values of the shadow play and operetta in relation to the social context highlights the implications of the oppositions.

### The contrasts in the shadow play in relation to the place of men in society

The shadow play comprises numerous characters, the majority being male Ksatriyas. As some characters have ambiguous positions in the conflict, the qualities associated with each camp can only be drawn up on a relative basis, see Figure 3.3.

**Figure 3.3**

| *Pandawas* (+ gods) | *Korawas* (+ ogres) |
| --- | --- |
| following one's duty (*dharma*) | greedy, uncontrolled (*momo*) |
| restrained (*dharma*) | wild, ferocious (*galak*) |
| modest (*dharma*) | proud (*bangga*) |
| refined, poised (*alus*) | coarse (*kasar*) |
| supernaturally powerful | supernaturally powerful |
| of the right (*sakti tengawan*) | of the left (*sakta pengiwa*) |

The plays are always acted out in the public domain and the goals are public ones. During the course of a performance, it emerges that the Pandawas are better Ksatriyas than the Korawas, and more suitable as heirs to the throne. Both sides are, however, said to be indispensable, for the evil of the Korawas is seen as offsetting and complementing the goodness of the Pandawas. In fact most puppeteers after a play symbolically bring back to life any member, regardless of their camp allegiance, killed in battle, by reciting ritual incantations.

The contrasts between the Korawas and Pandawas relate to the social life of the Balinese. The epic touches on the complex rules of inheritance and succession in a Ksatriya family. Primogeniture is the ideal rule, but it is mitigated by preference for selecting the most suitable heir, irrespective of genealogical considerations. If a prince is refined, poised and restrained, it implies adherence to the Ksatriya *dharma*. He does not squander his energies in ignoble pursuits, but possesses the requisite traits to be a good warrior, an able administrator and a virile lover. Traditionally such a Ksatriya was thought to possess supernatural power of the right, but as elsewhere in the world, mystic power is considered ambiguous, neither good nor bad. Although since colonisation and the Local Land Reform Rules introduced in 1960 the power of the Ksatriyas has diminished and wars are no longer fought out between kingdoms, princes still have wealth, keep retainers and hold public positions.

Refinement and restraint are, though, not only qualities associated with high castes in Bali. In men of all castes it is an index of their suitability for major roles in public affairs, whether this is in the egalitarian village council which administers most public business within the community, or in the irrigation association. A man who is coarse in language and behaviour is not thought capable of contributing to public debates or able to enforce decisions. Women rarely participate in public affairs, the implication being that their presence is as disruptive in public as men's in the private domain (see following discussion on operetta).

The shadow play is, however, also a sacred theatre. It presents what Skorupski (1976, p. 25) calls a cosmocentric view of the world. In this context the division of the Pandawas and Korawas is linked to the cosmic dualities, ruwa-bineda: right:left:: female:male::day:night::water:sun, and so forth. Like the division of the Pandawas and Korawas these are complementary oppositions considered intrinsic to world order.

**The contrasts in operetta in relation to the place of females in society**

There are much fewer characters in operetta than in the shadow play. The principal ones are Galuh and Liku. Their main qualities are shown in Figure 3.4. The other characters, depending on whom they are associated with, reflect similar qualities.

Operetta plays itself out in a closed and intimate circle. It tells of problems within the family which relate to those in life.

Madness in Liku's sense is a well-known state in Bali which does not imply illness to the people. It is primarily used to

**Figure 3.4**

| Galuh | Liku |
|---|---|
| sweet, delicate (*manis*) | mad (*buduh*) |
| graceful (*lemuh*) | clumsy (*kenyat*) |
| modest (*dharma*) | proud (*bangga*) |
| refined, poised (*alus*) | coarse (*kasar*) |

describe someone who is 'madly' in love to the degree of folly. Madness may, however, be manifest in other contexts. Two main qualities are associated with it: excess or extreme lack of control and no feeling of shame. Such a person transgresses social boundaries and shows no awareness of rules of etiquette. Madness can be demonstrated in any activity, even one approved of. For example, a man may be described as mad if he reads incessantly the manuscripts or if he exhausts himself overworking in the ricefields and hence has no time for his family and friends.

Galuh, in contrast to Liku, is sweet, modest and refined. These are considered cool qualities. It is of interest that in popular exegesis women are linked to water (and the god Vishnu) and men to fire (and the god Brahma). This dichotomy, the Balinese point out, should also be found in the family where it is related to kin ties. Descent in Bali is of a patrilineal variety, with women marrying into the compound. Daughters-in-law ideally are assimilated with ease into the household. More affection is generally also felt for daughters than sons in Bali. This belief accords with the cosmic dualities brought up earlier. In the domestic sphere ties through women ought to be cool, while ties through men are referred to as hot, and it is conceded that there is often tension between agnates (Hobart, 1979). So Galuh exemplifies the ideal in marriageable woman.

## A comparison of the shadow play and operetta in relation to the social context

The survey of the contrasting values expressed by the shadow play and operetta highlights the differential place of males and females in society. Although the distinction between the sexes is no longer so sharply defined, they still tend to be seen as forming a complementary relationship over the public and domestic domain, with males and females being respectively responsible for stability in the community at large and the household.

Additional relevant points emerge if the two genres are compared within an overall framework, taking into consideration their various dramatic components, see Figure 3.2. It is evident that the shadow play and operetta are each enveloped in a 'mystique' which has a two-fold purpose. First, the incomprehensibility of the shadow play to females and operetta to males stresses the separation between the sexes. At the same time, many of the spectators themselves have to rely on the servants to understand the other characters, whom they otherwise mainly appreciate visually. This mystique, it can be argued, validates the status of each dramatic genre in the eyes of the public, which is available either to males or females only.

Apart from their mutual incomprehensibility to the opposite sex, the orientation of the two dramatic genres is different. In the shadow play the actors are puppets. The dark silhouettes outlined on the screen direct attention to certain core values in society. The stories derived from the sacred texts reinforce the impact of the shadows. It is worth pointing out as a sideline that French academicians of the eighteenth century held drawing to be superior to painting, as the former appealed to the mind, and colour to the eyes, or to the emotions (Blunt, 1973). The shadows have further religious implications. Through their unsubstantiality they provide an idiom which has transcendental overtones.

Operetta dwells on the sensuous and qualitative. The songs, which tell of Galuh's suffering, evoke lingering feelings of tenderness, pity and sadness. Their effect is enhanced by the attractive appearance of the girls on the stage, their sumptuous costumes and stylised dance.

It is interesting to note that the responses of the adult spectators, when asked, reflect the varying significance attributed to the shadow play and operetta. Men emphasise the didactic and religious role of the shadow play. Educated men say that the shadows, called by the Sanskrit term *maya*, illusion, refer to the illusionary nature of all categories of manifestations and that they act as a bridge, or *titi*, between this world and the next. So they serve as a vehicle of a transcendental order which hovers beyond the perception of the common man. Thus the knowledge communicated from the puppeteer to the audience gains in persuasiveness as he is said to be a mouthpiece of the gods during a performance. The Balinese seem here to be echoing Platonic ideas, for the shadows, Plato writes in *The Republic*, show the ascent of the mind to the highest intelligible region where the final thing to be perceived is 'the form of the good; once seen, it is inferred to be responsible for whatever is right and valuable in anything' (Lee, 1981, p. 321).

Women, on the other hand, say they enjoy operetta as it invokes a complex of feelings, referred to as *ngelangunin*, which is best translated as enchantment tinged with sadness. The term implies a poetic sentiment which transcends the personal emotions, and as such has proximity with the Indian idea of *rasa* (Osborne, 1968, pp. 174–5).

Children, to whom I next want to turn, are in general not lucid when asked to discuss the significance of theatre. Some boys may say that they enjoy the shadow play out of historical interest; also because of the moral system and cosmology which are enacted on the stage.

## CHILDREN'S EDUCATION THROUGH THE SHADOW PLAY AND OPERETTA

The education received through the shadow play and operetta is an active process of teaching and learning by which the growing child gradually becomes acquainted with and assimilates his cultural heritage. Schools have been set up by the Dutch throughout the island since the beginning of the twentieth century, and most children have at least four years of schooling; boys tend to go longer to school than girls, as do children from the capital, Denpasar, or larger villages. However, the training received at school, as elsewhere in the world, is systematic and purposive, directed primarily at imparting knowledge and skills which are of practical use in life. The education the Balinese child receives through theatre is unsystematic, irregular and diffuse. In contrast to such institutions as initiation schools, ceremonies or secret societies, described at length at other societies, it is also not overtly transmitted. Although the didactic function of the shadow play (and to a lesser degree the masked dance, which is not discussed here) is recognised, children as well as adults watch performances as they are stimulating, amusing and entertaining. Further, as the stories are often known, being drawn from a fixed repertoire which belongs to the public domain, the spectators pay special attention to the visual element and the improvisations. The message, moreover, transmitted through theatre is reiterated and hence intensified by other cultural forms such as paintings, reliefs, statues or comic books, which are nowadays widely distributed and frequently based on the epic stories, with characters represented as shadow types. Of these forms, however, theatre is the most sophisticated and subtle medium of communication, combining varied stimuli—appearance, costume, dance, voice, language and music.

## Children at performances

Children constitute the front rows of any audience, their attention being riveted on the servants who clown around and tell spicy, bawdy jokes. Young children, up to about ten or twelve years old, are drawn to any performance irrespective of the dramatic genre, while small infants sit on their parents' laps for hours at night, sometimes until late into the morning, often lapsing into sleep. As adolescence is reached, in line with the sexual dichotomy which runs through social life and thought, boys frequent the shadow play more and girls the operetta. So the system of morality, together with the history and cosmology represented in the plays, is largely unconsciously adopted, and the moulding of the individual to the social norms occurs imperceptibly and indirectly as a pleasurable 'by-product' as it were of the cultural routine. It should be pointed out here that the select patterns of meanings expressed by the shadow play or operetta have already been presented in the home context to the child as rudimentary and unstable schemes during what Piaget (1977, pp. 25–7) has termed the first stage of a motor and individual nature up to two years old. These values are crystallised in theatre where they are given visual form and where they acquire complexity and depth. This makes them more accessible to the growing child who progressively assimilates them while gaining an increasing awareness of their significance in the society.

## Adults' attitudes to theatre: teaching methods

Adults place high value on their culture and are fully aware of the fact that its continuity depends on its transmission to their descendants. Traditionally boys were, and to a high degree still are in the smaller villages, deemed the active perpetuators of the culture, special stress being laid on their intellectual skills which entail philosophical, religious and literary knowledge and verbal ability. Few intellectual achievements were demanded from females. In the religious sphere they only had to know how to make the varied offerings requisite for the numerous household and temple festivals. Girls had primarily to learn to become good housekeepers. They also had certain economic duties later, which, like those of men, related above all to rice cultivation.

In this light it is unsurprising that nowadays adults still encourage mainly boys to attend dramatic performances, especially the shadow play which has such a high repute because of its religious nature. Adults whom I interviewed lucidly explained that it is on the stage that such abstract ideas as rank, good and evil, or refinement and coarseness, which derive their existence from the imperceptible world called *niskala*, in contradistinction to the perceptible world, or *sakala*, are made tangible. The tension which is built up during the play relates to events which revolve around a juxtaposition of attitudes or an opposition of interests. For example, the concept of baseness may be better understood in terms of its opposite, nobility. Thus the child during a play observes a variety of characters of different moral worth. This applies to both the shadow play and operetta. Anthropologists and psychologists (see Fortes, 1970, pp. 240–4; Piaget, 1977, p. 32) have often drawn attention to the importance of learning through imitation. This method is also clearly recognised by adult Balinese in their appreciation of theatre: the characters provide vivid examples which can be imitated, *ketulad*, by the individual in daily life.

The educational value placed on theatre is also evident from the frequency with which adults refer to stories which they have seen dramatised recently in order to instruct the young on the moral axioms of society and the standards of correct behaviour. Again the stories are primarily drawn from the shadow play and it is boys who are so taught. There are in general a few men in a village renowned for their story-telling ability, and they narrate in the evening when children and grown-ups gather around them. Other villagers just allude to anecdotes or to characters from theatre. Two stories are included, for they highlight the methods adults may use to teach boys on issues thought crucial in the community. (The stories are taken from an indigenous repertoire of myths known as *Cantakparwa* which involves heroes from the great epics.) Both were recounted in the village in which I lived during my research period.

Yudistira went to fetch water with his brothers in the forest. While there, they died; only he remained alive. His genitor, the god Dharma, then came to him in the form of an ogre and tempted him to choose out of his brothers one to be brought back to life. Yudistira chose either Nakula or Sahadewa. The god Dharma was pleased as thereby Yudistira showed his fairness and love for his younger brothers born from another mother. So Kunti would be represented by one son, Yudistira, and Madri by one of the twins, either Nakula or Sahadewa. See illustration below.

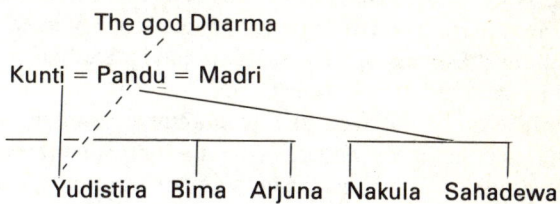

– – – = genitor (the genitors of the other brothers are not shown here)

**The five Pandawa brothers**

Men in Bali, especially if they belong to the high castes or are wealthy, may have a number of wives—nowadays this does not usually exceed three. These are either co-wives, or the man may marry several times in succession. This may result in familial tension, not only between co-wives or father and his sons, but also between male siblings, which centres on inheritance problems. The villager who told this story has sons from three successive marriages. He is here pointing out that they should all try to act like Yudistira and be equable with each other, and so ensure harmony in the home. The next story concerns a man's relations with women.

Subadra went in tears to the monkey god, Hanuman, to complain of the beahviour of her husband, Arjuna. He was a philanderer and not constant with any woman. Hanuman was well aware of Arjuna's faults and suggested that they should both take on the forms of ogres and steal Arjuna's weapons and so remove much of his power.

Meanwhile Arjuna went to the tournament given by the

king Suryaketu where he won the hand of the king's beautiful daughter. On leaving the tournament grounds Hanuman and Subadra, in disguise as ogres, confronted Arjuna and demanded that he give them the newly obtained princess. Arjuna refused and fighting broke out. Although Arjuna stood out by his bravery, he and his supporters were defeated and his weapons were removed.

During the battle Arjuna's faithful servant, Merdah, ran off into the woods crying bitterly. One of the gods (Ismaya) descended and consoled him and told him that he could defeat the ogres by removing his clothes and lifting his arms above his head. Merdah returned to Arjuna and acted as suggested. The moment his dress was laid aside, Hanuman and Subadra were forced to emerge in their true shapes.

Arjuna was abashed on seeing Hanuman and his wife, Subadra, in front of him and enquired their reason for making war. Hanuman explained that he was not treating his wives properly and that they were unhappy. He advised Arjuna to rotate on a fixed basis the nights he spent with each wife, so each one would have equal amounts of time with him. Arjuna agreed to mend his ways.

By referring to this story a father is tartly reprimanding his son, who is wayward with women and a philanderer, to mend his ways before he actually considers marriage, for particularly then women must be treated with respect in order to have harmony in the home. Arjuna is known for his great refinement and bravery. These qualities though must go hand in hand with self-control in all matters.

Adults often also instruct children by comparing them to characters in theatre, implying in this context that the growing boy or girl should or should not conduct him or herself like a particular character. This is shown in the following examples.

*sekadi Arjuna*      like Arjuna
The implication being that the boy should become like Arjuna who is refined, handsome, skilled and brave.

*sekadi Bima*      like Bima
The boy should try to act like Bima who in Bali is always described as honest, constant and bold.

| | |
|---|---|
| *nènten sekadi Dursasana* | not like Dursasana (the second Korawa brother). The boy should not behave like Dursasana who is coarse, proud and disdainful of others. These are vices abhorred by the villagers, who value solidarity. |
| *sekadi Galuh* | like Galuh The implication being that the girl should try to be like Galuh who is sweet, modest and graceful, and hence appealing to men of worth. |

A detailed study of the moral values, norms and standards of correct conduct a Balinese has to learn in the course of his or her life cannot be undertaken here. For the limited purpose of this chapter, however, a note should be added on refinement and coarseness, concepts which have often been mentioned in the discussion and which come to the fore in all dramatic performances. Refinement or sweetness, *alus*, is achieved through, or reflected in, self-control and inner balance; coarseness or loudness, *kasar*, is expressed in selfishness and uncontrolled feelings on Java, (see Geertz, 1960, p. 232). Refinement and coarseness are, in part, associated with caste, but individual traits may further determine the degree to which they are demonstrated. While refinement is linked principally to the high castes, it is a quality highly regarded in any male or female.

Although children are not punished harshly unless they actually violate village rules, qualities such as refinement or restraint are deemed necessary for satisfactory social adjustment. Villagers condemn coarseness or other negative attributes primarily by ridicule and public criticism. In fact, the reaction of the adults or older siblings around him is the child's best way of learning whether it is behaving properly. Growing up, in other words, is the evolution of the individual's social personality ever closer to the cultural ideals of the Balinese and theatre is an important vehicle in this process.

**Play in relation to social development**

I shall only make a few comments on the child's learning process through play in relation to theatre as this is a complex subject of its own which would require further research. Special consideration is given to two learning techniques which I observed in my village of research, mimesis and identification.

Children, when neither at school nor helping their parents, play a variety of games, prominent among which are ball games, hop-scotch and mimicking in play. Small groups of children from about four to twelve years old may gather together on a household pavilion and act out roles or situations which always appear to be based on known drama or dance genres. Boys tend to draw on the shadow play, modern drama or the *barong*, the masked lion dance. It is generally boys about seven years old who make simple puppets of banana leaves and bamboo rods, with one of them parodying the puppet performer. Girls are less involved in dramatic games than boys. Older ones sometimes join groups enacting scenes from modern drama, which is becoming increasingly popular with the young, the stories being romantic and light-hearted. It is more common, though, to see young girls with old towels wound tightly around their waists projecting into roles from operetta or other dances.

It is in their play-acting that children explore the different dramatic stimuli and the meaning they encapsulate, as well as gaining a deeper understanding of the themes and concepts expressed through theatre. The shadow play is of special importance here. As mentioned earlier, its iconographic principles are reflected in the other forms of theatre. So, to a greater or lesser degree, children abide by its rules, which are considered sacred and hence respected. This implies that the co-operation which is required of children in their dramatic games takes place within a mystic framework, set down by tradition.

The extent to which children learn to conform to the artistic tradition, in particular the shadow play, is demonstrated by a study carried out by Belo (1970, pp. 240–59) of boys' drawings. Twenty boys were chosen and asked to draw anything they pleased. They were divided into four groups of the following ages: nine to ten, seven to eight, five to six and three to four years old. Boys from the last two groups drew spontaneously subjects largely derived from daily life. As the boys grew older, the drawings became ever more reminiscent of scenes from the shadow play, with characters stylised like puppets. Mead (1970, pp. 338–9) also pointed out that children seem to express their fears through traditional art forms. Belo's and Mead's respective studies emphasise the importance of theatre in relationship to the cognitive development of the child.

I also want to suggest that children's sense of body-self and their role in society is reinforced through both watching performances and play-acting at home. A number of scholars such as Belo (1970, pp. 86–94) or Holt and Bateson (1970, p. 329) have already drawn attention to the extreme awareness that the people have of boundaries pertaining to the body, the territory and society. It is in this context that theatre teaches children how to classify appearance, expressions, dress, behaviour, movements, and by extension voice and speech, which as we have seen are interrelated and fixed on the stage. These classificatory schemes act as powerful frameworks of interpretation in terms of which new experiences can be ordered. This became evident when a few foreigners passed through my village. They were identified with characters from theatre, whom on first glance they resembled, and so they were drawn into the Balinese world and made comprehensible. For example, a large Australian whose face was reddish from the sun stayed for several hours in my village. To the villagers he appeared clumsy, pompous and overbearing and thus like the Korawa servant, Dèlem. A group of teenage boys applied the following proverb to the foreigner—*dageg Dèlem*, proud and conceited like Dèlem.

The village abounds with such proverbs relating to theatre, but they are largely used by adults in conversing with one another. As brought up earlier, grown-ups more often teach children by straightforward comparisons to characters from theatre. Such identifications are also made by children of all ages in their process of learning to adjust to the world.

## CONCLUSION

As we have seen, the Balinese place high value on theatre, the men being primarily drawn to the shadow play and women to operetta. It is one of the main vehicles through which the cultural heritage is perpetuated and disseminated. As such, theatre is intrinsic to the process of socialisation by which moral values and attitudes are inculcated in individuals which, in line with the sexual dichotomy which runs through traditional life, are befitting of their roles in society. Performances are frequently given throughout the island which are attended by packed crowds of spectators. Gilbert Lewis (1980, p. 19) has discussed what he refers to as the special 'alerting quality of ritual'. The same can be said of Balinese theatre. The stimuli are highly standardised and the stories often known. As a result the spectators' attention need not be constant; it is sporadically 'alerted' to what is considered noble or base in society. These symbolic truths held in common are enacted on the stage where they serve to order and structure, and possibly alter experiences, especially of the young.

Although the focus here has been on the didactic significance of the shadow play and operetta, each play is an artistic creation where life is presented as a single reality which partakes of an ideal order. Hence the instruction is veiled and only seen in glimpses. A play sustains the attention of the audience not through instructing, but by stimulating and entertaining.

## HUMAN LIFE CYCLE FROM BIRTH TO ADULTHOOD

### Boys

| *Formal activities*: Rituals marking status changes/ Schooling | *Informal activities*: Duties/Play and recreation |
|---|---|
| **Birth to 6 years** | |
| *lepas aon* (fall of umbilical cord) *ngerorasin* (12th day naming rite) *kambulan* (42nd day rite after birth, terminating impurity of mother) *nelubulam* (105th day rite after birth) *oton jumu* (1st birthday) *oton* (subsequent birthdays) | Assimilating new experiences, including those derived from attending all genres of dramatic shows and rituals from babyhood onwards, first to rudimentary then to more differentiated cognitive 'schemas'. Strict rules are already imposed on child: e.g. the use of the right hand for most activities or folding the hands for worship. |
| **6 to 10 years** | |
| *sekolah dasar* (primary school) Attended by all boys. | Duties comprise escorting ducks or water buffaloes to the river. Frequenting all genres of dramatic shows. Playing such games as hop-scotch or with kites or dragonflies. Also beginning to mimic dramatic |

roles in play. Boys may make miniature lion masks, *barong*, or simple puppets. Often boys at this period play easy musical instruments, e.g. cymbals or gongs. Adults are continually encouraging boys to imitate their behaviour and speech.

*10 to 14 years*
*sekolah menengah pertama, SMP* (secondary school I) Attended by all boys.

Assisting in rice cultivation and other male duties. Sexual dichotomy is established during this period. This implies that boys mainly watch—and are encouraged by elders to do so—the shadow theatre and the masked dance; also contemporary drama. Boys continue to mimic dramatic roles in play or enact scenes from these genres of theatre. At this stage many boys are accomplished musicians and join musicians' clubs (*seka*). Rules of etiquette and decorum should be learnt by now.

*14 to 18 years*
*sekolah menegah atas, SMA* (secondary school II) Attended by many boys nowadays.

Assisting in the rice cultivation and other duties. Continuing to watch male genres of theatre and playing in the orchestra. Adulthood attained during this stage. Thus courtship also occupies attention.

*Generally after 18 years*
*mesangih* (toothfiling rite)
*mesakapan* (marriage ceremony)
These two rites are often performed together. Marriage

As theatre plays an integral part of village life, adults continue to watch shows. These are predominantly of the genres mentioned earlier.

is the last rite of the life-cycle ritual system (*manusayadnya*)[a].

*Further education*
Few village boys continue in education because of lack of funds and contacts. Popular possibilities are teachers' training colleges or Udayana university.

---

[a] Life-cycle rituals (*manusayadnya*) are one of the five recognised ritual cycles on Bali. The others are rites for the dead (*pitrayadnya*), rites for gods (*déwayadnya*), for demons (*butayadnya*), and a more obscure cycle of rites for priests (*resiyadnya*).

## Girls

| *Formal activities*: Rituals marking status changes/Schooling | *Informal activities*: Duties/Play and recreation |
|---|---|
| *Birth to 6 years* Same as for boys | |
| *6 to 10 years* *sekolah dasar* (primary school) Attended by all girls. | Helping to make simple offerings (mainly of such natural substances as palm leaves, flowers, rice and so forth) and generally assisting in the household; also taking care of younger siblings. Attending all genres of theatre. Sometimes girls join in boys' games, but one of the main recreations is dancing with old towels or shawls. (Girls never play musical instruments, although they may sing.) |
| *10 to 14 years* *sekolah menengah pertama, SMP* (secondary school I) | Generally assisting in the household and with younger |

| | |
|---|---|
| Attended by most girls nowadays. | siblings. Helping make more elaborate offerings for the many rituals. Duties in most small hamlets still entail carrying water in a jar on the head back from the river. With the establishment of sexual dichotomy, beginning to frequent such female genres of theatre as operetta or pure dance shows. Sometimes also mimicing roles from these at home. Scenes though from contemporary drama may be enacted with boys. |
| *14 to 18 years* | |
| *sekolah menengah atas, SMA* (secondary school II) Formerly few village girls went to SMA, but now a fair number reach this level. | Assisting in the female duties in the household and rice cultivation. Continuing to watch female genres of theatre. Heterosexual interests occupy some of the time. |
| *c. 18 years* | |
| *mesangih* (toothfiling rite) *mesakapan* (marriage ceremony) Girls tend to marry earlier than boys. *Further education* Few village girls continue in their education. | Adult women continue to watch female genres of theatre. |

## BIBLIOGRAPHY

Belo, J. (1970) (1935) 'The Balinese temper'. In J. Belo (ed.), *Traditional Balinese culture*. New York: Columbia University Press.

Blacking, J. (1977) 'Towards an anthropology of the body'. In J. Blacking (ed.), *The anthropology of the body*. London, New York: Academic Press.

Blunt, A. (1973) (1953) In N. Pevsner and J. Nairn (eds), *The Pelican history of art: art and architecture in France 1500–1700*. Somerset: Butler and Tanner Ltd.

Brandon, J.R. (1970) *On thrones of gold*. Cambridge: Harvard University Press.
Conklin, H. (1955) 'Hanunoo colour categories'. In *Southwestern Journal of Anthropology*, 11.
Douglas, M. (1980) (1966) *Purity and danger*. London: Routledge.
Fortes, M. (1970) 'Social and psychological aspects of education in Taleland'. In *Time and social structure*. London: Athlone Press.
Geertz, C. (1960) *The religion of Java*. Illinois: the Free Press of Glencoe.
Else, G.F. (tr.) (1967) *Aristotle's Poetics*. Ann Arbor Paperbacks.
Gombrich, E.H. (1966) 'Ritualized gesture and expression in art'. In J. Huxley (ed.), *Ritualization of behaviour in man and animals*. London: Philosophical Transactions of the Royal Society, ser. B 251.
Goody, J. (1977) (1978) *The domestication of the savage mind*. Cambridge: Cambridge University Press.
Hobart, M. (1979) *A Balinese village and its field of social relations*. (Unpublished PhD thesis)
Holt, C. and Bateson, G. (1970) (1944) 'Form and function in Balinese dance'. In J. Belo (ed.), *Traditional Balinese culture*. New York: Columbia University Press.
Langer, S. (1976) (1953) *Feeling and form*. London: Routledge.
Leach, E.R. (1966) 'Virgin birth'. In *Proceedings of the Royal Anthropological Institute*. London.
Lee, D. (tr.) (1981) (1955) *Plato: The republic*. Penguin Classics.
Lewis, G. (1980) *Day of shining red*. Cambridge: Cambridge University Press.
McPhee, C. (1966) *Music in Bali*. New Haven, London: Yale University Press.
Mead, M. (1970) (1940) 'The arts in Bali'. In J. Belo (ed.), *Traditional Balinese culture*. New York: Columbia University Press.
Osborne, H. (1968) *Aesthetics and art theory*. London: Longmans.
Peacock, J. (1968) *Rites of modernization*. Chicago: University of Chicago Press.
Piaget, J. (1977) (1932) *The moral judgement of the child*. Penguin Books Ltd.
Singer, M. (1966) 'The Rādhā-Krishna Dhajanas of Madras City'. In M. Singer (ed.), *Krishna: myths, rites and attitudes*. Honolulu, East-West Center Press.
Skorupski, J. (1976) *Symbol and theory*. Cambridge: Cambridge University Press.
Sperber, D. (1979) (1975) *Rethinking symbolism* (trans.) A. Morton. Cambridge: Cambridge University Press.
Strathern, M. (1980) 'No nature, no culture: the Hagen case'. In C. MacCormack and M. Strathern (eds), *Nature, culture and gender*. Cambridge: Cambridge University Press.
Zoete, B. de and Spies, W. (1973) (1938) *Dance and drama in Bali*. Oxford: Oxford University Press.
Zoetmulder, P. (1974) *Kalangwan: a survey of Old Javanese literature*. The Hague: Nijhoff.

# Part II:
# Cognitive Development and Indigenous Psychology

# 4

# From Child to Human: Chewong Concepts of Self

Signe Howell

Indigenous ideas regarding cognitive development have been largely ignored as an area of study for social anthropologists in Britain. Nor was this an issue that I planned to investigate when I first went to do fieldwork among the Chewong of the Malay Peninsular. However, I was interested in studying the Chewong concept of self, that is, what it means to be a human being, and this is a topic which, I would argue, is central to any discussion of cognitive development; since the process of acquiring knowledge of all kinds can be delineated only by eliciting the socially agreed expectations of what it is that a child is to become. What I shall attempt to do in this chapter, therefore, is to discuss Chewong notions of what constitutes a child and an adult (i.e. a 'human'), and then examine the process whereby the one is changed into the other. This will involve reviewing all the stages in the developmental cycle. I shall be arguing that in the Chewong case, this cycle starts before birth and continues beyond physiological and social maturation. Thus it is necessary to modify, or even abandon, Western models of cognitive development to take account of a society such as the Chewong, in which the range of the process is extended and the stages differently perceived.

In the early days of my fieldwork I made very little progress in establishing Chewong notions of what constitutes the human being. People appeared to have few clear cut ideas about it.

Later I realised that expected normal attributes of an adult man or woman are not made explicit by describing ideal types, but are revealed by the articulation of perceived shortcomings in small children. Adults will make comparisons in concrete situations; and by paying close attention to their comments on the behaviour of children, as well as their own behaviour *vis-à-vis* them, I began to build up an understanding of beliefs and values regarding humanity and, following on from this, what one is to expect from a human being. In other words, by emphasising how children fail to measure up to certain standards, the Chewong express the characteristics of humanity in negative rather than in positive terms. For example, by being told that the reason for the frequent illnesses of small children was due to the fact that their *ruwai* ('soul', this will be returned to later) was not fully stable, I learnt that the *ruwai* is a very important aspect of the person, and that its condition is the chief indicator of the state of a person at any given time. Similarly, by listening to admonishments of childrens' boisterous behaviour, I came to realise that extravagant behaviour of any kind is not regarded as appropriate human behaviour.

All strong expressions of emotions are regarded by the Chewong as potentially destructive, and are controlled by numerous rules. In an earlier paper I have discussed the role of these rules in Chewong life, and I suggested that one of their effects is to discourage emotionality (Howell, 1981). The rules are constantly being referred to with respect to children, who learn early to control emotional expressiveness in their behaviour.

Although it will be impossible to talk about cognitive development among the Chewong without reference to the rules, I wish in this chapter to ignore them as much as possible. Instead, I shall concentrate on the process of growing and acquiring knowledge, and Chewong attitudes to this process. This will involve examining Chewong ideas concerning the elements that make up the person, how each element functions, how they are formed, how they relate to the other elements, and how, if at all, each may be affected in its development. Related to this is the question of the degree to which the Chewong view the individual as an independent agent, and to what extent it is thought that the individual may be shaped by outside influences. These ideas all affect attitudes to childrearing; parental behaviour towards their children and their expectations from them.

**THE CHEWONG**

The Chewong are a small group of aboriginal people of the tropical rain-forest of the Malay Peninsula. Traditionally they are hunters, gatherers, and shifting cultivators, but today they are divided into two main groups one of which has been drawn to some extent into the wider Malaysian society and as a result has given up its traditional way of life. The other half still lives deep inside the forest and their contact with the outside world is confined to the occasional sale of jungle produce in return for knives, salt, cloth, and tobacco. It was among this section of the Chewong (the Eastern Chewong) that I conducted most of my fieldwork and about whom I shall be speaking. Contact between the two groups is not maintained today, but each knows of the existence of the other.

The Eastern Chewong live in small settlements widely scattered throughout an area of about 190 square miles which they regard as their traditional territory. The settlements are changed every one to three years when they clear new fields by the slash and burn method. Their staple today is cassava. They have no domestic animals except dogs, and rely on the forest to supply them with meat and other foods, and I suspect that their relatively settled existence is of recent origin. They frequently abandon their fields for days, or even weeks, in order to go hunting and foraging. The composition of any one settlement undergoes continual change, but most commonly consists of two or three houses occupied by one or two pairs of elderly parents together with some married children.

Their kinship system is cognatic with their social organisation extremely informal with no political hierarchies. There is no machinery of law and punishment founded in human society. Rather, a large number of different superhuman and non-human beings are drawn into the conduct of daily affairs via the medium of the large number of rules already mentioned, the transgression of which result in superhuman retribution. In view of this, I have argued elsewhere (Howell, 1984) that at one level of discussion Chewong society must be regarded, not as consisting just of the 130 persons that make up the Eastern section, but also of the numerous superhuman beings who inhabit their universe. These beings are drawn directly into Chewong daily life and they influence almost every individual or collective action. Chewong society can be said to be co-existent with their cosmos. This wider social universe is maintained and recreated through processes of exchange which occur daily as well as on specified ceremonial occasions. In view of the above, it is not possible to distinguish a 'sacred–profane' dichotomy in Chewong thought. To do so would be meaningless as the so-called ritual and the so-called mundane activities are intertwined, both on the level of thought and action. Furthermore, the distinction between humans and superhumans is not a rigid one. It is possible for human beings to transcend the boundary and to join the rank of the immortal, inviolable superhuman beings.

Another aspect of Chewong society which it is important to understand in the present context, is that it is marked by peaceful co-existence. This is common to all the oboriginal groups of the Malay Peninsula. None of these has any history of warfare, and overt acts of aggression are very rare. (see e.g. Dentan, 1968, 1978; Endicott, 1979). I never witnessed a single one, not even a verbal combat. Whenever finding themselves in a potentially violent situation, it is the practice of the Chewong to withdraw, rather than to confront it. They fled from the marauding Malays of earlier centuries, and still run away in panic at the approach of strangers. Should hostility arise between individuals, one of those concerned will remove himself to another settlement. Both interpersonal relations and individual bearing are restrained. This fits with the general suppression of extravagant behaviour. Only two emotions are openly acknowledged and encouraged in children. These are fearfulness and shyness which again correspond to the absence of aggressive behaviour. I will return to them below.

## HUMANS AND SUPERHUMANS

It is important to understand that according to the Chewong all species of conscious beings, whether human, superhuman, or those animals and plants attributed with consciousness (*ruwai*) are, at one level of discourse, 'people'. That is they are all rational beings with the same fundamental characteristics as those of humans. But since it is human beings who serve as models for all other species of conscious beings, I wish to suggest that the Chewong attitude towards their environment, both natural and supernatural, is 'humancentric'. What is seen to differ between 'human beings' and the rest is the actual manifestations of the various characteristics, and the Chewong can be said to believe in the 'psychic unity' of all conscious beings.

Arising out of this, but not an issue that I am going to explore in detail in this chapter, is that the Chewong concept of human emerges not only in connection with ideas regarding children, but also in ideas connected to their relations with the superhuman beings. A child is not a human being, but an embryonic one, and the process of *becoming* goes on until, after marriage, the first child is born. For social purposes, once this stage is reached, a Chewong is a human being. However, this stage may also be regarded as the starting point only, at which the human being is an embryonic superhuman being. Now begins the process which ultimately, in the person of a big shaman, leads to the transformation into a superhuman being. One may therefore see an analogy in the relationships pertaining between a child and a human, and that between a human and a superhuman. Just as I found I learnt about Chewong notions of the person by listening to their talk of how children fail to conform to an implicit model of a human being, so I similarly enhanced my understanding by being told how humans fail to measure up to the standards of the superhuman ones. Again, by listening to statements couched in terms of negative achievement, one was able to construct positive values. The Chewong compare themselves to the superhuman beings (at any rate to some of them) in terms of failure: they are not inviolable, they are prone to accidents of all sorts, they fall ill, they die. The same is not true of superhuman beings. So just as children are more vulnerable and unstable than humans, so humans are the same *vis-à-vis* the superhumans. However, as children are changed into humans, so humans may be changed into superhumans. The key factor in both changes is the acquisition of knowledge. Children learn from adults, adults learn from the superhuman beings. Most adult men and women have some direct personal contact with one or more of the helpful superhuman beings, and they receive much knowledge from them which aids them to control their environment and which is passed on to the community at large. Thus, learning, in the Chewong view, is a process that continues throughout a person's life, reaching only an illusory completion upon the achievement of humanhood.

**THE CONCEPT OF KNOWLEDGE**

The Chewong attach enormous importance to the possession of knowledge (*haeratn*). The type and quantity of knowledge is what distinguishes the different stages of the development of one person from another, and one category of beings from another category. The word *haeratn* is used to include all kinds of knowledge and it is both a verb and a noun. One might expect that *haeratn* could be divided conceptually into two main types, that is the kind of knowledge concerning practical tasks and the more theoretical issues. However, just as I argued above that it is invalid to make an analytic distinction between ritual and ordinary acts among the Chewong, so I would also argue that it is similarly inappropriate to separate two domains of knowledge. The most practical of tasks, such as the making of cane backbaskets, cannot be performed without cosmological considerations. As a young girl learns how to make a proper backbasket she is simultaneously taught always to face the joints in the cane upwards lest the breath of the carrier becomes imprisoned in the body which has fatal results. Breath is the chief manifestation of life, and by implicating it in the basket-making procedure, a whole set of associated ideas and values are also implicated, thus widening the significance of the act into extra-human domains. These two aspects of backbasket-making (and most other practical tasks) are mutually interdependent.

For the successful transition from child to human to be accomplished, the accumulation of all kinds of knowledge has to be effected. It is my suggestion that this accumulation, as it takes place during infancy and childhood, is intimately and affectively linked to the development and growth of the body and of the various other elements that constitute the person. At the point when the body has completed its physical growth, the other elements are thought of as fully integrated into a self. Without the appropriate acquisition of knowledge the integration of the self could not be achieved. In other words, the transition from child to human can be said to include three processes: the growth of the body, the assimilation of the elements of the self, and the acquisition of all kinds of knowledge. The formation of these three aspects of the person occurs in a mutually dependent and reinforcing manner, resulting in the integrated self of the adult (i.e. human) person.

Having said this, it will be necessary to briefly outline what the pertinent elements of the Chewong person are. For present purposes these can be described as: the body, consciousness as manifested by the *ruwai*, the liver, the smell, and the eyes (for further elaboration see Howell, 1984). The body does not require any further explanation here, except to say that the Chewong also refer to it as the 'cloak' (*bajo*) of the 'real person' (*ruwai*). The *ruwai* is both the vital principle of a being (and as such associated with breath) as well as his or her essence or consciouness. It is said to have substance, and it leaves the body during dreams and trance states. It may become lost, or stolen by harmful superhuman beings, the result of which is illness and—if it is not returned—death. The smell of a person is uniquely his (her) own. Like the *ruwai* it may become detached from the body and lost, but unlike the *ruwai* it does not have a substance. The liver is the seat of an individual's actual states of consciousness; both intellectual and emotional, and it can be said to represent the personality. Again, it is more unstable during childhood, when tantrums are ascribed to it. The eyes, through which reality is perceived, are different in each species of being. This means that the actual reality is different according to the quality of the eyes that observe it. Children's eyes may be adversely affected and as a result they see the world upside down, or spinning. These five elements of the person, together or independently, determine the way a person acts. Finally, in the present context and of a slightly different order, is the name by which a person is known.

Children are characterised as 'not strong' and 'not knowing'. Their bodies are not strong, their *ruwai* are not strong, their smell is not strong, and their liver and eyes are easily influenced. More particularly, what is weak are the bonds between these various aspects of the person. These are not yet stabilised, and as a result they become either actually dissociated from the rest as in the case of the *ruwai* and the smell, or upset as with the liver and the eyes. The weakness of the links results in disequilibrium, manifested in illness. The fact that children are ill much more often than adults is taken as proof of the above assertions. The growing period of the child is one in which the different parts become properly fixed and are placed in a permanent and stable relationship, forming a unified whole. From now on illness is much rarer, and can in most instances be explained in terms of serious transgression of the rules.

Furthermore, the boundaries between the various elements in a child are fluid. Whereas an adult may freely scatter his (her) hair trimmings and nail parings, those of the child are not yet independent 'things'. A child's smell may be infused in them. Therefore, when they are cut, steps must be taken to ensure that any lingering smell does not fall into the wrong hands. All that is cut is first placed on the child's head 'to make it return', and subsequently kept in the roof of the house, wrapped in a leaf. If the pieces are thrown casually away, a passing superhuman being may come across them and consume the smell. Numerous other prescriptions and proscriptions exist to protect the child from a disintegration of the self and from the attacks of harmful beings.

Secondly, children 'do not know'. What is meant by this is that they do not know how to behave and act properly both with regard to the rest of society (including the superhuman beings) as well as towards themselves. This includes a full understanding of the implications of their acts. Only through partaking in the 'original knowledge' (*haeratn asal*) does an individual become a human being. Chewong original knowledge is contained in their myths, in their songs, in their spells, in the rules which direct behaviour, as well as in much unformalised information. It is passed on verbally via these media, and it is also transmitted in most daily acts and rites.

As will be clear from the above discussion, the environment for a child is not identical to that of the adult. It has to be modified in certain ways in order to accommodate the perceived shortcomings of children, and to protect them from various dangers. The child is much more vulnerable than the adult. In view of this, the role of the adult can be seen to fall into two main parts: that of protector and that of educator.

To sum up the discussion so far, I have suggested that Chewong society includes numerous superhuman beings with whom the human beings maintain continuous relationships, and that the ultimate stage of cognitive development is the transformation from human to superhuman. This can only be achieved, however, after a series of processes which first of all transform a child into a proper human being. For this to be accomplished the Chewong child must be in possession of a fully developed body, he (she) must have acquired the appropriate traditional knowledge, and the integration of the various elements of the person must have been effected. Furthermore, I have also suggested that these three processes are mutually interdependent, and that they can take place only by adults providing the correct environment and instruction.

## PROCESSES OF CHANGE

The Chewong life cycle may be divided into six stages: prenatal; from birth to name; infancy and childhood; adolescence; married life; and old age. The transition from one stage to the next is marked socially more clearly in some cases than in others, but none is subjected to elaborate ritual. Only the first four of these stages are of relevance in the present context, and I shall discuss each in some detail in terms of Chewong ideas regarding cognitive development, emphasising how their views and values affect adult expectations from their children and their behaviour towards them. There is of course another stage, namely that of superhuman. However, this is not an invariable part of the cycle, and I will not discuss it in any detail here. Much of what I shall be saying with regard to the other stages, and the category 'human', is derived from my understanding of the superhuman category.

**Prenatal**

Once a woman realises that she is pregnant (usually when the new life makes itself felt) both she and her husband enter into a relationship with the foetus. It is now thought of as a being, and is referred to as 'child in the stomach' (*wong lam aig*). From then until the birth both parents are equally responsible for the correct development and growth of the foetus in all its aspects: physical and 'mental'. This parental responsibility is formulated in terms of dietary restrictions and certain confinements of movement. Any breaches of these prohibitions may have a detrimental effect on the foetus.

A foetus is said to be 'built' by the semen, a regular deposit of which is required right up to the time of birth. Whereas the father thus builds the baby, the mother houses and feeds it. Furthermore, the menstrual blood which ceases upon conception is said to build the placenta, the child's 'older sibling', which has to be ritually disposed of and which reunites with its 'younger sibling' (the child) upon the latter's death. These roles are explicitly seen as complementary.

The prenatal stage is the one in which parental responsibility is at its strongest since congenital malfunctions of any kind are attributed to the behaviour of one or other of the parents during this period. The following example will elucidate: One boy who was born with club feet, six toes on each foot, and deficient eyesight was said to be thus affected while 'in his mother's stomach' because the mother failed to heed the rule that forbids a pregnant woman to be in contact with a corpse. In this instance it was only the physical development that was affected, the boy's mental faculties being perfectly normal. Another boy suffered very badly from epilepsy, and had apparently done so since infancy. This was explained in terms of the father having failed to observe a particular food prohibition while the baby was yet unborn. The Chewong say that this laid his *ruwai* open to the attack of a particular species of superhuman being.

The foetus, then, is fundamentally dependent upon its parents' behaviour. However, it is thought of as having some identity as well. It is believed to be able to see what is happening outside 'its house' and to be able, in a limited degree, to act upon this knowledge. For example, if a woman frequently breaks the rule of *punen* which states that all food caught in the forest must be brought back to the settlement and shared out to all those present, and instead eats it in secret and alone, her child in the stomach sees this and may decide to delay its birth: 'it does not want to be with such a stingy mother'.

In view of these examples it might be argued that the cognitive process begins before birth. The foundations for the later individual are then laid, and these may be laid wrongly. Moreover, the foetus is already beginning to observe and even to act upon its observations. Here it is of interest to note that the eyes are said to be the first part of the foetus to be built. Thus the foetus has some degree of self, but it is extremely vulnerable and it has no power to combat the effects of parental transgression of pregnancy rules.

**Birth to name**

The next stage is that which begins at birth. The event itself is called 'coming to earth', and is said to take place after every part of the body is formed. A foetus may delay this event, but it is unable to prevent it altogether. The birth is surrounded by several prescriptions and proscriptions, but these now operate with regard to mother and child only. The father's direct physiological involvement ceases upon birth, whereas that of the mother continues until weaning. The most elaborate birth rules operate only for the first week or so. After that the mother is subject only to restriction on certain foods whose detrimental effect is passed to the child via the milk. For this first week (the precise time is not specified, it is up to the mother to do as she sees fit) the child is in a liminal stage. It is particularly vulnerable to superhuman attack and therefore has to be highly protected. It is also undergoing its first 'formation'. Until the time when it is brought out of the house to make its first encounter with the rest of the society, the newly born child is slowly being exposed to the cultural domain. These are: the house, clothing, fire and cooking (heated water). It cannot leave the house, it sleeps next to the fire which is kept going night and day, and it is completely covered in a cloth, and it can be washed only in heated (i.e. culturally transformed) water. This is the only time when the hot state is preferred, and actually encouraged; the cool state which at all other times is sought after, is thought of as healthy, restorative and generally good, and is chiefly associated with the superhuman worlds. Heat, by contrast, epitomises the human condition, which is, I suggest, why the new-born infant is being immersed in it. If the baby dies at this point it does not receive the mortuary rites, a further indication that it is not yet a member of the society.

Once the mother is fit again and the postpartum bleeding has ceased, she starts to move about and if the baby looks as if it is going to survive, she brings it out of the house with her. Some time after this (again no specified time is prescribed) the child receives its name. This is not marked by a ceremony, but is simply stated one day by the mother or father, either of whom may have received it in a dream, or just decided upon it. This name becomes rapidly known throughout all the Chewong settlements, and from then on is always used in referring to the child. From this moment the child is incorporated into the society. No distinctions are made between male and female names, no name being thought more suitable for one or other sex.

It can be seen from the above that birth may be regarded as a process which continues for some time after the actual appearance of the baby. But once the baby has survived the particularly persistent superhuman attacks of the early days, and has undergone the process of exposure to the quintessential human artifacts and conditions, once it is given a name and has been introduced to the rest of the society, it is truly born, and can be said to have entered the stage of infancy and childhood.

**Infancy and childhood**

The next stage, one not overtly identified by the Chewong, is that which can be seen to extend from the name-giving to adolescence which, in the Chewong case, begins between six and eight. During this time we can see the child starting off from a basis of complete dependency upon its parents, subject to a number of protective measures, and reaching, at its conclusion, a point when it achieves some degree of autonomy and abandons parents in favour of peer group.

The named category of persons during this period is that of children (*wong*). This term may be qualified according to the stage a child has reached in regard to certain aspects of development. Thus they may say, 'it is a child who cannot walk yet', or 'who does not yet know how to speak'. The usage of 'yet' is significant as it indicates specific expectations. *Wong* may also be used with a gender qualifier, such as 'woman-child, or man-child', but these terms are rarely applied, and no equivalents for boy and girl exist in the Chewong language. Similarly, the language does not have person pronouns indicating gender; when referring to someone, 'it' is always used. At this point it may be useful to take a brief look at Chewong sex roles and associated ideas and values.

The elements of the self are not distinguished in any way on grounds of gender, and we have already seen that personal names are not sexually differentiated.

As regards adult sex roles, certain occupations are chiefly associated with one or other sex, but these are not divided into rigid categories. On the whole, men and women work together, and most adults are able to perform the whole range of practical tasks required. The most important social–economic group is that of the married couple, together with their children, and it is not unusual to find one such unit living on their own in the jungle. What sexual divisions of labour do occur, are grounded in physiological differences, which the Chewong, of course, fully appreciate. The fact that only women may give birth to, and suckle, babies does not give them any special status, but because most adult women tend to be either pregnant or feeding babies, they have less freedom of movement, and for this reason the men tend to do the hunting and to carry out prolonged heavy work, while the women tend to look after the children, cook, plant the fields, and gather wild tubers. But it must be stressed that both sexes frequently participate in the tasks associated with the opposite sex, and this is no subject for comment by the rest of the community. Value judgements are not attached to gender, or gender-associated behaviour, nor are these made the basis for further social or symbolic distinctions.

This is reflected in Chewong attitudes to, and treatment of, children. There is no cultural preference for babies of either sex, although I was told that mothers prefer to have sons, and fathers prefer daughters. Adults display some interest in the sex of a child, and like to point playfully to their sexual organs, calling out their respective name. When news of the new-born is carried to other settlements, the sex of the child is always mentioned. However, once a child is born, the treatment it receives is identical in both cases and all rules apply equally to boys and girls. No difference based on gender is expected in terms of character traits or childhood interest, nor in the relative speed of their physical and mental growth. The development in these respects is attributed to the actual qualities of the child in question, usually associated with the type of liver that he (she) is thought to have. I return to this below.

Chewong children are given few toys. Those that they have are the same for boys and girls. Their first possession is usually a knife. It is not unusual to see an infant, barely able to sit, hacking away at the ground, or at a dry cassara with a blunt old knife.

Mostly, small children of both sexes attempt to copy the activities of adults. They never indulge in competitive games, a fact which possibly links with Chewong non-aggressive behaviour.

These early years are the most dangerous in terms of a child's development, and it is up to the parents to provide the best environment for growth. Some of the precautions necessary have already been referred to and various foods are forbidden them until they have reached the time of puberty. Children should not be allowed to bathe in the river lest their *ruwai* or their smell flows away with the water. Hair and nail parings must be preserved lest the child's smell is thrown away with them. Children must not be allowed to roam freely at certain specific times when harmful beings are about (such as at dawn and dusk). Furthermore, infants should not be left alone at any time because their *ruwai* may get lost as it goes in search of their parents, or they may then be attacked by superhuman beings. All this means that the small child is never far from either of its parents. Until it can walk it is always strapped to its mother's or father's body during work and leisure. It sleeps at night on its parent's mat. It is rare for a baby to be looked after by other adults or even older siblings. It therefore develops a very close physical link with both parents, but tends not to know the rest of the community very well.

**Adolescence**

The transition from childhood to adolescence is not explicitly marked in the form of initiation rites. However, there are other social markers. At the age of about seven children can be seen to shift gradually away from parents in order to join a peer group consisting of older children of the same sex. This move is slow and intermittent, and is very much dependent upon the child itself who oscillates for a long period between parents and peer group. When the transition is finally accomplished, the youngsters spend most of their time together with the peer group, sleeping with them in a special corner of the house, and having virtually no contact with youngsters of the opposite sex. This is also the time when they begin wearing loincloths, because, it is said, they have become shy (*lidya*). The sexes are now linguistically distinguished. They are no longer children (*wong*), but have become maidens (*kokn ködah*) and bachelors (*bujaegen*).

Very few special prohibitions are in operation with reference to maidens and bachelors. Only a few of the dietary restrictions specific to children still have to be observed. In general, as they get older they become subject to those rules that govern adult (i.e. human) life. That is, they begin to take responsibility for their own actions.

Adolescence is an active learning period, but the attitude of adults is even more permissive than during infancy. They do not seek actively to teach anything at all, but leave the adolescents to their own devices.

On the other hand, it is assumed that every maiden and bachelor will have mastered the customary tasks by the time they approach marriage, and most in fact do so. All adult activities are participated in by the adolescents if and when they wish, and the general assumption is that, as men and women, everyone is equally able and proficient. Any variation in the quality of achievement between individuals is ignored. Again, as in children's games, competition is absent and personal excellence is not commented upon. At this level the individual is subordinated to the society. What is of ultimate importance is the continuation of society—a communal task—not individual glory or gratification.

This concludes my discussion of the four developmental stages which are passed through in order to become a human being. Before ending, however, I would like to elaborate on the points made concerning Chewong attitudes to learning and how these relate to the concept of the self.

**LEARNING AND SELF**

From the deeds and words of the Chewong with regard to the instruction of children, two contrasting pictures emerge.

On the one hand they seem to favour the belief that learning is best obtained from example and individual initiative, on the other hand, in the specific case of the rules governing behaviour, a belief in the efficacy of specific and enforced instruction is displayed.

They recognise the importance of the cultural environment, being fully aware that all their ethnically different neighbours lead their lives according to different codes, but this does not worry them. 'This is our way, our traditions', they explain and assume that their own children will grow up to conduct their lives in conformity with these traditions. They profess an extreme relativistic view of culture and assume that each species of conscious beings (whether human or superhuman) adhere to their own rules of rationality. A discussion once arose whether, if one of their babies were to accompany me to England, it would start to speak English or their own language. The concensus of opinion was that it would speak English, as 'there would be no one else to listen to'. This suggests a preference for the nurture rather than nature view of child development. However, in their own childrearing practices, the only concrete example of this actually being applied is in respect of the rules governing behaviour, the knowledge of, and adherence to, which are absolutely necessary for the successful existence and continuation of life of the individual and the society. The rules are involved in virtually every act and utterance, as the Chewong recognise, and many of their comments on small children concern their ignorance of the rules. Children are constantly admonished for behaving without consideration to them, and throughout the early years, a child is frequently being stopped in its activities by adults calling out the name of one or other rule. If a child has transgressed and the anticipated catastrophe ensues, for example a thunderstorm, adults enter into conciliatory measures on behalf of the child. While doing so, they inform the superhuman beings responsible for the thunderstorm that it is 'only a child' who has offended, and that he (she) did so because he (she) did not know.

In all other aspects of cognitive development it is assumed that a child will grow and develop without specific parental interference. As long as the correct foundations were laid while the child was in the womb, all the right procedures adhered to in bringing it into the world, and the correct environment for growth provided, then the basis for development without assistance in the form of instruction has been laid. A child is left to perform various tasks whenever it chooses to, and to approach an adult if and when it requires specific guidance. Thus no attempts are made to teach motor skills or speech, nor to speed up the acquisition of these. No importance is attached to rapid development, and there are no clear ideas as to how soon a child ought to be able to sit, crawl, walk, talk or whatever. I never heard parents discussing a child's progress, or lack of it. The same absence of explicit expectations can be found at all levels of cognitive development. It is up to each individual to absorb knowledge of all kinds from watching, listening, participating, and by asking questions. The Chewong are explicit about this: 'We wait for a maiden or a bachelor to come and ask us how to make a basket, or how to say a spell', they told me. If no one asks, then they believe that the knowledge will die out. This passive attitude to training is manifest in all situations. For instance, the little boy who was born crippled was never encouraged to overcome his handicap. His parents would always carry him around with them, saying that he was unable to walk. When I returned to the Chewong after an absence of two years, this boy had in fact taught himself to hobble around quite effectively. The explanation given was simply that he was very energetic, or rather that his liver was energetic. The initiative for learning had lain wholly with him, and no one thought to generalise from the experience.

This focus upon the liver as the seat of individuality deserves some elaboration. In common with many other societies of South-East Asia, the Chewong regard the liver as the physiological seat of inner states of all kinds, and as the locus of what we call personality. The quality of a person's liver is used as an explanatory device for particular actions. Relatively few types of personality are distinguished, but two examples of 'states of the liver' commonly referred to may serve to illustrate the point. Some people are said to have energetic livers (or simply to be energetic, the liver is not always invoked, although it is always seen as the ultimate source). The crippled boy just described is one instance. Another is a woman who is persistently hardworking, making mats and baskets, planting cassava, etc. Her efforts too are explained by the statement that her original liver is energetic. This fact does not single her out for admiration, nor would signs of laziness single her out for condemnation. Each behaviour is simply a manifestation of characteristics with which she is born, and particular characteristics do not appear to be consciously developed or discouraged. I could find no evidence that adults deliberately tried to encourage desirable characteristics in children.

A second example of a commonly identified state of the liver, is the timid, or fearful, one. When I was first with the Chewong I was struck by the fact that timidity in children appeared to be looked upon with favour, and from certain adult behaviour patterns it appeared to be actively encouraged. I later came to revise this view, and concluded that timidity is regarded as a quality shared by everyone in the group, in contrast to outsiders of various ethnic groups who are described as 'brave' (for which a Malay term is used, there being no Chewong equivalent). 'We jungle people are very fearful (*höntugen*) and timid (*lidya*)', they always say. Adults are constantly mentioning how frightened they are of going into the Malay trading station to sell their cane, and how frightened they are of meeting tigers or soldiers while out in the jungle. Stories of Malay slave raiders of the past are kept alive, and hostile intrusions from the outside are always anticipated in fear. I have seen whole settlements scatter in panic at the sudden approach of strangers. Anything new, or unusual, is met with suspicion and exclamations of 'I'm frightened!' Within this general atmosphere of timidity, the Chewong say that children are particularly timid. They do not make a connection between their own behaviour towards the children and children's own behaviour. When toddlers begin to explore away from their parents, or to take an active interest in the world around them, they are never encouraged. Rather, the toddler is stopped short by loud exclamations of 'don't!' elaborated by 'it is hot', or 'it is sharp', or, 'there are Malay tigers, snakes, millipedes', etc.

States of fear are sometimes consciously provoked in children by adults for their own amusement. Thus a child may be told that a Malay is waiting to take him away, or that a tiger will catch him. This always induces attacks of violent screaming and crying in the child, whose parents as a result display every sign of satisfaction as well as amusement. 'So and so is very fearful,' they would explain to me, usually adding that all jungle people are fearful. I suggest that to be energetic (or angry, generous, jealous etc. (see Howell, 1981 for a list of indigenous terms applied by the Chewong)) is seen as idiosyncratic, and peculiar to the personality of the individual; whereas a timid liver is regarded by them as an inherent characteristic of the Chewong self. In neither case can the characteristics be overcome, but I would argue that the timidity of the Chewong liver is actively encouraged—and hence a learnt attribute—even though the Chewong themselves think of it as inherent.

In summary, therefore, the Chewong appear to believe that adult instruction of children is in some respects necessary to ensure that they turn into human beings. Where this is explicitly acknowledged is in the area of the rules of behaviour. Subject to their following the prescriptions and proscriptions, in all other respects children will acquire other knowledge and skills by exposure, by the structure of the self (the unique Chewong self), and by their own initiative (the quality of their original liver).

Attitudes towards the acquisition of esoteric knowledge are equally open. Those who become shamans, usually after marriage, i.e. achieved status of human, are said to do so because of the energy they put into studying with existing shamans and in establishing relationships with spirit guides. All knowledge is freely available to anyone, child or adult, man or woman, who wishes to obtain it, but it has to be asked for. Because of this it is up to the individuals how much they wish to continue their quest for esoteric knowledge so as to advance from the status of a full human being to that of a superhuman being. Though only a minority achieve it, this transformation is open to any adult; no prerequisites are necessary in terms of sex, kin status, or life situation.

Despite the strong emphasis on the individual which may be detected in Chewong ideas and practices there is an explicit part of Chewong ideology that no person is in any way better than anyone else. Even when differences in achievement are manifest, these are not socially acknowledged. On the contrary, they are ignored; except on certain specific occasions when special abilities are needed, such as in the case of a particular shaman's healing power. Even so, the shaman has no means to use his specialist knowledge for other purposes or in other contexts. Similarly, the good hunter produces more meat than the others, but this is a fact which is ignored. Also, he has to share all his meat. The insistence on the rules of sharing all foodstuffs and other things brought back from the forest, together with the suppression of the expression of emotionality and the sanctions against aggressive and competitive behaviour of all kinds, all prevent the emergence of individuals as leaders. 'We Chewong are all the same. All men are good hunters, all women are energetic' they insist, often in the face of flagrant empirical evidence to the contrary.

## CONCLUSION

In this chapter I have been arguing that in order to examine the process of cognitive development in a given society, it is first necessary to establish the indigenous ideas and values with regard to what is thought to constitute the human being, i.e. what is the self that is developing and acquiring knowledge. In my study on the Chewong, I have concluded that the cognitive process starts in the womb and continues until death (and in the case of the big shamans, beyond death). There is a threshold at the time of the birth of the first child, when the individual has, from a social point of view, become a human being. At this point the body is considered fully developed and the ability to reproduce oneself has been demonstrated. The various elements of the self are fully integrated and stable and 'traditional knowledge' has been acquired to the extent that the individual knows how to behave and to exploit his (her) environment at minimum danger to himself (herself) and the rest of the society. I have suggested that these three processes are equally part of cognitive development and they occur simultaneously and interdependently. I have also shown that, apart from the obvious physiological differences between the sexes, the concept of the person is not sexually differentiated and cognitive expectations are identical in both cases.

On achieving humanity, the process is from one point of view complete. However, from a different perspective the quest for knowledge has only just begun. All that has been accumulated until this point can be seen as the foundation for a further quest for knowledge through interactions with superhuman beings. It is assumed that every Chewong will become human in the sense outlined, with little specified instruction from adults except in respect of the rules governing behaviour, and without undue exertion on the individual's part. But it is then open to the individual to choose how far to continue the cognitive development process, the final culmination of which is a transformation of all aspects of the self—the body, the *ruwai*, the liver, and the eyes—to attain the status of a superhuman being.

**ACKNOWLEDGEMENTS**

Fieldwork among the Chewong was carried out between 1977 and 1979 and was supported by the Social Science Research Council. A return visit was made possible by my being appointed to the Susette Taylor Travelling Fellowship 1981–2, granted by Lady Margaret Hall, Oxford University; and by a grant from the Equipe de Recherche d'Anthropologie Sociale: Morphologie, Echanges of Centre National de la Recherche Scientifique and Ecole des Hautes Etudes en Sciences Sociales, Paris.

**FROM CHILD TO HUMAN: CHEWONG CONCEPTS OF SELF**

**Chewong terms pertaining to growth and development[a]**

*Infancy and childhood (0–7/9)*

| | |
|---|---|
| *wong* | generic term for 'child'. Used for all children (boys and girls) from time of perceived foetal presence until 'adolescence'. |
| *wong lam aig* | child in the stomach |
| *wong the* | new child |
| *wong ba* | child carried |
| *wong kanin* | small child (this is a relative rather than absolute term) |
| *södn han haeraten* | does not yet know |
| *wong ka manung* | child (who) has become large |
| *wong ka badoden* | child (who) has become old |

In the last two categories the child is now expected to 'know the rules' and to start to behave 'properly'.

*Adolescence (7/9–13/15 (girls), 15/17 (boys))*

| | |
|---|---|
| *kokn ködah* | woman maiden |
| *bujaegen* | bachelor |

Sexually differentiated terms are used for the first time. The application of terms coincide with movement from parents to same sex peer group. No generic term.

| | |
|---|---|
| *ka ködaha*[b] | has become maiden |
| *ka bujaegen* | has become bachelor |
| *ka pakai wed (ti)* | has (started to) wear loincloth (male and female cloths differentiated) |
| *ka oplug bo* | breasts have fallen |
| *ka inyeden ai* | has refused meat (first menses have occurred. Menstruating women are forbidden meat.) |
| *ka haeraten ko boweig* | has learnt to hunt monkeys |
| *södn han abn bi je (te)* | does not yet sleep with a wife (husband) (i.e. not married) |

*Adulthood (marriage to ca 50)*

| | |
|---|---|
| *kokn* | woman |
| *tungkal* | man |
| *ka wo je (te)* | has got wife (husband) |
| *te (je) södn the* | husband (wife) still new |
| *ka abn bi te (je), tapi södn ho wong* | has slept with husband (wife), but still no child |
| *ka wo wong nai (bir, ped, padn) kur* | has had one (two, three, four (the limit of Chewong counting)) children |
| *ka yedi beri* | has become human (following the birth of the first child; man and woman) |
| *ka yao ruwai* | has met a spirit guide |
| *ka wo wong besok* | has many children |

*Old age*

| | |
|---|---|
| *bi badoden* | old people (sexual distinction applied less frequently, although old man, old woman may be used) |
| *kokn badoden* | old woman |
| *tungkal badoden* | old man |
| *ka badoden* | has (become) old |
| *ka hadeiten inyeden ai* | has stopped refusing meat (menopause) |
| *bi ka okriden* | body has dried up (may be used specifi- |

| | |
|---|---|
| | cally to post-menopausal women, or to old people in general) |
| *oraez limon* | teeth fall out |
| *sog puteh* | white hair |

Notes:
  a. Not having made a systematic study of such terms, those listed here represent terms employed spontaneously by the Chewong and which I picked up as part of my general studies. Other terms may be employed, such as *södn han kom klugn* (not yet able to speak), but these tend to be with reference to a particular instance, not as a general abstract indicator.
  b. All expressions starting with *ka* (has, had; indicating a past event) may be substituted with *sodn* (not yet; indicating a future event).

## BIBLIOGRAPHY

Dentan, R.K. (1968) *The Semai, a non-violent people of Malaya*. New York: Rinehart and Winston.
—— (1978) 'Notes on childhood in a non-violent context'. In Montagu, A. (ed.), *Learning non-aggression*. Oxford University Press.
Endicott, K.M. (1979) *Batek negrito religion*. Oxford: Clarendon Press.
Howell, S. (1981) 'Rules not words'. In P. Heelas and A. Lock (eds), *Indigenous psychologies*. Academic Press.
—— *Humans and superhumans; a study of the Chewong of Peninsular Malaysia*. Oxford University Press.
—— (1984) *Society and Cosmos; Chewong of peninsular Malaysia*, Oxford University Press.

# 5

# Personal Autonomy and the Domestication of the Self in Piaroa Society

Joanna Overing

For the Piaroa, a jungle people who dwell along tributaries of the Orinoco in the Guiana Highlands of Venezuela, growing up is a magical process of learning wizardry. It is the Piaroa understanding that the capabilities which allow one to exist within society are forces that come from the crystal boxes of gods who dwell beyond 'the sky of the domesticated' beneath which exists society. All intelligence is said to come from this celestial source. Thus, to achieve the maturity to accomplish any social deed, that is, to act morally, to be fertile, to garden, to hunt, to fish, to play music, or to do shamanic deeds, the individual must take various and continuous 'lessons in wizardry' (*maripa ỉeau*). These lessons are the means through which one incorporates the forces from celestial space into oneself. Because such forces for culture are both wild and dangerous, one may take them only gradually into the self and acquire no more than one is personally able to master, or to domesticate. To a large extent the individual may decide upon and choose the number and kind of forces that he/she wishes to incorporate as an inner clothing. Since maturity is always relative to the particular capability in question, the Piaroa do not differentiate sharply between developmental stages, and thus do not judge maturity as an absolute value that one has or has not achieved. They do, however, place extreme value upon personal autonomy, moderation in behaviour, and high intelligence (a rich 'life of thoughts'). It is the association of such values of maturity with the Piaroa theory of social personhood and the acquisition of the social that I wish to examine in this chapter.[1]

The Piaroa understanding of personhood entails a theory of mind or cognition that is based upon a presupposition of metaphysical dualism. Such topics as the relation between reason and emotions, between knowledge, reason and madness, between consciousness, reason and social behaviour, are issues that play an important part in daily Piaroa talk and concern that deals with everyday decisions involving principles of action, choice, and responsibility. Before continuing with the discussion of the Piaroa ideals of social maturity and their equation of such maturity with the taming by the individual of wild and poisonous forces of power acquired from the crystal boxes of the gods, I shall place the Piaroa within their political and economic setting.

## THE POLITICAL AND ECONOMIC SETTING

The two to three thousand members of Piaroaland were traditionally divided, until about 1970, into twelve to fifteen territorial units. Each territory, isolated geographically as well as politically from the next, is located along a stretch of one of the large right bank Orinoco tributaries or along several adjacent small tributaries within a headwater region. The territory is the largest social unit within Piaroaland and is normally comprised of six to seven large communal houses, the membership of each house ranging from 14 to 60 individuals. The multiple-family house is a semi-endogamous, kindred structured, residential group serving various functions within Piaroa society as an economic, kinship and ceremonial unit. Houses are separated one from the next by approximately one/half day's walk along jungle paths. The population is a highly dispersed one with great distances separating both houses and territories. In contrast, life within the communal house is carried out within densely populated spaces. Each family within the house is assigned its individual compartment; but no partition separates one hearth from the next. The central area of the house provides a communal space for work, visiting and ritual.

Although all social relationships within Piaroaland are conducted through the idiom of kinship terminology, the organisation of the territory is based upon factional politics played out among wizard leaders. The existence of the territory as a bounded, physical unit depends solely upon the specific set of alliances made between wizards and their followers, and the political organisation of each territory is predicated upon a loose and competitive hierarchy of wizard leaders (see Overing Kaplan, 1975).

The term the Piaroa use for referring to, but never addressing, a leader is *'ruwang'*, the only status label used by the Piaroa outside of kinship terms to think about and to classify social relationships. *'Ruwang'* can be variously translated depending upon context as 'master', 'shaman', 'wizard', 'sorcerer', 'priest', 'big-man'. Throughout this chapter I shall refer to the leaders as wizards, the most general of the translation possibilities, and the one that refers specifically to their powers, which are of the same source but much greater in number than the powers of wizardry acquired from the gods by the ordinary Piaroa layman. The Piaroa view their wizards, those who have achieved the status of *ruwatu* (pl.), as leaders of extraordinary power. The wizard is a 'warrior' against forces and beings who dwell in worlds beyond society. In his role as both political and religious leader, the wizard uses as weapon the knowledge he has of the other worlds to which he travels and the capabilities he has acquired from them to deal with these worlds and to handle relationships between them and the terrestrial world of social reality.

For the Piaroa, the universe is comprised of a plurality of spatially separated worlds. Such worlds are in continual interaction as beings who refuse to stay at home wander from their own world to the worlds of others. There are the worlds of the powerful tapir/anaconda gods beneath the earth from whom the force for all creation on the earth's surface originally came. There are the Piaroa lands of creation and afterworlds from whence the souls of the dead come screaming to earth to steal both people and culture. There are the worlds of the dangerous Thunder gods and Sun gods. Finally, there is the uncontrolled world from the mythic past. All forces from these worlds beyond earth of both the present and the past are wild, and it is their entrance into the Piaroa world that gives it life, disease and death. The wizard's duty is to control these forces so that life is advanced while disease and death are kept at bay. To have legitimate power within society, the wizard must use his powers benevolently to establish the well-being, the survival, and the wealth of his community.

The wizard leader, however, has very little power of coercion over the acting out of social matters. Indeed, it is he who teaches formally against such coercion, as the knowledgeable teacher of the ethical values of personal autonomy, equality, and tranquility. The Piaroa place a strong value upon the freedom of the person, have an aversion to political tyranny, and demonstrate concern over the ambiguous relationship between personal freedom and both socio-political right and constraint. As I have mentioned elsewhere (Overing, 1985), the ideal that the good society should allow for both personal freedom *and* the attainment of harmonious relationships with one's fellowmen did not have its sole origin in Enlightenment thought. Piaroa society is one with no civil law as we would ordinarily label it, no suprafamilial means of judging, controlling, and punishing ordinary misdemeanors (Overing, 1985). There are no courts, no formal council of elders. The Piaroa see custom and law to reside within the person and not without, as the section below on the learning of wizardry will detail. Logically, then, there is no need for an authority system to impose itself formally upon the members of the community.[2] As I shall discuss below, instead of civil or criminal law that punishes, it is therapy that cures which is the means through which Piaroa citizens keep themselves personally in line. Ideologically and in fact the Piaroa absolutely forbid the use of physical violence and/or physical coercion in any form, whether by wizard or layman, adult or child.

In the Piaroa view, they have eradicated coercion as a social force within their society by both refusing the possibility of a political ownership of material resources and allowing neither the political control of another's labour, the ordering of it, nor the political ownership of its products. No person in Piaroa society can order the labour of another; corporate group structure is not tied to the ownership of scarce material resources. Very briefly, sovereignty is in the hands of the gods; for it is they who own and guard all material resources and the capabilities to use them. Humans may tap these powers and as individuals use them; but they have no right to own them, nor indeed the means through which they would be able to do so.

The Piaroa rely on four food sources, that from garden cultivation, from collecting, from hunting, and from fishing (Overing Kaplan, 1975; Overing and Kaplan, in press). All products from the jungle are shared equally among members of the multiple-family house, while garden products are privately owned by the individuals whose labour produced them (or literally created them, see below). Land, however, is owned neither by individuals nor groups. A garden belongs to a family only so long as its members involve themselves in the production of it, and any person can take from the fruit trees remaining in old, untended gardens.

In the organisation of labour, men tend to be involved in intensive labour during the dry season, when they cut down the forest for gardens and engage in collective hunting and fishing expeditions. Women's intensive labour, in contrast, is concentrated in the wet season, when they plant, weed, and harvest crops. It is also during the wet season that women do the heavy work of manioc production. It might be mentioned that the Piaroa have a highly specialised technology for obtaining food from the forest: the men are skilled blowgun hunters and are famous throughout the Orinoco Basin for the quality of their curare and fish poisons. Their trapping devices for both fish and animals are varied and intricate.

Besides gender, age status is an important element in the division of labour. For each task a particular category of people is thought to be appropriate, and anyone within the category can fulfil the job. For some tasks the category is highly specific and might be tied to a specific ritual status, as might well be the case in the manufacture of some artifacts, where particular chants must be sung during the manufacturing process to make them efficacious. In turn the chore may well be kinship based. For some labour, especially with collecting duties, any person within the communal house who can work and wishes to do so may participate, whether man, woman, or child. In general, the division of labour within the communal house is highly fluid such that its members can be divided in accordance to several principles, e.g. groups of men for hunting and fishing; groups of women for gardening, firewood collecting, and food preparation; groups of men and women for collecting, preparation of game, and smoking animals; groups of children comprised of males and/or females in collecting endeavours. The boundaries of most categories of work units are equally flexible: if necessary, a man will cook, although cooking is normally a woman's job. Young men, because of the prohibitions placed on them as young hunters, must often cook their own daily meals. Men might help with manioc preparation if sufficient help is not available, as he might also aid his wife in giving birth in an emergency situation. A woman may help her husband on a hunting trip. In sum, loosely organised work parties within the multiple-family house characterise Piaroa economic life.

The organisation of labour is the most predictable with garden work, for here kinship obligations come into play. Normally, younger kin and affines work in the gardens of older kin and affines within the house until deaths occur in the older generation, at which time the pattern is reversed, e.g. widows work in the gardens of their daughters and/or daughters-in-law. In women's work, young girls and widows form a floating labour force within the house. Boys and young men perform the messenger services between houses within a territory.

A further comment should be made about the organisation of labour and its relationship to the associated values of personal autonomy and tranquillity. The Piaroa place high value upon autonomy in personal decisions with respect to labour. If a man wants to hunt he may do so; if he does not, he does not hunt. Instead, he does other things, for example, he manufactures artefacts. The Piaroa consider it very rude to comment upon such decisions, whether made by men, women or children, and it is especially odious to comment upon their relative worth. The Piaroa also place high value upon tranquillity in labour relationships. They justify their marital preference for house endogamy and cross-cousin marriage as a means of generating a co-residential organisation that will insure the most peaceful creation of relations of economic interdependence. By marrying within the house, both the husband and wife take on few new responsibilities or economic partners than those that existed before their marriage. From childhood, the bride and groom have each assisted and worked beside their same-sex in-laws in the course of working for their parents. Young people who are in danger of being married off into another house lament loudly about the dangers of such a prospect, the worst being the loss of tranquil work relationships.

As will be discussed in the sections below, it is through the learning of wizardry that each individual receives the capabilities for food acquisition and the responsibility that the knowledge of it requires.

## THE 'LIFE OF THE SENSES' AND THE 'LIFE OF THOUGHT': A THEORY OF MIND[3]

The Piaroa understand human beings to have both a 'life of the senses' (*kákwá*) and a 'life of thought' (*ta'kwarü*).[4] Such dualism of mind and body distinguishes humans from animals, who normally have only a 'life of the senses', and also from the immortal celestial gods, who have no 'life of the senses', but do have a 'life of thought'. Such ontological distinctions exist at the level of grammar and are expressed through verbs designating existence. One verb, taken from the noun *kàkwà* (the life of the senses) is *kü*, and denotes the ability to walk, to hear, to eat, to defecate, and so on. One says of animals and of humans, but not of gods, that they exist in this sense: *ime yo kü* ('there is a wild pig'); *u'bo yo kü* ('there is a man'); *tu küsà* ('I live'). A second verb that designates existence, *a'kwarü*, is derived from the noun *ta'kwarü* ('the life of thought'). Unless an animal is domesticated and has had chants of domestication sung over it by a wizard, it is generally said not to have *ta'kwarü* (Overing Kaplan, 1982). As human or as god, one can say *tü akwarusà* ('I live, I exist, I am'), but normally one cannot say 'the wild pig lives' (*ime a'kwarü*).[5]

To have *ta'kwarü*, a 'life of thought', entails the acquisition and learning of both cultural capabilities (*ta'kwanya*) and responsibility, or consciousness (*ta'kwakomenà*). *Ta'kwanya* can best be translated as the knowledge of, and the capabilities for using, the customs of one's own people, including its language, its social rules, its processing of food, its ritual. The Piaroa have the *ta'kwanya* for making blowguns, curare, and producing manioc, while White people have the *ta'kwanya* for making machines and tinned food. *Ta'kwakomenà*, on the other hand, refers to one's own responsibility for such capabilities, and is one of the most commonly used words in everyday Piaroa discourse.

As an abstract concept, *ta'kwakomenà* varies in meaning depending upon the context of its use. When one asks a Piaroa why he/she is doing something, he/she is most likely to reply '*cha'kwakomenà*', a first person possessive form which can be variously translated as 'I do it because it is *my* will' or 'because *I* want to' or 'because it is *my* custom' and 'it is of *my* people'. The last two translations, 'it is *my* custom' and 'it is of *my* people', are two different answers where the stress in the one case is upon one's own idiosyncratic manner of doing something, while in the other it is one's society's idiosyncratic ways. The expression *ta'kwakomenà* can equally well refer to one's responsibility, guilt, or fault. It further refers to comprehension: the sentence, '*tü ahúkusà cha'kwakomenà*', can be translated depending upon circumstance as 'I listen to whom I wish' or as 'I am able to understand' (Overing, 1985).

*Ta'kwakomenà*, then, refers to one's motivation or intentionality in using custom, one's comprehension or consciousness of it, one's responsibility for its use. The term overlaps with, or includes, concepts that we tend to distinguish: 'will', 'consciousness', 'rationality', and 'conscience'. Thus, it is through *ta'kwakomená* that one is able to master both one's emotions (*kákwá*) and the knowledge of and capabilities for one's culture (*ta'kwanya*). As an ontological scheme the relationships between *ta'kwarü* ('life of thought'), *ta'kwanya* (knowledge and capabilities), *ta'kwakomená* (rationality, will, and so on), and *kákwá* ('life of senses') are as follows (also see Overing, 1985):

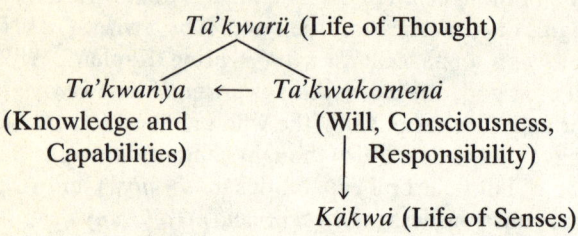

For the Piaroa there is a connection between virtue and the mastery of both 'the life of the senses' and 'the life of thought'. The good life (*adíuná*) is the tranquil one (*adiupawí*) where moderation is achieved in both. The person with good character has what is said to be the imagination to live tranquilly (*máriyá adiunákü*), or literally 'the wizardry to live tranquilly'. Such a person has attained a balance between his/her 'life of senses' and 'life of thought', and has equally mastered and developed them. One achieves such mastery through *ta'kwakomená*, one's will, consciousness, and sense of responsibility.

All formal learning among the Piaroa is of *ta'kwarü*, first of will and responsibility (*ta'kwakomená*) and then of *ta'kwanya*, the capabilities for and knowledge of culture. All learning is considered to be a domestication process through which one slowly and continually throughout life controls aspects of self taken within one. Young children before they have had their first lessons on mastery of self are called '*u'ur'o*', 'the newborn of animals', an expression that designates their undomesticated state as one of a pure 'life of senses', without the benefit of *ta'kwarü* (a life of thought), and thereby one that is yet unfit for social living.

While the Piaroa vocabulary about selfhood is a complex and rich one, they have a relatively sparse lexicon through which they express developmental stages in a person's life. They distinguish between male (man) and female (woman), and the old and the young of each category:

|  |  |  |
|---|---|---|
| Male human (man) | u'bo | Young man: *muáya* |
|  |  | Old man: *bü'o i'so* |
| Female human (woman) | i'sa'hu | Young woman: *muáyahu* |
|  |  | Old woman: *bu'a i'sahu*. |

Children are often referred to by the more general terms designating merely gender: *u'bo* and *i'sa'hu*.

The lack of regard the Piaroa demonstrate for distinguishing distinct developmental stages is not surprising; for in Piaroa theory one's self in all its various aspects is in a constant state of transformation (also see Overing Kaplan, 1982). Although all Piaroa undergo formal training at age six or seven and again at eleven or twelve, there are no ceremonies through which a person's status is straightforwardly transformed from that of childhood to adulthood. Maturity is a highly relative business, and one may consider one aspect of the self to be child-like, one's 'life of thought', for instance, and another to be mature, one's 'life of the senses'. One's *ta'kwakomena* (will, responsibility) may be well-developed, but not one's *ta'kwanya* (knowledge and capabilities). Moreover, one may lose mastery over what has previously been attained. Particular knowledge and capabilities, and this is more true for men than for women, are gradually learned throughout life, and maturity must therefore always be judged relatively in terms of 'maturity for what?'. Finally, since the acquisition of much knowledge is made only through personal choice, a person may remain a child with respect to particular knowledge for all of his/her life.

## THE LEARNING OF *TA'KWAKOMENA*: THE WIZARDRY TO LIVE TRANQUILLY

The child's first *maripa ťeau*, 'the learning of wizardry', occurs when he/she is six or seven years of age when the leading wizard of the community gathers together a group of children of appropriate age to teach them *ta'kwakomenā*, consciousness, will and responsibility. Learning *ta'kwakomenā* is the first step toward acquiring *ta'kwarü*, a 'life of thought', and before these lessons a child is not expected to be able to perform any tasks for normal living. The Piaroa with whom I lived expressed envious amazement once over the abilities of a four- or five-year-old boy who was visiting them. He was particularly close to his father and enjoyed joining him in short hunting expeditions. He specifically surprised my friends when he helped his father clean a small animal in preparation for its cooking. He was supposed to have neither the will nor the knowledge to do such a chore.

A child until the day it can walk is never placed upon the ground, but carried by its mother, grandmother, and older female siblings. It is first carried on the back in a basketry sling and then allowed to crawl up and down the person, where it has ample freedom to develop its arm and leg muscles. It sleeps in its mother's hammock. On the day the parents decide that the child can walk, at usually about 18 months or older still, the entire communal house joins the parents to praise the child as it takes its first steps on the plaza which surrounds the front of the house. After this ceremony, the child increasingly leaves its mother's hearth to play with the mixed-gender pack of free-roaming, small children who are an ever present fact of plaza and house life. In general, young children are cared for and trained by both parents. The children are open, curious and join whichever adults or older children whose interest attracts them. Since Piaroa society totally disallows the display of physical violence, and children are never physically punished, the children have no model of such action. Their play, although robust, is accompanied by very little obvious dissension. As was similarly the case with adults, I never witnessed anger expressed by children of any age through physical means. Strong anger is expressed by both adults and children through pointed silence.

Basically, in the lessons for *ta'kwakomenā*, the wizard teaches the children the art of living, the wisdom of leading a tranquil life, which is but the ideal of adulthood, and how to go about achieving it. They are taught what in our own moral philosophy are called 'the other-regarding virtues' (Overing, 1985), those that enable one to take responsibility for one's actions towards others. The virtue of living tranquilly with others is favoured in general by the Piaroa over the more self-regarding virtues such as personal courage, ambition, talent, and industry. When young men mock themselves, a characteristic aspect of Piaros humour, they often tell of a lapse in their own personal courage, when for example they were terrified during a ritual of biting ants or when lost in the forest on a hunting expedition. The wizard also teaches the children social deficiencies, especially those of ill-nature, cruelty, malice, arrogance, jealousy, dishonesty, and vanity. Such deficiencies are considered to be those most disruptive to peaceful living. The wizard chants to the celestial gods to incorporate these moral lessons into the child.

The wizard also uses story-telling, especially episodes from the mythic past to elaborate his moral lessons. Myths, in general, have high pedagogical value for the Piaroa. As I have discussed elsewhere (1985), the myth in its telling among the Piaroa is a unique event that is created by the performer for a particular audience. Although the dramatic events of the entire mythic cycle of creation are more or less known by all, the exact combination of event with event and the stress of one event over the other, or one character over another, are rarely repeated. The narrator performs for his audience; he entertains, making use of the comic and the tragic, for didactic gain. Stock characters are marched out by the teller of the myth to dramatic effect in order to underline a particular moral lesson. There is the knowledgeable, but diabolical and mad buffoon (the creator of all culture); there is the promiscuous and perfumed wandering hunter, the promiscuous and perfumed wife; there is the good gardener and the quarrelsome brothers. Consistently, the tales tell of characters whose out-of-control behaviour leads to their own unhappiness and personal disaster, and sometimes to danger for others. The quarrels of two brothers transform themselves into poisonous snakes; the wanderers never find peace; the greed for too much knowledge leads to the needless death of an old grandmother; two brothers-in-law are condemned to continue their quarrel until the end of time at the edge of the world; the lives of the violent end in horrific pain.

The wizard emphasises in the first *maripa ɫeau* the value of mastery over the emotions, mastery over the 'life of the senses'. These are the lessons required of a person before he/she acquires most other capabilities. Desires, or emotions, per se, for the Piaroa are neither good nor bad: they are merely wild until a person's will (*ta'kwakomenā*) determines their form and thereby *tames* them. The wizard also teaches the proper use of kinship terms and proper behaviour toward types of kinsmen. In brief, he is giving the children the means through which they can behave socially with others which will enable them to lead a life in harmony with them. As mastery over such skills is developed, *ta'kwakomenä* (will, responsibility) can then be further matured to care for other knowledge and capabilities beyond the first *maripa ľeau* that one learns as one grows older, e.g., hunting, fishing, gardening, the making of artefacts, childbearing, and ritual.

*Ta'kwakomenä*, it must be remembered, refers not only to responsibility, but also to personal autonomy. The wizard teaches about 'the good life', but does not order it. Free will comes only with consiousness, and first of all the consciousness of self with respect to others. The Piaroa obviously consider that responsibility to others is but one aspect of the development of personal autonomy. It is upon the child's own decision which virtues he or she in fact develops, as too it is a personal decision later about what other aspects of knowledge and capabilities that one develops, over which one must take personal responsibility, just as one must also do over one's own social relationships (see also Overing, 1985).

There is one constraint. A child whose tendency is to throw temper tantrums is never allowed adult lessons in wizardry through which he would be enabled to travel to other worlds and tap powers that reside in them. It would be too dangerous for society; for he has not illustrated sufficient mastery of *ta'kwakomenä* to control such powers if he should take them within himself.

Before a child has undergone *maripa ľeau* or *ta'kwakomenä*, parents consider it as yet unsocial and therefore unable to take responsibility for any domestic chores. As part of the initial lessons in wizardry, the wizard also chants to the gods to give the child its first *ta'kwanya*, the knowledge and capabilities for gardening, acquiring food from the forest, and so on (see next two sections). With the lessons on morality and the receiving of some *ta'kwanya* the child is expected then to take increasing responsibility for its actions and thereafter to co-operate with others in everyday activities. As children begin to participate in daily tasks, they gradually leave the mixed-gender pack of children to join the company of young people who are of their own gender. By puberty it is only with their same-sex age mates that children are by convention free to banter and joke without constraint (Overing Kaplan, 1975).

Boys, by working unsystematically with adults and instructed by them, slowly learn the skills of hunting, fishing, and the making of artefacts. They are a source of help in all difficult and collective activities, such as house-building, clearing and burning of fields, and large ceremonial preparations. For the most part, however, boys are called upon to perform tasks that they themselves enjoy and in which they express an interest. The boys, generally anxious to travel about as much as possible, will join almost any group leaving the house for reasons of work or pleasure. They are given high freedom of choice about both the amount of work they do and its type. Parents are highly considerate of the personal idiosyncracies of their children; although girls have less leeway than do the boys. A young daughter will help her father distribute game or follow her mother into the fields; but by the age of nine or ten girls are fully participating in the total range of tasks normal to female status. Unmarried young people, male and female, from the age of ten or eleven provide a labour force upon which all adults of the communal house may draw. They do not work only with their parents, but with anyone within the house who needs them or with whom the children are so inclined to work. A boy, for instance, may form an affectionate relationship with a father's brother or mother's brother, and therefore learn most skills from this kinsman rather than from a parent. The development of affectionate relationships with specific adults of one's choice is extremely important to both boys and girls, and a subject much discussed by them.

## THE BEADS OF KNOWLEDGE AND LIFE

For ornament the Piaroa wear necklaces, leg and arm bands which were traditionally made from a special granite that the Piaroa say is the outcroppings of faeces of the most powerful and dangerous force of the universe, the tapir/anaconda, which lives beneath the earth. The beads are called 'the beads of life', *kákwàwa reu*, and are as the label *kákwàwa* designates the force for the 'life of the senses' (*kákwà*), which enables one to have desires and impulses. Each child at birth, through the chanting of a wizard, receives its first set of internal beads from the celestial goddess, Cheheru. The celestial gods then gradually give to each

Piaroa during ritual most of his/her knowledge and capabilities which fill up the 'beads of life' enclosed within the body. Both *ta'kwarü* (the 'life of thoughts') and *kákwá* (the 'life of the senses') are given by the gods,[6] and as such concretised as filled up 'beads of life' within one.

The number of beads one wears tells of the knowledge that one has. Thus, as one becomes more knowledgeable, one increases one's strands of beads, and a great wizard is laden with them. Traditionally the Piaroa also wore both face and body designs. The design on face or body and the strands of beads worn on chest, legs, and wrists are but pictorial and outside representation of the types of beads, which forces of knowledge (*ta'kwanya*), are held within the body serving as its inner clothing. The stamped body markings of women are called 'designs of menstruation' (*iwa máruwá*), and speak of their knowledge of fertility. Likewise, the face designs of men are the marks of their knowledge of hunting, fishing, chanting, and sorcery. (Piaroa women are also allowed to acquire the knowledge of chanting and sorcery, but they rarely decide to do so. I heard of one example.) Men's face designs which indicate the forces of knowledge within their beads are called '*k'eráu párátámi*'. *K'eráu* is not only the name of the red dye used for these stamped designs, but is also the name of the disease of madness, a form of paranoia caused by the poison of the sun and unmastered knowledge within one (Overing, 1985). As will be explained below, the Piaroa understand most forces of knowledge to be highly poisonous, and by labelling the designs of knowledge on one's face as 'madness' (*k'eráu*), they are referring to the danger of poisonous forces contained within their 'beads of life'. Such danger is averted by the individual through continual development of *ta'kwakomená*. The hunter may have within him the capabilites (*ta'kwanya*) to hunt, but not the mastery over it (*ta'kwakomená*) sufficient to dispel the poison of such knowledge. Until he achieves such mastery, he lives the life of a promiscuous and arrogant wanderer, poisoned by the uncontrolled knowledge within him.[7]

It is within the Piaroa myths of creation that we find an explanation for the equation of knowledge and capabilities with poison, madness, and evil (Overing Kaplan, 1982; Overing, 1985). In Piaroa cosmogony the creation of most knowledge on earth carried with it madness and the incapability for moral behaviour. Kuemoi, the creator god of the abilities to use the earth's resources grew to maturity on powerful and poisonous hallucinogens, and it was this poison, and later that of the sun and other venom, which gave him the strength to create cultural resources, food and the means through which to acquire and process it. As owner of so much poisonous knowledge, his mastery over self was so lacking that he is portrayed in mythic commentary as an evil and diabolical buffoon, and as one who always displayed such excess in behaviour that he exemplifies the despicable within the Piaroa code of morality.

With the creation of cultural capabilities, mythic time became one of violent disorder where the creator gods fought continual battles for the ownership of the poisonous means to use the earth's resources. Such attempts to privatise resources and the capabilities to use them in mythic time led to violence, thievery, and social disorder. The poison of unmastered knowledge fed, and indeed was the cause of, the greed, the murder, the cannibalism, and the incest of mythic time, all asocial compulsions mocking the morality upon which the Piaroa consider society to be dependent for its continuity and tranquillity. In the Piaroa view, a major lesson from mythic history is that the private ownership of material resources and greediness for the capabilities to use them entail the impossibility of any moral order.

The powers mighty enough for the original creation of culture on earth proved, then, to be forces too destructive, wild, and poisonous to remain free as unbounded forces within a social world. No orderly social life would be possible if such forces roamed free for the taking. On the other hand, for society to exist and to continue, these powers must still be a part of it both to provide for life and to protect it. Mythic time finishes with the celestial gods capturing poisonous knowledge within their crystal boxes. Thus, in present-day time the powers for using the earth's resources are housed safely *outside* of the world where social life is played out, as too are the forces to tame it. The immortal gods who live within their celestial temple each possess crystal boxes within which are locked up their specific powers, concretised as their quartz stones, their crowns, their beads, their hunting powders, the words of their songs, and finally the light of the moon which cleans knowledge of its poison. All are powers—the knowledge of and the capabilities necessary for human existence on earth—that they now give to the Piaroa to fill up their 'beads of life'. Until he/she receives some of these forces, the child is therefore incapable of participating in social life. It is the responsibility of the wizard to bring these forces back into society, usually upon an individual's request, safely contained within beads as first protection against their poison. It is the duty of the individual to develop the *ta'kwakomena* necessary to master poisonous knowledge within one, and to accept no more of it than one can handle.

## THE LEARNING OF *TA'KWANYA*: THE WIZARDRY TO ACQUIRE FOOD AND TO BE FERTILE

After the first *maripa ɫeau*, stages in development are not strongly marked for either males or females. It is particularly the case with men that one slowly over time increases his knowledge, abilities, and mastery over self. Many ceremonies for both males and females are privately conducted, often at the most in the company of a wizard. Marriage as a ritual is a private one between bride and groom: the groom presents the bride with game, which if she accepts him as husband she cooks and gives to him. They then move their hammocks to a compartment of their own within the house. The marriage may not change the duties of bride or groom, for it may be years before they clear their own garden. Similarly, for pregnancy most ritual is carried out privately by the parents: both must follow stringent food taboos before and after the birth of the child. Also to protect the mother and the unborn child, the father must during the pregnancy each night join in the chorus to the wizard's protective chanting for the house as a whole. Funeral ritual is not elaborate: the wizard chants to send the soul of the deceased to its home of creation (Overing and Kaplan, in press). The corpse is placed by close family members into a cave in a neighbouring mountain.

For a woman, her most important *maripa ɫeau* comes at puberty. Again, the ceremony is a highly private one conducted for her at a stream by the wizard. He chants to fill her beads of life with the knowledge of fertility. Her capability for fertility is said to be her *ta'kwanya*, her *a'kwa* (thoughts), just as hunting or sorcery is the *a'kwa* of a man. The knowledge of fertility that she acquires from the gods also gives her control over it. Later, when she owns her own garden, it too is said to be her *a'kwa*, as also are her children.[8] During the girl's seclusion for her first two menses, her mother teaches her to spin cotton and to weave. Her life does not immediately change, for women do not usually marry until the age of 15–18 (and men between 18 and 25).

All boys when about twelve or thirteen undergo their second *maripa ĩeau*, which gives them specifically the internal clothing of the hunter. The age of boys varies for this ceremony, because it is held during the *Sari* festival, the great increase ceremony when animals of the hunt are brought up to earth by the wizard from their subterranean homes of creation (Overing Kaplan, 1975, 1982; Overing, 1985). The boy as part of his *maripa ĩeau* for the hunt joins the men to play musical instruments not allowed the sight of women, and he is not permitted to do so until the adults decide that he has the self-control to keep a secret from the women. All knowledge taken internally is thought to be private and often dangerous to others. The means by which animals are transformed from human to animal, and thus made edible, for their journey to the earth's surface is said to be especially dangerous knowledge for women.

The wizard conducting the *maripa ĩeau* for the boys chants over a four-day period the 'Origin of Hunting' chant, blowing from time to time its words through a flute into *sariha*, a sweet potato and manioc beer.[9] The chant tells of the goddess Cheheru giving the hunter his internal set of clothes, the blowgun, the crown, the medallions of song, the crown of song, the blowgun of song, the thoughts for hunting. As the initiate drinks the beer and takes hallucinogens, he begins to incorporate the internal bead designs the goddess also gave to her first hunter. During the ritual the boys should be able to see the words of the 'Origin of Hunting' chant, to see the 'path of the beads' that they receive through the ritual. They should see the waterfalls inside the mountains of the gods which are described by the chant; they should hear the songs within the waterfalls which are their sound. Piaroa men say that when they hear this sound of falling water, they think they have immortality, that they like the gods will never die. Later, after the *sariha* ceremony, the boys also undergo a wasp or biting ant ordeal to guarantee their hunt.[10] After this *maripa ĩeau*, boys, when they can manage the sleepless nights, join in the men's chorus to the nightly protective chanting of the wizard.

With this *maripa ĩeau* for the hunt, and similar but more powerful ritual undergone later in life, the initiate slowly increases his internal beads of knowledge, the source of his fertility as hunter, fisherman, or chanter. The *maripa ĩeau* for adult men is more elaborate and lengthier than for boys, and men undergoing these rites may choose among the specialties. The same ceremony serves for all three, and the goddess Cheheru is the source of power for each. For strength in any given area, or all three, a man must undergo these ceremonies throughout his life. Some men choose to take no more knowledge from the goddess than that they received as a young teenager.

The greatest *maripa ťeau* is that given for the learning of sorcery, for becoming a wizard. It is also the most important increase ceremony of the Piaroa, and can only be presented because of its dangers by a powerful wizard. Only the few men who wish to become wizards or who wish to increase their power as wizards undergo this ritual as initiates. Great wizards may undergo it as often as twice a year. A boy who plans his future as a wizard may begin by the age of twelve or thirteen. As part of the ceremony, one takes very strong hallucinogens, under the influence of which the initiate's 'master of thoughts', homunculus who dwells in his eyes, travels to the celestial gods for gifts of beads of power and knowledge. In all other *maripa ťeau* it is the wizard's homunculus who travels to obtain knowledge for his initiate, to move forces of culture into the social world from their protected encasement within the crystal boxes of the gods. It is because the initiate himself must approach the gods and bring poisonous knowledge back to this world that this ceremony is the most dangerous of all *maripa ťeau*.

The initiate's 'master of thoughts' takes from the crystal boxes of the gods their crowns, their leg bands, their multi-coloured strings of beads, their 'blown' powder for defence, their thrones of songs, the words of the songs, the light of the moon. It is the light of the moon that the Piaroa describe as the 'light of chants', and which enables the wizard to see the words of songs within the beads inside his body. It is this light that also comes from the words of the songs themselves, and as a wizard chants this light for him turns night into day as it emanates from the words of the chants. It provides both a protective shield around him and allows him to see worlds which for the ordinary man would be invisible. This light of the moon, visible only to the wizard, allows him to defend his house against its enemies (Overing Kaplan, 1982). With the forces that the powerful wizard takes from the crystal boxes of the gods, he can battle against the powers of mythic times, wild untamed forces from other worlds that endanger the health and the life of members of his community.

To acquire great powers of both sorcery and chanting, one must undergo these ceremonies many times.

The powerful hallucinogens taken during the *maripa ïeau* for great wizardry also give the initiate the means for becoming a bountiful provider as one who maintains the fertility of the land. One of the most notable increase visions for the initiate is that of seeing conjoined, in the centre of the vision, a sample of each type of animal of the hunt from beneath the earth in miniature form. Such a vision speaks of the wizard's future power for transforming animals from human to animal form when transporting them up to earth from their homes of creation.

Thus, in the Piaroa theory of knowledge, men who undergo these most powerful of lessons in wizardry are the best hunters in Piaroaland. A person's knowledge and ability is for the Piaroa literally determined by how much *maripa ïeau*, the formal learning of wizardry, that one goes through. It was once said to me of a man who daily brought in the most game in the house where I lived that he was not a great hunter, for he knew nothing about hunting. He was set in contrast to the wizard of the house, who was described as a great hunter, although he rarely hunted and was often, because of the drugs he took, clumsy at it. The practical hunter had not gone beyond his boyhood *maripa ïeau* for the hunt, and the capabilities given to him by the gods during that ceremony allowed him the skills necessary for the killing of game in the forest. To behave correctly, morally, and to have the skills for normal everyday economic activities require for both men and women no more than the wizardry lessons undergone when six or seven years old and later at twelve or fourteen. To take within oneself a larger number of capabilities from the crystal boxes of the gods gives one a greater awareness of the worlds of the cosmos, its forces, a knowledge perhaps through travel of what the cosmos is. These capabilities also give the wizard the knowledge to transform forces from other worlds, and it is through his powers for transformation that he makes fertile the forest and supplies it with game for the benefit of the practical hunter.

What it means to be a hunter, then, must be placed in wider context for the Piaroa than is the case in our own usage and understanding. For them hunting is the cultural ability to acquire animal meat and to make it edible for human consumption. The hunter who strikes down a wild peccary with a blowgun dart is participating in only one aspect of this process. The wizard transforms human to animal flesh, transports it to earth, and then, after the earthly kill, transforms the animal flesh into edible vegetable form (Overing Kaplan, 1975). With these capabilities, he is the greatest of all hunters.

It is important to note that also in Piaroa epistemology information and skills taken in casually through everyday listening, experience, and discussion are undervalued, except when associated with the level of formal training, the incorporation of beads of knowledge, with which they are associated. Unless one has been through the formal training for a particular ability, one says and believes one is ignorant of it. No matter how much commentary one hears, and that of the wizard is daily and considerable, given for the benefit of appropriate learners through his chants and stories, one is able to understand such instruction only if the beads within one are filled with the force, the specific capability, to do so. Old women, for instance, are frequently extremely knowledgeable, to the extent that much of their speech is filled with the metaphors of chant language, a consistently obfuscatory and grammatically anomalous 'old talk' that speaks the authentic relations among things and the authentic (true) names of things. Although young people are intimidated by the rich language of the old, who are given respect for their esoteric speech, the old women wail, and do so in formal chanting, of their own ignorance of the sacred, of their inability to do a wizard's job, and thus of their dependence upon men.

## PERSONAL AUTONOMY, PRIVACY, AND THE DOMESTICATION OF THE SELF

In this concluding section I shall discuss the relationship between individualism in Piaroa society and the Piaroa concept of selfhood. The ideology is one that places great stress upon self-control, and not social control. Proper behaviour is of course highly valued by the Piaroa, and its code continuously taught. Nevertheless, the Piaroa are as allergic to a notion of social 'rule' as to the idea of 'the right of command'. A Piaroa marries correctly into the appropriate category of kinsman, because to do otherwise is unthinkable: to marry correctly is not so much a rule, but the natural order of things. I was emphatically told that there was no residence 'rule'. There are kinsmen with whom it is proper to live, but the final choice is always left to the individual as a private decision. I have discussed above the Piaroa attitude toward work, an area where no one can order another to compliancy. The leaders can request help in preparing for ceremonies or house-building; they cannot order it. One is the absolute proprietor of one's capacity to labour. Basically, one cannot order another in most decisions because to do so would be rude beyond belief. It would be tampering with the inner self of another, and therefore an intrusion on the other's privacy. The Piaroa associate such intrusion with shame.

One's inner self is comprised of unsocial, wild, and unspeakable forces. All powers within one are private to the self and must be privately controlled and domesticated. It would be indecent to disclose their shape, colour, or characteristics. The capacity to menstruate and the capacity to hunt are equally shameful for disclosure to the outside world. Both are considered the fertility and the intelligence of the person with whom they dwell, and as such they are both privately tamed primal energies.

It is not only knowledge that is a private matter, but one's named soul which the wizard calls into one at birth is as private and unsocial a power as the forces later taken from the crystal boxes of the gods. A child is addressed by name until its first *maripa ťeau* lessons, a practice which reflects the child's unsocialised status, the recognition of its lack of control and therefore lack of shame. Thereafter to address the child by name is considered equivalent to exposing its genitals to public view. One's named soul is the immortal aspect of self which returns to its home outside this world when one dies. In this home it lives a totally non-social existence, stripped of association with all the knowledge and fertility that was necessary for social life. All domestication of self is lost at death (Overing and Kaplan, 1984). Because it is a non-social aspect of self, it is highly shameful to expose the named soul in social life.

The social world, then, is where wild elements—the named self, the forces for culture, and the life of the senses—are tamed privately by individuals to provide an inner self for each. The individual demonstrates his/her success at the domestication of the complex inner aspects of self through controlled and moderate behaviour. If one loses restraint over oneself, one becomes a nuisance or even a danger to society (Overing, 1985). If one indulges in incest, steals, is promiscuous, laughs wildly, or in other ways, even with sorcery, ignores social obligations through excessive behaviour, one is not punished. Rather, one is judged ill, and as with all illness, one then goes to a wizard to be cured in order to master the undomesticated and poisonous knowledge within one which affected one's ability to act responsibly (Overing, 1985). The wizard then helps the patient in his/her private battle to regain mastery over both the 'life of thoughts' and the 'life of the senses' within him/her.

As always with fact and theory, the truth lies somewhere in between. The Piaroa greatly fear the shame of any loss of personal autonomy, as their distaste for commands well illustrates. For the Piaroa, the demonstration of a lack of control over the self is mockable, the foolishness of excess, and its shame, as well as its dangers, is best portrayed in the example of the mad buffoon of mythic time, the first owner of all cultural capabilities. Thus, the individual is prevented from excessive behaviour not only by wizardry skill, but also through the thoroughly social means of mockery and teasing which are liberally used by one's peer group in Piaroaland (and it is through these techniques that I inadvertently made friends with wilful teenage boys). As Girard has pointed out (1978, pp. 124ff), all forms of comedy are associated with a loss of autonomy and self-possession. Laughter strips its object of both its sovereignty and its individuality. Each Piaroa knows that his/her own show of excess will be met by disdain, and in a society where high value is placed upon one's freedom of will, the threat of the loss of personal autonomy is a sharp check on such display (also see Overing, 1985).

Finally, Piaroa individualism, as that of the West, focuses upon the happiness of the person living within society. Stemming from the Piaroa view of human social nature, is a moral philosophy that speaks of the necessity of personal restraint. It is human nature to have conjoined within the person wild desires and poisonous knowledge, both of which must be mastered by personal will. It is through such mastery that a happy life can be achieved, the tranquility which is valued above all else by the Piaroa. It is here, in the mode of attaining happiness, that we have a contrast with Western thought. In Western individualism, in most of its various manifestations, the subject is seen as creatively acting on and sometimes against society as object; whereas in Piaroa individualism the subject restrains him/herself from imposing the self upon society. Yet, at the same time, culture, which is the wild card, has its own will, and it is culture that, through choosing individuals, imposes itself upon society.

Thus, the Western notion of the individual is somewhat akin as a construct to the Piaroa notion of culture.

## NOTES

1. The fieldwork upon which this paper is based was carried out in 1968 and 1977 with M.R. Kaplan, to whom I am deeply indebted in general for data collected jointly. The research in 1977, upon which much of this presentation is based, was financed by the SSRC Grant HR5028, Central Research Funds of the University of London, London School of Economics Research Funds, and the Institute of Latin American Studies Travel Funds. The SSRC also later gave me a Research Grant (HRP6753) which allowed me the time to analyse data acquired in 1977. My fieldwork was not directly focused upon socialisation, but upon the Piaroa theory of personhood and mind, an emphasis this paper reflects. The topic at hand is highly related to some of the issues upon which I have recently been focusing; thus, much of the data presented in this chapter is scattered through various published and unpublished papers written over the past few years. See the bibliography.
2. See Overing (1975) for extensive discussions on the politics of wizardry.
3. See Overing (1985) for a lengthier discussion of the Piaroa theory of mind.
4. The distinction is similar to the Platonic one between the 'pleasures of the senses' and the 'pleasures of the mind'.
5. Since plants and objects have neither a 'life of the senses' nor a 'life of thoughts' a third positional 'verb' provides their reference, as 'upright', 'close', 'horizontal', 'lying on a rafter', and so on.
6. I do not know whether *ta'kwakomena* is incorporated into the beads of life, concretised there as knowledge is. The Piaroa do say, however, that *ta'kwarü* is within the beads, which would then include both *ta'kwanya* (knowledge) and *ta'kwakomena* (will, responsibility).
7. See Overing (1985) on the association of beauty and cleanliness with the mastery of *ta'kwanya*.
8. I know of no specific garden ritual for a woman's knowledge, which may well be a lapse in my field notes.
9. The words of a wizard's chants for protection against disease and the curing of it are likewise blown into both water and honey to be drunk by patients and members of his house. See Overing Kaplan (1982), Overing and Kaplan (in press) for greater detail on this process.
10. See Overing and Kaplan (in press) for greater detail on these ordeals and the *Sari* ceremony in general.

## BIBLIOGRAPHY

Girard, R. (1978) 'To double business bound'. *Essays on literature, mimesis and anthropology*. Baltimore: The Johns Hopkins University Press.

Overing Kaplan J. (1975) *The Piaroa; a people of the Orinoco Basin: a study in kinship and marriage.* Oxford: Clarendon Press.

—— (1982) 'The paths of sacred words: Shamanism and the domestication of the asocial in Piaroa society'. Presented in symposium on 'Shamanism in Lowland South American Societies' [J. Overing Kaplan, organiser], 44th International Congress of Americanists, Manchester.

Overing Kaplan, J. (1984) 'Dualisms as an expression of difference and danger: marriage exchange and reciprocity among the Piaroa of Venezuela'. In K. Kensinger (ed.), *Marriage Practices in Lowland South American Societies.* University of Illinois Press.

—— (1985) 'There is no end of evil: the guilty innocents and their fallible god'. In D. Parkin (ed.), *The Anthropology of Evil.* Blackwells.

Overing, J. and Kaplan, M.R. (in press) 'Los Wötuha'. In *Los Aborigenes de Venezuela*, vol. 3. Caracas: Foundacion La Salle.

# 6

# Concepts and Learning among the Punan Bah of Sarawak

Ida Nicolaisen

This chapter explores ideas concerning human nature and cognition, and their implications on actual socialisation practices among the Punan Bah, a tiny ethnic group of the Bornean rain-forest. The study focuses on Punan Bah conceptions of adults as to the understanding of children at various age levels. It presents some observations on children's acquisition of knowledge of the reality in which they grow up, especially on their assessment of self and of social differentiation, a critical aspect of Punan Bah culture.[1]

**THE SOCIETY**

The Punan Bah are a minor ethnic group of central Sarawak. They were classified by Leach (1950) in his socio-economic survey of the various ethnic groups here, as belonging to what he termed the Kajang complex, comprising a number of small groups, which presumably lived in central Sarawak prior to the larger and more well-known Iban, Kayan and Kenyah. The Punan Bah are one of the larger Kajang groups, but still number only about 1500 persons. Half live in three settlements along the Rejang river in the seventh Division while the other half lives highly scattered in four settlements in the fourth Division. They take their name after the Bah and Punan rivers, tributaries of the Rejang, the region believed to be their land of origin.

Like most indigenous groups in Borneo, the Punan Bah live in longhouses, magnificent timber constructions, which may accommodate up to 350 persons. They consist of a gallery running all along the frontside of the house and from here doors open up into the rooms of the various families. The gallery is predominantly the men's area. It is here they spend the major part of their spare time. Also boys stay here when not playing at the river. Women on the other hand stay mainly in the rooms, although this pattern of behaviour is rapidly changing. The longhouses vary greatly in size, and so do the rooms. The latter are usually between $3 \times 5$ to $4 \times 8$ meters. Most families have an additional kitchen of sufficient size to allow the family to take its meals there. But most rooms are crowded, with an average family size of 9.4, and when a family goes to sleep at night there are persons lying all over the place.

With up to several hundred persons under the same roof, with an additional one hundred dogs, plus chickens, fighting-cocks and with a cultural pattern according to which very little use is made of the surrounding area either for social purposes or for activities like the making of tools, the beating of sago, pounding of rice, chopping of firewood, weaving of mats or even at times the building of canoes all of which may take place within the house—with all this confined activity it seems no wonder that restrained behaviour is highly valued. The Punan Bah move slowly, never hastily or noisily, and never rush hither and thither. Conversations are quiet and children are admonished not to shout.

Punan Bah society is hierarchical, consisting traditionally of three classes: aristocrats, commoners and slaves, the last only being possessed by aristocrats. Today slavery has ceased to exist in its original form, and some longhouse communities are even without aristocratic families.

The social system is founded upon a bilateral ideology, the kinship terminology being of the Eskimo–Hawaiian type. Residence is predominantly uxorilocal, and households are usually formed by extended matri-families. Authority over family resources and heirlooms as well as economic decisions on family affairs, for instance on the size of brideprice, is vested in the eldest person of a sibling group, who stays on in the natal family, i.e. stays on in the room. Due to the predominance of uxorilocality these family heads are therefore generally women.

The Punan Bah maintain a living partly by swidden-agriculture with hill-rice as the main crop, partly by hunting, fishing and gathering. Until shortly after the Second World War rice cultivation was based on collective labour. Families would join together in large groups and work each other's fields in turn, women and men, old and young all would lend a hand according to their ability and to the division of labour by sex. The cultivation of rice is still to a large extent carried out by workgroups, usually based on kinship, but nowadays the Punan Bah exchange workdays with the result that families that are at a disadvantage in terms of labour can find it difficult to grow the rice they need. Ordinary Punan Bah families, (i.e. commoners), still perform corvée labour on the rice-fields of the aristocrats, who besides using the store of rice for their own and their families' consumption and for the entertainment of visitors to the longhouse, are expected to provide for or at least contribute to the subsistence of any family which falls short of rice. Any major catch of game and fish brought to the longhouse was traditionally shared among all families, including prescribed shares for the aristocratic one. The improvement of the means of transportation on the rivers and the subsequent introduction of deep freezers by Chinese shopkeepers has brought about a change in this pattern. Game and fish can now be exported to markets downriver, and a major part of these items are therefore now sold. However, food is still to a large extent shared in Punan Bah society, although not in the institutionalised ways as before.

The rivers, mountains and the jungle set the physical frame for Punan Bah life. They know this natural setting by heart and from its richness create a living. These surroundings have also a spiritual dimension which offers emotional satisfaction and coherence in their lives, while at the same time placing demands on them. The Punan Bah believe that the world was created by the god Bua about twelve generations ago. They are themselves his descendants. The first few generations of Bua's offspring were still endowed with supernatural powers, and these ancestors, the Etun Oa, still live among them and are called upon whenever they are in despair. The Etun Oa have their longhouses next to those of the Punan Bah and, although invisible, these houses and their spiritual inhabitants are as real to the Punan Bah as their own material community. There are other invisible 'societies' in Punan Bah territory: the spirits of which some are anthropomorphic as against the 'true spirits' which do not stay in organised communities but wander hither and thither and are often envious and vicious. Omens were formerly observed to avoid their evil designs, but this practise was given up upon the adoption of the Bungan cult, a revivalist religious movement which spread among the ethnic groups of the Borneo interior in the 1950s. Instead the goddess Bungan is implored to keep the evil spirits in check and protect her adherents. The pattern of interaction with the spiritual world is considered one of exchange. Spirits must be ritually invoked and served with blood, food and drinks according to their nature to establish or reinforce relationships of mutual obligation. Benevolent spirits may otherwise lose interest in human beings and refrain from offering their assistance, while the malevolent ones have to give up their evil designs once they have accepted the offerings, or they will themselves face an ill fate.

Cultural competence demands an intimate knowledge of this reality, of the visible as well as the invisible dimensions of the environment. Individuals can only achieve a happy and successful life if they adapt to these conditions and acknowledge and respect the autonomy of living creatures as well as spiritual beings. The latter are ever present and demand respect each in their way, or they may get offended and take revenge. Deferential behaviour is therefore the very foundation of all interaction. Those of an inferior position or younger age must respect those of a superior or elder. One must learn to be afraid, the Punan Bah say, or one is bound to end up in misery.

The Punan Bah are obsessed with status and their personal standing in society. The fight for social recognition and for prestige, for 'news', *denge*, as it is often called, is fought at many levels and in many ways.

Society is, as mentioned, hierarchical with aristocrats, commoners and formerly also slaves, previously with differential access to the means of production, and with an obligation on the part of the commoners to perform corvée labour for the aristocrats. But class differences manifest themselves in a number of ways with regard to rights and duties as well as to behaviour. Punan Bah see these differences as originating in descent, and the class structure as a given, ideal order perpetuating itself through class endogamy. However, descent can be manipulated, and social mobility occurs as well within as between classes. The aristocratic class is numerically small. There is only a single family in each longhouse. The slaves are today more or less incorporated in the class of commoners, but status differences between the two are still socially significant. Status distinctions between the commoners themselves are not based so much on variance at the level of subsistence, due to the extended co-operation and sharing of food, although a skilful handling of such assets is of significance. Nor is the possession of wealth, or valuables like bronzes, old china, etc. which are exchanged as bridewealth, decisive. Such distinctions are dependent as much on the personal behaviour and achievements of the members of the various families, on whether they possess the self-restraint, diligence and blameless manners necessary to compel the respect of others.

Concern about personal standing goes far beyond the struggle between the classes. It permeates every aspect of daily behaviour also within the families to an extent which can be difficult for an outsider to appreciate fully. The constant focus on personal status and related appropriate behavioural norms is intimately linked with, on the one hand, an outspoken anxiety of not living up to given expectations and emotional outlets here, such as the feeling of shame, and on the other a pronounced self-assessment. Punan Bah adults are masters of the art of impression-management, of elegantly camouflaging their self-praise. They can express themselves with the greatest subtlety about their own qualifications and at the same time in a refined way sap those of others by means of a sophisticated use of apt metaphors.

From the age of two to three years children begin to be concerned about their personal standing and sensitive to the responses they receive in interaction with others. The older they grow, the more they are on their guard, reacting promptly to any deviation from expected response with signs of shyness, by feeling ashamed or by becoming angry if they feel that they lose face. All these reactions are designated by the term *menjar*, though in actual fact it covers a range of meanings.

Punan Bah children thus grow up in a society characterised on the one hand by economic co-operation, an extended sharing of food and services, and consideration for and respect of others, while on the other obsessed with social status and self-promotion. Although the atmosphere is highly competitive, strict rules govern the ways in which the fight for public recognition can be carried on.

**CONCEPTS OF THE HUMAN BEING**

The Punan Bah view the human being as a physiological as well as a spiritual phenomenon. The foetus is created out of male sperm; the woman functions as a receptacle that shelters the foetus during the period of gestation. In accordance with this view, a child's class-affiliation is determined solely by that of its father. When a child is born it is endowed with *etun*, i.e. life-giving forces. These are described as the souls of the souls, and they together with the souls proper make up the invisible spiritual substance of human beings. Females get six souls, males seven, though why this is so, and which soul it is that females do not possess, no one can tell.

The Punan Bah believe in reincarnation. When an ancestor wants to return to this world his of her main soul, the soul of the body or the 'true soul', as it is also called, and its *etun* enter a descendant. The souls of male ancestors enter male descendants only, those of female ancestors their female descendants. Persons who are not blessed by ancestral presence remain sterile. While the ancestral *etun* ensures that the child begotten by the descendant is born and stays alive, his or her true soul does not enter the child immediately upon birth but takes refuge in the breasts of the child's mother. Due to this separation of body and soul small children must be in intimate contact with their mothers all the time. If a mother leaves her child for more than a short while, the child may fall ill and eventually die. For the same reason a new-born child is considered little more than a mere body of blood, bones and flesh. Only gradually as the soul of the body and the other souls take up residence in the child, does it become human.

The souls arrive in a given order reflecting Punan Bah understanding of the motor and cognitive development of children. The true soul enters the child more permanently around the time it has its first tooth, at the age of about five to eight months. Only from then on is the child considered a proper human being. Only then is it named, and only then can it be buried in the prescribed way if it dies. For only then is there a point in carrying out the death-rituals, which serve to guide the soul of the body along on its final journey to the realm of the dead. Though this soul stays with the child from the age of five to eight months, it may occasionally stray off and follow the child's mother even till the child is about seven years old. It is to ensure that it does not get lost, that one can hear a mother calling out for the soul of her child when for instance leaving her farm. 'Come back with me, smell of Kedi' she shouts, when stepping into the canoe, the word smell being a metonym of the soul, thus urging the soul of her son Kedi to return with her in case it has been following her to the field. The true soul is visualised as identical in shape and looks to the body, but it is able to transform itself into such a tiny shape, that it can sit on the tip of a knife, as it may do during seances with spirit-mediums.

The soul of the stomach is the second soul to enter the child. It may arrive almost immediately upon birth revealing its presence through the child's wish to suck, or it may come after a few days. Then comes the soul of the eyes, which is there when a child can follow the lamps with its eyes, and later again the souls of the arms and the legs, linked with the development of motor faculties. Following these, the soul of the ears enters the body. The latter is critical for cognitive development. If a child has 'no ears' i.e. if this spiritual capacity is deficient, and this reveals itself if the child does not listen and pay attention to what adults say, its cognitive development will be hampered and the child in the end doomed to be a failure. Here the Punan Bah do not only think of physical disabilities but also of people who do not live up to general expectations of appropriate social behaviour. The last to arrive are the souls of vulva and penis respectively. These do not enter the body till the child has reached its teens, and becomes sexually mature.

The souls of children are elusive as already indicated. They can easily be scared away, and children must be handled with the greatest care at least till they are about four years old when they become more secure. Moreover, children have no powerful guardian spirits, *otu tua*. As these are considered a pre-requisite for staying alive, since it is only due to their intervention that attacks of malevolent spirits are warded off, children are highly vulnerable. They are an easy prey and die more readily than grown-ups.

These beliefs have implications for socialisation practices. Young children are for instance never punished physically so as not to scare off their souls. Older children, say from five and upwards, may be given a smack on the legs, but not on the head or the back, as the child's *otu tua* is believed to reside here, clinging invisibly to the back of the child. Rather than beating older children, adults will punish them either with smoke from a burning stick, chasing the child with it or in grave cases holding the head of the child into a basket filled with smoke, or the child is pinched in the arm or the thigh. But physical punishment of children is a rare phenomenon, and it is resorted to only if an adult loses her temper, or if a child will not stop crying. For under no circumstance should one let it go on weeping. A child may do so if one of its souls is not staying put within the body. If this is the case, it must be calmed immediately and brought to rest if fatal consequences are to be avoided. But children also cry just because they are angry or sullen, and in such cases, if nothing else works, the crying may be brought to a halt with a punishment, with the justification that crying attracts the ever lurking malevolent spirits.

## COGNITION AND COGNITIVE DEVELOPMENT

The human mind, intelligence, character and emotions are located in the internal organs of the human body. The liver is considered to be the very centre of life, and it is from here that the breath, *ingad*, stems. *Ingad* not only means breath, it also denotes the human spirit. It embraces consciousness as well as character, conscience and emotions, qualities all located with *ingad* in the liver. The intellect and the ability to reason are placed on the other hand in the gallbladder.

The size and appearance of the two organs reflect the faculties of the individual. Persons with good characters, who demonstrate that they have feelings for other people, are said to possess big, red livers, while small, black ones are indicators of wicked predispositions. Bad behaviour is often described with the simple statement, that the person in question has 'no liver'.

It tallies with this view that the Punan Bah used to take omens of the livers of sacrificed pigs. Similarly, a person's intelligence is dependent on the size of his or her gallbladder and mental diseases, it is believed can be caused by a dislocation of the gallbladder.

Whether a person has the one or the other predisposition is generally considered incidental. Although the foetus is created solely out of male sperm, mental faculties and character do not derive from the father. Considerate persons may well have children that do not know how to behave, it is claimed; and mentally less well-developed men can have bright children. Nor does one explain these variations as mere replicas of the ancestors reborn, but rather as a matter of fate, *ukon*. Physical appearance is believed by some to derive from the father, by others from the ancestors. Physical handicaps are ascribed to the improper behaviour of the parents, mainly the father, during the period of gestation. This does not imply that a person's character and intellectual faculties, his or her predisposition, is a simple given fact, nor that human beings are born either good or bad, intelligent or stupid. Punan Bah notions are more complex although far from clear on this issue. Human growth is cumulative in their view, and can be compared to that of plants. Like these, individuals must be nourished to thrive. Children in particular are frail and sensitive, just like young seedlings, and must be taken good care of. The assimilation of humans and human growth to that of plants is a recurrent theme in Punan Bah beliefs and rituals. They believe for instance that the supreme God, *Otu Telangan*, has a tree for each living person planted in his heaven. If this tree, the 'life-tree' is growing well so is its human counterpart. Ill-health is referred to metaphorically by saying that the 'leaves are dropping' and at curing rituals a branch of a tree called *Kaju Da'an* is put up next to the altar, and offerings are made to this symbolic representation of the 'life-tree', while the old men urge *Otu Telangan* to do likewise and look after its counterpart in heaven, so that it will recover and regain strength.

Punan Bah understanding of cognitive development tallies with these ideas. It is conceived of as a gradual process, and not in terms of a set of stages, through which an individual passes, defined e.g. by age. The Punan Bah have rarely any idea of their actual age. They do, however, know among kin and fellow longhouse dwellers who is the older, as relative age plays an important role in social behaviour. Only between age mates is deferential behaviour modified.

Linguistic categories group people according to their position in the life cycle. This classification is not based on age, but reflects social categories: *benie*, i.e. babies, which are considered only partly human, as they have not yet been fully endowed with souls; *kolovi*, i.e. children from the age of walking up to that of sexual maturity, when they will be called *kolovi oro* and *kolovi elei*, i.e. child-woman and child-man. These terms cover unmarried adults in general, all bachelors and spinsters, as long as they are sexually mature, including divorced persons. Upon marriage they will be called *oro* or *elei*, i.e. woman and man.

No rites of passage mark the transition from one stage in the life cycle to the next today, except for the making of a separate bed for a girl, when she is considered old enough to receive nightly visits by young men. But this takes place without any rituals or celebrations, and need not even coincide with the beginning of the girl's menstruation. The formal establishment of relations between boys and a specific category of guardian spirits which formerly took place in connection with headhunting rituals, ceased to exist about the time of the Second World War. This ritual did not imply any change in the boy's social position and it might take place at any age from four or five years up to adulthood. It was solely dependent on the outcome of headhunting expeditions, and there could be long gaps between the holding of these rituals. There are no marriage ceremonies either; the man simply moves to the girl's room and eats there. Only if virilocal residence is later adopted will the transfer of the bride be ritually marked. With the introduction of the Bungan cult, some families have begun to perform minor rituals at births and marriages to ask the goddess for protection.

Human beings thus develop gradually, they mature. 'A child is like an unripe fruit, it must ripen, only then will you know the taste of it', it is said metaphorically. Character formation and the accomplishment of intellectual skills develop steadily through infancy and adulthood. This is an imperceptible process without leaps or sudden dramatic changes. But the two do not necessarily go hand in hand. A person may well turn out a good character but only modestly well equipped intellectually. This is a topic frequently and openly discussed. A woman may sit and talk about her husband in his presence, e.g. describing him as a nice and well-meaning person, a good provider, one with a good *ingad*, while at the same time deploring his lack of intellectual skills due to which he will never rise in society.

While one may begin to assess the character of a child in terms of its moral behaviour already from an early age, say about three to four years, intelligence is, as the Punan Bah understand it, *inter alia* linked with the capacity to express oneself in abstract terms, and to do so eloquently with an apt use of metaphors. The concept thus refers to a communicative competence. If a person is 'intelligent' he or she knows how to speak. There is, however, more to it than this. Intelligence implies cultural competence, it is dependent on knowledge, traditionally of *adet*—the traditions and norms of the society. Intelligence does therefore only emerge gradually, and does not manifest itself properly till adulthood. At that stage of life on the other hand, it is critical with regard to the respect in which an individual is held. It is a precondition for the achievement as well as the maintenance of social status. No adult, not even an aristocratic longhouse leader will be truly respected, unless he is able to speak meaningfully and spiritedly on *adet*, though there are indications that this is changing.

Over the last ten years, schooling has become an increasingly prominent feature in the socialisation of children. Punan Bah adults are highly conscious of the changes going on in Sarawak, not only of the direct impact that these have on their own society. They realise that a new way of life is around the corner, and that their traditional culture is doomed to disappear. Knowledge of the wider social setting of which their own society is only a part has always been highly valued, but they believe that it will become critical as is definitely the case. 'The future is for those who know how to hold a pencil' as they sometimes express it, and adults increasingly hold the opinion, that school learning, the 'new wisdom', not only paves the way for their children to get a good position outside their own society, but that it will also be a powerful tool for climbing the social ladder and gaining influence within it. This shift in evaluation of the kind of knowledge which is of importance in the changing life situation, is influencing the concept of intelligence. The concept is now used ever more frequently to characterise persons, who possess and make sensible use of this new kind of information, rather than those who operate mainly within the traditional sphere of knowledge. In the long run it may affect the notions of the intellectual faculties of the two sexes, as also sex roles are undergoing drastic changes these years, though so far, it is maintained, there are no such differences. Women have the same intellectual dispositions as men in the view of both sexes. This is probably so because although women and men are socialised into different roles and they do to a certain extent acquire different cognitive skills, women have the same knowledge of *adet* as do men. They are even better informed on current social affairs. Women can devote themselves much more to such issues than men, and they are therefore at an advantage when social problems arise, opinions have to be formed, and judgements made. Women manifest their intellectual capacities less frequently in public speeches than do men, and they rarely obtain the same oratorical practise. Women may therefore ask male relatives to speak for them e.g. in court cases. But they may nevertheless express themselves with great subtlety in a narrower circle, and so live up to the requirements of 'intelligence'.

The Punan Bah with whom I discussed cognition and how

cognitive development takes place had no definite answers or solutions to these questions. They found it difficult to grasp, they said, how individuals learn 'the human way'. Nevertheless they do possess elements of an explanation, as we have seen. They believe that cognition is possible only through an intricate interrelationship between innate conditions (the liver and the gallbladder), the senses (the soul of the ears and the soul of the eyes), and the spiritual capacity that is potentially inherent in these and the other souls. In a proper combination, these factors enable the individual to make sense of the information she or he gets from the surroundings, including the moral instructions that a person is subject to both as a child and as an adult. I shall not push the view of the Punan Bah on cognition much further or try to establish a coherent logical construction out of the abovementioned elements, that the Punan Bah do not do themselves. It would make them uneasy if I did, for they are highly cautious whenever they express themselves about the nature of things or causes of events. From this point of view they would make excellent scientists. Their conclusion is, that we humans know little about these questions, and that, ultimately, it is a matter of fate whether a person learns 'the human way' or not. Some never do, and the Punan Bah consider quite simply, that they have no livers, i.e. they are no good. Such persons are like the chaff carried away when winnowing the pounded rice.

The Punan Bah have a general view of their intellectual faculties and of their selves which is rather negative. They come back to their lack of understanding and lax morals again and again. 'We Punan Bah are bad', is a recurrent statement, and discussions on how to improve this state of affairs are countless. The deplorable situation is neither believed to be caused by evil spirits nor is it because their guardian spirits fail to assist them. Rather it is only due to the positive influence of these forces that people do not behave more foolishly or quarrel all the time. No, the low standard is due to their own carelessness, to the fact that they do not exert themselves, they do not care to take the pains to develop and thus live up to their own normative values. No opportunity is missed to touch upon this painful subject and to moralise. Moral instructions, *tabara*, are an institutionalised part of all major social events. This general attitude does not imply, however, that individual behaviour is self-effacing, quite the contrary: self-assertion is pronounced.

## LEARNING PUNAN BAH CULTURE

The Punan Bah frequently use the expression 'the human way', *lengan linou* to denote their culture and cultural behaviour in general. In discussions on the upbringing of children the critical elements of 'the human way' are crystallised as the aims of socialisation, as the 'musts' that children have to learn to cope in an honourable way with this world of status-obsessed characters and touchy spiritual beings. In Punan view children must first and foremost learn self-restraint as well as rules governing interpersonal behaviour and relations with the spiritual beings. Less weight is put on other aspects of the culture such as the more technical skills required to make a living.

I have already mentioned that adults see little point in any systematic teaching of small children, due to the belief that only from the age of about five when the souls stay put, will children have the ability to reason, and only from then on can one begin to admonish them with any hope of success. Still even from that time on socialisation practises are rather incidental. Adults rely more on setting children a good example than on formal instruction. The latter is only offered occasionally and then with a subtlety that tallies with general normative behaviour. Admonitions are paraphrased to the extent that children do not always catch the meaning. Scoldings are rare, as it is believed that such behaviour exposes the children to grave risks, to *tula*. *Tula* implies that guardian spirits leave their protégés for shorter or longer periods, for instance out of shame on a deserved reprimand to the person they guard. A child may therefore fall ill or even die, if it is severely scolded. Adults make use of one educational device, however, and that is to frighten their children. They threaten them with evil spirits and with *penjamun*, i.e. persons who practise human sacrifice and therefore come to abduct children. They point out visiting Europeans claiming that they will give the children injections, etc. These attempts to frighten children are sometimes so successful that the children scream with fear, but this will only make the adults laugh. For children should be afraid they claim, or they will never take advice nor pay respect to their elders.

Children, even the older ones, are rarely offered straightforward explanations on social matters, beliefs, ideas, values or rituals. They must use their eyes and ears and reason a great deal on their own. They are not encouraged to ask questions or to seek explanations on why things are the way they are. When they do so, they will usually be cut short with a remark like 'that is how it is', or 'that is customary'. What little instruction they get comes mainly from elder siblings, and when children reach the age of eight, they teach one another in peer groups.

I may add perhaps, that I felt this absence of formal teaching quite trying myself, and not very helpful to my endeavours to familiarise myself with the culture. But children have an amazing gift of participation, and they learn to behave though they are given limited instruction.

It is difficult in a short account to do justice to the characteristics of the adult–child relationship and its peculiar combination of close physical contact but limited mental interaction in day-to-day situations. They do make up for the latter in one respect however, and that is in the joint interest in myths and fables. These play a prominent role in this society also as an educational device. Myths about the ancestors are highly appreciated as entertainment, while at the same time they are listened to as instructions. 'The myths are our laws', say the Punan Bah. 'They provide us with guidelines for every aspect of human behaviour, and with solutions to all our problems. If we could just use our ears and listen properly to what they tell us and act accordingly, then we would have a much better life; then we would progress'.

The myths tell of the aristocratic ancestors, of their love-life and marriages, of their social and ritual life, and of men's bravery and fate on headhunting expeditions. The myths underline the crucial importance of knowing one's place in society and of respecting those of senior age or higher social position. They paint the troubles and the supernatural wrath that misbehaviour calls down upon the disobedient. Ideally ancestral myths are transmitted in a special singing tune and in an archaic language, which is unintelligible to children, till they reach their teens. A performance of a single myth may take up to four nights, and it must be completed, or the souls of those who have listened to it are endangered, as they may stay on with the ancestral heroes of the myth on their adventures in distant realms. Grandparents may, however, retell these myths in a short form in the evenings while lying with their grandchildren on the sleeping platforms, to amuse and instruct these. In explaining the myths, they occasionally teach children about norms. The Punan Bah also possess a vast number of animal fables, which are told more often to children. These fables are regarded as less educational by adults, but both kinds illuminate what is good and bad in Punan Bah society, what can be done and what not, both *vis-à-vis* human beings but also towards animals and the invisible inhabitants of the environment.

What then are the aspects of cognitive development, to which the Punan Bah attach special importance? The Punan Bah are as mentioned obsessed with social status and the improvement of their personal reputation. Every Punan Bah wants desperately to be held in esteem and to climb the social ladder. They want to rise, *bau*, as they say, rise in respect within the longhouse community and eventually win renown outside it. Personal qualifications and behaviour dependent on age and sex are crucial in this game. They are the prime movers of social mobility. For this is a society, where, for instance an attractive girl of the commoner class may captivate an aristocratic boy, and end up, if not in marriage, then in a love relationship, which in any case will consolidate her and hence her family's reputation despite a rule of class-endogamy. No wonder that the Punan Bah are keenly interested in the behaviour and development of their children.

In order to obtain the respect of others, it is particularly important to exercise self-restraint and to comply with the rules of etiquette. Tranquil behaviour is strongly valued in Punan Bah society. A person has to achieve control over him or herself. Only those who know how to *luerd*, to remain calm whatever happens, who do not give in to their emotions verbally or physically, can compel the respect of others. One must conduct oneself with dignity. Bodily movements must be confined, noisy behaviour avoided, if one is not going to be frowned upon. Perfect bodily control is exemplified in the traditional dance, where a single individual at a time graciously moves arms and feet on a mat in front of a silent audience. Emotions must be restrained whether they be jealousy, grief, or anger, or positive ones like joy and love. Or they must be expressed in a formalised or ritualised way. Adults, for instance, show no sign of recognition, they do not nod, shake hands or use any other kind of greetings when somebody leaves or arrives. A son may have stayed for years in another community, but when he returns on a visit, walks up the longhouse ladder, crosses the verandah where people are sitting, enters the room, puts down his knapsack and sits down, no one will say a word or hardly even look up from what they are doing, but for the children. There are no outward demonstrations of emotion, let alone of happiness. Only if his return is caused by a death in the family will this reserve be broken and ritual lamentations take place immediately upon his arrival. Otherwise a while will pass till one begins talking, while the visitor is offered a cigarette, and family members drop by as is expected and proper. The Punan Bah explain the necessity to exert self-control and to behave, for instance as just described, as compulsory if one wishes to be held in respect.

The other 'must' is to become knowledgeable about the social reality, the visible as well as the invisible. One must know how to conduct oneself, how to move around, i.e. where, when and how, according to age and sex, kinship and class distinctions. One must know how to choose one's words, from the correct terms of address to the subtleties of rhetoric, in which the Punan Bah place such value and take such pleasure. Those who are tactless, or who only engage in small talk can never compel the respect of others. They would do better just to keep quiet.

Cognition and behaviour are considered closely interrelated. A child's understanding of social relations or norms is disclosed by a demonstration of shame. Or as the Punan Bah put it: 'to know the human way is to know how to feel ashamed'. Let us take a closer look then at how this is brought about, how children acquire the above-mentioned qualifications and learn to behave as boys and girls of various age levels and not as monkeys.

## CHILD DEVELOPMENT AND INTERACTION WITH PARENTS

Children are desired among the Punan Bah. To have no descendants is considered a great loss, not only in this world, but it is believed to be a hindrance to a future rebirth. Women generally wish to have two or three children only, and quite a number procure abortions to limit their offspring, sometimes with grave consequences. Girls were formerly preferred, but both men and women maintain that boys and girls are equally desired today. When expatiating on the reasons for this, they will say that they want a girl to look after them when they get old, and a boy who can speak up for the family. Nor does the sex of a child matter in cases of adoption. About 15 per cent of all marriages prove childless. Such couples will normally be given custody of one or two children of their siblings, or adopt children of more remote relatives, but there are no indications that the one sex is preferred to the other. From my enquiries and observations during the one and a half years I stayed with a Punan Bah family, it would seem that male and female babies are treated alike in all respects. There are no differences in breast-feeding practises, the ways one takes care of the baby, caresses it, or handles cleanliness, to which one incidentally has a relaxed attitude. One fondles the sexual organs of girls as well as boys, kisses their behinds and accepts their nakedness till they are about three years old. But from then on the upbringing of the two sexes will begin to differ; at first almost imperceptibly, later more distinctly. From that age the sexual organs of girls will be covered a bit more systematically than those of boys, though both boys and girls will be teased mainly by their elder siblings and cousins, if they do not put on clothes.

Babies are taken care of by their biological mothers. Only twins, and babies whose fathers have died before their birth or who have been the object of dreams must be given away to others for care. Upon delivery, the baby is washed and wrapped in cloth and placed on a tiny mat next to its mother. Till she has recovered all attention will be directed towards her and not the baby. It is her one worries about, the baby is, as we have seen, hardly considered human. It is the mother who bathes and nurses the baby, and she will be in close bodily contact with it for months, not to separate from its soul. For as long as she continues bleeding, she remains in the room and takes on no work. Her own mother, sisters, or husband perform the household duties: fetching water from the river, doing the cooking and washing. There is great variation as to when and to what extent women resume their duties. But one thing is for sure: the baby will never be left on its own. If it is not in the arms of its mother, it will be lying on the lap of the father, or on that of a grandmother. At night it sleeps between its parents. As the child gets older and suckling comes to an end, the care of it may pass to a grandmother or an elder sister, and will definitely and almost completely do so, if a new baby arrives. But the child is carefully looked after all the time, also to protect it from malevolent spirits and prevent its soul being scared away.

The Punan Bah do nothing to speed up the development of their children's motor skills: rather the contrary. Children of up to three years of age lie or sit in the arms or on the laps of adults or within their reach for the major part of the day, if they are not carried around on the hip of someone. When a child can crawl, it is allowed to do so on the sleeping mat of its parents. But it is discouraged or prevented from crawling on the sleeping platforms of the other married couples, except when it is taken care of by its grandmother, or another adult woman. It is also discouraged from touching any of the belongings of the other family members. If a child is on its way to do so, someone will soon grab it, kiss it and put it on his or her lap. The spatial movements of small children are thus highly restricted, and even infants of between two-and-a-half and four years do not run around at will, but do already conform with the pattern of restrained bodily movement and spatial mobility. They do not go out on the gallery alone. Girls will not do so at all on their own initiative, and will even at an older age do so only in company with other girls, and if they have a specific task to perform, such as pounding rice or running errands. Small boys will begin to sneak out on the gallery to enjoy the company of elder cousins or brothers, or to sit on the lap of their father or grandfather, when they are four or five years of age.

Children thus exert proper spatial behaviour from an early age, i.e. two to three years, and I believe, that by learning this they acquire a basic knowledge of social relationships. They experience their social universe, the extended family, in terms of entities each with its own platform, those of the married couples with their small children, while other members have no specific territorial claim, such as the young men, who sleep here and there and have simply a bag for their personal belongings. This spatial division reflects to some extent the qualitatively different social relations that the child will find itself engaged in with various family members. Children also experience their social world as divided up along another (gender) line likewise spatially marked: the cleavage between those staying in the rooms, the women—and those at the gallery, the men.

Cognitive skills of social relations are, of course, instilled in numerous ways. Among these the learning of the etiquette surrounding family meals seem to be of special importance. Punan Bah children go through no traumatic weaning experiences. Breast-feeding runs parallel with the other foods and may continue till the child is three or four years old, even longer, if there is no new baby. It is usually completed at the age of between eighteen months and two years. The Punan Bah do not normally cook special food for babies. As soon as they are about six months old they join in at family meals and are fed with tiny bits of rice and soup, sitting on the laps of their mothers. Later they will be given cooked vegetables, fish and meat. A child begins to eat by itself picking up food from the plate of its mother, and at an age of between two-and-a-half and three the child is able to eat completely on its own and gets its own plate.

Proper behaviour or etiquette is acquired gradually. This includes when and where to sit down, the posture to adopt during meals (so that one does not put others in spiritual danger), with whom one may share one's plate and/or bowl, and how one helps oneself to food. One must learn, for instance, that one must always take rice from the same place, in order that one does not expose oneself to spiritual danger by upsetting the helping spirits of one's elders. Children are also taught to concentrate on eating and not to talk too much during meals. Children are helped to observe proper behaviour through motor instruction and sometimes with a slight admonition or correction, but they are mainly left on their own and are as always expected to make use of their eyes.

Through observation of the correct behaviour at and around meals, children not only acquire what is considered proper manners, but also a basic knowledge of social relationships and to some extent the ideational rationale behind these. They learn basic facts about the division of labour, that, for example, women cook and serve food for men. They also acquire more sophisticated knowledge, observing for instance that their mother never shares her plates with any other man but her husband. Later they realise that this is so because of *barou*, the fatal illness which women may inflict upon men, polluting them through careless or deliberate behaviour. Similarly, it is because of *barou* that girls must sit with their sarongs tightly around their legs, so that these are covered, that under no circumstances must they step over the legs of their brothers, or other male relatives, or worst of all shake their sarongs, while these are present. Children also learn of kinship and affinity, realising e.g. that non-kin and in-laws do not share plates nor the small bowls with vegetables, cooked fish and meat with one another. They become aware of the social consequences of ageing, that persons belonging to the elder generation must be treated with the utmost respect, that one cannot simply help oneself to rice from the same side of the bowl as old people, if they are not one's grandparents. They become aware, also, of their own social standing within the family through these rules of etiquette. They are confirmed over and over again in their own rights. They too are treated with consideration, they too should have their needs fulfilled and be respected or their guardian spirits may retaliate. Moreover, basic values are instilled in children as they learn to help themselves to food at the right time and in a well-mannered way, to restrain themselves, taking care that whatever food there is, is shared by everyone. They are told too that any transgression of these rules of etiquette is *tula*. Only little by little do children find out that this implies supernatural sanctions on the part of the guardian spirits.

## GENDER AND THE RULES OF ETIQUETTE

The word *tula* is, however, also used as a mere word of warning mainly among children as when we say: 'for shame', or utter some other expression of disapproval. Older sisters and brothers of, say, seven or eight years may say this to a young child if, for instance, it dirties itself while eating.

A child is said to show its understanding by following the rules, or if not, then by showing signs of shame when exposed to its failures to live up to the expectations. Children show that they are ashamed by looking down, turning their faces away, or by outright hiding at the shoulder of an adult or running to the sleeping platform. Parents are very proud, if their children know how to feel ashamed from an early age.

A great many rules of etiquette are properly internalised by the age of three. This is demonstrated for instance by the active engagement of girls of that age, when a family receives visitors. It is evident that girls take great pleasure in copying the roles of adult females. I noticed when visitors had been offered a rolled cigarette by the hostess that small girls even down to an age of two-and-a-half years, when they are hardly able to walk steadily, will all by themselves go to the kitchen, fetch a burning piece of firewood and bring it to the guest so that she can light the cigarette. When they are about three or four years this will be taken as a matter of course; while when they are younger, the visitor may encourage the girl by saying *yet*, *yet*, 'go on, go on', demonstrating her appreciation. At the same time, the women present will, of course, keep a close eye on the little girl, so that she does not burn herself. A child who plays with fire on the other hand will be reproached. Children at such a young age are also able to apply their knowledge of appropriate manners outside the family arena, as shown by the following example:

A girl of closer to two than three years of age is visiting a family with her mother. They have sat down on the mat in the middle of the room, the girl on the lap of her mother.

The hostess gets some biscuits and serves the child. The girl instantly grabs one of the biscuits, but when it is half way to her mouth, she probably remembers that one should not begin to eat immediately in order not to appear greedy. I do not know what really went on in the head of the girl, but she did put back the biscuit on the plate turning her head shamefully onto the shoulder of her mother. Only after some time, upon repeated encouragement by her mother and the hostess to take another biscuit, did she finally look up and take one, and one only. Her father looked at me and said proudly: 'she knows how to feel ashamed'.

From about five years of age children are usually aware of and sensitive to the competitive atmosphere of the community, to the pre-occupation with status and the fight for recognition and esteem. Children at that age begin to react systematically in accordance with Punan norms and to demand respect in their own right. The following examples illustrate this:

A boy of between five and six enters the room and is told by his grandmother that she has some coffee and biscuits for him. (To drink coffee and have biscuits is highly appreciated among the Punan Bah. This is what one serves guests at major ritual occasions, and if one can afford it, on weekdays too. But the Punan Bah are short of money and grow only a little bit of coffee, so there is still an aura of luxury surrounding the drinking of it. So it is something that the boy is offered.) The boy, however, goes to the sleeping platform and sits down there and not on the mat where food is served, and one can see from his looks that he is sullen with anger. Why is this so? The answer is that we—those of us who are staying in the room and who have already had coffee and biscuits—that we did *suau* him, we have disrespected him. He had not been called upon to the gallery, as one does with men. We had left him with his playmates. No one had taken the trouble to go and look for him. In this case the grandmother goes to the kitchen, and brings back a tray with a coffee pot, a cup and a plate with biscuits, which she places at the mat. But the boy turns his back to the room and remains on the sleeping platform. No one utters a word. Then the grandfather gets up, sits down on the mat, pours a cup of coffee and begins to *parap*, i.e. he sings a hymn of praise, as the Punan Bah sometimes do, when they want to pay homage to high-ranking or honoured guests. The reaction of the boy is immediate. He screams with anger while everyone is laughing.

This incident demonstrates that the boy is well aware of the etiquette according to which men and big boys are called upon when food is served. It is evident moreover that he behaves as if he belongs to this category of people. But he is not yet accepted as doing so. His assessment of self is out of touch, but this is disregarded, the grandmother serves him politely. However, when he does not change his behaviour and his grandfather *parap* him, as a correction, the boy is unable to take the joke and screams. The reaction is prompt: the whole family simply laugh at him, and the humiliation is total.

I shall not go into the Punan Bah sense of humour as such here. It suffices to say that laughter can also be a serious sanction in this society, and one laughs at one another, when persons are unable to control themselves.

A boy of about five comes into the room, slams the door behind him and throws himself sullenly at the sleeping platform. An adult looks up and asks 'What now?' well aware that the boy has left some others playing at the gallery. '*Do suau oa*' they insulted me, answers the boy, offering hereby a sufficient explanation to those present in the room.

In this case no one laughs and ridicules the boy, nor is he encouraged to forget the matter and go playing again. For he has to demand respect from his peers, not only for his own sake, but for that of his family, and in this case his assessment of self is approved by the adults.

Differences in gender roles are traceable already at the age of two, as we have seen, but become more marked at the age of five to six. Small children are as mentioned not believed to have sense, their souls do not stay put within their bodies till they are five or six. From that age adult expectations will grow steadily. But their demands on girls and boys differ, and the two sexes to some extent grow up in different surroundings. The girls remain in the rooms, where they begin to perform various household duties, first on a small scale, later more systematically. They fetch water in the river, help their older sisters and cousins with the arduous task of pounding rice. They serve at meals, do the serving and wait upon guests. They also take care of minor siblings and run innumerable errands. Girls are gradually made familiar with the female world and female obligations, and they take upon them their part of the burdens quite smoothly.

The world of boys is different. At the age of about six they are hanging around the gallery, watching their older siblings and the men making fishing nets and repairing tools, tasks that they cannot themselves perform. They listen to the stories told, stories of the behaviour and nature of animals and the spirits of the jungle; of the problems that men face in cutting timber, and of the hopelessness of the economic situation of them all. They explore the vicinity of the longhouse with their peers to chase small animals like squirrels and sometimes birds. And they spend a great deal of time playing in the river. At the age of eight they can paddle properly and can accompany men, when these go fishing. At the age of ten, they may be taken along hunting wild boar. They are now of some use. Boys are not introduced as systematically to the men's work, nor can they as easily take upon them such obligations. Only at an age of about fourteen to fifteen are they considered old enough to go hunting on their own, and with peers, and they are not able to find their own way in the jungle till the age of about 18 or 20. Girls and women rarely become familiar with anything beyond the immediate surroundings of the longhouse and the riverbanks. They never leave the longhouse except in the company of other women or of men if they have to go a bit far.

Girls and boys thus grow up differently, and adult expectations of their efforts, accomplishments and behaviour vary. Girls are expected to pass easily into the female role and act responsibly at an early age, while boys are given much more leeway and are left more on their own and with their peers. Not till the age of nine to ten are they expected to work to any extent.

This seems to influence the development of children and their views of the self. Girls identify themselves rather easily with their roles. They are self-confident and carry themselves with a calm dignity which is moving. But they declare frequently that they are scared of many things, that they are afraid of anything beyond the familiar longhouse arena. Living more in a vacuum, with more diffuse role-expectations on the part of adults, boys seem to have greater difficulty in adjusting and defining themselves. They are more restless and self-centred, more enquiring and also more self-assertive. This is demonstrated in numerous ways, but again quite distinctively at meals, an important arena of male–female interaction. Here boys expect to be waited upon even to an extent that adult men do not. It should be recalled here that gender roles are not particularly rigid in Punan Bah society. There is a division of labour between the sexes, as we have seen, but no one is precluded from any activity due to his or her sex, except, in former times, women from headhunting and headhunting rituals. Men especially will often take upon them women's work. They pound rice and they may even cook and serve meals within the family circle. But children feel ashamed to engage in work of the other sex, and are often most particular about gender behaviour. My findings indicate that boys demonstrate this more passionately than girls, and do so in a highly self-affirmative way as the following episode indicates.

## A CHILDREN'S SUBCULTURE

A boy of ten comes into the room, sits down on the mat and says: '*do*, I want to drink'. His sister gets up from her work, goes to the kitchen, fetches a glass of water, and brings it to her brother. He empties the glass, puts it on the mat and leaves the room immediately.

In this room one must pass by the pitcher when entering and the boy could most easily take a drink by himself. Men frequently do so during a meal, and no adult man would come rushing in the way the boy did, and then demand to be waited upon. But boys do so, and they create situations like the one described over and over again, where they demonstrate their gender consciousness and assess themselves. This more rigid gender behaviour may be seen as a reaction and adjustment to the overall emphasis on status. Children internalise this, but are well aware of their own young age and ensuing inferior position in the society. While they can do nothing about this, they may well stress their sex, and by playing on the differences in gender roles focus on themselves. In effect, children have developed a kind of sub-culture, a slight alteration of the rules of the game, that offers them a way of manifesting themselves. Adults do not interfere. It is left to the children to play out their expectations and in due time adjust to the adult pattern of gender behaviour.

From the age of nine or ten, both boys and girls are supposed to have an understanding of the overall demands posed by the Punan Bah way of life. They are expected to be old enough to realise that life is not only play, that one cannot just do as one pleases, that one has to struggle for one's existence. Moreover that one can only hope for an improvement in one's living conditions, that one can only acquire the modern industrial goods, the fine clothes and the tape-recorders, radios and watches so desperately desired by the young people, through work.

Children should know that there are many tasks to be performed every day, that one must fetch water, chop firewood, work at the farm, go fishing and hunt wild boar and cook to stay alive, and that all this work is equally important. The Punan Bah do not discriminate between household work and other kinds of work, only between wage-work and their traditional undertakings.

Children are expected to see the necessity of all this, to have a sense of the coherence in life and of their own responsibilities. Children of that age should be aware of the morals of the society as well as of general behavioural norms. But this is not always the case. They are often unwilling to work and make themselves invisible when they know that there are demands of one kind or the other in the air. Or they simply lie down on the sleeping platform, turning their backs to the room and demonstrating thereby the greatest disrespect of the other members of the family. But again, these will almost never show any sign of emotional disturbance, or turn to verbal repercussions. It struck me again and again while I stayed among the Punan Bah that they put up with incredibly bad behaviour, and this goes for adults as well as for children, without expressing verbal disapproval. But communication can take other forms, and it certainly does among the Punan Bah. The following situation illustrates this point.

> It is still morning, about 7.30. A married couple, a man, and a twelve-year-old boy have already left the room to cut swidden, One woman is down at the river bathing herself and her one-year-old child, washing her clothes and fetching water at the same time. Janap, a girl of seven, is doing the dishes from last night. Two old women are sitting on their platforms smoking. Jegud, a boy between four and five is rolling around next

to them while Gun a boy of nine is smoking. We have had nothing to eat yet. Nobody is talking, but the family is not very talkative except for the grandfather, who talks and jokes a lot. But he too says nothing this particular morning. He is getting ready to leave, tying the jungle knife around his waist, putting on his hat and finding his fishing net. He is in no hurry, but steadily putting the things he needs together. Gun continues to smoke. Jegud watches his grandfather and Gun, and after some time, begins to sob. (We all know why he is crying, *pali*, a word which the Punan Bah most likely would translate by the English word hunger, because that is how they feel about it, although it actually connotes a situation where there is no meat or fish for a meal. Then you eat *pali*, rice with no accompanying meat or fish, something which the Punan Bah detest.) Jegud's sobbing does not make any of the adults intervene, and Gun continues to smoke, as if nothing is happening. Jegud is now crying loudly, the grandfather tosses about with his gear, Jegud puts ever more effort into his crying; it becomes trying. The atmosphere is tense, Gun gets up suddenly and leaves the room. The grandfather takes off his hat, puts down his gear and sits down rolling himself a cigarette.

Janap brings in some plates and a bowl of rice from the kitchen. Jegud calms down, lies down on the sleeping-platform with his back turned towards us. The grandfather begins to eat, the two old women continue their smoking—they, Janap and the children's mother, will eat a little later, and so will probably Jegud. Gun makes himself invisible for an hour or so.

I witnessed scenes like this one quite often during my stay with the family. What happened was the following: the Punan Bah do not like to have a meal without meat or fish to go with the rice or sago. Vegetables are acceptable but not sufficient. When there are no leftovers from the evening meal, it is the duty of men to get up early in the morning to catch fish for the morning meal. As the young men were busy this particular morning working in the fields, it was up to the old man and definitely also to a boy of Gun's age to provide for the women and children. For the grandfather cannot fish alone, while he throws the fishing net there must be someone at the stern to steer the canoe.

Gun knew very well that it was expected that he went along, but he did not want to and therefore there could be no fishing, and nothing to eat with the rice. We had to eat *pali*. The adults, however, said nothing. Adults rarely force children against their will. They are afraid to scare off the souls of the children. They give in, although they feel disappointed.

Five-year-old Jegud could not, however, control his feelings. He is well aware of many aspects of the gender pattern and of the obligations of the various age groups, including that of his brother Gun to provide for him and the women when needed. He tried to put pressure on Gun by crying first quite calmly but then increasingly louder and out of anger. Not only because he would like to eat fish—there are many mornings when he eats rice alone without complaining—but because he felt that his brother ignored his wishes, that he 'disrespected' him.

As stated earlier, I did not go to the Punan Bah to study cognition or the cognitive development of children. My presentation here must be taken for what it is, an outline of some observations and findings on the topic. I was struck, however, by the difficulties of understanding cognition in this society. These are generated by values and features of the behavioural pattern. First of all by the importance attached to deferential behaviour. Not only are younger persons expected to behave with the greatest respect towards the elder generation, but even among peers reverential regard is outspoken. Respect is expressed not only in etiquette but also through a severe limitation of the content of verbal communication. One does not readily air one's thoughts or lay open one's worries even within a narrow family circle or necessarily between husband and wife. As an outsider, one is struck by the fact that life in a Punan Bah longhouse on the one hand is characterised by spatial intimacy and by an extended sharing, while the individual on the other hand has so restrained possibilities of expressing him or herself mentally and to some extent also emotionally. This behavioural restraint can appear as a lack of personal interest in one another's problems. This is not necessarily the case, but it is a fact that the Punan Bah know only little about each other's feelings and thoughts. The restrictive behavioural frame is further accentuated by the value attached to the exertion of self-control. One is expected to keep quiet and refrain from comments or what is considered criticism of the behaviour of others. A considerable amount of significant communication in a Punan Bah family and in the society as such is non-verbal. An assessment of what goes on in the heads of people, not least in those of the children, is correspondingly difficult.

**NOTE**

The fieldwork on which this paper is based was carried out from February till August 1973 and from September till August 1974–5. Another six months were spent among the Punan Bah in 1980–1, but as the society is undergoing rapid change, the ethnographic present here described is limited to the early 1970s.

The aim of the research project was neither to study cognitive development nor socialisation practises. The data presented are such as I collected during my efforts to familiarise myself with Punan Bah culture in general. The fieldwork received financial support from the Danish Social Science Research Foundation.

## INDIGENOUS CONCEPTS OF GROWTH AND DEVELOPMENT

The most commonly used expressions are the following:

*For physical growth:*

1. *Suan*: thrive grow. The word is used as well for human beings as for plants and trees.
2. *mabu*: shoot up, grow tall
3. *makin ajo*: grow big, grow
4. *mabongo*: grow in size

*For cognitive development:*

1. *maseang*: progress, advance, show improvement (pamaseang: development. The word may denote human development as well as the development of a country).
2. *menjeluang*: assume shape, develop
3. *bakale*: gain knowledge, learn
4. *madju*: show improvement, make progress e.g. in school, in life in general
5. *ma'akien*: gain knowledge, obtain insight

The Punan Bah do, however, often prefer to express themselves metaphorically, using expressions like:

6. *lelurua*: to sprout. The word also denotes the cutting of teeth
7. *ngalanei*: shoot, put forth

Or they make use of more complicated metaphors like for instance:

8. *mavut*: which literally means to paddle forwards while correcting the course. Figuratively it means to go straight, improve

More often than not the Punan Bah will, however, express themselves with negations, i.e. they will talk of the lack of growth or development. They use for instance words like:

9. *usoa*: unripe
10. *esang vi tuo*: not yet ripe
11. *aleang aleang*: lagging behind in
12. *stenga*: only half, only partly
13. *kureang*: short of
14. *maiput*: choked, blocked

**BIBLIOGRAPHY**

Leach, E.R. (1950) *Social science research in Sarawak*. London: His Majesty's Stationery Office.

# Part III:
# Cognitive Development, Gender and Hierarchy

# 7

# Children's Perceptions of Gender and Hierarchy in Fiji

## Christina Toren

'It is inherent in the nature of hierarchies that certain non-gender based principles of social organisation take precedence over gender itself as a principle of social organisation.' This quotation from an interesting paper by Ortner (1981, p. 396) on gender and hierarchy in Polynesia immediately raises two questions. First, is it ethnographically true that gender is subordinated to rank in hierarchical societies and second, if one believes it to be true, how can one demonstrate it? Here I wish to argue that the answers to both questions can be found by considering together the nature of the cognitive processes available to the single human actor and the nature of the inevitably social acts in which such processes must deal. In the present study this entails examination of one aspect of the process of children's cognitive construction of hierarchy in Fiji together with an analysis of the way that social organisation is represented by adults. As we shall see, this approach throws up some interesting contradictions and calls into question the use of purely anthropological methods in ascertaining the nature of the principles of social organisation for any given society.

Contemporary anthropologists, irrespective of whether they take a more 'cultural' or a more 'sociological' perspective, tend to assume that a set of collective representations, or an ideology, or the pattern of symbolic or cultural constructs can provide us with an understanding of important distinctions within a given culture and, more radically, with an understanding of how these important distinctions organise the subject's view of his or her world. This assumption is virtually always implicit rather than explicit, simply because the apparently most significant set of collective representations, or symbolic constructs, or ideology, may emerge out of analysis as the creation of the anthropologist and, at best, can give us only a partial understanding of the subject's view of his or her own culture or society. And this may be the case even where the anthropologist is specifically concerned to do justice to indigenous categories and indigenous perspectives with respect to that society. I have suggested elsewhere that this problem arises out of the conflation of representation with the processes of thought, an approach that may explain the strong relativist stance taken by anthropologists such as Geertz and Evans-Pritchard in his later work, an approach that has been questioned by a number of anthropologists.[1]

Clearly the primary task of the anthropologist *is* to discover the various principles of order for a given society and this inevitably entails an examination of modes of representation and the interconnections between them. Far from wishing to dismiss such a procedure I have to point out that my own data have largely been gathered and analysed using well-tried anthropological methods. However, as one whose initial training was in cognitive psychology, I have to object to the almost imperceptible slide that makes representation virtually identical with thought. Apart from the fact that representation is *not* the same as thought, the conflation of the two categories can lead to further systematic errors so that the anthropologist unwittingly privileges certain data, giving them a prominence that they may not necessarily deserve.

This is perhaps the case with Ortner who, despite her concern to appreciate 'actors' categories' and her sensitive analysis of the ethnography, uses 'hierarchy' as an analytic category. Like Needham, Geertz and other contemporary theorists, she starts with the necessary working assumption that 'culture . . . has the properties of a system' (Ortner, 1981, p. 4). This is fine as far as it goes, but a problem arises at the point where it is further implicitly assumed that the 'properties of the system' will conform to the logical implications of the analytic categories used by anthropologists to describe the system.

Thus, in her use of 'hierarchy' as an analytic category, Ortner assumes that the principle of rank differentiation or 'genealogical seniority' must override gender in any hierarchy where social status is said to be fundamentally a matter of hereditary ranking and people are born into given statuses. In crude terms this means that in such a hierarchy, aristocrats will always be seen as superior to commoners and that it is only within rank that men are superior to women. The point to be made here is that Ortner has no way of demonstrating how subjects or 'actors' (to use her term) actually articulate notions of rank with those of gender and age seniority and so, for all her emphasis on 'actor-centred analysis', she willy nilly privileges an anthropological construct of hierarchy over actors' categories. I do not mean to argue here that Ortner is necessarily wrong in her reading of the relative dominance of rank, seniority and gender in Polynesian hierarchy. However, I do question whether she has been able to arrive at the nature of Polynesian actors' categories by anthropological analysis alone. As we shall see below, what individual actors represent as being unambiguously the case may produce a confusing and highly ambiguous situation from the point of view of the analyst. Moreover, because Ortner assumes that gender may be axiomatically isolated from a hierarchy that depends on a principle of hereditary ranking, it is hardly surprising that actors' views of hierarchy and gender emerge from the ethnographic data as distinct categories. She is then able to maintain that gender is subordinated to hierarchy in Polynesia—but her conclusion is foregone, an artefact of her theoretical stance.

The present paper will show how the meaning of constructs such as hierarchy can be best understood by looking not only at the ways they are represented, but at the form of the exchange relations in which they are manifested and, finally, at the course of cognitive development. It is in the examination of the process of children's acquisition of hierarchy that we can find out its component principles, how they are articulated with one another and evaluate both the extent to which they interact, and the extent to which one component actually dominates over others.

For my own ethnography it will be seen that, in the course of their cognitive development, children in two central Fiji villages construct specific notions about the nature of hierarchy. As we shall see, children's notions of hierarchy at once conform with adult *behaviour*, and are at odds with what adults have to say about Fijian hierarchy. In fact, adult behaviour constitutes rank, age seniority and gender as interacting and equally dominant principles of social organisation, principles that cannot be isolated from one another. However, as we shall see, this is not readily apparent from the nature of indigenous categories.

The complex intertwining of the ideas involved and of the behaviour that is governed by the interaction of notions of gender with those of rank and seniority, is encapsulated in a spatial construct that is of central importance at once for the symbolic ordering of society and for its empirical manifestation in people's behaviour. This spatial construct is represented in the observation that 'the chiefs sit "above" and the ladies sit "below" ', an observation that I both heard repeated and saw expressed in behaviour day after day during the eighteen months I spent in the chiefly village of Sawaieke, the leading village of the eight villages of the Sawaieke *vanua* (country) on the island of Gau, central Fiji.[2]

This observation expresses an all-pervasive concern with the disposition of people within any given space—indoors or outdoors. Basically there are only two positions: *i cake* ('above') and *i ra* ('below'). I refer to the axis described by these two terms as 'symbolic *cake/ra*' to differentiate it from the logical construct that describes the relation between objects on literally different planes. However, this usage should not be taken to mean that I conceive of a sharp break between the two. Rather the 'logical' and the 'symbolic' describe the poles of a conceptual continuum; so, for example, when a visiting high chief sits on a chair in that part of a building that is called *i cake*, 'above', he is at once symbolically and literally above all those who are seated on the floor in that part of the building that is called *i ra*, 'below'. I shall return to this later on, after I have given some brief outline of indigenous accounts of hierarchical relations.

## THE CONTRADICTION BETWEEN HIERARCHY AND EQUALITY

The type of hierarchy described by Ortner as general to Polynesia is formally very similar to my own data for an island in central Fiji. There, as in Polynesia, social status is said to be fundamentally given by birth. There is no argument about the fact that the different patrilineal clans or *yavusa* are, and should be, ranked with respect to their traditional obligations to the chiefly clan (i.e. that from which a paramount chief of the eight villages of the Sawaieke *vanua* are chosen).[3] Despite its apparent clarity this principle is actually full of ambiguities. Thus, while there is no question that 'the chiefs' rank above all others, the reference of this term varies. *Ko ira na turaga*, 'the chiefs' may denote either all legitimate members of the chiefly clan (male and female) *or* the chiefs of each of the different clans as a group.

The latter may also be referred to as *na malo* (lit. 'the cloths') or *na turaga ni vanua* ('the chiefs of the country').[4] From the analyst's point of view, the relative rank of the various clan chiefs is ambiguous as is, therefore, the ranking of the clans.

In conversation, informants give somewhat different accounts of the nature of this ranking depending on their own clan affiliation. The clan from which a paramount chief is chosen is said to rank highest by virtue of its members' chiefly birth, and it is followed by the clan that 'makes the chief'. However, the effective power to perform (or to delay) installation allows members of the 'chief-making' clan to assert their own superiority and to maintain that, at least until the installation of the paramount, their own clan chief ranks highest. At the same time, members of the chiefly clan take it for granted that their clan is the highest ranking irrespective of whether the paramount has been installed and point to the fact that all legitimate members of their clan are of chiefly birth and entitled to the honorific prefix *Ratu* or *Adi* ('sir' or 'lady') before their given name. Similarly, members of the clan who are 'people of the land' assert their position to be above that of the clan who are 'people of the sea', while the latter maintain the reverse to be true. A fifth clan, said to have been traditionally either warriors or priests is variously said to rank second after the chiefly clan or third after the clan that 'makes the chief', or is simply ignored as 'not really a *yavusa*'.[5] Within clan, the exogamous lineages (*mataqali*) are ranked over against each other in terms of their ritual obligations to the lineage from which clan chiefs are chosen, while within lineage the *tokatoka* (the smallest kinship group beyond the domestic group) are ranked according to whether their respective ancestors are represented as older or younger brothers in relation to each other.[6]

Exchange relations provide the key to an explanation of the ambiguity in ranking across clans. These are such that 'the chiefs' (irrespective of the reference group denoted by the term) are said to owe their position to 'the people' (*na vanua*, 'the country'); the people owe allegiance to the chiefs but only if the latter show their worthiness by a proper reciprocity and by redistribution of *all* goods they receive as tribute. Thus, clan chiefs, high-status men of the chiefly clan and especially the paramount chief, are the locus of exchange across groups; and women of the chiefly clan are the locus for exchange between all-female groups. Between 'the chiefs' and 'the people' the exchange relation is that of tribute and redistribution—it denotes hierarchy.

However, the underlying value in exchange *between clans* is that of perfectly balanced reciprocity. Thus the relation between *vanua* ('land') and *wai* ('sea') stresses equality in a mutually dependent relationship; 'people of the land' do not eat pig or other 'land' foods in company with 'people of the sea' who do not eat fish. So the members of each group symbolically exchange the product of their labour. The chiefly clan is also associated with the sea, as is the warrior/priests' clan, while the clan that 'makes the chief' is associated with the land. The relation between 'land' and 'sea' is explicitly one of equality and balanced reciprocity. So, if there is a fund-raising drive for the church, the school or some other village project, village members divide into two competitive groups, according to their association with either 'land' or 'sea'.

The relation between 'land' and 'sea' in terms of balanced reciprocity is apparent in the layout of houses in the village. Sawaieke, like all other villages in Gau, is situated on the coast; houses of the chiefly clan lie on its central axis with houses of the 'chief-making' clan beside them, just as sea is contiguous to land. On the village peripheries, houses of 'sea people' are on one border beside those of the chief-making clan (sea beside land); houses of 'landspeople' stand on the other border beside those of the chiefly clan (land beside sea). Again, the 'honoured door' of any house (i.e. that reserved for the owners or high status guests) is also the 'sea door' and it faces onto 'the land door' (also tabooed) of the house beside it. This orientation of houses to one another is that of *veiqaravi*, 'facing each other'.[7] However, the apparent emphasis on balanced reciprocity and mutual equality is rendered ambiguous in that a number of houses belonging to the chiefly clan are built on high *yavu* or named house foundations; the relative height of the *yavu* traditionally denotes the relative status of its owners.[8]

In Fijian social organisation there is an endemic contradiction between the hierarchical principle, with its insistence on a definite rank order across clans and individuals, and the equality implied by balanced reciprocity in exchange relations between 'land' and 'sea'. This contradiction is also given by the equality of cross-cousins when compared with all other categories of kin relations; these are hierarchical and give authority to the senior party, e.g. elder brother over younger brother. Note that the relation between cross-cousins typically obtains *across* domestic groups while the core of hierarchical kinship is *internal* to the domestic group. Thus the orientation of houses in terms of *veiqaravi*, 'facing each other', symbolically constitutes in part the relation between cross-cousins (i.e. between affines, since cross-cousin is the only marriageable category of kin).[9]

By contrast, the spatial construct given by *cake/ra*, 'above'/'below', describes the space *inside* buildings and in part symbolically constitutes hierarchical relations in the domestic group.[10] I have no space to go into the details of hierarchy in the domestic group; however it is important to point out that here hierarchy is symbolically manifest in the activity of the meal.[11] The cloth is placed on the mat to conform with the symbolic *cake/ra* axis of the house space and the members of the domestic group take their places according to their status by gender and age seniority. The senior man of the household sits *i cake* with his wife at the pole *i ra*; other members are seated according to sex and age in relation to the senior man, males in general being seated 'above' females. Women serve and 'wait' on men; a woman begins her own meal when her husband has finished, or is at least half way through eating.

This is not necessarily to say that all women are 'below' men; the position of women in the domestic group and in the wider hierarchy is ambiguous. Whatever its sex, the birth of the first child is ritually celebrated and as *na ulu matua*, 'the eldest', a woman is respected by younger brothers and her opinion sought when major decisions are taken. However, she has no jural rights in land or house and is economically dependent on father, brother or husband; she has only usufruct rights in lineage landholdings and her children benefit from these rights only through operating the privileges of the *vasu*, i.e. the right of a man's sister's child to take what s/he wants without asking from her or his mother's brother.[12] In general, women's labour is highly valued, especially with respect to the production of mats for ceremonial exchange; but women's contribution to food production and meals is devalued in comparison to men's. Women fish for their families, but fish is just one of a number of *i coi*, 'relishes', while men produce *kakana dina*, 'true food', i.e. the root crops without which there is no meal; men also produce, cook and present the *magiti*, 'feastfood', for ceremonial exchange. Men's cooking in the earth oven is rated above that of women's over the fire; food that is baked (*vavi*) being 'tastier' than food that is boiled (*vakasaqa*). A woman's sexuality should be *marorori*, 'taken care of', by male kin, female virginity on marriage being highly valued; female sexuality is 'weak' but sex with an older woman is dangerous for young men. Finally, while men tend in conversation to represent all women as 'lower' than men, they *do* show their respect to older women of chiefly birth and the behaviour of such women reveals their awareness of their high rank.

These ambiguities with respect to women's status are operated by the distinction between women as wives and women as sisters. Women as sisters are the object of 'respect'. Marriage converts the equality of cross-cousins across sex into a hierarchical relationship whereby it is axiomatic that a husband has authority over his wife whatever her status by birth. This transformation begins in betrothal and marriage ritual where the woman becomes an object of exchange. Thus the 'side of the man' in the marriage exchanges *must* be seen to give more than the 'side of the woman', otherwise the groom and his kin are 'ashamed'. The symbolic transformation of the equality of cross-cousins across sex into the hierarchy of husband and wife is often marked, in the early months of marriage, by the violence of the young man towards his wife.[13]

The ambiguity of women's position in the wider hierarchy of the village and the ambiguity of clan ranking raise the question of how Sawaieke villagers yet managed to assert that all individuals could be unambiguously ranked in relation to one another. In part this is attributable to the fact that any given individual's relation to others is governed by the kinship relation in which s/he stands to those others, all relations being constituted in the idiom of kinship. However, if hierarchy is to emerge as fundamental to the social order then the equality of cross-cousins has to be at once contained and subordinated to ranked relations across kin.

Across sex and within the domestic group, this transformation is accomplished by marriage such that the in-marrying woman takes up a position that is unambiguously *i ra* in relation to her husband. However, the problem of 'women' in relation to 'men' still remains, as does the problem of the equality of cross-cousins within sex. This requires that balanced reciprocity in exchange relations between cross-cousins and between clans be transformed into a hierarchical exchange. This transformation is symbolically constituted in the *yaqona* ceremony where balanced reciprocity in exchange relations is transformed into 'tribute' and hierarchy is unambiguously manifest.

## YAQONA-DRINKING AS AN IMAGE OF THE SOCIAL ORDER

The ritual exchange of *yaqona* (*piper methysticum*), called kava elsewhere in the South Pacific, is of primary significance for the symbolic constitution of the contemporary hierarchy in Fiji. Ceremonial drinking of the pounded root infused in water is mandatory at weddings, funerals, circumcisions, the welcoming of visitors, and ceremonial exchanges; in other words, it is an integral part of virtually any occasion of ritual importance and is also drunk on an everyday basis at routine social gatherings.

It is when people drink *yaqona* that relative statuses are most clearly revealed. In *yaqona*-drinking, the position of the *tanoa*—the large wooden bowl in which the drink is prepared and from which it is served—defines the space around it such that it becomes both bounded and highly significant. One side of any *tanoa* is that which 'faces the chiefs' (*qarava na turaga*). Once the *tanoa* has been positioned—and this is nearly always in accordance with the already given 'above' and 'below' of the space inside a building—the space around it is no longer ambiguous or, if the drinking is to take place out of doors, neutral. All who sit *i cake*, 'above' the *tanoa*, are of higher status than all those who sit 'below' it.

In Figure 7.1 we see the typical seating arrangements for a village-wide gathering: the chiefs, with the paramount chief in the 'top' central position, sit *i cake* and face 'down' the space; those of lower status sit in their due order beside or behind the *tanoa*, facing 'up' towards the chiefs. One never sits with one's back to the *tanoa* and the chiefs, and the open space between the *tanoa* and the semi-circle of chiefs is left free; those of high status are always separated off from those of lower status and the latter may cluster together while the former never do. If only men are drinking then it is young men (*cauravou*) who are seated at the pole *i ra*, while if men and women are drinking together it is women who occupy this position. Within the gross division given by *cake/ra* one is always seated 'above' or 'below' other people present according to one's own status relative to these others.

In *yaqona*-drinking relative status finds expression on the symbolic spatial axis given by *cake/ra* and is further confirmed by the order in which the drink is served. The first 'three' bowls are most important, these being drunk by the three highest-status persons present.[14] After chiefs and elders have drunk in their due order serving becomes general so that instead of one server being

**Figure 7.1**: Typical seating pattern inside village hall when people are gathered to drink *yaqona*.

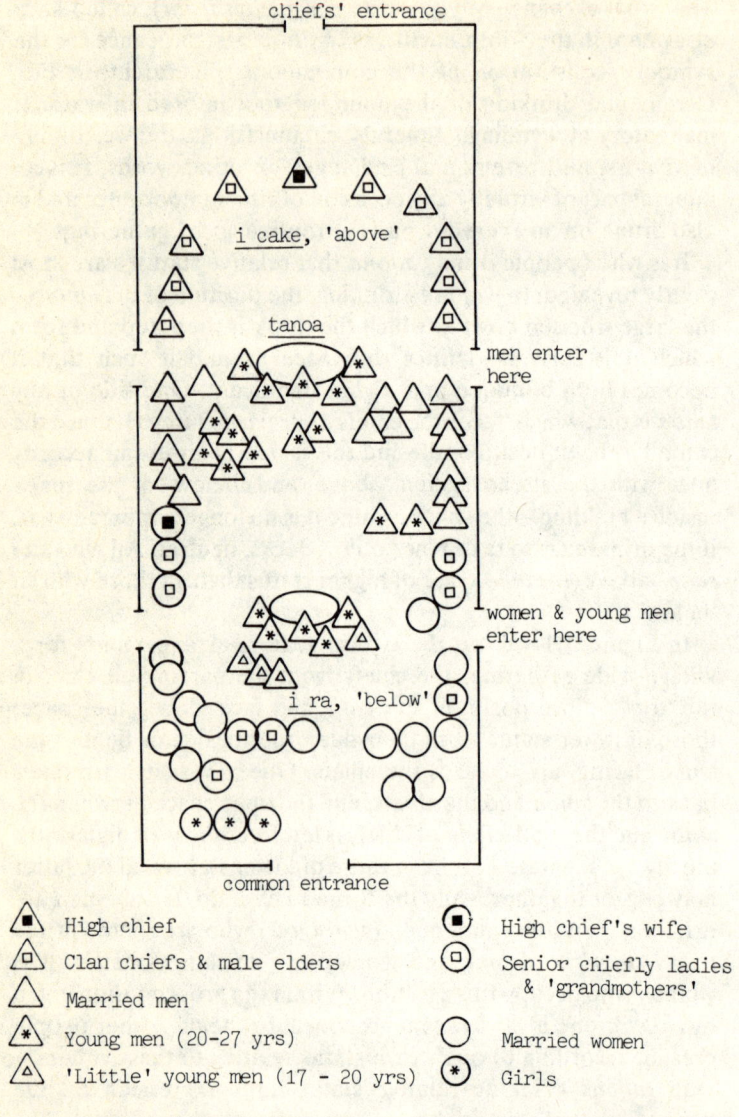

at work there may, in a large gathering, be several. This means that relative status in terms of drinking order is not so clear but even so, it is always true that those of higher status are served before those 'below' them, e.g. an elderly chiefly lady before an elderly woman who is a commoner, married women before girls.

A paramount chief is installed in office by drinking a bowl of *yaqona* served him, in the appropriate ritual context, by the hands of the chief of the 'chief-making' clan. Once he has drunk the chiefly *yaqona* his every command must be fulfilled on pain of his mystical power causing illness to those who fail to do their duty; a high chief does not will this punishment, it simply occurs because *e sa tu vei ira na sau*—'the command (or prohibition) is his', i.e. has become as it were intrinsic to him and mystically effective so that his will is simply asserted since no dereliction of duty can be concealed from one who now has the powers of a god.

The act of presenting the bowl of *yaqona* that installs a chief is of such importance that it is in itself symbolic of power, so much so that, as I mentioned above, the question of *who* actually was the high chief of Gau was an ambiguous matter for villagers in Sawaieke since the man who held the title had not yet been formally installed; for some the man in authority was held at that time to be the man who could perform the ceremony of installation.

In the contemporary political context the power of the high chief of a small *vanua* ('country') like Sawaieke does not extend very far and is best described as 'influence'; even if such a chief be unscrupulous he cannot easily exploit his people because, unless formally installed in office, he is not thought to have any means of visiting retribution on those who deny him. Also, all adults have voting rights, in village meetings as well as in general elections; in law, all adults are jural equals and matters concerning all should be subject to democratic processes. A high chief's political influence prior to installation tends to depend largely on the respect in which he is held by the community at large.

In the nineteenth century, prior to British colonisation and in the early days of the colony, chiefs had real political and economic power, including the power of life and death over their subjects, and this power was itself derived from the mystical power or *mana* that was bestowed on any given chief by the *kalou vu* or 'ancestor god' who was the original 'owner' of the land. The chief himself was not thought to be a direct descendant of the ancestral 'owner' of the land, rather his *mana* was conferred upon him by virtue of his installation as chief by those who were considered to be the jural 'owners' of the land. Today, in Sawaieke district, a paramount chief still depends for his *mana* on proper installation in office by those who are said to be the original owners of the chiefly village of Sawaieke. However, it is said that the *mana* of a paramount chief is not what it was, that this is because Christianity has diminished the power of the *kalou vu* ('ancestor gods') because 'no one attends on them anymore'.

It is in this context of a marked diminution in the actual politico-economic power of chiefs that *yaqona*-drinking has become of central importance. The present-day mode of *yaqona*-drinking is said to be *vakavanua*, 'traditional', and eminently Fijian, in spite of the fact that people are aware that historically women and young men were not permitted to drink *yaqona* at all. Women were actually excluded from *yaqona*-drinking groups, while young men were allowed only to prepare and serve the drink to older men, that is, to those classified as *turaga*, a term which refers specifically to chiefs but also to married men. There has also been a marked increase in frequency of drinking over the past sixty years or so. Today *yaqona*-drinking is the prime ritual manifestation of the 'traditional' order and one where chiefs are seen to occupy a preeminent position over against others who are seated in their due order 'below' them. Here the imagery of *yaqona*-drinking stresses a hierarchy that is dependent on political, economic and spiritual factors that are different in kind from those that obtained in the recent historical past and at the same time effectively denies that irreversible changes have occurred. Thus what is said to be *vakavanua* or 'traditional' is not a mere 'leftover' from an earlier era, but is itself continuously being constructed and transformed.[15]

The drinking of a bowl of *yaqona* is the crucial act of chiefly installation. When a chief installs a chief he is, in 'making him drink' (*vagunuvi koya*) disposing of *yaqona* as a chief does and, at the same time, in actually serving the other man, he gives himself the junior position. As a symbolic act of chiefly tribute and subservience this rare and highly significant ceremony may be contrasted with the everyday but equally significant *sevusevu* from which it takes its meaning. *Sevusevu* precedes or accompanies *yaqona*-drinking; it is the presentation of *yaqona* in its 'raw' form, i.e. the roots of the plant. Essentially the *sevusevu* is a form of tribute to chiefs which, once presented and accepted, confers on those who present it the freedom of the place where they are and entails obligations of hospitality etc. from those who accept it.

At its most simple *sevusevu* requires merely a brief ritual acceptance by one of those present round the *tanoa*. This is a much attenuated form of a solemn ritual that entails traditional dress, formal speeches of presentation and acceptance of a whole uprooted *yaqona* plant, and proceeds to the ceremony of *yaqona vakaturaga*, 'the chiefly *yaqona*', that is the mixing and serving of the first 'three' bowls. This is the *sevusevu* for a very high status visitor. The form taken by rank relations exemplified by chief and commoner is made manifest in *sevusevu*: *yaqona* is given 'raw' as tribute to a chief who re-distributes it as drink that can only be accepted.

The drinking of *yaqona* is an act that is constitutive in part of a ritually defined social order and so it is hedged about with prohibitions and ceremony. Having joined a drinking group, one should not leave it until all the *yaqona* has been drunk. *Yaqona* is the chiefly drink and is dispensed as it were by the chiefs to the people. This is so even when no actual chief is present. To reject the *yaqona*, to pour away what remains in the *tanoa* when those assembled have had enough, is not considered possible. Proper modes of deportment should be observed in the preparation and serving, in the acceptance and thanks for a bowl, and in the polite acknowledgement of another's drinking. One never prepares and drinks *yaqona* alone; to do so is to lay oneself open to charges of witchcraft since it is by pouring libations of *yaqona* to the ancestor gods that one taps their power to bring evil upon one's kin and undeserved favours to oneself; conversely, curing rituals entail the public drinking of *yaqona* and an open appeal to the ancestors for help. Drinking *yaqona* is the quintessential social act; so drinking alone cannot be countenanced and is the idiom used for witchcraft practices. The corollary of this is that most adult Fijians regard *yaqona*-drinking as virtually obligatory; a refusal to drink at all is effectively a denial of society and a rejection of the status quo. One should drink if only to show respect to the chiefs under whose auspices the *yaqona* is offered.

The installation of chiefs, the *sevusevu*, the evil acts of the witch and the beneficial ones of the curer, all suggest that drinking *yaqona* in the proper ritual context is an expression of *mana*. *Mana* may be glossed as 'spiritual power' but in general the term refers to a special kind of 'effectiveness' whether this be the efficacy of a herbal remedy to cure, that of the *yavusa* chief whose *mana* installs a high chief in his office, or that of the speech for *sevusevu* in which the formula *Mana . . . e dina* is always repeated. This formula expresses the notion that the words of the speechmaker (concerning perhaps prosperity and peace between kin) have by their very pronunciation brought about the state to which they refer.

It seems likely that historically the notion of *mana*, whose source is always a transcendent power, would have provided the key to symbolic *cake/ra*. As we shall see, it is the position of the high chief in *yaqona*-drinking that exemplifies the pole that is *i cake* on the symbolic axis. It is also the case that, on the scale of human effectiveness, he is said to have the most *mana* and in this sense he is closest to the ancestors. The ancestors were 'above' the chief but it was he who was the channel for the *mana* that they dispensed 'downwards' along the *cake/ra* axis from ancestor, to chief, to commoner. The witch who 'drinks *yaqona* on his own' initiates the flow of *mana* only to misdirect it for his own selfish ends; by contrast the *mana* of a high chief was traditionally supposed to be for the good of his people in so far as it resulted in prosperity for all or victory in battle.

This is not to say that the notion of *mana* provides a complete explanation for what *cake/ra* currently means for villagers in the *vanua* of Sawaieke. For while the notion still exists, the salience of 'ancestral power' has been much reduced in the face of Wesleyanism. The ancestors still stand at the back of a paramount chief, indeed the lowliest person has ancestors to call on, but they are said to be weak by comparison with the Christian God. The authority of a high chief comes at once from ancestral *mana* and from *na kaukauwa ni Jiova, na Kalou cecere*, 'the strength of Jehovah, the high God', and is ratified by association with his divine nature.[16]

The above analysis suggests that hierarchy in the chiefly village of Sawaieke is constructed in part by reference to the images that people form of social behaviour in particular contexts. In this paper I have concentrated on the context of *yaqona*-drinking because it takes in the widest possible social group, since it is by definition open to any person who brings a *sevusevu*. Moreover the ritual of *yaqona*-drinking symbolically resolves the contradiction posed by balanced reciprocity in a society where a principle of hierarchical ranking is taken for granted; balanced reciprocity in exchange relations gives way to 'tribute to chiefs'. This transformation is paralleled by a transformation in symbolic space; thus the orientation of houses in terms of *veiqaravi*, 'facing each other', implies balanced reciprocity in relations across groups but in *yaqona*-drinking *veiqaravi* denotes hierarchy in attendance upon chiefs; the chiefs and the people 'face each other' but now the chiefs are *i cake*, 'above' the *tanoa*, and the people are *i ra*, 'below' it—the relation between them being transformed by the medium of *yaqona* through which chiefs have access to the *mana* of the ancestors from which they partly derive their authority. The *sevusevu* and the drinking of *yaqona* form the paradigm for all presentations to chiefs and for their redistribution. Thus *yaqona* ritual symbolically transforms a fundamentally balanced exchange into one that is hierarchical. The image of an ordered and stratified society exemplified in people's positions relative to one another around the *tanoa* is one that is encountered virtually every day in the village of Sawaieke.

The rest of this paper looks at how the image of Fijian society that is projected in *yaqona*-drinking enters into children's construction of the 'meaning' of symbolic *cake*/*ra* ('above'/'below').

Here I have to remind the reader that representation in terms of symbolic *cake*/*ra* ('above'/'below') is common to the space inside all buildings in the village. For all enclosed spaces and certain contexts out of doors this symbolic representation of space places certain behavioural constraints on the way that it is used.[17] In the house *i cake* may be seen to be the place of senior males of the family and *i ra* the place of females; in most public buildings *i cake* is seen to be the place of *yavusa* chiefs and *i ra* the place of females. Church space is used somewhat differently; *i cake* is still the place of chiefs, but the space 'below' them is occupied by the congregation such that males and females, each on their own side of the church, are more or less on the same level with one another for a given status category, an observation that underlines the ambiguity of women's position in the contemporary hierarchy. The data suggest that representation of social hierarchy is merged with symbolic representation of space—but is this indeed the case? What does symbolic *cake*/*ra* actually mean to those whose behaviour it appears to govern, do they understand it to be an attribute of certain spaces or an attribute of people in relation to one another? The ambiguity of women's status raises a further question about the nature of this social hierarchy. Does gender interact with notions of rank and age seniority in the construction of hierarchy? Or does hierarchy—as Ortner maintains for Polynesia—override gender and age by stressing rank (Ortner's 'genealogical seniority')?

By participant observation and anthropological analysis alone

one cannot fully answer these questions and it is here, I suggest, that the psychological method comes into its own. Data on the course of children's cognitive development—in this case with respect to their acquisition of the meaning of symbolic *cake/ra*—is, I would argue, essential here. This is not to say however that the psychological method *on its own* would have yielded any useful results; analysis of the data gathered by participant observation is essential for achieving an initial grasp of the underlying significance of symbolic spatial constructs in this Fijian context.

The necessity for combining the two methods should be borne in mind in assessing the data on children's cognitive construction of symbolic *cake/ra* presented below.

**THE DEVELOPMENTAL EVIDENCE**

I begin with some brief general details about child development in Sawaieke village. Children's acquisition of symbolic *cake/ra* takes place in a context where the emphasis is on peer group learning and on an early grasp of the principle of seniority. This is brought home to the child via interaction with others with respect to food exchange, affection, orders and discipline. A difference in age of 12–18 months is sufficient to allow the older party to act as loving 'parent' as well as disciplinarian. A toddler's experience of older children is that they dispense both desirable tidbits of food, cuddles and kind advice as well as slaps and sharp words. As the child grows up s/he too begins to act *in loco parentis* to younger children and is encouraged, and indeed expected to do so, by parents and other adults. Children of any age should be obedient, quiet and undemanding in the presence of adults. Adult interaction with children under school age tends to be confined to dispensing food, physical expressions of affection, injunctions against disapproved behaviour and disciplinary smacks or lectures. There is comparatively little play and/or conversation between adults and children though it does occur now and again; on the whole children rely on their peers for this type of interaction: as lively and forthcoming 'authorities' with younger children and as humble audience with older children. The pattern appears to be 'set' in infancy and goes along with a timid and self-effacing style of self-presentation in the company of those senior in age; this is commonly ascribed to 'shyness' or 'shame' (*madua*) or to 'fear' (*rere*). These sentiments are inculcated in the child via ridicule, mockery, laughter or outright disapproval on virtually all occasions that the child draws adult attention to his or her behaviour. By the age of four or so, most children give the impression that they positively do not *want* to be noticed by adults or, rather, by most people who are senior to them. This behaviour is carried through in adult life: deportment that combines humility with a quiet dignity is considered 'chiefly', while the quintessence of bad manners is to presume beyond one's station.

It will be apparent to the reader that children are not admitted to *yaqona*-drinking, though a toddler or two may be present on informal occasions, especially those at home. However, children have ample opportunity for observation. The habit of 'peeping' (*iro*) is adopted by children as young as four or five; so any lively gathering in the house or village hall attracts small groups of children, who range themselves outside the building and peer at the proceedings through the chinks and crevices in the bamboo slats or other material that forms the walls. School children may be called upon to penetrate a *yaqona*-drinking group in the pursuance of some small task such as the delivery of a message. Despite their formal exclusion from *yaqona*-drinking and other adult activities children are thus in a position to form their own ideas about their nature.

I use the term 'child' advisedly here, since one is not considered to be fully adult until married (usually in one's early 20s). However, 'little young men' (*cauravou lalai*, boys aged about 15 and over) are admitted to *yaqona*-drinking at around age 17, primarily as mixers and servers of the drink; *gone yalewa* (lit. 'girls' but, more properly, 'young women' from age 15 or so onwards) begin to attend village-wide gatherings at around age 17 or so. Within the category of 'children' (*gone*) the developmental stages most often acknowledged are those of 'baby' (*gone dramidrami*, lit. 'a sucking child'), 'little children' (*gone lalai*), i.e. toddlers and those aged up to five or so and 'school children' (*gone vuli*), i.e. primary school children and those in the early years of secondary school; the term *gone tubutubu* (lit. 'grown-up child') is sometimes used in reference to early adolescence.

Fijian children have, by law, to attend primary school and most continue in secondary school until age 16 or so; there is an average of one primary school for every two villages.[18] The developmental data I refer to here comes entirely from my analysis of drawings and commentary upon them provided by the

67 children who, in 1982, made up the entire roll of the Sawaieke District Primary School and who came from the villages of Sawaieke and Somosomo (a small village some 3 km from Sawaieke). Because Fijian children tend to be quiet and withdrawn with adults, I spent several months towards the end of 1982 working in the school—the headmaster and other teachers kindly allowing me this opportunity to encourage the children to become used to talking to me. The children ranged in age from 5:10, the youngest child in Class 1, to 14:2, the oldest child in Class 6. The drawings, commentary upon them and the essays written by older children were the first tasks that I set. They were devised very freely in order to get relatively un-structured information on children's understanding of status distinctions, of symbolic *cake/ra*, and to find out the extent to which they would themselves make use of this dimension to differentiate status. All investigations were conducted in Fijian.

For their drawings children were instructed as follows:

> Just imagine that there is a big gathering going on in the village hall in Sawaieke. All the people are sitting in the village hall: the women, the young men, the girls and the men. They are drinking *yaqona* and having a good time. Please draw nicely everything that you can. Show all the people who are there drinking *yaqona*.

The children did these drawings in their school classes, each individual being sufficiently separated from the next to ensure that there was no possibility of systematic copying. Later they gave me their drawings and in individual conversation with each child I labelled the drawings in accordance with their answers to the following series of questions:

> Who are these people? Are there any women here? Where are they sitting? Please point them out. What about the men, are there any men? Please point to them, where are they sitting? Is the high chief here? What is his name? Where is he sitting? Are there any young men? Show me the young men, where are they sitting? Is there a chiefly lady here? Where is she? What is her name? Where is she sitting? And what about the girls, are there any girls? Where are they sitting?

It was often unnecessary to ask all the questions since once they were started off, many children came out spontaneously with the desired information. One of the early answers might forestall further enquiry e.g. one boy aged 9:0 in Class 3 told me there were three chiefs sitting 'above' and that all the rest of the figures he drew were young men. Were there no women or girls? No, there were none. When I had to ask the full series of questions, I changed them about so as to minimise any bias arising from order effects across children. My questions distinguished three statuses for each sex: a high chief and a chiefly lady, men and women, and young men and girls. However the children spontaneously distinguished up to five different statuses as being possible for men and four for women. Figure 7.2 shows the reader some of the drawings.[19]

Owing to the difficulty I should have in analysing the *cake/ra* problem in tandem with developmental variation in respect of the way children approached the problem of perspective, I have entirely ignored perspective in the present analysis to concentrate on what children *told* me was the case. In other words I might be told that the figure pointed out to me as 'the high chief', *na turaga levu*, was seated 'right up high', *i cake sara*, and that others were seated 'below', *i ra*, even when the layout on the page would not necessarily have led me to this conclusion. Ignoring perspective then, the drawings were analysed to discover:

(a) the pattern of opposition given for the positions *i cake* and *i ra*.
(b) the number and kind of rank distinctions made for each sex,
(c) marks of distinction that set one person off against the others.

*Patterns of opposition* (see Table 7.1). When the poles *i cake* and *i ra* are taken together, a total of 37 oppositions can be distinguished from one another across all drawings. But if we look at the position *i cake* alone, then we find only six variations possible within it; while for the position *i ra* taken alone we find 17 possible variations across all 67 children. Looking at the two poles of the opposition as they varied together, the 37 different types were further broken down into ten distinct types of drawing. The results across all 67 children are shown in Figure 7.3 together with a description of the various opposition types.

In reference to Figure 7.3, the reader will see that the progression from Drawing Type 1 to Type 10 is in accordance with the

**Figure 7.2(a):** Girl 7/0. Drawing Type 4: ▲ i cake △ ○⊙ i ra.

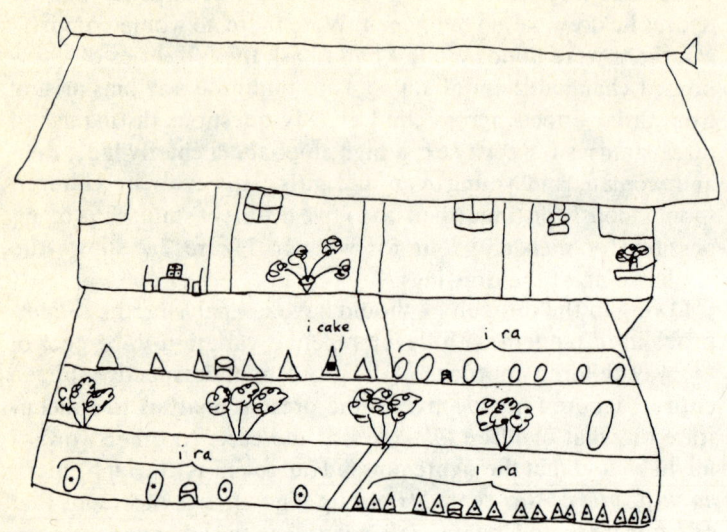

Girl 8/3. Drawing Type 4: ▲ i cake △ ○⊙ i ra.

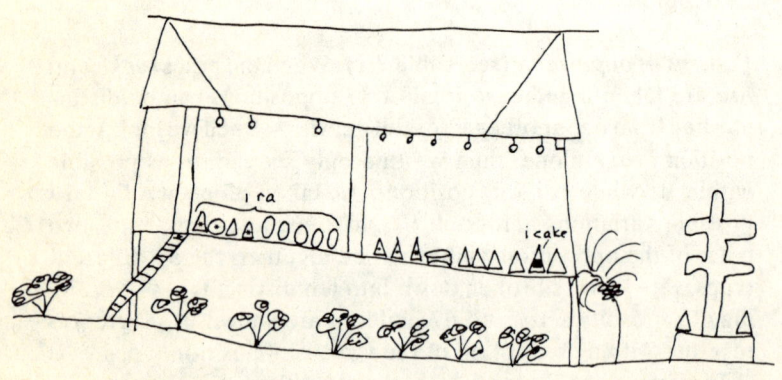

**Figure 7.2(b):** Boy 7/3. Drawing Type 5: ▲ i cake ○ i ra.

Boy 9/2. Drawing Type 5: ▲ i cake ○⊙ i ra.

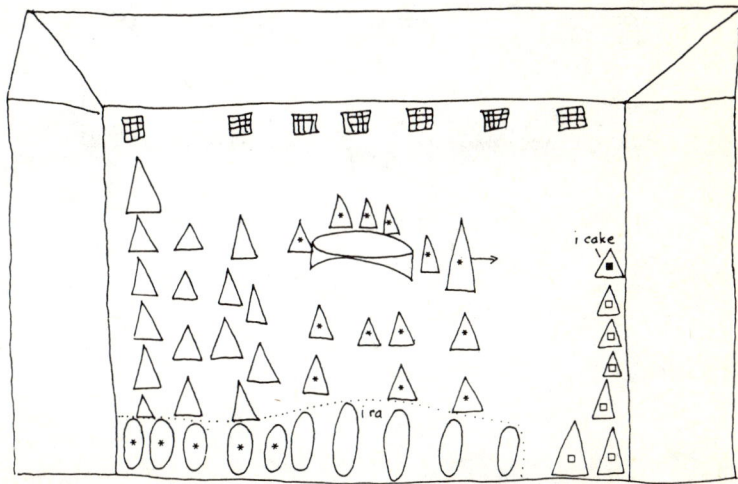

**Figure 7.2(c):** Girl 8/6. Drawing Type 6: ▲▲▲i cake ▲⊙ i ra.

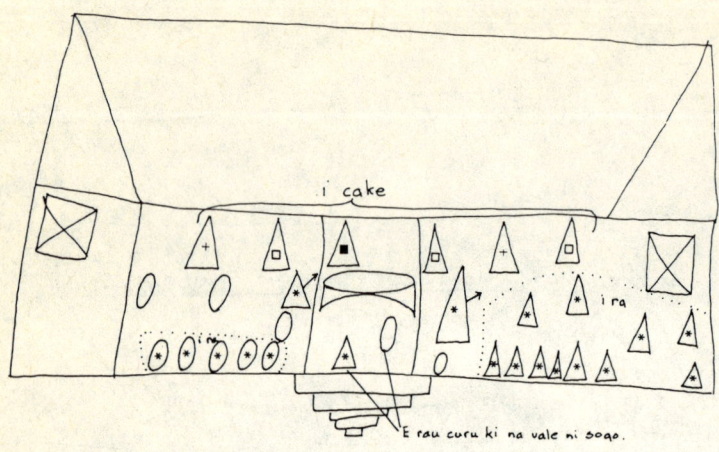

Girl 11/0. Drawing Type 6: ▲i cake ▲⊙i ra.

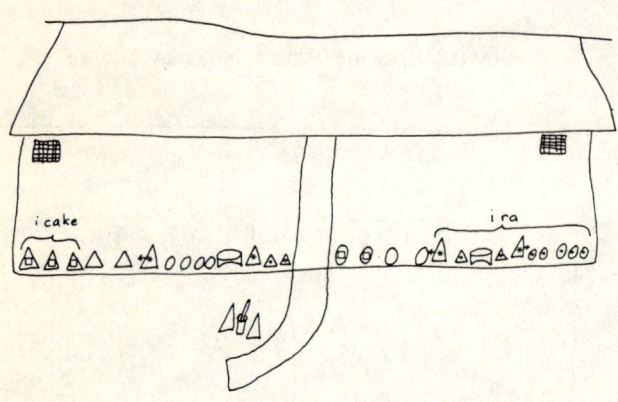

**Figure 7.2(d):** Boy 8/4. Drawing Type 6: 🔺🔺i cake 🔺i ra.

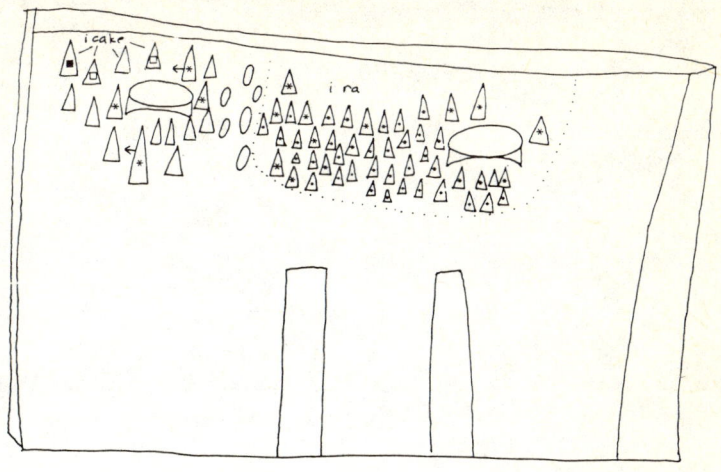

Boy 11/10. Drawing Type 6: 🔺🔺i cake 🔺i ra.

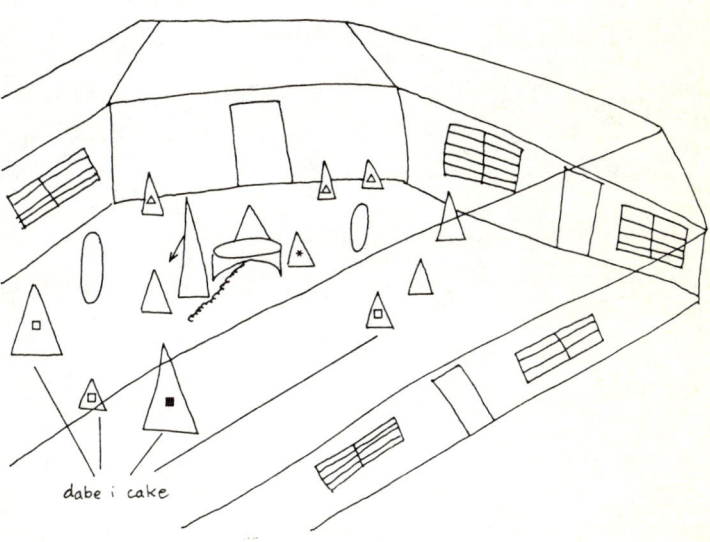

**Figure 7.2(e):** Girl 10/8. Drawing Type 7: ⚠⊙i cake △○△△⊙i ra.

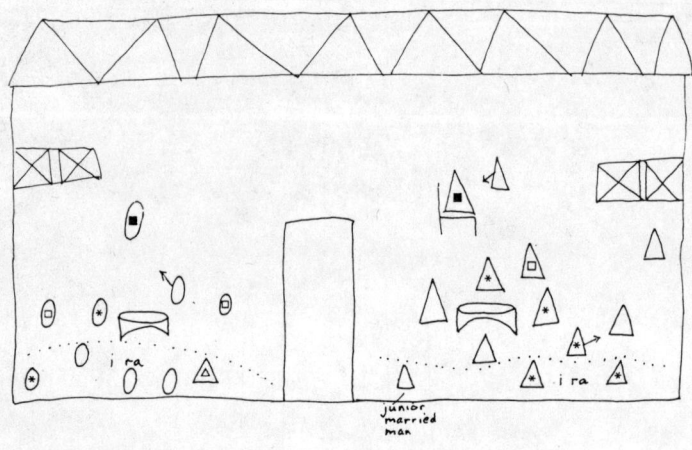

Girl 11/6. Drawing Type 7: ⚠⊙△⊙i cake ○+children i ra.

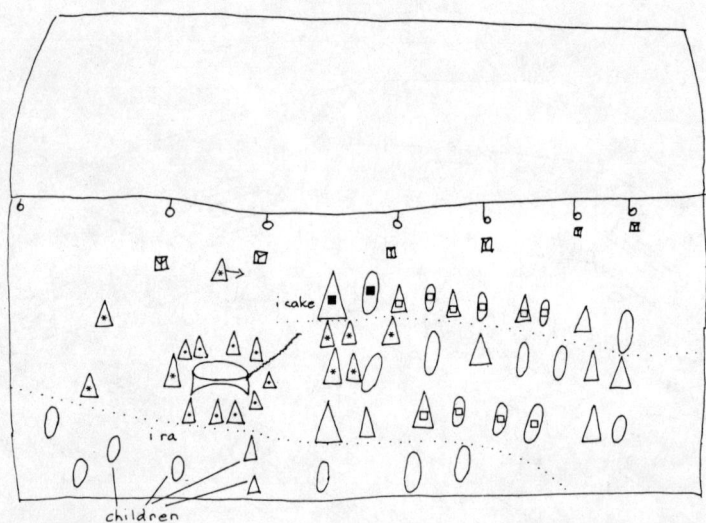

**Figure 7.2(f):** Boy 9/10. Drawing Type 8: ▲▲i cake ⊙○i ra.

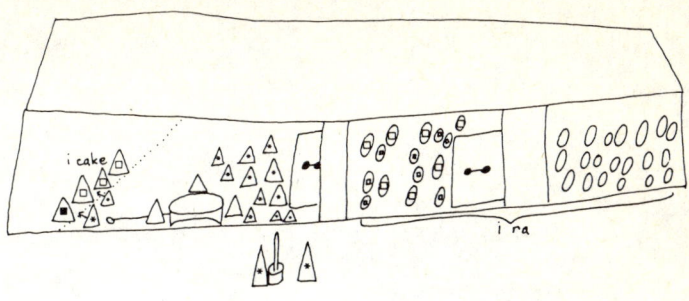

Boy 11/9. Drawing Type 8: ▲▲i cake ○i ra.

**Figure 7.2(g):** Boy 12/10. Drawing Type 9: △△ i cake △◉◉ i ra.

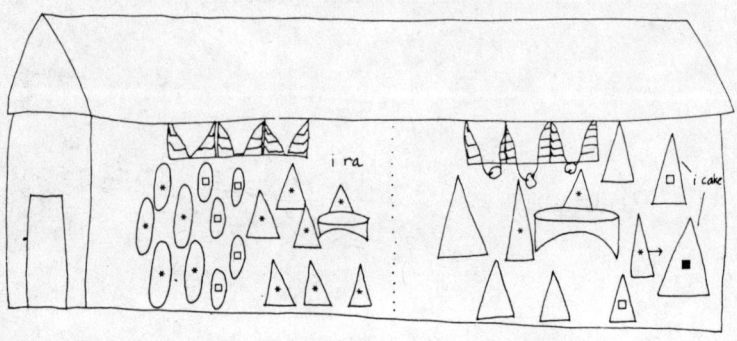

Boy 13/8. Drawing Type 9: △△ i cake △◉ i ra.

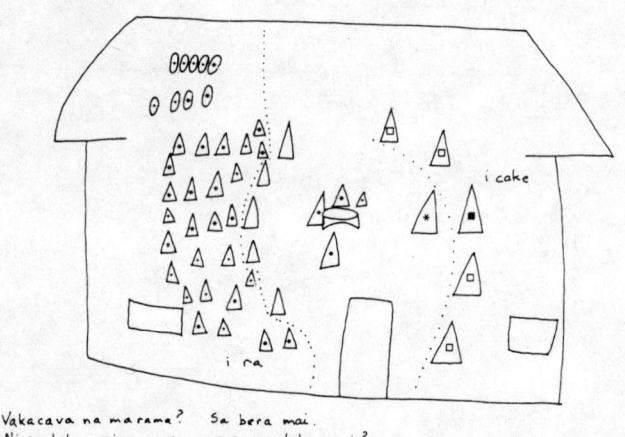

Vakacava na marama? Sa bera mai.
Ni ra lako mai na marama e ra na dabe evei?
E ra na dabe sara i ra.

**Figure 7.2(h):** Girl 13/0. Drawing Type 10: ⧈⧈i cake ⧈⊙i ra.

Boy 14/2. Drawing Type 10: ⧈⧈i cake ⧈⧈○i ra.

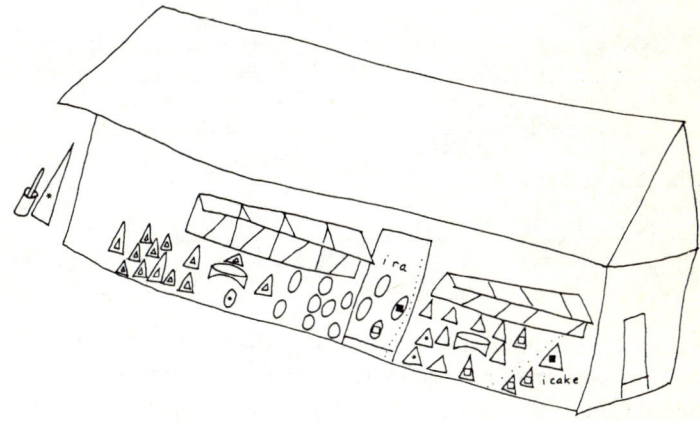

## Table 7.1

| Drawing Type | Pattern of Opposition | | Number of children |
|---|---|---|---|
| 1 | ? | ? | 1 |
| 2 | ▲ | ? | 2 |
|   | △ | ? | 1 |
| 3 | ▲ | △▲ | 2 |
|   | ▲ | ▲ | 1 |
| 4 | ▲ | ▲○/▲○⊙ | 8 |
|   | ▲ | ▲⊙ | 1 |
|   | △ | ▲▲○⊙ | 1 |
| 5 | ▲ | ○/○⊙ | 12 |
|   | ▲ | ⊙ | 3 |
|   | △ | ○ | 1 |
| 6 | ▲ | ▲ | 3 |
|   | ▲ | ▲▲○ | 1 |
|   | ▲ | ▲▲○/▲○⊙ | 2 |
|   | ▲ | ▲ | 1 |
|   | ▲ | ▲⊙ | 1 |
|   | ▲ | ○ | 1 |
|   | ▲ | ▲⊙ | 2 |
| 7 | ▲⊚ | ▲⊙ | 1 |
|   | ▲⊚ | ▲△⊚○ | 1 |
|   | ▲⊙ | △▲▲○⊙ | 1 |
|   | ▲ | ▲⊙ | 1 |
|   | ▲⊚ | ○ | 1 |
|   | ▲⊚ | ▲⊙ | 1 |
|   | ▲⊚ | △▲⊚○⊙ | 1 |
| 8 | ▲ | ○/○⊙ | 5 |
|   | ▲ | ▲⊚○⊙ | 1 |
| 9 | ▲ | ▲○/▲○⊙/▲▲○ | 5 |
|   | ▲ | ▲⊙ | 1 |
| 10 | ▲ | ▲▲○ | 3 |
|   | ▲ | ▲○⊙ | 1 |

Total no. of different oppositions: 37

Possibilities i cake:

| | | |
|---|---|---|
| ? | Drawing Type 1 | 1 |
| ▲ | Drawing Types 2, 3, 4, 5, 6 | 35 |
| △ | Drawing Types 2, 4, 5 | 3 |
| ▲ | Drawing Types 6, 7, 8, 9, 10 | 22 |
| ▲⊚ | Drawing Type 7 | 1 |
| ▲⊚ | Drawing Type 7 | 4 |
| ▲⊙ | Drawing Type 7 | 1 |
| | Total: | 67 |

Possibilities i ra:

| | | |
|---|---|---|
| △▲ | Drawing Type 3 | 2 |
| ▲ | Drawing Types 3, 6 | 4 |
| ▲○ | Drawing Types 4, 9 | 4 |
| ▲○⊙ | Drawing Types 4, 6, 9 | 9 |
| ▲⊙ | Drawing Types 4, 6, 7, 9 | 8 |
| ▲▲○⊙ | Drawing Type 4 | 1 |
| ○ | Drawing Types 5, 6, 7, 8 | 15 |
| ○⊙ | Drawing Type 5 | 5 |
| ⊙ | Drawing Type 5 | 3 |
| ▲▲○ | Drawing Types 6, 9, 10 | 6 |
| ▲ | Drawing Type 6 | 1 |
| ▲△⊚○ | Drawing Type 7 | 1 |
| △▲▲○⊙ | Drawing Type 7 | 1 |
| △▲⊚○⊙ | Drawing Type 7 | 1 |
| ▲⊚○⊙ | Drawing Type 8 | 1 |
| ▲○⊙ | Drawing Type 10 | 1 |
| ? | Drawing Types 1, 2 | 4 |
| | Total: | 67 |

median age of children whose drawings display a given opposition. The pattern of opposition for each drawing type is given in symbol form with a key at the bottom of the page. Children are grouped according to age and sex: a small circle represents a girl and a small triangle a boy, their ages being plotted on the horizontal axis. So, for example, the youngest child to produce a Type 5 Drawing may be seen to be a boy aged 6:3, while the oldest is a boy aged 9:7.

**Figure 7.3: Distribution of drawing types by age and sex of child.**

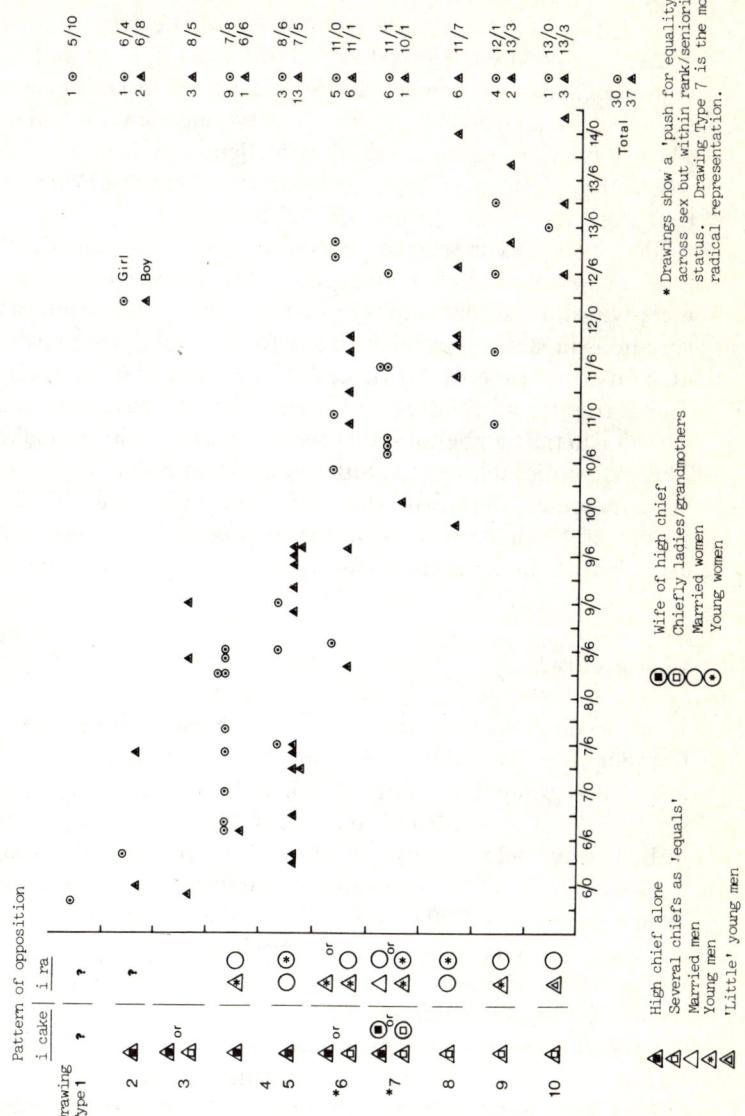

### Who sits i cake?

The first problem to be answered concerns who sits *i cake*. Looking just at the pattern of opposition shown for Drawing Types 2–10 and excluding Type 7 (to be discussed below), it is clear that the matter of who sits *i cake* is a relatively unambiguous one for the children. Thirty-five out of 67 children showed the high chief *i cake* alone while 22 showed a small group of chiefs including the high chief, as *dabe i cake*, 'sitting above' together. Thus 57 out of 67 children said that the figures in their drawings whom they designated chiefs (i.e. *ko ira na turaga, turaga ni vanua* or *o ira na malo*) were 'sitting above'.

Thus high rank is seen to pertain to a very few individuals; other people are classified into groups that are very much more inclusive, and less highly differentiated with respect to internal variations in status that might make for example, one married man superior to another by virtue of higher rank or age seniority. This is true for all children and is indifferent to developmental variation in the number of status distinctions that children make. There is a noticeable change with age such that children aged 8:6 and over tend to show two to four chiefs together *i cake* with only 15 out of 43 children showing the high chief *i cake* alone. In accordance with these data *i cake* is defined as the place of chiefs.

### Who sits i ra?

The question of who sits *i ra* is a much more difficult one. Drawing Types 4 and 9 show females, considered as an undifferentiated group, intermingled with and therefore on the same symbolic level as unmarried young men. The entire group is said to be *i ra* or 'below'. However, Drawing Types 5 and 8 show females only as seated *i ra*, differentiated from and definitely 'below' young men. Type 10 may be read as similar to Types 5 and 8 in that here females are shown intermingled with 'little young men' (*cauravou lalai*) and, as a group, are said to be 'below' young men (*cauravou*).

However, there is a strong interaction here between the task and the sex of the child who carries it out. For Types 4 and 9 it is girls (13 out of 16 children) who say that young men too are seated *i ra* with women. For Types 5, 8, and 10 it is boys (22 out of 26 children) who say that women only are *i ra* or, in the case of boys doing Type 10 Drawings, *i ra* alongside 'little young men' (*cauravou lalai*), this being the humblest of male statuses. Thus, girls prefer to say that young men are *i ra* along with women and girls, while boys prefer to say that only women and girls are *i ra*. This preference holds for older children (12:0–14:0) with five out of six girls continuing to place young men along with women *i ra*, and five out of seven boys either giving women the 'low' position or seating them alongside 'little young men' and 'below' young men.

## A 'push for equality' across gender

Drawing Types 6 and 7 are particularly interesting and I shall comment upon these before returning to a more general discussion. They show what I refer to as a 'push for equality' across gender and within rank/seniority levels, with Type 7 being the more radical representation.

The main point here is that the disposition of figures shown in these drawings is virtually never seen in real life. Thus Type 7 Drawings may show the high chief seated beside his wife *i cake*, with other chiefs seated beside their wives, and so on 'down' through the rank/seniority levels, with young men and girls seated together *i ra*. Husbands and wives practise avoidance in public gatherings and certainly do not sit side by side. In the typical situation, shown in Figure 7.1, men and women cannot be said to be mingled together but instead form discrete groups according to their gender and rank/seniority status. Only two or three times in 18 months did I attend a gathering where the situation came anywhere near being similar to that shown in Drawing Types 6 and 7.

One of these times occurred during the New Year holiday season in 1982 when the ladies of Sawaieke (some 20 or so) visited the neighbouring village of Nawaikama (about 3.5 km from Sawaieke) in response to an invitation from Nawaikama men. No Sawaieke men accompanied the ladies on their visit. Sawaieke women, considered as a group, rank above or on the same level as Nawaikama men, because Nawaikama owes allegiance to the chiefly village of Sawaieke. So, on this occasion, several high-status women from Sawaieke sat 'above' the *tanoa* side by side with Nawaikama chiefs; Sawaieke women as a group sat towards the 'top' of the room and along one side, on a level and sometimes intermingled with, Nawaikama men. In this case all Nawaikama young men (*cauravou*) were definitely 'below' Sawaieke women.

However, this pattern was extremely unusual and arose largely because no Sawaieke men were present and because it was a holiday occasion from which lots of fun was expected—dancing, flirtatious banter and other daring behaviour. It should be said however that when Sawaieke women visit villages that owe allegiance to their own, several chiefly ladies from Sawaieke are always invited to take their place 'above' the *tanoa* and will do so as a matter of course. However, if their own men are present these ladies are bound to adopt seating positions that are unambiguously 'below' their men (husbands, elder brothers, fathers-in-law etc.). It is only when unaccompanied by their own men that chiefly ladies from Sawaieke can, in another village, sit on a level 'above' the *tanoa* that is side by side with the traditional chiefs of that village.

The unusual nature of this type of situation means that the children who did Drawing Types 6 and 7 can only rarely, if ever, have actually seen anything like the situation that they depicted. Type 6 Drawings are less extreme than Type 7. They show the high chief or a small number of chiefs together *i cake* and it is only for rank/seniority levels below 'chief' that one finds a 'push for equality', that is, women may be intermingled with men, girls with young men. Type 6 Drawings vary quite widely in disposition of figures, however they all share a certain feature: i.e. that at least some, possibly more senior, women are said to be on a level with or just 'below' men and unequivocally 'above' young men.

Given that *yaqona* is drunk everyday somewhere in the village, and that each week there is at least one mixed gathering of men and women in the hall for the same purpose, it seems unlikely that children would choose to depict a highly unusual situation when asked to do a drawing that shows members of both sexes drinking *yaqona* together. It is possible that these children were extrapolating information from their knowledge of seating arrangements in the body of the church, where, as I pointed out above, women and men are on the same level as each other for statuses 'below' that of clan chief. Whatever its source, it looks as if some children were asserting what would be the case according to rank and age seniority *if gender was not a factor*. It is interesting too that 11 out of 18 children who asserted a certain equality across gender within rank/seniority level were girls, while of the seven who make the most radical representation in Type 7 Drawings, six were girls.

It looks as if, around age 11:0, some, but not all, children had constructed an understanding of relative status in terms of an interaction between rank and age seniority that they then applied rigidly to the ordering of status relations, ignoring the gender principle that makes females in general inferior to males on the *cake/ra* axis. It could be said to be the 'over inclusiveness' of their application of the rank/seniority principle that led children to depict exceptional situations—mostly ones they can never have seen e.g. a man seated beside his wife in a public gathering.

Reference to Figure 7.3 shows that the preference for Type 6 and 7 Drawings is most prevalent between the ages of 10:0 and 12:0, with 12 out of 17 children in this age group choosing to make an assertion of rank/seniority over gender as the main principle in ascribing social status. Type 7 is the most radical choice in that it asserts equality across gender within status for most rank/seniority statuses from high chief's on down. This radical assertion of an interaction between rank and seniority in ascribing status does not occur before Class 4 nor beyond Class 5. Two older girls, both in Class 6 (the final year of primary school) made Type 6 Drawings showing the less extreme assertion of the rank/seniority principle, where married women are seen as 'above' young men, who are ranked on the same level as girls. All other children in Class 6 represent a situation that shows a high chief or a small group of chiefs *i cake*, with women and girls, or women, girls and young men at the pole *i ra*. Those who are seated *i ra* are apparently regarded as a group whose members are of more or less equal status. It will be noticed that any grouping that puts *all* females over the age of 17:0 or 18:0 on the same symbolic level as young men effectively ignores rank/seniority differences among women.

*Rank/seniority distinctions.* In connection with this, and referring to Table 7.2, note that children who produce Type 7 Drawings are using three, four and five rank/seniority distinctions for men and two, three or four for women; those who make Type 6 Drawings—the less radical choice—tend to make fewer distinctions within women, the majority showing only one or two categories of women (9 out of 11 children).

### Table 7.2

(i) No. of rank/seniority distinctions made for MEN by children doing Drawing Types 6, 7, 8, 9 and 10

|               | 5 | 4 | 3 | 2 | 1 |                         |
|---------------|---|---|---|---|---|-------------------------|
| Type 6        |   | 4 | 3 | 4 |   | re. 11 chn  8:4 –12:10  |
| Type 7        |   | 2 | 4 | 1 |   | re.  7 chn 10:1 –12:6   |
| Types 8, 9, 10|   | 7 | 9 |   |   | re. 16 chn  9:10–14:2   |

(ii) No. of rank/seniority distinctions made for WOMEN by children doing Drawing Types 6, 7, 8, 9 and 10

|               | 4 | 3 | 2 | 1 |                         |
|---------------|---|---|---|---|-------------------------|
| Type 6        |   | 2 | 5 | 4 | re. 11 chn  8:4 –12:10  |
| Type 7        | 3 | 3 | 1 |   | re.  7 chn 10:1 –12:6   |
| Types 8, 9, 10| 3 | 3 | 7 | 3 | re. 16 chn  9:10–14:2   |

Looking now at Table 7.2 (ii), if we compare the number of rank/seniority distinctions made for women by children doing Drawing Types 6 and 7 with those by children over 9:9 who have made other choices, we can see that the latter children make as many rank/seniority distinctions for women as other children. Nevertheless they are declining to *use* them. Despite their ability to distinguish female statuses they seem to prefer to class all women together, or to class all women together with young men, and effectively assert that the different categories may be conflated such that all members are considered to be sitting *i ra*.

Thus it seems fair to say that while young men (or 'little young men' when both distinctions have been made) may be considered as defining the place that is *i ra* when status differentiations are made for men, the fact that women are treated as an undifferentiated group and placed as such *i ra*—even when status distinctions have been made for them—means that fundamentally the term *i ra* is defined by its being the place of women.

### Developmental variation

With regard to overall developmental variation, the children's drawings show an early grasp of symbolic *cake/ra* in its crudest form: the high chief is *i cake* and females, or females and young men are *i ra*, but few rank distinctions are made within gender. In other words, the youngest children have not yet grasped the complexities of rank/seniority differentiation on the *cake/ra* axis. Table 7.3 shows that up to age 8:0 the majority of children are making two or three distinctions for men and one or two distinctions for women. At eight-plus they begin to further differentiate ranks of men using three and four distinctions, but still only one or two for women. It is not until age 10:0 that they begin to use with any reliability three or four distinctions for women; but over half of them are still making only one or two distinctions for women.

**Table 7.3**: No. of rank/seniority distinctions.

| No. of: | Distinctions for MEN | | | | | | for WOMEN | | | | |
|---|---|---|---|---|---|---|---|---|---|---|---|
| | 5 | 4 | 3 | 2 | 1 | 0 | 4 | 3 | 2 | 1 | 0 |
| AGE | | | | | | | | | | | |
| 5 yr+ | | | 1 | 1 | | | | | 1 | | 1 |
| 6 yr+ | | | 3 | 4 | 1 | | | 1 | 2 | 5 | |
| 7 yr+ | | 1 | 3 | 4 | 1 | | | 1 | 2 | 6 | |
| 8 yr+ | | 4 | 4 | 1 | | | | | 5 | 3 | 1 |
| 9 yr+ | 1 | 5 | 2 | 1 | | | | 1 | 3 | 3 | 1 |
| 10 yr+ | 3 | 2 | 2 | | | | 2 | 1 | 3 | 1 | |
| 11 yr+ | 3 | 5 | 2 | | | | 1 | 4 | 3 | 2 | |
| 12 yr+ | 3 | 3 | 1 | | | | 1 | 1 | 3 | 2 | |
| 13 yr+ | 3 | 1 | | | | | 1 | | 2 | 1 | |
| 14 yr+ | 2 | | | | | | 1 | 1 | | | |
| Total: (67 chn) | 15 | 21 | 18 | 11 | 2 | | 6 | 10 | 24 | 24 | 3 |

There is an interaction here with a child's sex (see Table 7.4) such that boys differentiate statuses for men more finely than do girls, while girls differentiate statuses for women more finely than do boys. That is, the majority of boys (i.e. 23 out of 37) make four or five distinctions among men, where the majority of girls (i.e. 22 out of 30) make three or four. The reverse finding holds for distinctions among women: the majority of girls (21 out of 30) make two or three distinctions among women, while the majority of boys (30 out of 37) make two or less.

Despite this interaction, there is a noticeable tendency around age 11:0, and despite the introduction (at age 10:0) of four possible distinctions for women, for older children to continue to distinguish only one or two rank/seniority statuses for women.

**Table 7.4:**

i. No. of rank/seniority distinctions made for MEN

|          | 5  | 4  | 3  | 2 | 1 | 0 | Total |
|----------|----|----|----|---|---|---|-------|
| By boys  | 10 | 13 | 4  | 8 | 2 | – | 37    |
| By girls | 5  | 8  | 14 | 3 | – | – | 30    |

ii. No. of rank/seniority distinctions made for WOMEN

|          | 4 | 3 | 2  | 1  | 0 | Total |
|----------|---|---|----|----|---|-------|
| By boys  | 2 | 5 | 8  | 19 | 3 | 37    |
| By girls | 4 | 5 | 16 | 5  | – | 30    |

For children over 11:0, it can be seen that eight out of 13 boys and five out of ten girls make only one or two distinctions among women. It appears that, while they are probably able to make more than one or two distinctions for women, these children do not regard such distinctions as of any great significance and tend to ignore them.

This accords with the way that drawings by children of 12:0 and over are fairly equally distributed over Types 8, 9, and 10 (i.e. ten out of 13 drawings). On the one hand they seem to be more conscious of ambiguity regarding the position of the high chief when compared with other chiefs, but they also reconstitute, as it were, a definition of *i ra* as the place of young men against all other ranks of men, or of women as an undifferentiated group over against the ranks of men and on a level with, or 'below' young men.

In other words, these older children have grasped both the principle of hierarchy as expressed in a relative ranking on the *cake/ra* axis, *and* the way that gender is a complexly interacting factor that tends to make status distinctions for women of marginal importance. Children doing Drawing Types 8, 9, and 10 no longer apply a hierarchical concept in its simple form like the majority of six- to eight-year-olds—who tended to focus on its extremes, chief 'above' and women, or women and young men 'below', and to refuse to use *all* the statuses suggested by myself. Nor do they make status differences the product of a rigidly inclusive interaction between rank and seniority, like some of the nine- to twelve-year-olds. That is to say, they no longer overregularise the rank/seniority principle such that older persons of chiefly birth are always 'above' younger persons whose rank by birth is less relevant. Rather, they have learned that the rank/seniority principle, though it may be expressed in general terms, also implies possible exceptions and that these are largely clustered around a gender distinction that makes females in general inferior to males.

In my own judgement, Type 9 Drawings are the most sophisticated representation, simply because they introduce an element of ambiguity at both ends of the *cake/ra* axis: that is, the possibility that several chiefs including the high chief might be considered to be more or less equals, and that the high chief is not, at least in Sawaieke, always unambiguously the 'highest'. In addition, young men are said to be *i ra* on a level with women and again this gives a truer picture of empirical fact, for whether young men as a status category may be said to be 'above' all women is a matter that varies according to the status of the women who are present and the sex of the person making the judgement. In connection with the relative sophistication of Type 9 Drawings, it is perhaps not surprising that they do not appear before 10:11 and cannot be said to be a popular choice—only six children making this type of representation.

*Marks of distinction.* There is little tendency up to age 7:6 to separate the high chief off from other figures, though he may be shown aligned with the *tanoa* (the *yaqona* bowl) and next to it. At age 7:6 children begin to leave more space around the high chief or, in a few cases, show him seated in a chair, so that he is literally above others. In using the chair to mark high rank, children are extrapolating information from contexts *outside* that of *yaqona*-drinking where, except in the case of a nationally important chief (like the Prime Minister, Ratu Sir Kamisese Mara or the Governor General, Ratu Sir Penaia Ganilau), no-one ever sits in a chair, and using it in their drawings to make the chief's position clear.

The four youngest to use a chair were aged 5:11, 6:6, 7:3 and 8:5. Two drawings by older children show a chair, but these are much more sophisticated. In the first, a Type 7 Drawing by a girl aged 10:8, the high chief is on the same level on the page as his wife and each of them is said to be *i cake* with the high chief having 'below' him a couple of elders, some married men and some young men, while 'below' his wife sit grandmothers, married women and young men. Telling me about her drawing this child said: 'Both the high chief and his wife are sitting right "up above", but it is different because the high chief is sitting in a chair and his wife is sitting on the mat.' That is to say, both rank above all others, but within their relationship the high chief ranks above his wife.

The oldest child to draw in a chair was a boy aged 12:7, who produced a Type 8 Drawing for which he described a small group of named chiefs as *dabe i cake*, 'sitting above'. He said: 'Look, these few chiefs are all sitting "above", but the *tanoa* faces towards the high chief and he is sitting in a chair.' I asked him if the high chief usually sat in a chair and he said: 'No, only here (i.e. in his drawing) so that he may be seen.'

Other rank markers include drawing the high chief larger than other figures and/or leaving more space around him. This starts at age 7:3 and continues to be used up to 12:10. Older children who show a number of chiefs seated together *i cake* tend to draw them the same size, but leave plenty of space both between the chiefs themselves and between chiefs and all other people shown. This strategy is introduced at age 8:6 and is still in use at age 14:0; as a marker it is a matter of empirical fact: chiefs *do* sit with more space between them, and between themselves and all others.

Finally there are two other rank markers. The first is given by the child's drawing the rope that leads from the *tanoa* to the high chief. This is used only on important occasions *before* serving begins, when it is coiled back under the *tanoa*; but it is an empirical rank marker and the children use it as such. The depiction of the rope occurs between the ages of 9:10 and 12:7, and most often between 11:6 and 11:10 (i.e. five out of eight children). A more subtle and more ambiguous marker is given by showing the *taki* or serving of *yaqona*; 23 out of the 67 children show one or more young men as servers. Most children show *yaqona* being served to the high chief and to one or two others. Older children may display a clearer understanding of the *taki* by depicting only one young man in the act of serving the high chief: five out of the 11 children over 12:0 who use this rank marker do so in this manner. In reality, no-one *ever* drinks or is served at the same time as the high chief. In choosing therefore to depict in their drawings a single young man serving the high chief, some of the older children appear to be drawing on knowledge that the order of drinking is very important, and that 'the high chief drinks first' and on his own.

## Children's essays on 'the gathering'

After completing their drawings, but *before* being questioned about them, children in Classes 3–6 inclusive wrote a story about 'a gathering'. This was intended merely as a 'check' on at least some of the drawings. Children were asked to write about a big gathering in the village hall where people were drinking *yaqona* and having lots of fun. The essay topic being so freely described, the essays were not necessarily related to the drawings; but in no case did the two forms of representation by a given child contradict one another, and often independently corroborated the coding type that I have ascribed to the drawings. Of a total of 43 essays, 32 refer either to 'rank markers' and/or describe the social status of participants by reference to their disposition in symbolic space.

Because the essays were virtually unstructured by myself and written *before* children were questioned about their drawings, the significance of spontaneous description like the following cannot be discounted. 'The chief sits above, the young men sit round the *tanoa*, the women sit below'—this by a boy of 9:2 who did a Type 5 Drawing showing the high chief *i cake* and women *i ra*. The following comes from an essay by a girl aged 12:6 who did a Type 7 Drawing showing a radical 'push for equality' across gender and within rank/seniority status:

> Takalaigau (the high chief) sits above. The men also sit above. Some of the men sit below. A few of the women sit above and some of them sit below ... those who look after the *yaqona* sit in the middle.

And finally, from a girl aged 8:5 who did a Type 4 Drawing showing the high chief alone *i cake* and women and young men together *i ra*:

> Takalaigau sits above and Ratu Laua [who was considered second in chiefly rank] comes next. The women sit below and so do the young men who look after the *yaqona*.

## THE CONSTRUCTION OF HIERARCHY

In conclusion, I wish to reiterate briefly some of the remarks with which I prefaced this paper. First, it is clear that the image of society to be found in *yaqona*-drinking is, for the villagers of Sawaieke, a powerful one. To recognise this we have only to see that the disposition of figures in children's drawings is (with the exception of the youngest child) entirely non-random. Second, it is clear that social hierarchy *is* merged with symbolic *cake/ra* such that children construct their notions of rank/seniority statuses and their interaction with gender in part by reference to symbolic spatial categories: e.g. to say that someone 'sits above' is the same as saying that this person is of high status. Third, it is clear that gender cannot be axiomatically isolated from the symbolic construction of a hierarchy that is *said* to be dependent upon one's status at birth, i.e. on whether one is born a 'chief' or 'a commoner' and, within rank, whether one has relative seniority in age in a genealogically senior line. Hierarchy, as well as gender, has to be considered from the outset as a culturally constructed notion, not as an analytic category. Whether gender *can* be isolated from hierarchy is a matter that can be decided only by looking at empirical data that is truly 'actor centred'.

Such data is, I suggest, to be found in the development of children's understanding of symbolic constructs. Sociological analysis of such constructs, however elegant it may be, cannot easily reveal the extent to which they actually organise people's understanding, that is to say, are central or fundamental to their notions about their own society. To say that a symbolic construct is central or fundamental is to assert that there is a complex of inter-linked core symbols that organise other notions and social behaviour. But this implies a *sequence* of learning for those core symbols and we can find out this sequence—and thus the relative salience of each part of a complex symbolism—by looking at the process by which children construct it. Children do not get their culture 'ready-made'; they have to construct it gradually over time out of data available to them from their interaction with, and observance of, other members of society.

Clearly, in looking at what *cake/ra* means for children in the context of *yaqona*-drinking I was following up an initial hunch of the kind common to anthropologists. Even without the developmental data I could have asserted that *cake/ra* was the central symbolic construct for organising villagers' ideas about rank, seniority and gender. What I could not have done so easily was to show conclusively that the cultural constructs of gender, rank and seniority are of *equal* dominance and must be considered together as of central importance for the symbolic construction of Fijian society. This becomes apparent in that the very youngest children used all three notions in an entirely regular way. That is to say, they constituted the two poles of the symbolic *cake/ra* axis by reference to rank (the high chief was always *i cake*) and gender (women or women and young men were always *i ra*, depending on the sex of the child); at the same time they made use of the seniority principle (i.e. 'older above younger') to order the disposition of people on the axis between the two poles. Moreover, the finding that the differential response of boys and girls centred on the issue of gender shows the process of 'learning hierarchy' to be affected by the fact of gender itself.

In Sawaieke one's position in the hierarchy is *said to be* primarily a matter of relative rank such that the distinction between 'the chiefs' and 'the people' seems to encompass all other distinctions; so Sahlins makes this the basis for his analysis of symbolic structures in Fiji (see Sahlins, 1976, pp. 24–46). However, what is said to be the case does not always accord with what is *seen* to be so and while the interaction between rank and seniority poses no problem, the matter of gender is rendered highly ambiguous. It is 'within-generation' kinship relations that pose a problem for the interaction between gender and age seniority. The ambiguity is such that men may recognise the formal authority of elder sister over younger brother while simultaneously asserting the axiomatic authority of a man over his wife.[20] This observation begs the question of which relationship, that of wife or that of sister, is most salient for the construction of hierarchy in Fiji. Type 7 Drawings showing women seated beside or on the same symbolic level as their husbands suggest that it is the inferiority of wives that is crucial for the construction of hierarchy among men; that women have to be symbolically excluded from the reckoning and relegated to their place *i ra* as wives, if men are to take their places relative to one another as heads of domestic groups, i.e. as *turaga*, 'chiefs' or 'married men' in a series of ranked clans.

Nevertheless, it is important to realise that the very ambiguity of gender relations within generation at the level of the village, is significant for the construction of Fijian hierarchy at the most inclusive of levels—that of the nation state. This is because it appears that rank distinctions operate more exclusively at the 'topmost' level of Fijian society than they do at the level of the village. I am referring here to the high rate of endogamy among the chiefly families of Bau, Cakaudrove, and Lau—these being the largest and most significant of the old kingdoms and those which are still of enormous importance in the current politico-economy of the democratic state. Thus, while social organisation in the village makes women as wives the crux of status relations amongst men, the ambiguity of the female gender construct makes it possible for women as sisters to be more salient at the level of those chiefly families who have national significance.

The contribution made by the present study to an understanding of the way that people come to be at once products and producers of their own cultures is not claimed to be definitive. However, it does suggest that such data have important implications for theory in social anthropology, and moreover, that further investigation of these matters requires a model of cognition that appreciates the full complexity of the developmental process; this demands an integration of theory in psychology and anthropology.

**NOTES**

1. See Bourdieu (1977), Sperber (1979), Toren (1983), Shweder (1984) and Bloch (1985) for recent discussions of the nature of the connections between culture and cognition.
2. Sawaieke village in 1982/3 had a total of 46 houses and a population of 257. The population of the eight villages of the *vanua* of Sawaieke was around 1300.
3. Clan affiliation is reckoned patrilineally, but kinship relations are reckoned bilaterally, see e.g. Sahlins (1962, p. 168).
4. *Malo* is the paper mulberry tree out of which barkcloth is made; the binding of a piece of barkcloth on his arm is part of a chief's installation (Capell, 1941, p. 133). Hocart (1952) tends to use the term *malo* for a lesser chief, i.e. not the paramount, but in Sawaieke, Takalaigau (the paramount chief) used the term to refer to all traditional chiefs of the *vanua*, including himself.
5. This *yavusa* was reconstituted in 1981 by reconciling to the clan the families of a band of brothers whose grandfather had broken away from it some 50 years before. From then until 1981 the clan had been a *mataqali* in the chiefly *yavusa*; the 'break-away' families having joined the *yavusa* whose members were 'sea people'.
6. I translate *yavusa* as 'clan' and *mataqali* as 'lineage' to distinguish higher and lower levels of integration; the terms are often used in this sense, though *mataqali* may refer to either level. In Sawaieke, it is at *yavusa* level that traditional obligations to chiefs are stressed. In the central government model of the Fijian village the *yavusa* is said to be co-terminous with the village, but in Sawaieke there are five *yavusa*, In general I agree with France (1969) and Clammer (1973) on the distor-

tions produced by the colonial administration's standardisation of what had been different principles of land tenure; however, it is *not* clear that the apparently unusual situation in Sawaieke is a direct product of the Lands Commissions' investigations. Oral history/myth attributes the large number of *yavusa* to an amalgamation of what were once separate villages, the remains of which are still to be seen.

7. Others have noted that the space of the Fijian village is divided amongst various groups in an ordered way though they do not attempt an analysis. See e.g. Thomson (1908, p. 62), Hocart (1929, p. 10); note that Phelps Hooper (1983, p. 231) observes that the notion of *veiqaravi* as 'mutually facing' is 'even reflected in the positioning of houses on the ground'. All three scholars worked in Lau.

8. The *yavu* as named house sites within the village are distinguished from *yavu tabu* ('sacred *yavu*') on clan and lineage gardening land and old village sites and associated with 'the ancestor gods' (*kalou vu*); this association apparently being derived from the fact that traditionally the dead were buried in the *yavu* of the house.

9. Kinship terminology is Dravidian, both the terminology and marriage preferences in the *vanua* of Sawaieke largely accord with descriptions given by Nayacakalou (1955) for Tokatoka, Tailevu, by Sahlins (1962, pp. 147ff) for Moala, and by Hocart (1929, pp. 33–42), Thompson (1940, pp. 53–65) and Phelps Hooper (1982, pp. 20–3) for Lau.

10. The symbolic association of the long walls of the house with 'sea' and 'land' is taken by Sahlins (1976, pp. 32–3, drawing on data from Hocart, 1929) to be isomorphic with the description of the internal space of the house in terms of symbolic *cake/ra*. My analysis is at odds with his in that I argue that the sea/land distinction is irrelevant for the disposition of people *inside* the space of the house, because what is important is that the orientation of houses is such that the 'sea door' of one faces onto the 'land door' of its neighbour. Thus the relation between 'sea' and 'land' is isomorphic with the relations between cross-cousins (i.e. relations between affines and equals) and thus symbolic of relations *across* domestic groups; by contrast the symbolic *cake/ra* axis of the internal space of the house in part constitutes the hierarchical relations *within* the domestic group.

11. Eating together defines the domestic group; food exchange is also a defining marker for groups at a higher level of integration; thus Hocart (1952, p. 22) defines *mataqali* ('lineage') as 'an assessment unit for feasts'; note too that in Lau the *tokatoka* ('sub-lineage') are called *bati ni lovo*, 'sides of the oven'.

12. The *vasu* relationship is formally established at any time from infancy onwards by the ceremony of *kau mata ni gone* (lit. 'carrying the face of the child') when the child or adolescent is taken by his father's kin to be presented to his mother's kin. The ritual exchange of goods must favour the mother's kin. See Phelps Hooper (1982, pp. 199–218) for a detailed account of this ceremony; he also notes (1982, p. 196) that the *vasu* 'may inherit land and titles in the mother's place'. See also Hocart (1915, 1929, p. 40), Thompson (1940, pp. 62ff), Sahlins (1962, pp. 169, 185), Belshaw (1964, p. 32).

13. This transformation is reiterated in the symbolic devaluation of

the wife's contribution in the daily exchange of food at meals. As I pointed out above, it is only in respect of food production and cooking that a woman's labour is consistently devalued by comparison with that of a man. Sahlins (1976, pp. 24–46) says that 'wife-takers' are superior to 'wife-givers' in Moala. However, my data suggest that the two 'sides' are notionally equal; that it is the superiority of the man over his wife that is crucial, not that of his 'side' over hers.

14. In fact six bowls are served and drunk, but the alternate bowls are discounted because they are served to chiefs' *matanivanua* or 'heralds' who do *not* rank after them.

15. In this respect I have to disagree with McNaught (1982) who views 'Fijian culture' as having been 'lost' as a result of the impact of colonialism and a monetary economy. See Toren (in press).

16. This divine ratification is symbolically manifest in church services where the high chief occupies a pre-eminent position *i cake* in the space of the church. Note that data given here about the chiefs and *yaqona* tend to confirm Leach's (1972) analysis of the kava ritual in Tonga. I should also point out that the myth of origin of *yaqona* discussed by Bott (1972) and Leach and said by Sahlins (1982) to be 'widely told' in Fiji was apparently unknown in Sawaieke or, at least, I was unable to find it out. However, the *mana* of chiefs was, in the nineteenth century and earlier, in part symbolically derived from acts of cannibalism and the symbolic association of *yaqona* with cannibalism and both with the *mana* of chiefs is clear in the ethnographic record. For data on the sacred nature of chiefs, *yaqona*, cannibalism see for example Williams, 1858, 1982, pp. 24, 39, 140–4, 231, 296.

17. Symbolic *cake/ra* is also expressed on the vertical dimension in terms of body posture; politeness requires that when passing amongst others one should adopt a stooping posture, bending forward from the waist, and apologise *tulou, tulou*. There are noticeable differences in the extent to which people incline from the vertical in particular contexts; in general women are more likely than men to adopt the full *lolou* position and to walk on their knees inside a building.

18. Primary education is free, secondary education is not. Gau's junior secondary school serves the whole island, the pupils living-in as weekly boarders.

19. Symbols are used to differentiate sex and rank/seniority status, but otherwise the arrangement and density of the figures shown, their relative size and so on, are exactly as drawn.

20. Nayacakalou (1955, p. 47, 1978, p. 15) takes the point of view of some Fijian men in making an unqualified assertion that male status within the kinship group is always higher than female status. Calvert (1858, p. 299) says that sisters are expected to be subservient to brothers, but Geddes notes that his chiefly informant (Ratu Cakobau) told him that the opposite was the case. Geddes (1948, p. 191fn) attributes this to a strong Tongan influence in Bau. However, it seems more probable that the contradiction is in fact inherent in the nature of the interaction between gender and seniority.

## BIBLIOGRAPHY

Bloch, M. (1985) 'Cognition and ideology'. In R. Fardon (ed.) *Power and knowledge*. Edinburgh: Scottish Academic Press.
Bott, E. (1972, orig. 1967) 'Psychoanalysis and ceremony'. In J. S. La Fontaine (ed.) *The interpretation of ritual*. London: Tavistock.
Bourdieu, P. (1977) *Outline of a theory of practice*. London, New York: Cambridge University Press.
Calvert, J. (1982, orig. 1858) *Fiji and the Fijians*. Vol. 2. *Mission history*. Suva: Fiji Museum.
Capell, A. (1941) *A new Fijian dictionary*. Suva: Government Press.
Clammer, J. R. (1973) 'Colonialism and the perception of tradition in Fiji'. In T. Asad (ed.) *Anthropology and the colonial encounter*. London: Ithaca Press.
France, P. (1969) *The charter of the land*. Melbourne: Oxford University Press.
Geddes, W. R. (1948) *An analysis of cultural change in Fiji*. Unpublished PhD thesis, London School of Economics and Political Science.
Hocart, A. M. (1915) 'Chieftainship and the sister's son in the Pacific'. *American Anthropologist*, 17, 631–46.
—— (1929) *Lau Islands, Fiji*. Honolulu: Bernice P. Bishop Museum Bulletin 62.
—— (1952) *The northern states of Fiji*. Occasional Publication No. 11, London: Royal Anthropological Institute.
Leach, E. (1972) 'The structure of a symbolism'. In J. S. La Fontaine (ed.) *The interpretation of ritual*. London: Tavistock.
MacNaught, T. J. (1982) 'We are no longer Fijians'. *Pacific Studies*, 1–2, 15–24.
Nayacakalou, R. R. (1955) 'The Fijian system of kinship and marriage'. *Journal of the Polynesian Society*, 64, 44–56.
—— (1978) *Tradition and change in the Fijian village*. South Pacific Social Sciences Association, with the Institute of Pacific Studies, University of the South Pacific.
Ortner, S. (1981) 'Gender and sexuality in hierarchical societies: the case of Polynesia and some comparative implications'. In S. B. Ortner and H. Whitehead (eds) *Sexual meanings*. Cambridge, New York: Cambridge University Press.
Phelps Hooper, S. (1983) *A study of valuables in the chiefdom of Lau, Fiji*. Unpublished PhD thesis, University of Cambridge.
Sahlins, M. (1962) *Moala: culture and nature on a Fijian island*. Ann Arbor: University of Michigan Press.
—— (1976) *Culture and practical reason*. Chicago, London: University of Chicago Press.
—— (1982) 'Raw women, cooked men and other "great things" of the Fiji Islands'. In P. Brown and D. Tuzin (eds) *The ethnography of cannibalism*. Special Publication, Society for Psychological Anthropology.
Shweder, R. A. (1984) 'Anthropology's romantic rebellion'. In R. A. Shweder and R. A. LeVine (eds) *Culture theory—essays on mind, self and emotion*. London, New York: Cambridge University Press.

Sperber, D. (1980, orig. 1979) 'Is symbolic thought pre-rational?'. In F. M LeCron and S. H. Brandes (eds) *Symbol as sense*. London, New York: Academic Press.

Thompson, L. M. (1940) *Southern Lau, Fiji: an ethnography*. Honolulu: Bernice P. Bishop Museum Bulletin 162.

Thomson, B. (1908) *The Fijians, a study of the decay of custom*. London: Dawsons of Pall Mall.

Toren, C. (1983) 'Thinking symbols: a critique of Sperber (1979)'. *Man* (N.S.) 18, 260–8.

—— (in press) 'Drinking cash: the purification of money through ceremonial exchange in Fiji'. In M. Bloch and J. Parry (eds) *The symbolism of money and the morality of exchange*. Cambridge University Press.

Williams, T. (1982, orig. 1858) *Fiji and the Fijians*. Suva: Fiji Museum.

# 8

# Cognitive Development and Sex Roles on the Kerkennah Islands of Tunisia

Katherine Platt

In a traditional Islamic society, it is impossible to talk about the local conceptualisation of cognitive development without putting the discussion in the context of attitudes toward sexual differences and sex roles. In this culture, ideas about sexual differences inform expectations about physical, psychological, intellectual, social and moral development. In turn, these sexually weighted expectations profoundly influence the actual training of children and, of course, in the long run, adult social roles. The central issue of this paper is how the development of certain cognitive skills is influenced by cultural attitudes toward these skills and how this contributes to the learning of male and female sex roles.

Male and female children on these Tunisian islands learn certain cognitive skills in emphatically different ways. The emphasis on various intellectual skills and the expected schedule of development varies according to sex. In some important aspects, the ultimate cognitive capacity for the development of males and females is thought to be different. The sexual division of mental and moral development is articulated and idealised by a traditional Islamic value system which depends on the asymetrical distinctiveness of the sexes.

The material for this paper was collected during an eighteen-month anthropological field trip to the Kerkennah Islands which are a small archipelago lying twelve miles off the east coast of Tunisia. Kerkennah is a traditional Islamic society with a rural economy based on fishing, subsistence agriculture and labour migration. There are eleven villages with a total population of fifteen thousand. The data for this study was mostly collected by the standard ethnographic method of participant observation.

For the sake of accuracy, I refer specifically only to Kerkenni ideas and practices concerning cognitive development and sex roles. On the basis of comparative literature, travel and consultation with other researchers, however, I believe that much of what I say about Kerkennah would also be true of other rural Islamic communities in North Africa and the Middle East.

Ethnographically, it is often very difficult to distinguish between social and cognitive development because social roles assume a particular level of cognitive development and they are often dramatised by community rituals. In other words, there is frequently a coincidence between the social expectation and the actual achievement of a new level of development. It is also difficult to distinguish between emotional and cognitive development because the two processes are often integrated. The fact is that childrearing practices, methods of nurturing, punishment and physical training *also* teach or foster intellectual skills. For the purpose of this essay, these two methodological difficulties are coped with by (1) focusing on the learning processes that can be observed in the stages leading up to the major life cycle rituals of infancy and childhood but not on the rituals themselves and (2) specifying the development of cognitive skills within the overall context of child development. This paper will compare the major characteristics of early, middle and late male and female childhoods in terms of the expectations about and actual development of cognitive skills. The implications of these differences in male and female development for adult sex roles and more generally for an Islamic value system are also discussed.

There are three general themes of cognitive development which illustrate the different ways in which males and females are expected and encouraged to develop. These themes are: (1) the idea of self, (2) self-expression and verbal skills, (3) initiative and attitudes toward activity. The idea of self concerns the early experience of the social world and the exploration of the boundaries between the self and others. This theme is especially relevant in the young infant's early mobility and experience of separation from the mother. Self-expression and verbal skills become an important cognitive theme in the second and third years of childhood when the child achieves recognition as a separate social being. This is the beginning of the idea of personal efficacy, that is, the beginning of a sense of autonomy and the power to command and manipulate responses from the social environment. Initiative and attitudes toward activity as a cognitive theme is especially relevant somewhat later in childhood. It concerns decision-making procedures and the development and internalisation of social responsibility. At this stage the child starts to be regarded as a moral being.

In all these areas of cognitive development, the characteristic experiences of males and females are emphatically different. According to traditional belief, males and females by nature are profoundly different. Therefore, it is only natural and appropriate that their training and development follow different courses and end with different results. So profound are the differences between males and females thought to be that they begin to manifest themselves before the child is even born. Kerkennis state that male foetuses are active and kicking in the womb, while female foetuses lie still. This belief both initiates and summarises the essence of Kerkenni sex roles differences. There are various tests that can be performed with the mother's breast milk from the seventh month on which are said to indicate the sex of the foetus. For example, there is a test in which the mother-to-be expresses a few drops of breast milk into her hand and puts a louse in it. If the louse leaves the milk, it will be a boy. If it stays in the milk, it will be a girl. Another version of the same test involves burying a louse with a little sand in the mother-to-be's palm. If the louse climbs to the surface, it will be a boy. If the louse escapes from the side, it will be a girl. Similarly, there are other 'sure signs' such as the pallor or flush of the mother's complexion and the belief that female foetuses ride 'in the lap' and male foetuses 'astride the hips'. During labour, females are said to cause rhythmic pain which comes and goes while males cause constant pain. The significance of all these convictions is the universal concern over the sex of the baby and the prenatally fulfilled expectation that the behaviour of males and females will be distinct.

The sex of the unborn child is also an issue when dealing with malevolent and envious spirits. In general, boy babies are thought to be more desirable than girl babies, so preparing for the birth of a girl is sometimes used as a ruse to disinterest the envious spirit. For example, a mother who wants a baby and has lost many will go out begging from the single women in the village to buy earrings for the baby. In this way, she very publicly prepares for the birth of a girl and hopefully throws the envy of the jinns (and the single women of the village) off the scent of a healthy baby boy. Similarly, after the birth of a boy, a very fearful mother might publicly give the baby a girls' name and dress him in female clothing for a period to ward off misfortune caused by envious influences. These are little dramas put on for the evil spirits which highlight the conceptual discreteness of maleness and femaleness in this culture from the earliest moment.

Although the arrival of a girl and the arrival of a boy provoke widely different public and private responses (the exclamation on the arrival of a boy is, 'It's a follower of the Prophet'; for a girl, it is 'May the mother be well', with no mention of the baby), the actual treatment of brand new babies for the first two or three months is basically the same regardless of sex. This is considered an extremely dangerous period when the infant could easily be snatched away by illness or malevolent forces. During this vulnerable period, it is thought that the fewer influences the baby is exposed to the better. To make the spine grow straight the new-born is swaddled in linen like a mummy with only its head unbound. So the baby spends most of its first months with its limbs bound mostly in a dark room away from activity and stimuli. Although they are vulnerable, babies are not thought to be perceptive or cognisant during this early period. Perhaps because of experience with high infant mortality, Kerkennis are not confident in the vitality of their babies during the first months and treat them as if not yet quite alive. In fact, an early death is not treated terribly differently from a late miscarriage. For an infant who dies there is no mourning ritual. The baby is buried within two or three hours in the local cemetery, but customary visits to the grave on holidays are not made as they would be to the grave of an older child. Condolences all concern the speedy replacement of this infant with another.

**THE IDEA OF THE SELF**

The infant is introduced to its immediate social world 40 days after birth at which time the worst danger is thought to be over. From this time onward, the baby begins to be treated as a receptive being. It is in the context of the maternal relationship that the male or female sex role begins to be established.

In spite of the fact that male babies are generally more exuberantly welcomed into the world than female babies, it would be very misleading to suggest that males are more loved by their mothers than females. They are, however, characteristically treated in a different manner. In general, a female infant tends to be treated almost as an appendage to the mother while a male infant, on the other hand, seems to be almost 'courted' by the mother. This 'courtship' takes the form of the mother talking to the male baby with playful respect, putting him in the mock position of a man with power over her. She will call him 'ya baba', meaning 'oh daddy' or 'ya sidi', meaning 'oh sir'. She will play at submitting to the baby's will by acting afraid or pretending to cry because of something he did or did not do to her. The mother will beg for kisses and ask the baby 'Who do you love?'. The mother continues to expect a lot of physical affection from her growing son. She can demand a kind of intimate attention from her son which she cannot necessarily expect from her husband because of the shame of their sexual relationship. This difference in orientation of attention begins to set the tone for the child's concept of itself. Paradoxically, the oblique kind of interaction between the female infant and her mother minimises the boundary between the two of them in some way. It seems that at least in terms of interaction with the mother the female infant's individual self remains undistinguished and she is somehow treated as an extension of the mother's self. The more head-on cajoling interaction between the male infant and his mother encourages an earlier, more distinct idea of self in the male. In other words, more attention is paid to the expression of the independent male ego than the female ego. The different character of maternal interaction shows itself in the greater degree of verbal stimulation, teasing, coaxing, negotiating and physical attention paid directly to male infants. One way in which this difference of treatment of infants is explained by the Kerkennis is that male infants are said to be 'naturally' fussier, more difficult, more demanding, etc. and so they require more direct attention than female infants. The 'naturally' sweeter dispositions of female babies is quietly cherished—'Hadhakaho' (and that's the way it is), as the Kerkennis say.

An emphatic and visible way in which the distinctiveness of the independent male ego is socially recognised is through ritual. First of all, there is generally more ritual recognition of a male birth than of a female birth. Gifts to male babies are more lavish. In the mainland cities it is stylish to give new-born male babies little gold signet rings. This custom is sometimes followed in some educated circles on Kerkennah. No such gesture is made toward female babies.

The forty-day ceremony is a kind of social 'coming out' party of the infant. It is often very elaborate for a male baby, including his first haircut, first pair of trousers and first sitting up in a chair. There are many references to his being a little man and to the upcoming circumcision ceremony for which there is no female equivalent. Formal greetings to male infants at this stage are, 'God willing, may you be circumcised'. For a female infant they are, 'God willing, may you be happily married', for this is the first ritual in a female's life of which she is the focus. Forty-day ceremonies for females are much abbreviated, more like a tea party, and very often not observed at all.

Male infants are carried about a great deal more and longer than female infants. They are worried about and not encouraged to walk so soon. It is said that they learn to walk later than females because they have 'heavier blood'. This is one of the ways in which males are more ostentatiously cherished and fussed over. It happens that in the hope of producing more male offspring, a female infant will be more quickly followed by another pregnancy than a male infant. This requires the female to get on her feet more quickly to make room for the next babe in arms. In general, females learn physical independence earlier than males, but males develop a kind of psychological independency of identity or idea of self earlier and to a fuller degree than females.

This difference in distinctiveness of identity is signified by the difference in the naming of males and females. Almost all male names are from the Qur'an and have recognised religious meanings. If one asks what a boy's name such as Abdulkader means, one will not only be told, 'slave of the Powerful One', but also receive an exposition on the power of Allah and the appropriateness of this name for the character of the child in question. Sometimes if an infant is troubled or ill, a Qur'anic specialist is consulted and the child is given another name which is thought to be more suitable. Girls' names are not from the Qur'an (the name Miriam is the single exception) and they have no religious significance. Girls' names are chosen to be pretty, not to encourage special personal attributes. There are particular girls' names, however, which are thought to come in natural sequence with boys' names. For instance, if a girl's name is Dalenda, the next child is supposed to be called Hamda, a boy's name. So a family disappointed with the birth of a girl, might name her Dalenda in hopes of having the opportunity of naming the next child Hamda, the correct name to follow Dalenda. I have not heard of particular boys' names which are supposed to be followed by particular girls' names. The point is that boys' names have special, individual significance and there is concern about the appropriateness of boys' names. This is much less so for girls' names. Attitudes toward naming and its significance is one of the subtle areas in which the distinctive identity of males is highlighted in contrast to the case for females.

A crucial difference in the treatment and development of male and female infants is the weaning schedule. Female infants are generally weaned some time between one year and eighteen months. This relatively early separation is not treated as any kind of crisis because the female child will continue to keep constant company with her mother in the household and neighbourhood. Male infants are usually not weaned until two and sometimes more than three years of age. Not a great deal of attention is paid to the weaning of females and the mother expects the procedure to go quickly and smoothly. Males, on the other hand, perhaps because they are older and have developed more ways of expressing themselves are expected to be very difficult to wean. Males are often weaned not too long before they are circumcised. Circumcision marks a new period in the male child's life. At this point the little boy's social centre of gravity moves from his mother to the world of his male peers. This is quite an abrupt change in circumstances. There are no such abrupt changes for females. Upon weaning, female children are immediately and easily incorporated into the multigenerational community of women. The transition from being an appendage to the mother to being an appendage to the wider community of girls and women is smooth and takes place without ritual punctuation marks. From the loud recognition of the male's birth, to the naming ceremony, the hair cutting and the forty-day ceremony, to the weaning and circumcision, the steps and changes in a male's infancy are paid a great deal more attention to and treated with more drama. In their early orientation toward the world, males and females have very different experiences based on the way the 'world' responds to them. The smooth and undramatic absorption of the female infant into the multigenerational domestic world predisposes her toward a less demanding sense of self than her male counterpart; less demanding of recognition of her individuality and powers of assertiveness. Having 'blended in' socially at such an early age, she does not have the kind of separateness of identity that her male counterpart develops. The more dramatic and longer intimacy of the male infant with his mother and the later more pronounced separation from her predisposes him toward a more independent, distinct and demanding sense of self than his female counterpart. The Kerkennis think of these differences in orientation and presentation of the self as being part of the difference between male and female natures, not something that is socially or culturally induced.

**SELF-EXPRESSION AND VERBAL SKILLS**

Self-expression and verbal skills are tied to the idea of personal efficacy, the ability to command and control responses to the self. On Kerkennah, a great deal more stress is put on the development of these skills in males than in females. The result is that male children learn to expect that their social environment will respond to their demands and influence in a direct and immediate way.

In terms of adult sex roles, the ideal male is someone who can defend himself verbally, he has strong words and greets people well. The ideal female, on the other hand, is verbally reticent, a good listener, and has soft words. This difference in ideals of adult behaviour begins to be communicated to children very early. Before a male baby sucks for the first time on the day of his birth, a raisin is rubbed around the inside of his mouth that he may grow up 'with sweet words', that is, with eloquence.

In general, male infants experience more direct verbal stimulation than female infants. This is partially because of the longer nursing period. The mother will often chat and sing very specifically to the infant while it sucks. The 'courting behaviour' of the mother toward her son discussed in the previous section is also significant in this regard because her words and attention are focused directly on him as an independent being. Male infants and toddlers also come in for more direct individual attention in the form of verbal and physical teasing which aims to provoke a response from the child by an elder. A common form of verbal teasing is for an adult to say to a little boy: 'Are you a girl or a boy?' or 'Are you a man?'. This is supposed to provoke a proud or outraged reply from the little boy. Little girls are never subjected to an equivalent form of teasing about their sex. A common form of physical teasing is for an adult to playfully and gently slap and hit a little boy until he returns the blows. Little girls are not engaged in this kind of mock combat. Provocative teasing and verbal games teach the male child to respond to verbal stimuli in a direct and aggressive manner. A strong and even impatient response is reinforced in the male child. The female child who is not often subject to provocative teasing and whose relationship to the world of elders is more diffuse is discouraged when she shows signs of verbal aggression. She is reinforced for developing a mild and deferential verbal and non-verbal style of presenting herself.

A correlate of this difference in male and female verbal styles is the characteristic way in which males and females express anger. Little boys are not discouraged from being impatient or from expressing frustration in an aggressive way. They turn their anger on the world vociferously. A temper tantrum in a little boy is thought to be amusing; not so in a little girl. Brothers are allowed to hit their siblings in anger and in a disciplinary way but sisters do not administer blows to their siblings. Little girls, who are taught to have a receptive and deferential manner, are encouraged to quietly tolerate frustration. Females in this culture characteristically turn their anger in on themselves. The visible manifestation of this is the scratches seen on the faces of women who have torn their own faces with their fingernails. Women inflict these wounds on themselves in moments of intense grief, but even more commonly during times of domestic strife.

Just as male children are taught to respond directly to verbal stimuli, so they learn to expect a direct response to their own verbal demands. This expectation begins with the immediate response male infants get when they demand the mother's breast. After weaning, a similar cry will bring forth at least a crust of bread. Gratification of a female infant's needs is not so consistently immediate. Very early on the female child is expected to fit into the routine and schedule of the household and not to make an exception of herself. Her undemanding conformity to the patterns of the household is reinforced, most certainly in a loving and appreciative way. This habit of self-discipline is soon activated by the daily order of things which dictates that males are served first and all their physical needs looked after before attendance to female needs. Little boys, on the other hand, are taught to expect exceptional treatment and they begin to learn through this power of self-expression.

Sexual self-expression is another area in which the development of males and females is radically different. The sexuality of male children is recognised, tolerated and in some cases, celebrated. This is one of the main themes of the circumcision ritual. The child's newly circumcised genitals are proudly displayed by his female relatives to visiting well-wishers. Male infants and children are allowed to play with their genitals and are sometimes teased or stimulated genitally by their mothers or aunts. Infantile exhibitionism in males is considered very funny. Public nakedness and evacuation by male children up to about two years of age is completely tolerated.

The first moral lessons for females is sexual shame. Even before weaning female infants are held back from touching themselves genitally. From the time they learn to walk, they are taught to keep their legs down and together and not to lift their clothes. Bathing, changing and evacuation all take place in private. A female infant's genitals are always covered even within the household. This moral lesson, of course, becomes more intense as the girl gets older and she is generally prohibited from activities such as bicycle and donkey riding, kicking balls, swimming, etc. Here she might expose herself or, more seriously, jar her hymen. Female sexuality does not receive any informal or ritual attention until just before the wedding at the typical age of 18 or 20. Before this time, girls are very strongly discouraged from expressing any sexual feelings or concerns they have.

Another aspect of verbal behaviour and sexuality concerns censorship. Because of their relative verbal passivity, their easy membership in the multigenerational community of females and the lack of recognition of sexuality in young females, no adult conversation is censored in the presence of female children. Conversely, because male children are thought to be 'tuned in' to some degree both verbally and sexually, and because their individual presence is felt more socially, it is quite common for adult conversation to be censored for their sake. Even in the negative form of inspiring censorship, causing others to be silent or to change their verbal behaviour, this is another way in which the male child experiences his personal strength and efficacy in the social world.

In terms of verbal behaviour the female ideal is mostly a negative ideal; that is, she should be a good listener, verbally reticent and soft spoken in her manner. She should be brief and gentle and modest in her speech. As with her other behaviour, she should not draw attention to herself to be talked about. In general, the social rule for females is the less said and the less said about, the better. Almost the opposite is true for males who are meant to be listened to, to be verbally forthcoming and powerful in their delivery. A very critical thing to say of a female is 'she beats people with her words', whereas a very positive thing to say about a man is 'his words are strong'.

Throughout childhood and adolescence, males continue to have more opportunities to develop their verbal skills than females. The most obvious factor is formal schooling. Very few girls are given the Qur'anic schooling which often accompanies state education in the case of boys. There is a significant drop in female enrolment in the secondary school around the age of thirteen. This is largely because it is traditionally thought to be dangerous for pubescent girls to be out and about in a mixed-sex, non-family situation. It is also because primary education if often thought to be sufficient for a female's adult educational needs. Girls are often kept out of school from a very early age because they are making a significant contribution to household maintenance and childcare. This brings us to the theme of attitudes toward productive activity and social responsibility.

## INITIATIVE AND ATTITUDES TOWARD ACTIVITY

One of the most important and striking differences between male and female childhoods is in attitudes toward work and play. For female children the distinction between work and play or productive and recreational activities is blurred. The two categories easily merge. For males the distinction is very sharp. The implications of this difference for adult behaviour are vast, for even in adulthood, women make little distinction between work and recreation. They are both simply generalised into the single category of 'what women do'. In the male sphere, however, work and recreation are very distinct categories. One often sees little girls 'playing at work' such as making cakes out of sand and in the same hour actually assisting their mothers in the making of real cakes. This is also true of playing at cleaning, washing and childcare. Dolls and little brothers are easily and often substituted for each other. As soon as a little girl can walk, she is involved in the productive activity of the household—often only as a nuisance, but she is involved. By the age of four most little girls have some real responsibility in the household. Little boys are babied longer and are discouraged from imitating their mothers because 'that is women's work'. This is part of their face-to-face rather than side-by-side relationship with their mothers. After circumcision they are shooed out of the house to play with their peers. They might run errands or assist their fathers in a specific task but in general they do not socialise with their fathers or their fathers' peers. This would be disrespectful. Nor do they have regular responsibilities except for going to school. Boys are encouraged to play without obligations until about the age of twelve and very often a good deal longer. Even if a girl is in school, she will still be fully occupied with household jobs and activities during non-school hours. This is not to suggest in the least that girls do not have fun or do not play but only that their activities are not differentiated in this way, while boys' activities are.

This sharp distinction between work and play for males persists throughout adulthood. Grown men continue to have a special category of activity that could be called 'play' which is absent from the lives of girls and women. Adolescent and adult male 'play' usually consists of sports, public strolling and card and table games. Both males and females listen to the radio and, when it is available, watch television, but then it is with different styles. It is quite remarkable to see the females knitting, shelling, husking or braiding away at some task at the same time as they listen to the radio or watch television—always blurring the boundary between work and play.

This recreational sphere of activity, like most of male social life, is informally but distinctly age graded. This informal age grading begins shortly after circumcision when boys start to have some social independence and it continues throughout their lives. This informal separation according to age as well as sex has to do with issues of respect, rivalry and personal power that do not have the same relevance in the lives of females. For females, the boundaries between generations are blurred as are the boundaries between work and play.

The compartmentalised quality of male activities has important implications for the sexual division of labour on Kerkennah. There are a finite number of jobs which are considered male work. These mostly have to do with fishing, building, commerce and bureaucracies. Most of the vast number of other things that there are to do are done by women. This asymmetry in the sexual division of labour reflects the difference between male and female attitudes toward activity which, in turn, reflects the difference in the local conceptions of male and female natures. Male productive and recreational activities are clearly defined, distinguished and highlighted, as is the individual male ego. Female activities include many things without distinction between the activities or the doers. They are generalised and shared without much ado just as the female self is submerged and shared in the general female community.

A great proportion of female work is characterised by a corporate idea of productivity. This is related to the female child's early sense of responsibility, the early integration into the multi-generational female world and the lack of emphasis on personal autonomy. This generalised identification and low threshold between individuals often extends even to creative work. It is not at all unusual for girls to pick up each other's knitting and to knit a few rows or to work on each other's tapestries. By contrast, for a man to weave a few palm fronds into someone else's fish trap would be considered an extraordinary invasion of personal territory. Actually, it would probably be laughed at as effeminate behaviour.

This co-operative aspect of women's work also extends to childrearing. It is perfectly acceptable for women to feed, embrace, clean and discipline other women's children. Such acts are not considered trespassing another woman's domain. Men, however, would not discipline each other's children except within the extended family. Young girls pick up this shared quality of work, while young boys continue in their track of developing their sense of individual autonomy and separate personal skills and power.

The general posture of boys and girls toward objects and property are also very different. Boys are aggressive and dominating, charging around like little bulls 'conquering' objects by force. The fact that the objects may break in 'battle' is not important. Girls are protective and conservative, saving, storing and preserving things both in play and for real. In some ways young boys are expected to be irresponsible. One sees five-to-ten-year-old boys destroy household objects to use as toys while their sisters try to rescue the objects for their proper use. One five-year-old cut up a table cloth in a daredevil sort of way. His aunt laughed as she stopped him saying, 'He's such a little devil'. It is with an indulgent kind of affection and pride that young boys are called 'little donkeys' and the 'very devil'. Such unruliness and lack of purpose in girls would be altogether shocking and the girls would certainly have the very devil beaten out of them.

Little girls are expected to share treats with their siblings. Very often a younger sister will divide up a treat among her older brothers, something of which the boys are not thought capable. A three-year-old girl was given a piece of candy which she popped into her mouth. Her mother said jokingly, 'Aren't you going to let us have some, too?' So the little girl took the candy out of her mouth and offered it to everyone in the room, one by one. Finally, when her grandmother actually took it and ate it, the little girl did not balk. No one would expect such a thing from a little boy of the same age. Childish greediness in boys is thought amusing and natural. Conversely, the capacity to take up one's place in the group and not to be made an exception of is thought equally natural for girls.

There is a certain paradox in this expectation of irresponsibility and wildness in boys. Boys are expected and allowed to be wild and irresponsible when young precisely because when they grow up the development of their natural capacity for wisdom and responsibility and the sobering weight of their adult obligations are assured. Girls, who do not have this natural capacity for responsible behaviour, must be more self-disciplined from the beginning. In other words, boys can act like little animals because their true and ultimate nature is wise and responsible and girls must behave conservatively because their true nature is thought to be wild and animal-like. Hence, the very great and early emphasis on sexual shame for females.

In this society, morally and intellectually, males and females are believed to have different ultimate capacities. Females become physically independent and acquire personal responsibilities earlier than males. They are also thought to reach their full intellectual and moral growth earlier. Males are thought to develop more slowly and to go through more abrupt stages. They are also thought to continue to develop well past adolescence. According to Kerkenni thought, males achieve a level of rationality and capacity for moral and religious judgement (*baṣira*) that is not available to females. Females in many ways are thought to reach their highest human potential while still in maidenhood. This pinnacle includes a combination of spirit (*nafs*), purity of motive or intention (*niya*), intelligence in the form of social propriety (*akhlaq*), and most important, modesty and shame (*hishma*). With marriage, sexual knowledge and experience, women are more likely to deteriorate morally than to develop. Hence, modesty, obedience, and restraint, themes stressed since her infancy, are a woman's protection. This is in contrast to the parallel attributes of eloquence (*balagha*), influence (*qadr*), and judgement (*baṣira*) which are fostered in males. Males, who are little devils when young, are thought to continue to increase in rationality (*aqel*), morality (*akhlaq*), and wisdom (*alam*), reaching the peak of their development only in old age.

**TERMS**

| | | |
|---|---|---|
| *akhlaq* | اخلاق | character = deportment = morality |
| *'aqel* | عقل | intelligence, responsibility |
| *balaga* | بلاغة | eloquence |
| *balug* | بلوغ | male maturity |
| *bashara* | بشر | to preach<br>to be a man<br>to speak for the group |
| *baṣira* | بصيرة | judgement<br>perception |
| *hishma* | حشمة | sexual shame, modesty |
| *nafs* | نفس | spirit, flesh-centred self |
| *niya* | نية | intentionality |
| *shitan* | شيطان | devil |

|  | Male | | Female | |
|---|---|---|---|---|
| Stage | Ritual and social markers | Developmental characteristic | Ritual and social markers | Developmental characteristics |
| New-born | (loud) welcome | | (subdued) welcome | |
| | anti-evil eye rituals | | anti-evil eye rituals | |
| | naming (religious) significance) | | naming (insignificant) | |
| Infancy | 40-day ceremony (elaborate): first haircut, first sex-specific clothes, first sitting in a chair | *nafs* | 40-day ceremony (underplayed): first sex-specific clothes | *nafs* |
| | | | early weaning | *hishma* |
| | late weaning | | | |
| Childhood | circumcision | | | *'aqel* |
| | Qur'anic School | *shitan* | | |
| | Primary School | | Primary School | *akhlaq* |
| | | | personal religious observance, fasting | |
| Adolescence | High School | *'aqel* | (High School) | |
| | personal religious observance, fasting | *akhlaq* | engagement | |
| | | | marriage | |
| | | *niya* | | |
| Adulthood | engagement | *baṣira* | | |
| | military service travel study abroad | *balagha* *balug* | | |
| | marriage | | | |
| | regular mosque attendance | | | |

**SELECTED BIBLIOGRAPHY**

Abu Zahra, N. (1982) *Sidi Ameur: a Tunisian village*. London: Ithaca Press.

Cuisinier, J. (1970) 'Le cycle domestique dans l'organisation familiale traditionelle en Tunisie'. Paper delivered at UNESCO Colloque sur les Structures Familiales dans les Pays Méditerranéens, Cyprus.

Davis, S. Schaefer (1983) *Patience and power: women's lives in a Moroccan village*. Cambridge, MA.: Schenkman.

Dwyer, D. Hilse (1978) *Images and self-images: male and female in Morocco*. New York: Columbia University Press.

Eickelman, D. (1976) *Moroccan Islam*. Austin: University of Texas Press.

Johnson, P. Ryden (1979) *A Sufi saint in modern Tunisia*. Ph.D. Thesis. Berkeley: University of California.

Louis, A. (1961) *Les Iles Kerkena*. Tunis: Bascone and Muscat.

# 9

# Sex Roles and State Roles in Soviet Georgia: Two Styles of Infant Socialisation

Tamara Dragadze

This chapter offers an ethnographic report, in which relevant observed events, so long as they are not wrested from their socio-cultural context, may perhaps be useful as material for psychologists interested in cross-cultural studies. I will not attempt to generalise on the basis of my material on such issues as the psychology of cognition and 'psychological' behaviour in which I have no training. I shall, however, make a very sweeping statement! I will declare that children from an early age, in all cultures, are particularly sensitive to their parents' (and other family members') non-verbally expressed sentiments. I shall also declare that the attitudes of adults which are expressed non-verbally form an integral part of the socialisation process.

This chapter, divided into three parts, begins with a brief outline of the socio-political structure of the setting in which I did my fieldwork (mainly between 1969–72 but several return visits were made including autumn 1981). Then I shall describe sex roles and the attitudes and roles connected with the State which are considered normative. (I use the term 'State' loosely, and do not intend to elucidate the polemics associated with the concept.) Lastly, I shall describe briefly how some of these norms and roles are taught to children under the age of seven, before they start ordinary school.

**THE ENVIRONMENT**

Ratcha Province, in North Western Georgia, lies at the foot of the Great Caucasian Range. The three villages where I mainly worked had a mixed economy: there were collective farms and dairies where, untypical for Georgia as a whole, very little produce went to the State after the farmers' allocations because the soil was poor and mostly on steep slopes. Local industry played an important part, with an arsenic mine and processing factory nearby, a sawmill and a host of tertiary services to support these activities. The strategy of each family consisted in allocating members to different sectors of the economy in order to ensure access to food from the farms and cash from salaries. It was often a grandparent who was the collective farm member in a family, thus securing the right to several privileges, for example, the right to own three cows instead of one and a larger plot of land for one's own private use.

As in many other peasant societies, the State was generally viewed as an inevitable, quite uncontrollable and arbitrary factor to reckon with, somewhat like the weather in the sky. Rule was by decree. For example, annually a certain number of tons of wine were required to be delivered by the province to the central government, regardless of the State Farm yields, so that sometimes grapes were requisitioned from all residents in the region from their private plots. Decrees issued from the Georgian capital (and secretly blamed on decrees from Moscow) allowed at one time only 200 guests at a wedding, then 150 or 300, changing often.

Each year, although there were no full-time nursery schools in the village I studied most intensively, there was a morning class in the library for three to seven-year olds during the winter. The teacher was not local but her first cousin with whom she stayed was married to an Abari man who had used 'influence' to get her the job. Directives and books were received from central government sources, with their sometimes changing instructions on what to teach. Always though, children learned, for example, a song about 'Great Lenin' who lived in a house in Moscow. At seven children started school in the next village, where they stayed until they were 17. The director and most of the teachers were from the group of three villages close by. Trainee teachers, who sometimes found it difficult to get local accommodation, and some inspectors came from outside the region. The common concern of all the staff was to ensure that they complied with what was demanded of them by the central authorities. People in the province generally felt they had no control over government decisions.

Local officials themselves tried to present their role as

mediators between the villagers and the omnipresent forces of the Moscow–Tbilissi–Ambrolauri Region of Ratcha Province axis. As anyone even slightly familiar with Soviet studies knows, a feature of the State economy consists in continual shortages of food, clothes, building materials, medicines and so on which give rise to a Black Market. Another aspect is that the low wages of shop-vendors, doctors, teachers and others lead to the need for them to 'make money on the side'. On the one hand people relied on local officials to 'turn a blind eye'. On the other hand it was common knowledge that nobody could escape severe sanctions if someone along the line of authority decided 'to find out', hence the element of suspicion in most of these relationships.

The village structure was largely influenced by the kinship structure. The layout of the houses often coincided with the kinship ties of their owners. Houses were usually built on plots of land which allowed some garden produce to be grown and cattle to be kept in wooden sheds at night. When the sons of a family married (virilocally, brides coming in from other villages) the government gave planning permission more easily to build a new house on the parents' plot of land surrounding the main house than to build on plots on the edge of the village. It followed that, in this agnatically structured village (where people are related through male ties) one's most immediate neighbour was more than likely a brother or first cousin and further neighbours were remoter relatives. The exogamy rules deeply rooted in Georgian society and upheld by the tradition of the Byzantine Church make it improbable for anyone to marry someone with whom common ancestry is shared up to seven generations back. Marriage within the village is unlikely, where 'we are all cousins', as they say. Social and economic networks are created through marriage ties across the province, maintained by 'proper' behaviour within the marriage and the law of hospitality and co-operation among relatives, both 'blood' and affinal. Affection among siblings is highly lauded, the death of a brother or sister being accompanied by great displays of grief and lengthy mourning.

If one is to describe the situation loosely in terms of a 'great tradition' as opposed to a 'little' tradition, then it would be safe to say that for the villagers the aspirations and the codes of behaviour which derive from their 'great tradition' are associated with their national heritage, epitomised vividly in their minds by the Golden Age of the Georgian people, in the reigns of King

David the Builder and Queen Tamar (ninth to twelfth centuries) who are among their favourite 'folk' heroes. Epic poetry is recited by all, urging respect for the canons of chivalry, hospitality and bravery and reminding all that Georgian civilisation is vastly superior in every way to that of other peoples. Not only at weddings and special festivals but also when adjudicating in disputes, people resort to quoting familiar passages. Two- or four-line aphorisms which are typically included in the poems are great favourites, such as: 'What you give is yours, what you keep is lost'.

Although explanatory statements are made in historical terms, the Georgians of the village view the time-scale of their culture and ideal codes of behaviour as perennial, alive in perpetuity. Superimposed, however, upon the above is everyday life in a Soviet State, with its demands for public proclamations of faith in the regime, made by the villagers in the spirit of 'singing for your supper'. The decrees, the bureaucrats and all the artefacts of Soviet life as it touches them in the village form the *local* variations on the universal theme of national culture shared by all Georgians. Their tenets, in contrast, are transitory and forever changing, albeit within a recognisable, well-known framework. Crucial to my argument is the recognition of these two levels of reference, the one to a traditional sector of perennial, so called 'Georgian', national values and culture; at another level, more local and particularistic, are the values and codes of behaviour which are seen by them to emerge from the ramifications of the Soviet State system and which they must absorb and master in order to interpret and operate within its parameters. In other words there appear two traditions, the 'great' Georgian one and the 'little' one of a trivialised and local nature which, although derived from what could be termed a second 'great' tradition— the all-powerful Soviet State tradition—is not perceived as such by the villagers. The modifying effects of the latter appear rather as local irritants or opportunities in the quest for living up to the ideals of 'great Georgianhood'. This subjective view should be seen in the context that, after all, the Georgians have a documented history of their civilisation stretching over several thousand years: sixty or seventy years of Soviet rule are perhaps scant on such a time-scale.

## SEX ROLES

Sex roles are defined within the traditional realm described above, within one level of culture and experience. Much more space is needed than that available here to elaborate in any depth on sex roles in Georgian society. I only provide a general background into which to set the remarks I will make on socialisation later on. Although I do not myself like to indulge in historical explanation, many Georgian villagers told me that in the past, over centuries, men either had to leave home to fight in the lengthy wars in which Georgians were constantly engaged to defend their territory, or else they had to migrate seasonally to towns and even distant lands to work as craftsmen. Thus, they say, it was always the women who looked after the villages.

Women are the agents of social control and maintain order. If two men fight a woman can throw her head-dress between them and honour demands that they cease. When there are brawls people rush to get the men's mothers or other senior women to intervene. Women are seen as dependable; men are prone to unruly feelings of violent temper or jealousy and so on. Women are, above all, mothers. It is they who run the household, who have to be consulted on deciding on expenditure. They nurture but also direct.

It is the women also who are the guardians of literacy; formerly it was the bride who was supposed to have a copy of *Knight in the panther's skin*[1] when it became readily available in print, in her dowry. Today a woman is supposed to have good handwriting for acquiring a good reputation. When families seek out a bride for a son, brother or relative, it is considered to be a good quality that she should have done well enough at school to be able to help her future children in their studies and, above all, that she should have good handwriting. It is often the women who fill in official forms in ornate, tidy script. When occasionally letters to relatives must be written, a man will perhaps tell the woman what message must be conveyed, but it is she who will compose and write out the wording. The special relationship of women to literacy in Georgian village society is detailed and complex and cannot easily be subsumed briefly in a chapter about something else. It is possible, however, to offer two reasons here, in reference to sex roles, for the significance of female literacy. On the one hand, women are the guardians of social order and of 'civilisation'. They are also thought to be able to control their actions more effectively than men. A certain sense of artistry fits into this concept: unlike men, a woman will arrange food such as slices of cheese in symmetrical and pleasing patterns on a plate when she serves at table. She decorates the pastry of pies and she may know how to embroider. Locally men are believed to be unable to master their fingers in such a way, although traditionally men in Ratcha were famous as silversmiths and carvers.

Handwriting is learned by all at school but girls are expected to be better at doing '*supta tsera*' (clean writing). On the other hand, as well as having this ability, the female role is also, and above all, to be a mother. As such, if a mother cares for her children she will assume responsibility for their schooling without which they will eventually be unable to obtain satisfactory employment. Posters and poems abound in Soviet Georgia today (as well as in the nineteenth century) where a mother in her village headscarf sits with her children doing homework. It is her role as a good mother which prompts her to teach children songs and poetry, especially to her daughters although it is known that for a man to have prestige he should display the fact that he had a good mother. By reciting poems in well-spoken toasts, for example, he will reveal that his mother taught him well, and this in turn shows he is an honourable man. Yet it is not a display of oral literacy alone which will confer distinction on men or women. In Soviet times especially, although for women it has simply developed a trend started in the previous century, you must show that you can read and that you have read a good array of the Georgian classics. If you can't, then you are presumed not to come from a 'good home' and, above all, that you do not have a good mother, with all the disgrace that it hints at.

Little stress, apart from fidelity, is made on woman's role as *wife*; a good mother will automatically gain her husband's affection. Virginity is expected before marriage and, as said earlier, her village playmates are not considered as potential partners because of kinship ties with them. Men, on the other hand, are presumed to have had sexual experience when in the army, prior to marriage, with Russian girls in the areas they served in. (Soviet policy is that minority nationals never serve in their own republic.) Through acts of bravery, honour and generosity, a man must defend the 'blood' of the family. He is expected to work hard physically and to be strong and have well-developed muscles. Men are governed by their emotions. Women are thought to experience emotions such as fear or anguish physically, with pains in their chest and so forth. With appropriate physical aids such as tablets and herbs they can be treated and so overcome them in order to resume normal life and duties. Men, in contrast, are thought to get 'unruly blood' when they are upset, which they cannot control and which does not manifest itself in the form of localised physical pain but rather as an overall body heat which drives them to violence.

Within the household, the division of labour is sharply defined. Women cook, clean, serve the food and wash their infants and dress them. Men do household chores like mending lights, chopping wood and so on. They play with infants of both sexes and will carry them in their arms, but they hand them back to the women when any difficulty occurs.

Both men and women work outside the home, women bringing in salaries from the tertiary services and doing a little work for the collective farm (women do not as a rule do heavy work in the fields in the area I studied); they also tend to their poultry and other domestic animals. Among the elder generation, the grandparents, much of the responsibility for childrearing devolves on them as well as the greater participation in the collective farm work to which at times they take their grandchildren with them. In this sense, incidentally, it is a question of your position within the generations in a family rather than whether you are a man or woman which determines whether or not you will be faced with the problems of combining childrearing with your job; it is the grandparents who have to seek out ways of combining the two rather than the mother.

Schematically, the nature of sexual identity which governs the allocating of sex roles can be seen in the following way, but bearing in mind that this is a selective and not exhaustive list of relevant concepts:

*The nature of sexual identity*

| Female | Male |
|---|---|
| Society–village | Nature–outside world |
| Stability | Mobility |
| Continuity | Innovation |
| Wholeness/dependability | Fragmentation/unreliability |
| Nourishment | Defence |
| Emotion is physically expressed | Emotion is temperamentally expressed |

Finally, modesty is prized in both sexes, although men may expose more of their bodies (i.e. their chests and legs) than women. Also your sex determines what you can do in public or not. For example, men can get drunk in public whereas women, if they ever do, would only indulge themselves at the all-female winter evening gathering called a 'campania'. The notion of public and private, however, is not straightforward, and merits more discussion than will be given further on here.

## STATE ROLES

Here again, a comprehensive examination of 'State roles' is outside the scope of this paper and inevitably I must be highly selective and somewhat superficial in my treatment of the subject. By 'State roles' in this context, I refer, of course, to the roles people are expected to perform as citizens of a Soviet State manifesting itself in village life, in order for them to maximise advantage and avoid negative sanctions. The ones I have selected are roles and skills that highlight, by their nature, the contradictions with which the villager is faced in everyday life deriving from fundamental official expectations and basic activities.

It should be pointed out, however, that they are expected to be taught at home. School, youth group organisations and other 'official' bodies, although they present themselves as such, are not considered by the villagers to be authorities on morals or to have the capacity of teaching them. This belies the importance given to the Soviet system of education enshrined in the impressions held by scholars who study Soviet socialisation from very early on. For example, Margaret Mead and Elena Calas (1955), who thought they were writing about the Soviet system in general, regardless of ethnic background, remarked on the aim of Soviet education. It was, they said, 'to develop ideological purposefulness, strong convictions and principles, a sense of duty, perseverence, endurance, courage, unselfishness and selflessness, self-control and discipline, humanism, vigour, optimism and cheerfulness, generosity combined with care of property, and also politeness, modesty and sensitivity.' They end by pointing out the disparity between the ideal Soviet world where there would be 'a complete respect for all human beings in a society with a lack of hierarchy and with a lack of any sense of gulf between a group ruling and a group ruled', and, on the other hand, a leadership in the Soviet Union 'which has a deep contempt of the mass of the people'. Such contradictions, they conclude, result in education methods which lead to a doctrinaire view of the world.

For the villagers I studied, such contradictions did not plague them; they were likewise impervious to the moral content (I call it 'moral' for lack of a better definition) of school and 'official' education and socialisation. For boys and girls alike, those characteristics in the long list cited above which were also contained in the ideals of Georgian village behaviour, such as valour, cheerfulness (most of the time), politeness and so on, were all considered part and parcel of what should be taught at home by the family members.

School was for academic learning and if part of the price was to sit through and memorise lines about the glory of the Soviet system, then that was a small price to pay for the advantages of learning writing, history and literature and getting a school-leaving certificate which was necessary to enter any profession or get any job. We will discuss actual socialisation later but suffice it to say at this point that before the age of seven, children are already prepared by their parents to learn what they are taught at school by rote, without questioning its contents, whenever it is concerned with 'official' material such as political poems or slogans.

In day-to-day life, however, parents know that children will realise that there are great contrasts between what they are taught 'officially' and what they see with their own eyes around them. More important, however, is that it would be safe to say that they probably sense that the adults, members of their own family in particular, are well aware of the differences.

Thus a citizen should proclaim allegiance to the State and its rulers and believe that the Soviet regime offers the best conditions in the world, the best system, both political and economic, and that it gives sufficiently of everything a person may need. The reality as the villagers usually see it is different: it is a system in which they cannot participate at any decision-making level even in some intimately personal choices. Obtaining access to consumer goods is a continuous struggle, living on 'official' incomes is very hard, and so on. So in their roles as citizens, at this level, they have to be astute and forever vigilant about the availability of consumer goods, to provide extra income for their families whenever possible through 'moonlighting', for example, and develop the awareness that, far from assuming his or her responsibilities, the State produces a system where each person has to act for himself or herself.

Similarly, although the average villager only has to think about the matter when listening to the radio or reading a newspaper, all citizens are supposed to identify with all the other peoples of the USSR and not to see their own nation as intrinsically superior. In fact, Soviet power is seen as Russian power and usually the only interest, for example, in an All-Union Soviet football team is if Georgian players feature significantly. At an educational level, when at school, the villager again is prone to rejecting parts of the school programme such as Russian literature which are obligatory in favour of poetry which extols the Georgian nation and which supports their quest to be 'Georgian' above all else. Indeed, to get his or her own way when petitioning an official in the provincial capital, the villager will endeavour to remind the official of his or her role 'as a local patriot above all else, despite the authorities' views, far away.

A final example of the contradictions offered by the State which the villager feels is that, officially, all citizens should be concerned with serving the State and through it everyone else, rather than seeking personal advantage for themselves and kin and friends. Yet a doctor or teacher often expects 'gifts' for services rendered, to maintain his or her family which would be impossible on a salary alone. The 'hidden economy' thrives, without which, again, few villagers could survive with the life style they accept as minimum: under-counter sales in the shops, or buying grapes on the cheap in another province and passing them off as your own when the Government requisitions all villagers to contribute their own grapes from their private plots to make up the annual production plan decided in the faraway capital. Officially, the State requires its citizens to take on a collectivist role whereas the conditions it has created cause people to be highly individualistic, familistic too, and to develop secrecy with all except close family and kin.

## SOCIALISATION

It is considered by the villagers that a child is born with no knowledge at all. Everything has to be taught, from etiquette to self-identity, through patient explaining and cajoling. Children under the age of seven are rarely punished physically and even then not severely. Children are continually asked, 'Do you understand? Do you hear?' whether in a cross voice or not. Children of both sexes receive much physical expression of affection, with kisses and hugs from adults and other children alike. Until the age of six or seven they are not considered to be responsible for their acts and then, only slowly, are they attributed with any, up until the age of 14 or 15. A youth is still not considered to be fully developed, although girls are thought to mature more quickly than boys, and only marriage and parenthood bestow adulthood on the average villager, whether man or woman. Yet a person is still developing, it is thought, and only someone in their mid-thirties, approximately, is thought to have become a full-fledged adult with all the necessary knowledge and control over his or her actions. Until then, the plea 'He or she is only young' is often used as an excuse for misdemeanour. Georgians as a whole have a high life expectancy, anyone dying under the age of 80 being considered generally 'too young' to have died and therefore mourned intensely. This contrasts dramatically with the expected life cycle of some Third World countries for which anthropological literature is available on the subject. Although the character of a person is deemed to be hereditary in some of its aspects, the main onus is on the way a family brings up the person, and the son of a hot-tempered person is not expected to behave in the same way if his family can teach him not to, for example. Furthermore, although I have already mentioned it, I have to emphasise yet again that only the family is thought to have any effect in his upbringing; both school and influences such as those of youth groups of the Young Communists League are considered of no consequence.

**How sex roles are taught**

Most anthropologists writing about socialisation have usually had the confidence to present the material with no equivocation, as 'Among *these people* such and such beliefs and roles are transmitted to the next generation'. It is implied that some sort of perpetual culture maintains itself over time and socialisation is viewed in terms of it. In this sense, sex roles for the villagers fall into that category and their teaching pertains to the traditional style of socialisation which forms the bulk of ethnograpic reports.

A child is brought up in a house containing grandparents, parents, and sometimes unmarried uncles and aunts. There is, however, no disagreement of opinion between the members of the family or of the actual statements made.

Furthermore, the subject is discussed and children are taught sex roles by both family members and by other kin and village members whom small children meet and even in the nursery run for a few hours a day by the village librarian.

A sing-song tone is used, characteristic of that region of Georgia, by the way, and even admonitions are delivered with usual affectionate diminutives (e.g. *Shvili*=Child is replaced by *Shviliko*, the *-iko* suffix implying 'small' in an affectionate way). Sex differences in terms of inferior/superior are played down and a favourite verse is often quoted from the *Knight in the panther's skin* mentioned earlier: 'Lion cubs are lions, whether male or female'. The grandparents with whom they spend a lot of time share domestic tasks more than their parents whom they see less of. As stated earlier, it is sibling love that is encouraged between both siblings and cousins who constitute the major part of children infants are likely to encounter.

Until the age of around six, children may play or run about with their genitals in view, although after that it is strictly forbidden, among adults especially, and privacy for excreting is also sought invariably. Nevertheless, girls and boys are quick to understand the differences between them that are made apparent to them. Girls are allowed to cry when they have physical pain whereas boys are told not to accept physical pain as having any important reality. Girls must not cry too loudly but may cry for longer than boys. 'Be strong' is said to boys and girls alike, but to a girl the necessary explanation is added that 'You must be strong *because you are a girl*, one day to be a mother, to bear a family on your shoulders'. In contrast, a boy will be told, 'You must be strong *because you are a boy* and you must defend your people'.

To cry about physical pain provokes different responses, to a girl that 'She will know such pain in adult life that she can cry a little now', but a boy is told not to pay attention and not to cry otherwise he will never be able to do the brave deeds that are expected of him. A girl is told she must look after the things in her house so she better not wander too far away, except to visit her kin. A boy is not admonished as much, in comparison. A girl is taught not to stand when she drinks water because only cows and horses stand when drinking and people shouldn't. Although boys are told the same thing, I noticed it was not nearly as frequent and when I asked parents why, they simply said it wasn't as important for men as for women to keep the customs which make one really human.

Another example of using different explanations according to the anticipated sex role is when villagers deal with a problem familiar to those with adequate supplies: getting toddlers to eat up their food. A very frequent sight is that of a grandmother with a fork full of food running all round the house and yard after a playful (and sometimes wilful) child. Half singing she pleads with him or her to eat, saying to a girl that she must eat to become a pretty young woman, not a bag of bones (*dzvali da tqavi*: bone and hide) and to be strong enough to have a family and clever enough to do well at school. A boy is told to eat up to become big and strong to travel, to go hunting, to defend his people and so on. Never is it said 'Eat up because I told you to'.

Children, however, are not punished for not eating nor do adults ever resort to holding over the previous meal before new food is offered to a child. If the pleading and explaining with a stream of reasons fail, then adults will resign themselves to it and will resort to giving the children whatever known favourites are available, such as corn on the cob when in season, for example. Until they are of school age (seven years old) children of both sexes are never expected to care for younger siblings as a specific obligation, and in their games both boys and girls pretended to be parents. Boys, however, receive toy weapons as presents which girls do not. Girls would be given dolls. Girls are taught more poetry and songs than boys and are expected to know more about their kinship ties than boys of the same age. Again, oral communication is used as the primary source of teaching, although example as observed by infants of the adults round them plays, obviously, an important role. The sex role displays are consistent from family to family and from person to person. Neither is there ever argument or questioning on any point.

### How State roles are taught

At the beginning of this chapter, I noted the importance of non-verbally expressed sentiments. Now I would also like to add that, by and large, an anthropologist can identify certain ways in which the people she (or he) is studying express stress and anxiety, although she may have no specialist training in psychological behaviour, so long as she limits herself to those signs which are, on the whole, generally accepted as such by the community itself. Furthermore, they should be repeated not by one or two individuals but in a general way (although I would avoid the use of a statistically optimal number to qualify what I have described).

For example, there were gestures. Men in the village would rub their moustaches with sharp, nervous movements when under stress. Women would press their foreheads with the palms of their hands when agitated. There was the use of eye contact, to seek approval or disapproval from other members of the family, or other group, present when you were stating something and this use of eye contact displayed your uncertainty. Also, it was noticeable how people lowered their eyes if they did not really want to answer a question.

One particular characteristic of the region I did my fieldwork in was the way people sighed when they felt they were in a difficult or awkward situation, which children learned to imitate at an early age. Georgians from other regions can recognise that a person comes from Ratcha Province by the special way they sigh.

To smile with closed lips was also considered meaningful. Children would be told to 'show your teeth when you smile!' if they were shy, because if you smiled genuinely then you would not purse your lips at the same time which made it look false.

Finally, one of the factors I noticed for revealing stress was the use of speed and tone in speech. In my own Ratcha villages the usual sing-song intonation characteristic for the province was exaggerated more when talking with children. Adults used a kind of 'baby language' when speaking with toddlers, for example saying, like the toddlers themselves who find it difficult to pronounce 'r': *Ala* instead of *Ara* (which means 'No'). Even as they get older, children are still addressed with a strong sing-song intonation. When embarrassed, however, the speed of speech changed and became more rapid and the sing-song quality would fade.

It would be erroneous to give in to the temptation to read too much hidden meaning into particular gestures such as men rubbing their moustaches. Perhaps all men who have moustaches do that, regardless of their cultural context? Nevertheless, in Georgian symbolism, the moustache represents manliness and honour, to the extent that in pre-Soviet times it is said that a man would leave a hair of his moustache with the person from whom he incurred a debt as a safeguard. He would reclaim it only when the debt had been repaid.

Women of the older generation often wore headbands low over their foreheads, to be protected from the blowing winds and the cold air which were believed to provoke headaches. Intense emotion was thought to cause pressure to build up around the forehead, hence the reason for pressing their palms against their foreheads in times of stress to provide relief. That, at least, is one plausible but not exclusive explanation. The women themselves laughed embarrassedly and said they had no idea why they did it, when I ventured to ask them directly. (This is always an ill-advised approach for anthropologists in contrast to some psychologists' techniques.) As for the use of the eyes, for transmitting meaning, in contrast to Britain, winking was not used as a signal; rather the raising and furrowing of eyebrows and the use of meaningful glances signified that emphasis was being laid in a way that could not be expressed verbally.

My observations here refer to pre-school children between three and seven years old. Yet it would be very misleading to present the data as exclusive to that age group. The presence of siblings, older or younger, is one factor. Another is that my data here were not collected systematically nor on their own, but rather form part of my wider study of family structure (c.f. Dragadze, 1981). On the whole, certain areas of teaching children within the family, pertaining to State roles in particular where genuine opinions and attitudes could not be expressed explicitly, were invariably accompanied by indications of ambiguity and uncertainty which children learned to notice as a very important part of their socialisation process. In this sphere, some features are held in common which differ to those of sex-role socialisation.

(a) Whereas in sex roles teaching was usually accompanied by exegesis and elaborate explaining which formed the main method of the socialisation process used and which is often encountered in other cultures also, when studying it in what I call the 'traditional' realm, it is the case that behaviour necessary for coping as a member of the State is often taught as a command, without much accompanying explanation. The best example is that of *secrecy* about certain matters. In Georgian *secrecy* (*saidumlo*), from the word *dumili* for silence, is to be distinguished from '*piradi*' (personal) and '*kerdzo*' (private). Why one had to be secretive could not be explained openly and directly. A child is told: 'Don't tell anyone outside this house because I told you so, and that's that.' Or simply the answer 'Because' is given when a child asks 'Why?' (*ratom*=why; *amitom*=because). These kinds of response contrast markedly with those explanations reported above when telling a boy or girl not to cry according to their sex role.

(b) If pressed for a reason for a secret by a persistent child, each adult is likely to give a different answer.

For example, a child is told, 'Don't talk about what is growing on our plot'. This is because, although villagers can often see with the naked eye what produce is being grown it is not discussed except with extremely close kin so that, should an official ever come to question the villagers, they can more easily claim ignorance. The child might ask, 'Why mustn't I say it?' The father rubs his moustache and says, 'Because I still don't know what will grow there in the end.' When the same child pressed his or her grandmother for an explanation, she will perhaps reply, 'Because if you tell anyone, the birds might hear and will then eat all that's there.' So the child goes back to the father: 'Daddy, why did you say ... And granny said ... and Mummy said ...' Then, to all the adults' visible consternation, a child might say, 'I'll ask the teacher.' 'No, don't!' 'Why not?' 'Because I told you so!' Gradually the child will grow up with a sharp dividing line between listening to what outside authorities have to say and never supplying any information to them in return.

Parallels can be drawn, of course, with the environment of children brought up under other political systems whose families receive welfare benefits, for example, (Sutherland, 1975) or whose families are involved in tax evasion! In conclusion it would be erroneous to claim that the Soviet situation as I have described it is unique and devoid of strong albeit not totally identical parallels. But the sanctions in some more familiar areas are not so terrifying to the imagination as those that could be encountered under some other regimes, the Soviet one in particular.

(c) While a young child anywhere may conceive of certain things within a twilight zone of fantasy and reality, of fact and fiction, the definition of the borderline between them can take on, from the adult's viewpoint especially, whose anxiety is transmitted to the child, a significance of tremendous importance. I am not the only person who has witnessed the following type of conversation:

> A child of three will say, 'Is Great Lenin really our grandfather like the poem says which Teacher taught us?' (obligatory learning for three-year-olds).
> 'Yes, he is,' says a flustered grandmother.
> 'Does he always live in Moscow far away?'
> 'Yes, he's not Georgian,' says another adult.
> 'Did you live in Moscow? Do all grandfathers live in Moscow?' and all sorts of questions are fired.
> 'It's all rubbish,' chips in a fearless grandfather.
> 'Our teacher read us a story which says he loves us best of all, though. Is that rubbish too?'
> 'No, it isn't,' says the mother, furious at her in-laws with whom she lives, 'It's all true, what the teacher says,' looking anxiously at the other members of the family.

That sort of conversation, at least what it represents, can be witnessed frequently. But the response each family gives is different and it is hard for the ethnographer to see more than tentative patterns, elusive and undefined, in such an area of socialisation. Yet a psychologist might well be able to test out general hypotheses here and see whether they are culture-bound or not, at the very least.

If all children in a given community learn that much of what they are taught by school teachers and those whom their families might label as 'official authorities' is not to be defined as either 'true' or 'false', but should be discussed as little as possible, then is an individual child going to display signs of 'difficulty' or not? How would a psychologist define such displays of anxiety within this context?

(d) Adults themselves, as said earlier, have to contend with the handling of continually changing new government decrees. For example at one time you are permitted to have as many wedding guests as you want, another time there must not be more than 200 and so on. This undermines the rule of thumb most adults apply when deciding what facts children can talk about openly and which not. It also makes parents ambivalent when teaching children their roles to survive as citizens, where for example: (i) they must be secretive about certain matters, (ii) be persuasive towards all shop-keepers to sell you goods they say they don't have and which they will sometimes release for higher payment than the official price which you must offer always discreetly, (iii) never to say aloud that you do not take at face value what you are taught outside the home and so on, (iv) to emulate an adult's ambivalence in those areas which fit only with difficulty into the richly woven mesh of beliefs and codes of behaviour described and taught with such confidence from one generation to the next where traditions abound and even folk tales interlink intimately with the structures of local culture.

When socialising their young, instead of confidence there is hesitation, anxiety instead of ease, giving commands instead of explaining with reasons, providing individual responses instead of collective ones and so on. At the same time, what is also transmitted is that what really counts, is our great tradition; the rest is a grey area, silly at times, fearful at others.

## CONCLUSIONS

Difficulties arise when writing a report on the second type of socialisation, which includes, among others, the areas I have typified with the label 'State roles' (note that not more is intended than a label of convenience). Individual character among adults and even children, plays a great part in this field, especially when deciding whether or not an adult transmits unease to a child. An ethnographer has less repetitive data to base observations on which could represent a community as a whole. It would also be very wrong to generalise in an oversimplistic way about psychological dispositions in the style of American 'Culture and Personality' studies in the past.

It is possible, nevertheless, when watching parents and offspring interacting, to detect ways in which the former display signs of embarrassment and the latter react, at times in what would be considered a mischievous way (for example, the Lenin poem conversation was sometimes used by one sibling to gain attention over another when repeated several times over), all within the parameters of a given community's recognisable culture.

One conclusion I reached in such observations was that although the community had a shared structural situation *vis-à-vis* the State, there was no universally agreed way of coping with it and that conflicting opinions in themselves produced many of the same reactions by children in response to the adults' non-verbal displays of ambivalence. As I have said several times already, this contrasts sharply with the kind of attitudes and responses adopted by parents and offspring alike when dealing with what one could call 'traditional' areas of socialisation, as epitomised by the teaching of 'sex roles' to acquire identity and one's place in the community.

Although the 'traditional' area has formed the bulk of work on socialisation done by anthropologists, it would be interesting to note whether, in a general way, some similar patterns are emerging in other rapidly changing societies. Would it not be a good area for developing theoretical frameworks to study the uncomfortable? More particularly, given two levels of experience, cognitive development could differ significantly in response to the style used by adults to develop children's awareness of their own identity, in this case their identity as girls or boys, as siblings and cousins and co-villagers on the one hand, and as citizens of 'somewhere out there' on the other.

**NOTES**

1. *Knight in the panther's skin* is a twelfth-century epic poem written in intricate but still comprehensible Georgian language verses by Shota Rustaveli, who served at the court of queen Tamar. It extols the virtues cherished by Georgians and whole sets of verses are known by heart throughout the population.

**BIBLIOGRAPHY**

Dragadze, T. (1981) 'The sexual division of domestic space among two Soviet minorities'. In S. Ardener (ed.), *Women and space*. London: Croom Helm.
Mead, M. and Calas, E. (1955) 'Child training ideals in a post-revolutionary context: Soviet Russia'. In M. Mead and M. Wolfenstein (eds), *Childhood in contemporary cultures*. Chicago: Chicago University Press.
Sciama, L. (1981) 'The problem of privacy in Mediterranean anthropology'. In S. Ardener (ed.), *Women and space*. London: Croom Helm.
Sutherland, A. (1975) *Gypsies: the hidden Americans*. London: Tavistock Publications.

# Annotated Bibliography

## Recent Studies of Ethnography of Childhood

Christina Toren

This selected bibliography concentrates on material published since 1970; it is divided into two parts. The first, annotated section is intended to provide the reader with an overview of the wide variety of material available on childhood, childrearing, children's activities, children's construction of their own culture and related subjects, with special reference to children in non-western societies. The commentary aims to give the reader some idea of the theoretical perspective of the author(s) and the type of data under discussion.

The second section simply cites additional works that are likely to be of interest. Again, the emphasis is on material concerning children in non-western societies.

Both sections deliberately include a variety of different types of research from diverse theoretical perspectives. The bibliography is based on the assumption that advances in our understanding of the cultural construction of the notion of 'the child' *and* the child's construction of his or her own culture require an integration of apparently disparate types of data.

Note that this bibliography does not claim to be comprehensive; the emphasis is on English language sources and it excludes, for instance, most of the works cited in G. Jahoda (1982) *Psychology and anthropology*.

## SECTION 1: AN ANNOTATED SELECTION

Alland, A. (1983) *Playing with form. Children draw in six cultures.* New York: Columbia University Press.
 A cross-cultural study of drawing by young children (up to age 6/6 or so) from Bali, Ponape, Taiwan, Japan, USA and France. Ethnographic

detail is sketchy, little attempt being made to situate the subjects of the study within their particular cultures. However the study is interesting in that it does demonstrate the existence of distinct cultural 'styles' (even given strong individual differences between children within culture), in even the youngest children and in those in the Ponape sample who had little previous familiarity with visual art and no experience of drawing. A good case is presented for the argument that representation is not the necessary outcome of picture-making for children. The author's intention in carrying out the study was to demonstrate the existence of 'aesthetic universals', a goal which he freely admits he did not attain, though he does argue for a universal cognitive ability to appreciate 'good form' by explicit analogy with Chomsky's notion of a universal grammar. Given that the author is a professor of anthropology at Columbia University, the study would have benefited from an attempt to make it more anthropological, i.e. to make connections between how children construct their understanding of 'playing with form' and their simultaneous construction of other aspects of their culture.

Archer, W.G. (1974) *The Hill of flutes*. University of Pittsburgh Press.

Descriptive ethnography of the Santals of Bihar, Eastern India, with special emphasis on their poetry. A chapter covers pregnancy, birth, children's games and occupations, manners, prohibitions etc., rites to mark adolescence, relations between boys and girls. Information about parent–child relations centres on adolescence and marriage. The material on childhood experience and learning has large gaps and is not systematic.

Barry, H. and Paxson, L.M. (1971) 'Infancy and early childhood: cross-cultural codes 2'. *Ethnology 10*, 466–508.

Barry, H., Josephson, L., Lauer, E. and Marshall, C. (1976) 'Traits inculcated in childhood: cross-cultural codes 5'. *Ethnology*, 7, 83–114.

Barry, H. *et al.* (1977) 'Agents and techniques for child training: cross-cultural codes 6'. *Ethnology 8*, 191–238.

These three articles present information based on a world sample of 186 societies drawn from the HRA Files. Though inevitably patchy, they nevertheless constitute the largest collection of specially coded material available for cross-cultural hypothesis testing.

Blurton-Jones, N. (ed.) (1972) *Ethnological studies of child behaviour*. Cambridge University Press.

Collection of papers on, for the most part, the behaviour of European and USA children. The ethological perspective tends to concentrate on 'species specific behaviour' i.e. on universals, rather than on differences across cultures. The editor accepts the existence of class and cultural differences (pp. 26/27) but treats class and culture as variables that *affect* behaviour rather than behaviour itself as constitutive of these 'variables'. Some interesting material. Includes a paper by M. J. Konner on infancy among the Bushmen of Botswana.

Briggs, J.L. (1979) *Aspects of Inuit value socialization*. National Museum of Man, Mercury Series, Ottowa: National Museums of Canada.

An analysis of Inuit 'playfulness' and its role in childrearing. Shows how in Inuit society 'a great deal of the serious business of life is conducted in the playful mode'. In interaction between child and adult, play is a means of bringing the child to internalise the central values of Inuit society and at the same time 'charges' these values with complex emotional meaning, such that the values themselves become commitments. For instance, adults provoke children to play at the expression of extremely anti-social feelings (e.g. dislike being exaggerated in play as the intention to kill), and so these feelings are at once expressed and controlled. Argues that play contains the processes essential to the creation, maintenance and internalisation of the central values of Inuit society. Detailed and very well-observed data, sensitively analysed.

See also Briggs, J.L. (1970) *Never in anger. Portrait of an Eskimo family*. Cambridge, Mass.: Harvard University Press; and Briggs, J.L. (1975) 'The origins of non-violence: aggression in two Canadian Eskimo groups'. In W. Muensterberger (ed.), *The Psychoanalytic study of society*, vol. 6. New York: International Universities Press.

Bronfenbrenner, U. (1970) *Two worlds of childhood. US and USSR*. New York: Simon and Schuster, Clarion Books (1972).

Cross-cultural social psychological study. Data is culled from observations and interviews by the author on a series of trips to the USSR between 1960 and 1967. Comparison is made between this data and that from a variety of US studies of socialisation and childrearing. Data on the USSR particularly interesting but analysis suffers from the fact that no attempt is made to situate either the US or USSR children in an historical and/or sociological context. While the author is specifically concerned to show 'the impressive power ... of models, peers and group forces in influencing behaviour and development of children', society itself is taken for granted. The analytic perspective is largely derived from Bandura *et al*.'s 1960s' studies which argued that child behaviour was modelled on that of highly salient and 'powerful' others; the perspective is fundamentally a behavourist one since it relies on modifications of Miller and Dollard's (1941) 'social learning' theory.

Calhoun, C.J. and Ianni, F.A.J. (eds) (1976) *The anthropological study of education*. The Hague, Paris: Mouton Publishers.

A selection of papers presented to the IXth International Congress of Anthropoligical and Ethnological Sciences in Chicago, 1973. Papers possibly of interest include the following: M.J. King on 'enculturation' in Californian communes gives a brief account of commune organisation, composition etc. and describes how children are raised in each one. Two of the communes have an 'alternative religion' at their base—these are basically Eastern philosophies adapted to Californian requirements; the other is primarily organised in terms of economic convenience. King compares his own data with work on the Hutterian Brethren of Dakota. He looks at how the education/socialisation of the child tends towards dependence/reciprocity or independence/self-reliance and the implications of these findings for the stability of the commune.

H.E. Ellis attacks the notion of American blacks' 'failure' in education and shows how the nature of the educational process for blacks in urban schools is such that it inevitably reproduces the very conditions for its pupils that it is supposedly set up to relieve.

The collection includes a number of papers on adolescent and early adult socialisation in grammar schools in an urban area in the UK and in teachers' college (C. Lacey), on the social organisation of high schools—rural, suburban and urban—in the USA (C.J. Calhoun and F.A.J. Ianni), on school culture as a specific manifestation of American culture (H. Varenne); on problems of the wholesale importation of western methods/curricula etc. into the African context (E.B. Leacock); on Lakota (Sioux) views of the schooling process in South Dakota, plus other papers on theoretical issues in the anthropological study of education.

Camara, S. (1973) 'L'univers dramatique et imaginaire des relations familiales chez les Malinke'. *Psychopathologie Africaine*, 9 (2), 187–222.

An analysis of family relations, initiation and folk tales among the Malinke, this paper focuses on the 'drama of separation' that is to be found in initiation rites and various folk tales which describe or imply conflicts between mother and son. The author's perspective combines the anthropological with the psychoanalytic; he suggests that the ordeal of initiation and many stories are ways of dramatising the problem a boy encounters in his inevitable separation from his mother (with whom he has previously had a very close relationship). Interesting data but the paper would have benefited from richer first-hand material on circumcision.

Cannizzo, J. (1979) 'Rastamen, reggae and West African masquerading'. Paper presented at the 22nd Annual Meeting of the African Studies Association, Los Angeles, California.

Paper concerning masquerading by school boys in Sierra Leone. Boys masking associations create a world of their own, autonomous from adults and independent of ethnic origin, status, rank, religion etc. Shows how children construct a specifically 'child' culture.

For more detailed Information on the same subject, see also Cannizzo, J.E. (1978) 'Alikali Devils: Children's masquerading in a West African town'. Anthropology Ph.D dissertation. University of Washington, Seattle, WA.

Centner, TH.H. (1963) *L'enfant africain et ses jeux dans le cadre de la vie traditionnelle au Katanga*. Katanga: CEPSI (Collections mémoires CEPSI No. 17).

A beautifully produced 'ethnological' text with many photographs and illustrations, covering the variety of children's games in the Shaba province of Zaire. The account is based on research among the Luba, Sanga and Yeke (Bantu peoples). The author's perspective is influenced by the work of Ralph Linton of the Culture and Personality School. Superb descriptive account of children's play. The book begins with a discussion of the place of children in the traditional cultures concerned, plus a description of the various stages of child development and their recognition in ritual. This is followed by highly detailed accounts of play, games etc., especially those played in the *masansa* or children's villages (i.e. temporary play villages) such as games of imitation of ceremonies, family and village life etc., language games, hand and finger games and so on.

Charles, V. and Charles, S.X. (1979) 'Child rearing practices in an Indian slum'. *Tropical and Geographical Medicine*, *31*(3), 459–65.

Primarily concerned with the problem of infant health, this paper is itself an indication of the need for more extensive ethnographic data on the nature of parental attitudes, beliefs and childrearing practices. The authors found that while mothers were careful to see that their children were immunised against tuberculosis and other serious illnesses, their childrearing practices were likely to compound the problems caused by poverty, despite extensive efforts on the part of health workers to influence infant-feeding and other practices. A number of illnesses are believed to be caused by the evil eye and are for this reason thought to respond only to treatment by traditional healers. That such beliefs are resistant to change argues for the necessity of a more profound understanding of the wider context of belief and cultural practice.

Curran, V.H. (ed.) (1984) *Nigerian children. Developmental perspectives*. London: Routledge & Kegan Paul.

May be of interest if read in conjunction with relevant ethnographies; none of the authors display much appreciation of the way that culture enters into cognition.

Includes papers on the following subjects: looking strategies in Nigerian infants; the educational experiences of Nigerian infants; cognitive and affective aspects of infant development; developmental perspectives on memory; home and school: effects of micro-ecology on children's educational achievements; traditional childrearing practices of the Oje market women of Ibadan; handicapped children.

D'Anglure, B.S. (1980) '"Petit-ventre", l'enfant-géant du cosmos inuit. Ethnographie de l'enfant et enfance de l'ethnographie dans l'Arctique central inuit'. *Homme*, *20*(1), 7–46.

A comment on and re-analysis of Rasmussen's 1922 data in the light of that gathered throughout the 1970s; an attempt to correct the '*androcentrisme*' and the '*adultocentrisme*' of earlier ethnography. The author analyses the life stories of ten of the people met by Rasmussen the author, and by reference to the behaviour, concepts and rituals relative to children, argues that the whole system of Inuit life is conceived of in terms of reproduction of the material conditions of existence and of human reproduction itself. By these means we learn a good deal about adult attitudes towards children and the place of the child in the Inuit scheme of things.

Dennis, B.G. (1972) *The Gbandes*. Chicago: Nelson-Hall Co.

Data culled from fieldwork in Liberia and the author's own childhood there. Two chapters deal explicitly with 'the process by which the individual born into Gbande society becomes a Gbande'. However, information on infancy, pre-adolescence, adolescence and social control is all somewhat sketchy. The information on indigenous educational institutions, both informal and formal, is more extensive, though here too one wishes for much greater detail, especially with respect to instruction in the Poro school (of which the author, as a child, was himself a graduate) and its wider significance in Gbande society.

Dieterlen, G. (1978) *Systèmes de signes: textes réunis en hommage à Germaine Dieterlen*. Paris: Hermann.

Mostly devoted to data on adults, but includes C. Cartry on children's games among the Gurma of Upper Volta; M. Fortes on the significance of the first born in African family systems; S. Lallemand on Mossi notions of the 'baby-ancestor' and the transformation of the baby into the autonomous child.

Dinnerstein, D. (1978) *The rocking of the cradle and the ruling of the world.* London: Souvenir Press (Educational and Academic) Ltd., 1978.

An investigation of 'our species psychopathology' with respect to gender roles and the relations between the sexes: 'the prevailing symbiosis between men and women is something more than a product of societal coercion. It is part of the neurotic overall posture by means of which humans, male and female, try to cope with massive psychological problems that lie at the heart of our species situation.' The domination of early childcare by women has 'crippling consequences' for children, and more particularly for girls. Looks at mother/child relations in western contexts from a largely Freudian perspective. Shows little or no appreciation of the fact that her views are not necessarily applicable across cultures—even if they could be seen as acceptable in western contexts. The author is a professor of psychology at Rutgers University.

Dussan de Reichel, A. (1979) 'Child-rearing in a Colombian village'. *International Social Science Journal*, 31(3), 404–14.

An account of childrearing in a village in the foothills of the Andes, this article describes practices concerned with feeding and cleanliness, parental roles, disciplinary practices and sex-role identification.

Dwyer, D.H. (1978) *Images and self-images. Male and female in Morocco.* New York: Columbia University Press.

Analysis of data concerned with gender and derived partly from participant observation and partly from traditional tales etc. Chapters on the transition 'from girl to woman' and 'from boy to man' and on the complementary roles of mother and father in childrearing. Concentrates on the later stages of childhood and the transition to adulthood.

Ennew, J. (1986) *The sexual exploitation of children.* Oxford: Polity Press.

Examines cross-cultural evidence on the sexual exploitation of children in the light of contemporary theoretical and ethical perspectives, and of recent debates on childhood, sexuality and the family. The author analyses evidence for the involvement of children in prostitution, sex tourism and pornography and argues that child sexual exploitation must be viewed in the broader social context of power relations between men and women, between elders and juniors, between classes and between races.

Note that as an anthropologist, Ennew is also concerned with child labour and has produced the following reports published by the Anti-Slavery Society, London: *Child labour in Jamaica: its nature and incidence* (1980), *Young hustlers: work and childhood in Jamaica* (1981) and with P. Young, *Child labour in Jamaica* (1982).

Erny, P. (1973) *Childhood and cosmos. The social psychology of the black African child.* Washington, D.C.: Black Orpheus Press.

A phenomenological account of 'the Black African child', this study uses secondary sources as data. It aims to discover the psychological 'identity' of the child in African society, how African society views the role of the child and what 'it see(s) in him' (p. 9). Given these ambitious aims the bibliography is rather inadequate. The 'black African child' would appear to be a product of the author's own extrapolations from a mix of data on the Bambara, the Dogon, the Mossi and other, largely west African societies with sudden unexplained shifts to include southeast African data from the Banyamwezi (Tanzania), the Southeastern Bantu (Zambia) and the Chewa (Mozambique). However, we are not told where any of the peoples mentioned come from and the book does not include a map. At some points it is not even clear from which people(s) the data were derived, and by whom.

*Ethos*, Journal of the Society for Psychological Anthropology, Washington, DC. This journal routinely contains many papers likely to be of interest to anthropologists and psychologists concerned with child behaviour, childrearing etc. Some of these are cited below, with brief comments on selected issues.

*Ethos*, 1973 *1*(4), 478–89. See J.D. Herzog, 'Initiation and high school in the development of Kikuyo youths' self-concept'.

*Ethos*, 1974 *2*(3), 296–314. See J.E. and P.L. Kilbride, 'Socio-cultural factions and the early manifestation of sociability behaviour among Baganda infants'.

*Ethos*, 1975 *3*(2). Special issue re development of a 'central theme—the processes of cultural transmission' in the work of Margaret Mead. Includes a number of papers on socialisation, some of them mentioned here (see T. Schwartz below); some components of socialisation for trance (G. Bateson on Bali); socialisation for low affect among the Sebei (W. Goldschmidt); dream concepts of Hausa children (R.A. Shweder and R.A. LeVine); theorising about socialisation of cognition (M. Cole and S. Scribner) plus a number of other papers concerned with socialisation in young adults.

*Ethos*, 1975 *3*(4), 405–527. See C.P. Edwards, 'Societal complexity and moral development: a Kenyan study'.

*Ethos*, 1980 *8*(1); 40–8. See G. Erchak, 'The acquisition of cultural rules by Kpelle children'.

*Ethos*, 1980 *8*(4), 295–315. See R.H. and R.L. Munroe, 'Infant experience and childhood affect among the Logoli: a longitudinal study'.

*Ethos*, 1983 *11*(3), 152–65. See W. Keeler on the socialisation of shame in Javanese children, 'Shame and stage fright in Java'.

*Ethos*, 1983 *11*(4). Issue devoted to 'The socialisation of affect', edited by S. Harkness and P.L. Kilbride. Papers on children include: 'The cultural construction of child development' (S. Harkness and S.M. Super); 'Socialisation for high positive affect between Baganda mother and child' (P.L. Kilbride and J.E. Kilbride); 'Parental goals, ethnopsychology and the delvelopment of emotional meaning among the Ifaluk' (C. Lutz).

*Ethos*, 1984 *12*(4). Includes a typical 'cross-cultural' study by R.H. Munroe and R.L. Munroe, 'Infant experience and childhood cognition: a longitudinal study among the Logoli of Kenya'. This examines the association of early care patterns with both affective and cognitive measures and argues that this association may have far-reaching effects for the Logoli child. Also includes M.R. Welch on 'Social structural expansion, economic diversification and concentration of emphases in childhood socialisation'. This discusses the connection between specific modes of economic organisation and child training processes, argues that the type of economic organisation influences the content and form of childhood socialisation. Cf. L. Hendrix 'Economy and child training re-examined' in *Ethos*, 1985, *13*(3), 246–61.

*Ethos*, 1985 *13*(4). Relevant papers: N. Scheper-Hughes, 'Culture, scarcity and maternal thinking: maternal detachment and infant survival in a Brazilian shanty town'; also includes a discussion of work on the development of moral constructs by C. Pope Edwards; paper by M. Hollos and P.E. Leis on interaction in Portuguese rural families may also be of interest.

*Ethos*, 1986 *14*(1). A paper by Hy Van Luong, 'Language, cognition and ontogenetic development: a re-examination of Piaget's premises' discusses Piaget's ideas on language and cognitive development in the light of a cross-sectional study of Vietnamese children and their acquisition of kin terms.

Forssen, A. (1979) *Roots of traditional personality development among the Zaramo in coastal Tanzania.* Central Union for Child Welfare in Finland, Publication No. 54. Published in collaboration with the Scandinavian Institute of African Studies.

Attempts to assess the suitability of some widely used projective tests e.g. Human Figure and Family Drawing Tests, the Wartegg Drawing and Rorschach tests and a 3-D modelling test, by a child psychiatrist (A. Forssen) and an anthropologist (M.J. Swantz).

The data is derived from children in the rural Tanzanian village of Bunju. The author is concerned to understand the psycho-social development of the child in Zaramo society; the book includes chapters on the anthropological background to the environment and personality development among the Zaramo; psychological tests; modelling as a selection of child personality development in Zaramo society; music and dance in the life of the Zaramo child; and personality development in the light of the psychological tests and of observation among the traditional Zaramo. The authors' perspective is such that they see particular behaviours as 'reflecting' social values rather than being themselves constitutive of those values. We are given brief ethnographic details, though nothing on kinship and social organisation. Ethnographic data concentrates on details the authors feel important for interpretation of the various test results e.g. data concerning body and colour symbolism. Unfortunately there is not sufficient ethnographic detail here to fully evaluate the test results. Thus we are told that 58 per cent of boys and 85 per cent of girls (aged 6–18) modelled figures of both sexes when asked to 'model a person', but that 36 per cent of boys modelled male figures only while only 10 per cent of girls modelled female figures only. However, we are given so little information on notions of gender, on how the child constructs an understanding of gender, on its significance for social organisation, hierarchical relations etc. that we cannot understand the significance of these interesting differences across sex in response to the modelling task.

Fortes, M. (1974) 'The first born'. *Journal of Child Psychology and Psychiatry*, 15, 81–104.

Data from fieldwork among the Tallensi (North Ghana) with some cross-cultural observations. Primarily about the experience of first parenthood and its repercussions on the first born child in Tallensi society.

Gelfand, M. (1979) *Growing up in Shona Society*. Rhodesia: Mambo Press.

Detailed descriptive account of childrearing among the Shona, material derived from many years of familiarity with the Shona in his capacity as a physician. Includes accounts of childreading practices in the urban as well as the rural context, plus material on games, songs, avoidance rules, riddles etc. Lacks systematic data on infants and very young children.

Goldschmidt, W. (1976) *Culture and behaviour of the Sebei*. Berkeley, Los Angeles, London: University of California Press.

This ethnography is a product of the Culture and Ecology Project (established by the author) and concerns fieldwork carried out in 1961/62 among the Sebei of Uganda. It includes two chapters on 'infancy and childhood' and on 'the ritual transformation from child to adult'. The former includes information on general attitudes towards children, pregnancy and birth, infant care and response to infants by both parents, detailed information on weaning, naming, and material on naming, the significance of twins, children's tasks and education, play and discipline. There is also detailed information on boys' and girls' circumcision. Standard structural-functionalist analysis of ceremonies.

Goodman, M.E. (1970) *The culture of childhood: child's eye views of society and culture*. Columbia University Teachers' College: Teachers' College Press.

Primarily addressed to teachers to persuade them of the wide variety of differences between children of different cultures. Anti popularly accepted USA views of the nature of children and childhood. Uses secondary sources to discuss the following: infancy and early childhood: attention, patterns and learning; language and understanding. Self and others: identities, differentiations and attitudes in early childhood, and in the middle years; responsibilities, relationships and roles; values and conscience; concepts and knowledge; play, games and humour; the end of childhood.

Goody, E. (1973) *Contexts of kinship*. Cambridge University Press.

Data concerning the Gonja of Ghana gathered during fieldwork in 1956/57. Interesting chapters on interaction between parents and children, between parents themselves, and on relations between siblings. The author's concern is analysis of domestic organisation and there is therefore little explicit information on how children actually learn about kinship relations and their significance.

Goody, E.N. (1982) *Parenthood and social reproduction. Fostering and occupational roles in West Africa*. Cambridge University Press.

Parenthood and socialisation in West Africa. Concerned with the years of middle childhood and adolescence. Looks at the way in which parenthood is institutionalised in different societies and at how the tasks of parenthood as realised through these different institutionalised forms themselves help to construct the experiences of the child on the route to adulthood. Discusses how parent roles and patterns of socialisation are articulated with other aspects of a society. Fascinating comparative study of different West African groups, including West African families living in London. Argues that the different forms in which parent roles are delegated are correlated with different types of politico-economic integration. Includes a great deal of carefully observed and sensitively handled data on the outcome of specific practices for children with particular reference to fostering, wardship, apprenticeship etc.

See also, Goody, E.N. (1971) 'Forms of pro-parenthood: the sharing and substitution of parental roles'. In J.R. Goody (ed.), *Kinship*. London: Penguin.

Hamilton, A. (1981) *Nature and nurture. Aboriginal childrearing in North-Central Arnhem Land*. Canberra: Australian Institute of Aboriginal Studies.

A detailed, well-observed and often fascinating anthropological account of childrearing and child behaviour among Aborigines of northern Australia (Arnhem Land), most of the data being derived from observations of children up to age nine or so.

Herron, R.E. and Sutton-Smith, B. (1971) *Child's play*. New York, London: John Wiley & Sons Inc.

Series of papers on various aspects of children's play, mostly with respect to US children. Authors include G. Bateson, E.H. Erikson and J. Piaget. Papers grouped as follows: normative studies, ecological approach, the psycho-analytic tradition, comparative approaches, cognitive approaches, developmental approaches, theoretical overviews. Some interesting papers, giving a broad introduction to literature on children's play; less theoretically sophisticated than Schwartzman's *Transformations*; virtually no appreciation of the cross-cultural perspective or the necessity for including such data.

Hilger, Sister M. Inez (1960) *Field guide to the ethnological study of child life*. Behaviour Science Field Guides, vol. 1. New Haven: Human Relations Area Riles Press.

A still useful field guide to the ethnographer detailing the areas of interest and types of inquiry that should be made in order to produce relevant data on the ethnography of childhood. The guide was compiled by the author during her own fieldwork among North American Indians.

Hill, R. and Koenig, R. (eds) (1970) *Families in East and West. Socialisation process and kinship ties*. The Hague: Mouton.

Papers by sociologists for the 9th International Family Research Seminar in Tokyo. Primarily concerned with USA, Europe and Japan, but also with some other areas, these papers discuss aspects of child–parent relations, socialisation, schooling etc. Largely survey data, much of it concerned with family structure. The collection is divided into three parts under the following headings: problems of socialisation, relations between the family and extended kin, problems of methodology. Little or no attempt is made to understand the nature of social construction of notions of the child, childrearing practices etc.

Howard, A. (1970) *Learning to be Rotuman. Enculturation in the South Pacific.* New York: Teachers College Press.

An attempt to draw together 'the environmental, historical, cultural and social strands' of Rotuman social life so as to reveal the connections between social processes at the level of the community and learning processes in individuals. Part of a series on anthropology and education, this book pays particular attention to schooling and its place in contemporary Rotuma. Chapters on: education in a changing world, Rotuma and its people, infancy in the household and among kin, school years, the life cycle from a Rotuman perspective, life style, education and the Rotuman character, the impact of western education on Rotuman students in tertiary education, and a discussion of 'culture in the classroom'.

Ianni, F.A.J. and Storey, E. (eds) (1973) *Cultural relevance and educational issues.* Boston: Little, Brown & Co.

Includes a number of theoretical papers concerned with conceptualisation of issues and methodology in the field of anthropology and education. Some 'case studies', mostly on older school children and college students. Includes L.M. Hanks on indifference to modern education in Thai farming community; E.A. Parmee on 'factors affecting the education of Apache youth'; L. Comitas on 'education and social stratification in Bolivia' and M.C. Hodgkin on cross-cultural education in Australian schools.

*Journal des Africanistes*, 1981 51 (1–2).

The whole of this volume is given over to papers on childhood; these concern weaning, maternal care, birth practices, indigenous notions of the nature of the child and of proper socialisation, children's religious activities, children's drawings etc. It also includes an extensive bibliography on childhood (not including adolescence) in African cultures, with the emphasis on work produced between 1975–81.

The issue contains the following papers: a comparison of the period from pregnancy to weaning for children among the Basiari, the Fulani and the Boin of Senegal (M.Th. de Lestrange and B. Passot-Guevarara); childrearing among the Kotokoli of Togo and the Mossi of Upper Volta re breast-feeding, weaning and toilet training (S. Lallemand); the ritual processes surrounding birth among the Togo (C. Rivière); among the Diola (O. Journet); analysis of prescriptive practices re birth, breast-feeding, weaning etc. shows how among the Nzebi of Gabon these practices constitute a 'definition of the child's matrilineal and patrilineal identity' (A. Dupuis); an analysis of tales about children among the Sanan of Upper Volta shows how these construct a particular image of the child and parental responsibilities and of what will be expected of the child when s/he grows up (S. Platiel); Mossi children's songs are analysed to reveal the values they convey (O. Kabore); the relation between the space which is free to the child and his or her socialisation as a Burundi (N. Ndimurukundo); a fascinating paper about five-to-seven-year-old Bobo children's 'spontaneous' formation of groups on the age–set model and how these are made to carry religious significance in cults of possession and another using masks, these being manifestations of the adult view that 'all the virtues of old age' exist in young children (G. le Moal).

Kay, M.A. (ed.) (1982) *Anthropology of human birth.* Philadelphia: F.A. Davis Co.

While not strictly speaking concerned with children and socialisation, some of the papers in this book incidentally contain interesting data on social constructs of children and childhood and of mother–child relations, e.g. N. Scheper-Hughes on childbearing and infant care in rural Ireland.

Kessel, F.S. and Siegel, A.W. (eds) (1983) *The child and other cultural inventions*. New York: Praeger Publishers.

An interesting collection of papers largely concerned with devising a new approach to child psychology, i.e. one that acknowledges that 'somehow, whatever it is out there in the culture that says "this is what a child is" is being communicated to and being constructed by the child himself' (Kessen, p. 35). The avowed intention of virtually all the authors in this collection is one which denotes 'a paradigm shift': they wish to give a genuinely historical perspective to psychological studies. A number of authors (N. Edelstein and M. Cole for instance) make use of an anthropological perspective (explicit or implicit) but the methods remain those of experimental psychology or sociology and thus the data on which they rely itself remains inadequate. The collection includes papers on the 'traditional' and 'modern' systems in Iceland (W. Edelstein); on Victorian and 'colonial' fatherhood in Britain and the USA compared with '20th century fatherhood' (J. Demos); and the American child (W. Kessen). The remaining papers deal with theoretical questions regarding the nature of the questions psychologists can usefully ask and how these should be framed. This is a fascinating collection in so far as it demonstrates significant changes in the theoretical perspectives considered possible by psychologists; it seems a pity however that this multidisciplinary group did not include some anthropologists since a combined effort of the two groups is bound to be important for any genuine advances in both methods of data collection and of theory.

Kessen, W. (ed.) (1975) *Childhood in China*. New Haven, London: Yale University Press.

Fascinating data derived from observations of child behaviour and teaching methods in schools in contemporary China, with sections on the nursery, kindergarten, primary school and middle school. The data culled from direct observation is perforce confined to those areas which were open to the team of investigators (who included a number of distinguished US psychologists). However, the significance of the data is difficult to assess in the absence of any sociological or historical analysis (and this despite the presence among the investigators of two sociologists). To a certain extent this deficiency is acknowledged by the editor (p. 216); it could perhaps have been at least partially made up by including an anthropologist (or two) in his team.

Kimball, S.T. (1974) *Culture and the educative process*. New York, London: Teachers College Press (Columbia University).

Concerns the anthropological approach to learning and education, with a strong emphasis on theory and methodology. Part II on 'culture and learning' is most closely related to issues about how the child acquires his or her culture and the author refers to a variety of data under the following section headings: the cultural conditions of learning, cultural influences shaping the role of the child, social system and learning, communication behaviour as a function of social structure, individualism and the formation of values, the transmission of culture. Most substantive data is concerned with the learning process in western countries, particularly the USA.

Kimball, S.T. and Burnett, J.H. (1973) *Learning and culture*. Proceedings of 1972 Annual Spring Meeting of the American Ethnological Society, Seattle, London: University of Washington Press.

Includes theoretical papers on learning and culture (S.T. Kimball), language and socialisation (J. Brukman), and the anthropology of thinking (M. Cole). Others on 'the rituals of socialisation' include an account of the process which inducts the children of a Guatemalan elite into an aristocratic life style (G.A. Moore); the contrasting and conflicting experiences and behavioural expectations of native Hawaiian children in their families and in school (A. Howard); and the unintended socialisation of 'ethnic' slum children in a New York city school (C. Harrington).

Korbin, J.E. (ed.) (1981) *Child abuse and neglect. Cross-cultural perspectives*. Berkeley, Los Angeles, London: University of California Press.

An interesting series of papers by anthropologists on the position of children in a number of different cultures, with particular reference to child care, disciplinary and initiation practices and their cultural significance: on New Guinea (L.L. Langness), sub-Saharan Africa (S. LeVine and R. LeVine), South America (O.R. Johnson), rural India (T. Poffenberger), Turkey (E.A. Olson), Japan (H. Wagatsuma), China (D.Y.H. Wu), China (J.E. Korbin), Polynesia (J. Ritchie and J. Ritchie). The papers explore definitions of child abuse and neglect as a cultural construct, the nature of deviance in child-care behaviour in each culture, the effects of social conditions such as poverty and rapid socioeconomic change. Papers suggest that children are 'subjected to a lower frequency of idiosyncratic child abuse and neglect' in non-western societies.

See also J. Boyden and A. Hudson (1985) *Children: rights and responsibilities*, Minority Rights Group, Report No. 69; this has a useful bibliography for those who wish to follow up this subject.

Lee, R.B. and DeVore, I. (eds) (1976) *Kalahari hunter–gatherers*. Cambridge, Mass., London: Harvard University Press.

Includes three papers on childhood, all respecting data gathered during fieldwork in 1969–71: P. Draper, 'Social and economic constraints on child life among the !Kung'. This offers the reader a view of 'the niche of children in this society'; the data on the typical organisation of people in the space of the camp is interesting in so far as it allows speculation about how the !Kung child learns his or her culture. While we can glean quite a lot about adult attitudes towards children, their autonomy etc. there is very little data about explicit parental views. Paper shows !Kung children as the object of a high degree of adult supervision combined with adult respect for the children's personal autonomy; and little or no direction of children's behaviour.

M.J. Konner, 'Maternal care, infant behaviour and development among the !Kung'. Compares !Kung and USA children re motor development, very early cognition and degree of social interaction. The author finds that a high degree of physical contact and frequent nursing in the first two years for !Kung children is paradoxically correlated with reduced dependency in later years, when compared with data from studies on USA and English children. When compared with USA infants, !Kung infants are advanced with respect to neuromotor development and on certain measures of cognitive (sensori-motor) development. There is little discussion of how cultural factors enter into these findings or into childrearing in general in the two contexts.

M. Shostak, 'A !Kung woman's memories of childhood'. An adult !Kung woman remembers weaning, the birth of a younger brother, childhood relations with other family members and with other children, children's play and learning experiences, her marriage (as an adolescent), sexual experience and so on. The author's edited interviews provide a vivid account and one that gives us not only some notion of what it is to be !Kung but of a child's learning of her culture and !Kung views on the nature of children. The author's commentary provides additional information.

Leiderman, P.H., Tulkin, S.R. and Rosenfeld, A. (eds) (1977) *Culture and infancy. Variations in human experience.* New York, San Francisco, London: Academic Press, Inc.

A collection of papers arising from an interdisciplinary conference (including anthropologists, psychologists, biologists etc.) to explore the 'cultural and social influences in infancy and early childhood'. The emphasis is on research strategy rather than on theory and in general the papers are concerned to illustrate 'how caretaking practices interact with biological and maturational givens' (p. 1). While the editors assert that it is essential for the investigator to 'understand the broader cultural contexts within which child-rearing is studied' they go on to say that 'the questions underlying comparative child development studies are primarily psychological' (p. 6). The conjunction of these two statements argues a misunderstanding of culture and the way culture inevitably enters into development. Thus while the data is voluminous and highly detailed it does not tell us very much about *how* the child constructs his or her own culture over time—and neither are we given sufficient detail about specific cultures in which the studies took place. This is as true of the work by anthropologists as it is of that by psychologists. Thus Melvin Konner prefers to draw attention to the differences between USA and !Kung children in terms of differences between 'isolated monkey pairs' and 'group-living monkey pairs' respectively rather than to differences derived from the nature of society and culture in the USA and among the !Kung. In general the emphasis seems to be on the nature of specific types of interaction between caretakers and children and on the child behaviour with which this interaction apparently co-varies.

Leis, P.E. (1972) *Enculturation and socialisation in an Ijaw village.* New York: Holt, Rinehart and Winston, Inc.

Anthropological study of childhood among the Ijaw of Nigeria, fieldwork data being obtained between 1957 and 1959. The author attempts to discover why 'certain traits in adult culture' were stable and thus retained by children while others appeared to be rejected by them as a result of recent innovations. She argues that those 'behavioural' and 'ideational' traits which are most stable are those that are learned early. Traits which are in the process of disappearing are those which are both learned late and not consciously integrated into a 'pattern of traits'. 'Those traits perceived by a people as being interdependent with others, particularly with other elements unaffected by acculturation, will be less likely to change than those which are recognised by the people as being loosely related to other traits in an indigenous pattern' (p. 41). Leaving aside the question of the validity of a 'trait theory' of culture, the detailed information in this book is useful; it includes accounts of parental expectations, adult notions of the power (*kro*) of the infant child, as well as a full ethnographic description of childhood up to the age of 17. A brief introductory account of kinship, economic and political organisation and religion, provides a context for the often fascinating data on what Ijaw children have to learn and speculations on how they learn it. See also a later work by the same author, in S. Ottenberg (1982) cited below.

Levy, R. (1973) *Tahitians. Mind and experience in the Society Islands*. Chicago, London: University of Chicago Press.

Deals with data derived from fieldwork in the early 1960s in two villages on different islands in the Society Islands. Because the author's concerns are with psychodynamic organisation in adults—i.e. 'the more private, personal aspects of behaviour and how such aspects were related to the public world' (p. xvii)—the material on children is relevant largely to those concerns. Thus in an interesting chapter entitled 'Aspects of growing up', the author discusses parental attitudes towards children, weaning, toilet training, techniques of control in infancy and early childhood, the child's autonomy, what the child may be learning from his or her experience of these matters, and children's attitudes towards their parents. There is however, in addition to this chapter, a good deal of information on children, childhood, socialisation, child sexuality, adolescence and so on in other sections of the book. The author implies (p. 434) that a study of growing up in the Society Islands is to follow the present one.

Lindquist, H.M. (ed.) (1970) *Education: readings in the processes of cultural transmission*. Boston: Houghton Mifflin Co.

Includes papers covering Africa, Asia, Europe and the USA; little material on childhood though there are some sketchy ethnobiographical accounts re Taiwan and China, a very brief account of childhood in a Japanese village and of formal school education in Tokyo and in a French provincial town. Most of the material is concerned with aspects of adult socialisation; there is an interesting paper on the reactions of teachers in an English comprehensive school who were faced with giving up the cane and children's responses to the attitudes taken by different teachers, also a paper on American Indian children (Sioux and Cherokee) in USA schools. Little or no sociological analysis.

Macalandong, R.M. *et al.* (1978) 'Protection and pride in Maranao childhood'. *Journal of Social Psychology*, 105(1), 85–97.

Looks at the childbearing and childrearing practices of 160 Maranao mothers (Muslims in the southern Philippines). Discusses their use of both traditional and western medical practices to avoid birth defects, aid delivery, protect the child from supernatural forces and help him or her to develop courage and family pride. Argues for the necessity for understanding the Maranao conceptual system and for an understanding of *their* goals as parents, these being focused on the key notions of protection and pride.

Manning, F.E. (ed.) (1983) *The world of play*. Proceedings of the 7th Annual Meeting of the Association of the Anthropological Study of Play. West Point, New York: Leisure Press.

A collection of papers mostly concerned with *adult* 'play' and games. However, under the heading of 'the ludic construction of reality' the collection includes six papers on children's play: metaphor and play interaction in young children (M. Bamberg); the mechanics and products of peer play (N. Budwig, A. Strage and M. Bamberg); social play and intimacy (D. Kelly-Byrne); joking relationships between parents and children (K.F. Alford); child-structured as opposed to adult-structured play (H.B. Schwartzman). Data in these papers mostly obtained from US and other western children.

Marshall, L. (1976) *The !Kung of the Nyae Nyae*. Cambridge, Mass., London: Harvard University Press.

Includes information on children's learning about plant life, child care and training, naming, plus a detailed and interesting section on children's play and games. It is from this last section that we can glean most information regarding !Kung children's acquisition of their own culture. The data were gathered during fieldwork in the late 1950s and early 1960s. The author does not analyse her material, but it is possible to derive a good deal on the nature of children's learning processes from her data, especially when it is placed in the context of the other material in her ethnography and of data gathered by other ethnographers of the !Kung.

Mayer, P. (ed.) (1970) *Socialisation: the approach from social anthropology*. ASA Monograph 8. London: Tavistock Publications.

A number of interesting papers in this volume. E. Goody discusses kinship fostering in Gonja in middle childhood as an educational process, children's responses to it and the implications of the practice for their 'success' in later life. B. Lloyd gives Yoruba mothers' accounts of their childrearing practices for infants. B. Ward describes children's temper tantrums in a Hong Kong village and their implications for later individual development in terms of a marked psychological stability in adolescence and early adulthood and repression of aggression. P.I. Mayer writes on peer-group socialisation in the adolescent youth organisation of the Red Xhosa of South Africa; this includes an interesting account of the learning of fighting codes by adolescent boys, the law in the youth organisation and the conduct of sexual relations—all of which produce 'the well-controlled youth' of whom Red Xhosa adults are so proud. J.S. LaFontaine discusses teenage culture in Kinshasa; W. Wilder the socialisation of Malay children in adolescence, with particular reference to the development of sexual status and the complementary nature of relations between the sexes; he includes an account of Malay boys' circumcision and the socialisation of religious belief. A. Forge on 'learning to see' among the Abelam of New Guinea discusses girls' first menstruation and initiation rituals for young men and the significance of painting in the initiation ceremonies. J.B. Loudon writes on the significance of teasing and ridicule in the socialisation of Tristan da Cunha children and its continued use in adult interaction with respect to contests for power and influence in the domestic group.

*Medical Anthropology*, 1984 *8*(2).

This issue edited by Lauris McKee concerns 'Child survival and sex differentials in the treatment of children'. Includes comparative papers by C.M. Super and L. McKee, plus papers on Pakistan and Bangladesh (B.D. Miller), on Rajput girls in Khalapur, Uttar Pradesh (L. Minturn), and on Mexico (P.L. Engle, S.C.M. Scrimshaw and R. Smidt).

Merriam, A.P. (1974) *An African world*. Bloomington, London: Indiana University Press.

This ethnography concerns the Basongye people of the Eastern Kasai Region of Zaire, the data being gathered during fieldwork in 1959/60. The author's general aim is 'to know Basongye society and culture', his specific aim being 'to understand music as part of that society and culture'. The book includes a general description of the life cycle including some aspects of infancy and childhood, e.g. weaning, toilet training, disciplinary procedures, male circumcision, female scarification etc. (pp. 214–23) and friendships between children (pp. 263–4). There is no detailed and systematic data on children's acquisition of their own culture.

Middleton, J. (ed.) (1970) *From child to adult. Studies in the anthropology of education*. Garden City, New York: The Natural History Press.

Includes M. Fortes on education among the Tallensi from early childhood onwards: reprints from original monographs e.g. R. Firth on Tikopia, Raum on discipline and behavioural control for Chaga children, D. Eggan on the socialisation of Hopi children with special reference to the understanding of the meaning of kinship relations and the obligations these entail; Hogbin's early (1946) account of childhood (from weaning to age eight) among the Wogeo of New Guinea; a chapter from Nadel's (1942) *Black Byzantium* on Muslim education among the Nupe of Nigeria. Also K. Little on early socialisation and initiation among the Mende of Sierra Leone in the 'bush schools' for young initiates (at puberty); a section too from Ammar's (1954) *Growing up in an Egyptian village*. Plus other more general papers on theoretical issues and discussion of the educational process from an anthropological perspective.

Montagu, A. (ed.) (1978) *Learning non-aggression*. New York: Oxford University Press.

Collection of papers on socialisation of gentleness in children from a number of societies: the Fore of New Guinea (E.R. Sorenson), the !Kung of Botswana (P. Draper), the Inuit of the Canadian Arctic (J.L. Briggs), the Semai of Malaysia (R.K. Dentan), Australian Aborigines (C.H. Berndt), the Mbuti of Zaire (C.M. Turnbull) and the Tahitians (R.I. Levy). Some very interesting data, if not always as detailed as one would wish.

Munroe, R.L. and Munroe, R.H. (1977) 'Land, labour and the child's cognitive performance among the Logoli'. *American Ethnologist*, *4*(2), 309–20.

The paper concerns the Logoli of East Africa and discusses the responses of children aged 7–13 to tests concerning the conservation of quantity; it shows (i) that women's subsistence involvement is positively related to the size of their husband's homesteads, (ii) that 'compliance pressures' on children are positively related to mother's subsistence involvement (i.e. the more she works on the land, the more she restricts her children to the home and to helping her in her work) and, (iii) that children's cognitive performance is negatively related to the compliance pressures placed on them. It does not occur to the authors that 'compliance pressures' could significantly interfere with the children's responses to the experimental situation rather than with their ability as such to conserve quantity.

Munroe, R.H., Munroe, R.L. and Whiting, B.B. (eds) (1981) *Handbook of cross-cultural human development*. New York, London: Garland STPM Press.

This collection of papers by anthropologists and psychologists includes studies under the headings of theoretical perspectives, early experience and growth, cognitive and moral development, and socialisation and outcomes. Some of the papers are of interest (e.g. that by C.M. Super on 'Behavioural development in infancy'). However, because they are all concerned to survey and compare material respecting, for example, sex differences or the development of moral judgement we are not presented with material which increases our data on how culture enters into child development. Precisely because previous work in this area by anthropologists has been in general unsystematic and unquantified, while that of psychologists has been ahistorical and sociologically naive, earlier studies should not be relied upon as primary sources of data. The work in this book cannot be said to tell us much about how children acquire their own culture.

Musgrove, T. (1982) *Education and anthropology. Other cultures and the teacher*. Chichester, New York: John Wiley & Sons.

A readable and well-intentioned, if somewhat superficial, account of the various theoretical issues at stake in contemporary education across cultures. Rather an uncritical acceptance of the value of cross-cultural studies of cognition and naive use of anthropological data. Includes chapters on literacy, culture and thinking, rationality, 'learning to be modern', cultural relativism and the curriculum, education and the social order. Uses ethnographic data on children and adults throughout to illustrate specific points.

Oppong, C., Adaba, G., Bekombo-Priso, M. and Mogey, J. (eds) (1978) *Marriage, fertility and parenthood in West Africa* (Changing African Family, no. 4, part 1), Canberra: Australian National University.

This two-volume work contains a section of five papers on child care. E. Goody on one of the paradoxes of west African society, i.e. that parenthood is both central and 'sacred' yet at the same time there is a proliferation of institutions that entail the giving up of parental rights when children aged 6–12 go to live with pro-parents until adulthood (see also E. Goody, above). D.K. Fiawoo on foster care in Ghana. E. Schildkrout on changing economic roles in children in comparative perspective' which summarises changes in children's economic roles in

Europe and discusses the implications of this data for the study of childhood in Africa. W. Bleek on parental valuation of children in Kwahu, Ghana. P.A.C. Isichei on 'the basic meaning of a child through Asaba personal names'.

The data tends to concentrate on parental attitudes and values with respect to children, the notion of the child etc. However, given that a full ethnography of childhood demands attention to parental notions and child–parent interaction, these papers are of interest.

See also, Oppong, C. (1973) *Growing up in Dagbon*. Accra: Ghana Publishing Co. (MA Thesis 1965, Legon.).

Ottenberg, S. (ed.) (1982) *African religious groups and beliefs*. Published for the Folklore Institute by Archana Publications, Puri, Sadar, India.

This collection contains two interesting papers on children, the first by N.B. Leis, 'The not-so-supernatural power of Ijaw children' and the second by S. Ottenberg, 'Boys' secret societies at Afikpo'.

Leis discusses the socialisation of Ijaw children (Nigeria) for their 'egalitarian' society and the functional aspects of Ijaw beliefs about the young child's power to cause harm and suffering to its parents. These are taken to be a sign of adult attitudes towards children as 'individual agents', 'free agents over whom the parents have little control'. The paper is a convincing re-analysis of data presented in her 1972 book (see Leis, above). It shows how parental beliefs about the 'power' of children are less about 'the Ijaw belief system' than they are about how, by responding to children in terms of these beliefs, Ijaw adults 'are teaching their children to be the same egalitarian and independent persons they are themselves'.

Ottenberg's account concerns the way in which Ibo boys (S.E. Nigeria) form their own 'secret' societies which are centred on ancestral shrines in imitation of those to which all adult men belong; in any given village or ward of a village there are two boys' societies, one for boys between 5 and 10, the other for boys between 10 and 15. A fascinating account of the way that these autonomous, self-controlling groups socialise their members in gender roles and social control, stress male bonding, the separation of the sexes, and male domination over women; it is against women that the 'secrecy' of the boys' activities is directed.

Rabain, J. (1979) *L'enfant du lignage. Du sevrage à la classe d'âge*. Paris: Payot.

Probably one of the very best contemporary accounts of early childhood, this book is a product of fieldwork among the Wolof of Senegal. The analysis specifically attempts to understand how culture enters into the socialisation process and the author's recognition of the fact that subjectivity is itself a cultural construct, makes her analysis a particularly sensitive and interesting one. The study concerns children from the age of weaning (at about 22 months) to around five years old, the data being gathered by means of close participant observation of 25 children in two Wolof villages over a period of 18 months. Rabain shows how the child comes to realise his or her rightful place in the lineage of birth according to age, sex, and birth position. The analysis centres on exchanges of food, talk, physical contact and objects and shows how the nature of these exchanges themselves at once constitute particular kinds of social relations and provide the context in which the child is able to construct his or her own understanding of social relations.

Because this book is so very interesting I include a brief account of some of the material. Chapter 1 centres on food and the child's relations with others through food. Decisive weaning takes place between 22–24 months; at this time, in a special weaning ritual, the child is symbolically associated with siblings and the rest of his/her family as an eater of millet bread. Details of the ritual are specific to the sex of the child who is explicitly told to renounce the breast; the ritual insists on the new status of the child as a member of society and informs the construction of gender identity since eating separates the sexes. *La sevrage marque ainsi l'entrée de l'enfant dans la vie sociale, les tâches et les jeux avec les enfants de même sexe.* Rabain shows how, before weaning, the child does not want to approach other children, and how afterwards 'now he goes to the others, he plays'.

In Chapter 2 Rabain discusses the body as the locus of inscription of social relations. She shows how the nature of physical exchanges between adults and children and between children themselves sets up a situation in which close physical proximity is expected of those who are kin; by contrast the maintenance of physical distance, direct gaze and direct questions are taken to be a sign of evil intentions. Children learn to control and regulate any aggressive feelings towards others via the reactions of parents and older children; these reactions work to situate a given child's aggression within a social exchange and thus transform it into an expression of lineage identity with the other. Another very interesting chapter is that which analyses the way that the child's relations with other people are mediated by the exchange of objects; here again we are concerned with the construction of gender in respect of the child's perceptions of the relations between different persons and the objects associated with the sex specific division of labour. In her later analysis of the child as 'social partner' Rabain describes the shift that occurs around five years from primarily adult/child interactions to primarily child/peer interactions. She discusses the nature of verbal interactions, how these are initiated, by whom, and how carried on. The final fascinating chapter shows how *all* these exchanges, behaviours etc between parents and children and children and their peers relate to an implicit theory that the Wolof hold concerning the nature of heredity, i.e. that the child is, in some sense, an incarnation of a specific ancestor.

For a brief introduction to Rabain's work see also Zempleni-Rabain, J. 'Food and the strategy involved in learning fraternal exchange among Wolof children', in P. Alexandre (ed.) *French Perspectives in African Studies*, published for the International African Institute by Oxford University Press, 1973. This describes the way in which, on weaning, Wolof children are taken into the series of food exchanges that themselves define the nature of kin relations in Wolof society. The paper shows how the child is able to construct out of his or her experience an early 'awareness and respect for the "laws of brothers and equals"', rather than simply passively accept the imposition of 'adult rules'. In both this paper and the later book, the quality of the observation and the appreciation of both anthropological and psychological methods and analytical perspectives make Rabain's work exemplary.

Richards, M. and Light, P. (eds) (1986) *Children of social worlds.* Oxford: Polity Press.

A collection of papers discussing the relations between children, their families and broader social institutions, as well as their responses to divorce, the threat of nuclear war etc. Also includes material on the development of children's language and thought within the context of the child's communication with others. The basic assumption of this collection is that a child's psychological development can be understood only within its broader social context and with reference to the social relationships that children establish.

See also, M. Richards (ed.) (1974) *The integration of a child into a social world.* Cambridge University Press.

Reisman, P. (1983) 'On the irrelevance of child rearing practices for the formation of personality'. *Culture, Medicine and Psychiatry*, 7, 103–29.

A provocative paper that shows convincingly that major differences between the dominant personality types found among the Fulbe and the Rii of Upper Volta *cannot* be due to childrearing practices, because these practices are identical. The author accounts for the demonstrable differences between the two groups by taking personality as the manifestation of one's sense of self and this to derive chiefly from perception of one's location in the wider set of social relations. The paper includes a brief and useful critique of some child personality approaches and some interesting observations on the nature/nurture debate, and is well worth reading as an antidote to some of the more simple-minded literature in which 'personality' is treated as unproblematically dependent on child-rearing practices. The implications of Riesman's work are, of course, that our western focus on childrearing practices is itself an aspect of *our* social construction of the development of personality, rather than a strictly 'objective' point of view.

Roberts, J.I. and Akinsanya, S.K. (1976) *Schooling in the cultural context. Anthropological studies of education.* New York: David McKay Co. Inc.

Data here mostly concern children in middle and late childhood in school/formal educational contexts. The school is viewed as only one form of cultural transmission and a number of studies try to show how the school is embedded in the wider community and what kinds of interactions occur between school and community and the consequences of these interactions for the child. Papers include R. Redfield on education in Guatemala, C. Kileff on the educational experiences of a Shona boy, D. Eggan on instruction and affect among the Hopi, and a large number of studies on classroom behaviour cross-culturally, on theories of learning, education and so on.

Schildkrout, E. (1979) 'Roles of children in urban Kano'. In J.S. La Fontaine (ed.), *Sex and age as principles of social differentiation.* London, New York: Academic Press.

Account of the complementary roles of parents and children among the Hausa, showing how the social economic and political definition of adult roles cannot be understood without taking account of the roles of children. Particularly interesting re the social construction of adulthood and of gender out of qualitatively different childhood experience:

> In Hausa society certain tasks are inevitably relegated to children, for adults cannot perform them, limited as they are by the social definition of gender. The Hausa child does not simply imitate adult behaviour in rehearsal for adult life. Childhood is qualitatively different from adulthood for the child does not have to observe many of the rules that regulate the behaviour of adults. The suspension of these rules is a crucial part of the learning process, for it gives the child particularly the boy, whatever insight and understanding he may later have of the lives of women.

See also, Schildkrout, E. (1973) 'The fostering of children in urban Ghana: problems of ethnographic analysis in a multi-cultural context'. *Urban Anthropology*, 2(1), 48–73; and Schildkrout, E. (1980) 'Children's work reconsidered'. *International Social Science Journal*, 32(3), 479–89.

Schwartz, T. (ed.) (1975) *Socialisation as Cultural Communication.* Berkeley: University of California Press.

Papers reprinted from *Ethos 3*(2); includes W. Goldschmidt on Sebei socialisation for low affect and concentrates on Sebei mothers' emotional 'absence' in interactions with the child; R.A. Shweder and R.A. LeVine use the dream concepts of Hausa children to argue against the Piagetian notion of 'invariant sequence' in child cognitive development; their data show the noticeably different sequences by which children arrive at an understanding of dream as internal and unreal as opposed to external and real. Other papers in this collection concern the theory of socialisation and socialisation of adults.

Schwartzman, H.B. (1978) *Transformations: the anthropology of children's play.* New York, London: Plenum Press.

Interesting attempt to understand how children construct and transform through play the contexts in which they find themselves. Well-researched, with an impressive bibliography, the author wishes to show how any account of the anthropology of children's play is 'also a discussion of the history of anthropological ideas about culture'. She argues, via an account of the different theoretical approaches to play and detailed reference to ethnographic examples, that anthropologists should realise the central importance of play; the work also shows how 'play gives shape as well as expression to individual and societal affective and cognitive systems. These are play's products and they are extremely consequential' (p. 331). Chapter headings: the invention of childhood; describing play (i.e. ethnographic reports); staging play: evolutionary and developmental studies: preserving play: diffusionism and particularism; socialising play: functional analyses; projecting play: culture and personality; minding play: structural and cognitive studies; defining play: ecology, ethology and experiments.

Shweder, R.A. and LeVine, R.A. (eds) (1984) *Culture Theory. Essays on mind, self and emotion.* Cambridge, New York: Cambridge University Press.

Contains a number of papers directly concerned to devise the kind of theory and methodology that will allow social scientists to advance the study of culture and its acquisition. The book is the product of an interdisciplinary conference, the contributors united in the sense that they show a common adherence to the 'symbols-and-meanings conception of culture'. It opens with a useful critical discussion by Shweder on the various theoretical perspectives available to anthropologists, psychologists and other scholars interested in 'mind and culture'. However, while the book is in general concerned with questions of what culture is and how it might be acquired there is only one paper that deals specifically with data about children. This is E. Ochs and B.B. Schiefflin's excellent paper, 'Language acquisition and socialisation—three developmental stories and their implications'. They discuss the relationship between language and socialisation in three societies: white middle-class American, Kaluli (New Guinea) and Western Samoan. On the basis of data gathered during fieldwork they argue that 'children's language is constructed in socially appropriate and culturally meaningful ways ... that the process of acquiring language must be understood as the process of integrating code knowledge with sociocultural knowledge' (p. 307). This is not so say that they deny the significance of biological predispositions to language, but rather that, for instance: 'The biological predispositions constraining and shaping the social behaviour of infants and caregivers must be broader than thus far conceived in that the use of eye gaze, vocalization and body alignment are orchestrated differently in the social groups ... observed' (p. 299).

See also, Schiefflin, B.B. (1979) *How Kaluli children learn what to say, what to do and how to feel: an ethnographic study of the development of communicative competence*, Ph.D. Dissertation, Columbia University. Also, Schiefflin, B.B. and Ochs, E. 'Cross-cultural perspectives on the transition from pre-linguistic to linguistic communication'. In R. Golinkoff (ed.), *From pre-linguistic to linguistic communication*. Hillsdale, N.J.: Erlbaum, in press.

Tomeh, A.K. (1975) *The family and sex roles* (in series edited by K. Ishwaran, 'Interdisciplinary studies on family, kinship and marriage'). Toronto, Montreal: Holt, Rinehart & Winston of Canada.

A sociologist's account of the socialisation of gender in the family, primarily with respect to Europe and North America but with reference to cross-cultural data. The primary focus is on the changing status of women and much of the data is thus concerned with adults rather than children. Includes a chapter on sex role socialisation.

Virtanen, L. (1978) 'Children's Lore'. *Studia Fennica* 22 (Review of Finnish Linguistics and Ethnology). Helsinki: Finnish Literature Society.

How does play in the peer group prepare a child for adulthood? Are child norms the same as those of adults? What can adults learn from child traditions and 'the living culture of childhood'? These are questions the author attempts to answer with respect to her analysis of very extensive essay material provided by Finnish school children aged from 10 to 18. Chapter headings: the living tradition, the activity of the yard group, fun with rhymes, the 'deflating' tradition, the 'teasing' tradition, prose narratives, magic and beliefs, the function of the children's tradition. Demonstrates the stability of the traditional culture of children and attempts to analyse its 'function' in contemporary Finland.

Wagner, D.A. and Stevenson, H.W. (eds) (1982) *Cultural perspectives on child development*. San Francisco: W.H. Freeman & Co.

Papers included in this book are possibly of some interest to psychologists; however, with the exception of Super and Harkness' paper on the development of affect in USA children and Kipsigi children of western Kenya, there is no data here on how children acquire their own culture. From an anthropologist's point of view it might also be said to be lacking any understanding of what might constitute a 'cultural perspective'.

Williams, T.R. (ed.) (1975) *Psychological anthropology*. The Hague, Paris: Mouton Publishers.

Most papers are about adults. However there are three concerned to understand 'the nature of aggression and the striving for self-esteem and prestige in their various cultural settings' largely via an analysis of child behaviour. These are J. Bushnell and D. Bushnell, 'Projective doll play reconsidered: the use of a group technique with rural Mexican children'; R.R. Omark, M. Omark and M. Edelman, 'Formation of dominance hierarchies in young children'; and I. Eibl-Eibesfeldt, 'Aggression in the !Ko Bushmen'.

Williams, T.R. (ed.) (1975) *Socialisation and communication in primary groups*. The Hague, Paris: Mouton Publishers.

A large number of papers covering many aspects of child and adult socialisation. Those on children include G.M. Erchak, 'The non social behaviour of young Liberian Kpelle children and its social context'; S. Seymour on child rearing in India; J.A. Hostetler on aspects of personality in a Hutterite community in USA; M. Sanford on the lending of children among British West Indians in Honduras; C.B. Stack on who raises black children and transactions between 'child givers and receivers' in a black community in midwest USA; E.W. Smollett on social class and differential learning experiences in Canada.

Wolf, M. (1976) 'Child training and the Chinese family'. In M. Freedman (ed.), *Family and kinship in Chinese society*. Stanford University Press.

Based on data gathered during two years fieldwork in a village in northern Taiwan, this paper is explicitly intended to be in the tradition of Whiting and Child's 'Six cultures project'. It includes interesting data on the nature of parent–child interaction and shows how differential attitudes and behaviour by each parent vary according to the sex, birth order and relative age of the children. These variations in behaviour and attitude are further shown to be correlated with particular aspects of social organisation and the cultural values in terms of which this social organisation is played out. The paper further shows how the intricacies of relationships between parents, and between parents and other adults, affect children's understanding of their own position within the family, and how the strong cultural value placed on solidarity between brothers is paradoxically undermined by child training practices.

## SECTION 2: ADDITIONAL WORKS

Aboud, F.E. and Skerry, S.A. (1984) 'The development of ethnic attitudes'. *Journal of Cross-Cultural Psychology*, *15*(1), 3–34.
Bahl, L. and Singh, L. (1982) 'Some aspects of infant rearing practices and beliefs in rural inhabitants of Himachal Pradesh'. *Indian Pediatrics*, *19*(11), 921–5.
Bai, K.I. and Ratnamalika, D.P.N.V. (1981) 'Attitudes and beliefs concerning child care among women of Tirupati, Chittoor District, Andhra Pradesh, India. *Journal of Tropical Pediatrics*, *27*(5), 250–4.
Belmont, N. (1980) 'The exposed child' (in French, English summary). *Anthropology and Society*, *4*(2), 1–17, 164.
Benson, S. (1980) 'Mixed race children in South London: the management of an ambiguous ethnic identity'. *Cambridge Anthropology*, *61*(1–2), 150–61.
Buononno, M. (1978) 'Primary socialisation and parental roles in southern Italian peasant families'. *Rassegna Italiana Sociologia*, *19*(2), 315–25.
Callan, V. and Wilks, J. (1984) 'Perceptions about the value and cost of children: Australian and Papua New Guinean high school youth'. *Journal of Biosocial Science*, *16*(1), 35–44.
Carroll, V. (ed.) (1970) *Adoption in Eastern Oceania*. Honolulu: University of Hawaii Press.
Carter, A.T. (1984) 'The acquisition of social deixis: children's usages of "kin" terms in Maharaashtra, India'. *Journal of Child Language*, *11*, 171–201.
Caudill, W.A. and Schooler, C. (1973) 'Child behaviour and child rearing in Japan and the United States: an interim report'. *Journal of Nervous and Mental Disease*, *157*(5), 323–38.
Chan, A. (1985) *The children of Mao: personality development and political activities in the Red Guard generation*. London: Macmillan.
Chester, R., Diggory, P. and Sutherland, M.B. (eds) (1980) *Changing patterns of child-bearing and child-rearing*. New York: Academic Press.
Cole, S. (1980) *Working kids on working*. New York: Lothrop, Lee and Shepard.
Collard, C. (1980) 'The right birth order of children: study of guidar sibling relationships' (in French, English summary). *Anthropology and Society*, *4*(2).
Cottle, T.J. (1974) *Black children, white dreams*. New York: Delta.
Cowlishaw, G. (1982) 'Socialisation and subordination among Australian Aborigines'. *Man*, *17*(3), 492–507.
Cox, D.R. (1971) 'Child rearing and child care in Ethiopia'. *Journal of Social psychology*, *85*(1), 3–5.
Donohue, N. and Colletta, N.J. (1977) 'The child and his surroundings: the ecology of child development on a Malaysian rubber plantation'. *International Child Welfare Review*, *32*, 24–46.
Dreitzel, H.P. (ed.) (1973) *Childhood and socialisation*. Recent Sociology No. 5. New York: Macmillan.

Fraser, M. (1973) *Children in conflict: growing up in Northern Ireland.* New York: Basic Books.

Hake, J.M. (1972) *Child-rearing practices in Northern Nigeria.* Nigeria: Ibadan University Press.

Harkness, S. and Super, C.M. (1985) 'The cultural context of gender segregation in children's peer groups'. *Child Development,* 56(1), 219–24.

Hasan, K.Z. (1977) 'Effects on child mental health of psychological change in developing countries'. *International Journal of Mental Health,* 6(3), 49–58.

Hull, T. (1975) 'Each child brings its own fortune: an enquiry into the value of children in a Javanese village'. PhD Thesis, Australian National University, Canberra.

Kilbride, J.E. and Kilbride, P.L. (1975) 'Sitting and smiling behaviour in Baganda infants: the influence of culturally constituted experience'. *Journal of Cross-Cultural Psychology,* 61, 88–101.

Lallemand, S. (1980) 'Child adopting among the Kotokoli of Togo' (in French, English summary). *Anthropology and Society,* 4(2), 19–37.

Lewis, M. and Rosenblum, L.A. (1978) *The development of affect.* Plenum.

Lewis, M. and Saarni, C. (1985) *The socialisation of emotion.* Plenum.

Lozoff, B. (1983) 'Birth and "bonding" in non-industrial societies'. *Developmental Medicine and Child Neurology,* 25(5), 595–600.

Murphy, M.D. (1983) 'Coming of age in Seville: the structuring of a riteless passage to manhood'. *Journal of Anthropological Research,* 39(4), 376–92.

Nucci, L.P., Turiel, E., Encarnacion-Gawrych, G. (1983) 'Children's social interaction and social concepts: analyses of mortality and convention in the Virgin Islands'. *Journal of Cross-Cultural Psychology,* 14(4), 469–88.

Opolot, J.A. (1978) 'Child rearing and child care in Uganda'. *Journal of Social Psychology,* 106(1), 123–4.

Park, J.Y. and Johnson, R.C. (1984) 'Moral development in rural and urban Korea'. *Journal of Cross-Cultural Psychology,* 15(1), 35–46.

Rebelsky, F.G. (1972) 'Cross-cultural studies of mother–infant interaction: description and consequence'. *Human Development,* 15(2), 128–30.

—— (1973) 'Infancy in two cultures'. In F.G. Rebelsky and L. Dormon (eds), *Child development and behaviour.* New York: Alfred A. Knopf.

Richer, S. (1984) 'Sexual inequality and children's play'. *Canadian Review of Sociology and Anthropology,* 21(2), 166–80.

Rohner, R.P. and Rohner, E.C. (1982) 'Enculturative continuity and the importance of caretakers: cross-cultural codes'. *Behaviour Science Research,* 17(1–2), 91–113.

Ryback, D. (1976) 'Child-rearing and child-care practices among Israeli students'. *Psychological Reports,* 38(3), 922.

Ryback, D. (1980) 'Child-rearing practices reported by students in six cultures'. *Journal of Social Psychology,* 110(2), 153–62.

Semaj, L.T. (1980) 'Race and identity and children of the African diaspora: contributions of Rastafari'. *Caribe* (5), 14–18.

Sheper-Hughes, N. (1984) 'Infant mortality and infant care: cultural and economic constraints on nurturing in northeast Brazil'. *Social Science and Medicine*, 19(5), 535–46.
Shigaki, I.S. (1983) 'Child care practices in Japan and the United States: how do they reflect cultural values in young children'. *Young Children*, 38(4), 13–24.
Smith, P. (1979) 'Birth and destiny: iron children and butter children' (in French, English summary). *Cahiers d'Etudes africaines*, 19(1–4), 329–52.
Stein, H.F. (1978) 'The Slovak–American "swaddling ethos": homeostat for family dynamics and cultural continuity'. *Family Process*, 17(1), 31–45.
Stross, B. (1973) 'Acquisition of botanical terminology by Tzeltal children'. In M. Edmonson (ed.), *Meaning in Mayan languages*. The Hague: Mouton.
Sullivan, T. (1983) 'Native [Canadian Indian] children in treatment: clinical, social and cultural issues'. *Journal of Child Care*, 1(4), 75–94.
Thomas, D.R, (1975) 'Authoritarianism, child-rearing practices and ethnocentrism in seven Pacific Islands groups'. *International Journal of Psychology*, 10(4), 235–46.
Uyanga, J. (1980) 'Rural–urban differences in child care and breast-feeding behaviour in southeastern Nigeria'. *Social Science and Medicine*, 14(1), 23–9.
Weisner, T.S. and Gallimore, R. (1977) 'My brother's keeper: child and sibling caretaking'. *Current Anthropology*, 18(2), 169–90.
White, B. 'The economic importance of children in a Javanese village'. In M. Nag (ed.), *Population and social organisation*. The Hague: Mouton.
White, M.E. (1984) 'The changing roles of children in the economic and social life of the rural southern Appalachians during the 20th century'. *Tennessee Anthropologist*, 9(3), 114–28.
Young, N.F. (1972) 'Independence training from a cross-cultural perspective'. *American Anthropologist*, 74(3), 629–38.
Zern, D.S. (1970) 'The influence of certain child-rearing factors upon the development of a structured and salient sense of time [a cross-cultural study]'. *Genetic Psychology Monographs*, 81(2), 197–254.
—— (1980) 'Child-rearing practices and societal complexity: effect of disequilibrium on cognitive development'. *Journal of Social Psychology*, 110(2), 171–5.
—— (1982) 'The impact of values on development in a cross-cultural sample'. *Genetic Psychology Monographs*, 106(2), 179–97.
—— (1983) 'The relationship of certain group-oriented and individualistically oriented child-rearing dimensions to cultural complexity in a cross-cultural sample'. *Genetic Psychology Monographs*, 108(1), 3–20.
—— (1983) 'The relationship of pressure toward obedience to production in art and music: a cross-cultural study on the effects of certain child-rearing practices'. *Journal of Social Psychology*, 120(2), 213–21.
—— (1984) 'Relationship among selected child-rearing variables in a cross-cultural sample of 110 societies'. *Developmental Psychology*, 20(4), 683–90.

# Index

affection bonding 45–6
affective culture 19, 91–9
Ainsworth, M.D. 67–8
Akinsola, Esther 57
Aldis, O. 49
Alegria, J. 41
Alson, D. 43
anthropology, and child
    development 1–30
  American Culture and
    Personality School 10–12,
    14, 27
  British functionalist 6–10
  cognition 18–19, 38–9, 99
  dance and music 93–4
  ethnocentricity 5–6
  ethnographic case studies
    20–5
  evolution 1–2
  methodology and concepts
    15–20
  social 8–9
  socialisation 19–20, 26–30
Aristotle 117
arts 91–9
  *see also* Bali; Venda
attachment theory 45–6, 67–8
Ault, R.L. 101
autonomy, personal, Piaroa
    (*q.v.*) 174–91

Bacon, M.K. 11
Bali 22, 113–43
  dancing 92, 117
  education 116–17, 132–9
  gender roles 126–32
  human life cycle 140–3
  operetta 122–4
  play and social development
    137–9
  servants, clowns, jesters
    124–6
  shadow play 118–22
  social structure 114–15
  theatre 115–18

Bantu 2–5
Barbera, L. 5
Barkóczi, I. 94–5
Barry, H., III 11
Barth, F. 9
Bartlett, F.C. 7
Bates, E. 50, 52, 72
Bateson, G. 49, 96, 139
Beebe, B. 43
Beeghly-Smith, M. 52
Belo, J. 138–9
Berger, P.L. 80
Bernardi, B. 27
Berry, J.W. 13–14
Best, David 93–4
Blacking, John vii, 21–2,
    91–111, 117
Blehar, M.C. 67
Bloch, Maurice 109
Bloom, L. 72
Blunt, A. 131
bonding 45–6
Bourguignon, E. 11
Bowlby, J. 67–8
Brahmans 114–15, 117, 121
brain, lateralisation 71, 96–8
Brandon, J.R. 115
Bretherton, I. 50, 52, 72
Bronfenbrenner, U. 13,
    15–16
Brooks, J. 80
Brooks-Gunn, J. 52, 74
Bruner, J.S. 6, 49, 72, 92
Bundell, Kevin 75–7
Burnham, P.C. 16
Burrow, J.W. 1

Calas, Elena 295
Camaioni, L. 52
Campbell, D.T. 13
Campos, J. 52
Caselli, M.C.C. 73
Charnov, E. 52
Chewong 22, 27, 147–68
  emotions 148, 163–4

humans and superhumans 150–1, 165–6; knowledge 151–4; learning and self 161–5
life-cycle 154–61, 166–8; adolescence 160–1; birth to name 156–7; infancy 157–60; prenatal 155–6
liver 162–3
society 148–50
Child, I.L. 11
Chisholm, J. 52
Clifford, J. 17
cognition
and anthropology 18–19, 38–9, 99
and psychology 18, 38–9, 99–100
'artistic' 94–5
Piaroa 174–7
Punan Bah 200–4
Venda 102–5
cognitive development 18
Chewong, concepts of self 147–68
Fiji, gender and hierarchy 225–68
Kerkennah, sex roles 271–86
Piaroa, autonomy and self 169–91
Punan Bah, concepts and learning 193–221
Soviet Georgia, sex roles and State roles 288–306
Cohen, D. 41
Cole, M. 12, 16
communication, development of
cross-cultural comparisons 55–67, 73–7
first year 40–67
second year 67–81
concepts
anthropology and psychology 18–20
Chewong 147–68
Piaroa 169–91
Punan Bah 193–221
see also gender; hierarchy

Conklin, H. 120
Connolly, K. 92
co-operative motives, universal 21, 37–85
communication development: Lagos infants 55–67; western white infants 40–55
co-operative awareness 67–81; cognition and meaning 72–3; cross-cultural comparisons 73–7
Innate Intersubjectivity Theory 37–40
Crickmore, Leon 95
Csikszentmihalyi, M. 95
culture, acquisition of
cognitive development; autonomy and self, Piaroa 169–91; concepts and learning, Punan Bah 193–221; concepts of self, Chewong 147–68
gender and hierarchy; Fiji 225–68; sex roles and State roles, Georgia 288–306; sex roles, Kerkennah 271–86
non-verbal processes; dance and music, Venda 91–111; theatre, Bali 113–43; universal co-operative motives 37–85
culture, affective 19, 91–9
Culture and Personality School 10–12, 14, 27

Dager, E.Z. 19
dance 91–8
Bali 92, 117, 122–4
Venda 105–111
Dasen, P.R. 12
de Bono, E. 95
de Casper, A.J. 41
Dentan, R.K. 150
development, child, in anthropology and psychology 1–30
American Culture and

Personality School 10–12, 14, 27
British functionalist anthropology 6–10
cross-cultural psychology 12–15
ethnographic case studies 20–5
evolutionary phase 1–6
methodology and concepts 15–20
socialisation 19–20, 26–30
*see also* cognitive development; culture, acquisition of
Dore, J. 72
Douglas, Mary 18, 117
Dragadze, Tamara vii, 24–5, 288–306
Durkheim, Emil 8–9

ecology 13–14
Edinburgh, infant studies 40–55, 68–70, 80–1
education
  Bali 116–17, 132–9
  Chewong 151–4, 164
  Fiji 241
  Georgia 289, 295–6
  Kerkennah 281
  Piaroa 177–88
  Punan Bah 203, 205–8
Ellen, R.F. 16
Ellis, A.C. 2
Else, G.F. 117
Emde, R.N. 52
Emler, N.P. 81
emotions
  Chewong 148, 163–4
  Georgia 299
  Punan Bah 207–8
Endicott, K.M. 150
ethnocentricity 5–6
Evans-Pritchard, E.E. 18, 226
evolution 1–6
experimentation 15–16

fantasy 70, 75–6, 79
Farr, R.M. 18
Feld, S. 93

Feldman, H. 73
Feldstein, S. 43
Field, T.M. 41
Fifer, W.P. 41
Fiji 23–4, 27, 225–68
  hierarchy 263–6; and equality 228–32; children's perceptions of 240–63
  *yaqona*-drinking 233–40
Finnegan, R. 18
Firth, R. 6
Fortes, Meyer 6–7, 17, 29, 134
Fox, R. 40
Freeman, N.H. 52

Galuh 122–4, 129–30
Gardner, H. 93
Gardner, W. 52
Garvey, C. 49
Gay, J. 12
Geertz, C. 92–3, 137, 226
Gelfland, M. 6
gender 28
  Bali 113–43
  Chewong 158–9
  Fiji 225–68
  Georgia 288–306
  Kerkennah 271–86
  Piaroa 173
  Punan Bah 212–16
Georgia SSR 24–5, 27, 288–306
  environment 288–91
  sex roles 292–5, 298–300
  socialisation 297–305
  State roles 295–7, 300–5
Girard, R. 190
Goldin-Meadow, S. 73
Gombrich, E.H. 117
Goody, J. 117
Gosse, Edmund 92–3
Greenberg, R. 41
gymnastics 94

Hall, G.S. 1–2
Halliday, M.A.K. 52–3, 72
Hallpike, C.R. 18
Hamilton, V. 93
Harkness, S. 14
Harré, R. 80

Harvey, D. 49
Hawaii 92
Herron, R.E. 49
hierarchy
　Fiji 225–68
　Georgia 288–306
　Polynesia 225–8, 239
Hobart, Angela vii, 21–2, 113–43
Hofsten, C. von 46
Hogan, R. 81
Holt, C. 139
Horton, R. 18
Howell, Signe vii, 22, 147–68
Hubley, P. 40, 46, 48–51, 53–4, 57
humans, concept of 150–1, 197–200
Hungary 94–5

imitation 50–3
'imprinting' 41
Indian infants 75–7
infancy
　Chewong 157–60
　co-operative motives (q.v.) 37–85
　Fiji 240–1
　India 75–7
　Kerkennah 274–5, 279–80
　Lagos 55–67, 80–1
　Punan Bah 209–11
　Venda 108
Inhelder, B. 12
Innate Intersubjectivity Theory 37–40
intersubjectivity
　primary 42–5
　secondary 52–5
intelligence 102–4, 202

Jaffe, J. 43
Jahoda, Gustav vii, 1–30, 99
Johnson, J.A. 81

Kaberry, P.M. 6
Kagan, Jerome 73–5
Kaplan, M.R. 172, 184, 189
Keali'inohomoku, J.W. 92
Kerkennah 24, 28, 271–86
　childbirth 273–4
　cognitive development 272–3
　initiative and activity 281–5
　self 274–8
　self-expression and verbal skills 278–81
　stages of development 286
Kidd, D. 2–5
Kipsigis 14
Kligman, D.H. 52
knowledge 151–4, 181–4, 203
Korawa brothers 119, 128
Kowasa, Y. 52
Krige, J.D. and E.J. 6
Ksatriyas 114–15, 121, 128–9
Kugiumutzakis, J.E. 41, 50
Kuper, A. 6

La Barre, W. 15
La Fontaine, J. 9
Lagos, infant communication 55–67, 80–1
　environment 66–7
　home interaction 63–6
　laboratory studies 59–62
Lamb, M.E. 52, 81
Lancy, D.F. 15
Langer, S. 118
Langham, I. 1
Lavallee, M. 12
Leach, E.R. 116, 193
learning see education; socialisation
Lee, D. 132
Lee, D.N. 46
Le Vine, R.A. 52
Lewis, G. 139
Lewis, I.M. vii, 1–30, 99
Lewis, M. 52, 74, 80
Lewis, O. 67
Liku 122–4, 129–30
liver 162–3, 200
Lloyd, S. 52
Lock, A. 80
Logotheti, K. 38, 40, 54, 72, 79–80
Luckmann, T. 80
Luria, A.R. 12

MacNamara, J. 72

INDEX

McNew, S. 52
McPhee, C. 125
Malaya *see* Chewong
Malinowski, B. 6, 17
*mana* 235, 237–8
marriage 174, 188, 232, 290, 293
Marwick, H. 37, 42–3, 46–8, 54, 57, 68
Maslow, A.H. 98
Maurer, D. 41
Mayer, Philip 9, 19
Mays, K. 43
Mead, Margaret 10, 12, 45, 113, 138, 295
Meade, G.H. 80
meaning, development of 67–77
Mehler, J. 40
Meltzoff, A.N. 41
methodology 15–20
Mitchell, J.C. 16
Moore, M.H. 41
Morelli, G.A. 52
Moscovici, S. 18
mothers, and infants
  African 55–66
  white 40–52, 68–70
Mundy-Castle, A. 55
Munroe, R.L. and R.H. 14, 19
Murray, L. 40, 43
music 91–8, 105–11

naming 157, 189, 276–7
Naroll, R. 13
Needham, R. 226
Nelson, K. 72
New Guinea 14–15
Ngoni 8
Nicolaisen, Ida vii, 23, 193–221
Noirot, E. 41
non-verbal processes
  co-operative motives 37–85
  dance and music, Venda 91–111
  theatre, Bali 113–43

objects 50–5
Ochs, E. 44–5
operetta, Bali 113, 122–6
and roles 126–8, 129–32
Ornstein, R. 97–8
Ortner, S. 225–8, 239
Osborne, H. 132
Oster, H. 41
Ottenberg, S. 9
Overing, Joanna vii, 23, 169–91
Owen, B.M. 46

Pandawa brothers 119, 125–8, 135–7
Papousek, H. 48
patterning 40
Peacock, J. 113
Peery, J. 43
Piaget, Jean 2, 7, 10, 12, 38, 68, 99–100, 133–4
Piaroa 23, 27, 169–91
  autonomy, privacy, domestication 188–91
  beads of knowledge 181–4
  learning of *ta'kwakomenä* 177–81, 184–8
  politics and economics 170–4
  theory of mind, 174–7
  wizardry 170–1, 186–8
Plato 131
Platt, Katherine vii, 24, 271–86
play 77–8
  Bali 137–9
  Kerkennah 281–2
  Lagos 55–61
  Tale 7
  white, western infants 46–51
Pléh, C. 94–5
Plooij, F. 49
Polynesia 225–8, 239
psychoanalysis 10, 38
psychology, and child development 1–30
  'affective' culture 92–3
  cognition 18, 38–9, 99–100
  cross-cultural studies 12–15
  ethnographic case studies 20–5
  evolution 1–2
  learning theories 38–9
  methodology and concepts 15–20

socialisation 19–20, 26–30, 38
Punan Bah 23, 28, 193–221
  children and parents 208–12
  children's subculture 216–19
  cognition 200–4
  gender and rules 212–16
  learning culture 205–8
  society 193–7
puppets, Bali 119–20
Pygmy studies 13–14

Rabain, Jacqueline 1, 7, 28–9
Radcliffe-Brown, A.R. 8
Raum, Otto 8
Read, Margaret 6, 8
'recapitulation theory' 1–2
Reich, J.H. 52
Retschitzki, J. 12
Richards, A.I. 6, 9
Rivers, W.H.R. 9
Rogers, C. 98
Rogoff, B. 20
roles see gender; hierarchy

Sahlins, M. 265
Salapatek, P. 41
Samoa 45
Sander, L. 41
Sarawak see Punan Bah
Schieffelin, B.B. 44
Schwartz, T. 19
Schwartzman, H.B. 5
Secord, P.F. 80
self, concepts of
  Chewong 147–68
  Kerkennah 274–8
  Piaroa 169–91
  Punan Bah 193–221
self-actualisation 98, 101–2, 107–11
self-awareness 50–4, 72–4
Seligman, C.G. 9
sex see gender
sexuality 231–2, 280, 293
shadow play, Bali 113, 118–22, 124–6
  and roles 126–9, 130–2
Shakespeare, William 125
Shand, N. 52

Sharp, D. 12
Sherwood, V. 49, 72
Shotter, J.D. 49, 80
Shweder, R.A. 18
Singer, M. 113
Sinha, C.G. 52
Skorupski, J. 129
socialisation 1, 19–20, 26–30, 38–40
  see also culture, acquisition of
Somalis 9
soul 148, 150–3, 189, 198–200, 214
Soviet Union see Georgia SSR
Spencer, P. 9
Sperber, D. 18, 119
Spies, W. 117, 122
Spitz, R.A. 45
Sroufe, L.A. 52
State, and socialisation, Georgia 295–7, 300–5
Stern, D.N. 37, 41, 43, 53
Sternberg, C. 52
Stocking, G. 1, 17
Strathern, A.J. 15
Strathern, M. 127
Sudras 114–15, 121, 124–6
Sully, J. 1
Super, C.M. 14
superhumans 150–1
Sutherland, A. 303
Sutton-Smith, B. 49
Sylvester-Bradley, B. 43, 46, 48

ta'kwakomenà 175–81
Tale 6–7, 17
theatre 113, 115–16
  Bali (q.v.) 115–40
Thompson, R.A. 52
Tizard, B. 49
Tonkin, Elizabeth 38
Toren, Christina vii, 18, 23–4, 225–68, 307–33
tranquillity 150, 174, 177–81, 207
Trevarthen, Colwyn viii, 16, 21–2, 37–85
Tronick, E.Z. 52

INDEX

Tunisia *see* Kerkennah
Turner, V. 119
Tylor, Edward B. 2, 95, 100

Venda 21–2, 27, 91–111
   affective culture 91–9
   cognition 99–100
   dance and music 105–11
   intelligence 102–5
   self-actualisation 101–2
   world view 100–5
Venezuela *see* Piaroa
Vernon, M.D. 93
Volterra, V. 52, 73
Vygotsky, L.S. 12, 38–9, 99–100

Wachsmann, K.P. 94
Wade, T.O. 52
Wagner, R. 17
Wall, S. 67
Waters, E. 52, 67

Watson, J.S. 48
Wertheimer, M. 1
Wertsch, J.V. 38, 40
Whiting, B.B. 11, 19
Whiting, J.W.M. 11
Winn, S. 52
Winnicott, D.W. 44
Witkin, H.A. 99–100
Witkin, R. 91
wizardry *see* Piaroa
Wolf, K.M. 45
Wolof 7, 28–9
Woodson, R. 41

*yaqona* 232–40
Yoruba 55–67, 80–1
Young, J.Z. 95

Zoete, B. de 117, 122
Zoetmulder, P. 124
sone of proximal development 39

340